"'R. C. Sproul,' someone said to me in the 1970s, 'is the finest communicator in the Reformed world.' Now, three decades later, his skills honed by long practice, his understanding deepened by years of prayer, meditation, and testing (as Martin Luther counseled), R. C. shares the fruit of what has become perhaps his greatest love: feeding and nourishing his own congregation at St. Andrew's from the Word of God and building them up in faith and fellowship and in Christian living and serving. The St. Andrew's Expositional Commentary will be welcomed throughout the world. It promises to have all R. C.'s hallmarks: clarity and liveliness, humor and pathos, always expressed in application to the mind, will, and affections. R. C.'s ability to focus on the 'the big picture,' his genius of never saying too much, leaving his hearers satisfied yet wanting more, never making the Word dull, are all present in these expositions. They are his gift to the wider church. May they nourish God's people well and serve as models of the kind of ministry for which we continue to hunger."

—Sinclair B. Ferguson, Senior Minister,
First Presbyterian Church, Columbia, South Carolina

"R. C. Sproul, well-known as a master theologian and extraordinary communicator, now shows that he is a powerful, insightful, helpful expository preacher. This collection of sermons is of great value for churches and Christians everywhere."

—W. Robert Godfrey, President, Westminster Seminary California

"I tell my students again and again, 'You need to buy good commentaries and do so with some discernment.' Among them there must be preacher's commentaries, for not all commentaries are the same. Some may tell you what the text means but provide little help in answering the question, 'How do I preach this text?' R. C. Sproul is a legend in our time. His preaching has held us in awe for half a century, and these pages represent the fruit of his latest exposition, coming as they do at the very peak of his abilities and insights. I am ecstatic at the prospect of reading the St. Andrew's Expositional Commentary series. It represents Reformed theology on fire, delivered from a pastor's heart in a vibrant congregation of our time. Essential reading."

—Dr. Derek W. H. Thomas, John E. Richards
Professor of Systematic and Practical Theology, Reformed Theological Seminary;
Minister of Teaching, First Presbyterian Church, Jackson, Mississippi

"R. C. Sproul is the premier theologian of our day, an extraordinary instrument in the hand of the Lord. Possessed with penetrating insight into the text of Scripture, Dr. Sproul is a gifted expositor and world-class teacher, endowed with a strategic grasp and command of the inspired Word. Since stepping into the pulpit of St. Andrew's and committing himself to the weekly discipline of biblical exposition, this noted preacher has demonstrated a rare ability to explicate and apply God's Word. I wholeheartedly recommend the St. Andrew's Expositional Commentary to all who long to know the truth better and experience it more deeply in a life-changing fashion. Here is an indispensable tool for digging deeper into God's Word. This is a must-read for every Christian."

—Steven J. Lawson, Senior Pastor, Christ Fellowship Baptist Church, Mobile, Alabama

"How exciting! Thousands of us have long been indebted to R. C. Sproul the teacher, and now, through the St. Andrew's Expositional Commentary, we are indebted to Sproul the preacher, whose sermons are thoroughly biblical, soundly doctrinal, warmly practical, and wonderfully readable. Sproul masterfully presents us with the 'big picture' of each pericope in a dignified yet conversational style that accentuates the glory of God and meets the real needs of sinful people like us. This series of volumes is an absolute must for every Reformed preacher and church member who yearns to grow in the grace and knowledge of Christ Jesus. I predict that Sproul's pulpit ministry in written form will do for Christians in the twenty-first century what Martyn Lloyd-Jones's sermonic commentaries did for us last century. Tolle lege, and buy these volumes for your friends."

—Joel R. Beeke, President, Puritan Reformed Theological Seminary

ST. ANDREW'S EXPOSITIONAL COMMENTARY

ROMANS

ST. ANDREW'S EXPOSITIONAL COMMENTARY

ROMANS

R. C. SPROUL

:: CROSSWAY WHEATON, ILLINOIS

Romans

Copyright © 2009 by R. C. Sproul

Published by Crossway Books
 a publishing ministry of Good News Publishers
 1300 Crescent Street
 Wheaton, Illinois 60187

Cover design: Geoff Stevens

First printing 2009

Printed in the United States of America

Hardcover ISBN:	978-1-4335-0685-7
PDF ISBN:	978-1-4335-0686-4
Mobipocket ISBN:	978-1-4335-0687-1
ePub ISBN:	978-1-4335-2327-4

Library of Congress Cataloging-in-Publication Data

Sproul, R. C. (Robert Charles), 1939-
 Romans / R.C. Sproul.
  p. cm.—(St. Andrew's expositional commentary)
 Includes index.
 ISBN 978-1-4335-0685-7 (hc)1. Bible. N.T. Romans—Sermons. I. Title. II. Series.

BS2665.54.S57 2009
227'.1077—dc22

2009027809

SH		20	19	18	17	16	15	14	13	12	11	10	09
14	13	12	11	10	9	8	7	6	5	4	3	2	1

To my beloved Saint Andrew's congregation in Sanford, Florida,
who faithfully attend the exposition of sacred Scripture.

CONTENTS

Series Preface   11

Preface   13

1. Greetings (1:1–17)   15

2. The Gospel (1:8–17)   25

3. The Wrath of God (1:18–25)   37

4. Judicial Abandonment (1:22–32)   47

5. No Partiality (2:1–16)   57

6. Under the Law (2:17–29)   67

7. A Great Advantage (3:1–8)   77

8. Under Sin (3:9–20)   87

9. Righteousness Revealed (3:21–26)   97

10. Faith and Works (4:1–8)   105

11. Blessed (4:5–12)   115

12. The Righteousness of Faith (4:13–23)   125

13. Justified (4:23–25)   133

14. Peace (5:1–5, Part 1)   139

15. Hope (5:1–5, Part 2)   147

16. The Atonement (5:6–11)   153

17. Reconciliation (5:10–14)   163

18. Imputation (5:12–17)   171

19. The Reign of Grace (5:20–6:4)   179

20. Dead to Sin (6:4–11)   187

21. Slaves of Righteousness (6:12–23)   195

22. Delivered (7:1–6)   205

23. The Function of the Law (7:7–14)   215

24. The Conflict (7:14–25, Part 1)   223
25. The Will of Man (7:14–25, Part 2)   233
26. Set Free (7:19–8:2)   241
27. Spiritually Minded (8:1–11)   249
28. Adopted (8:9–17)   257
29. Subjected in Hope (8:18–27)   267
30. All Things for Good (8:28–30)   275
31. The Golden Chain (8:29–31)   285
32. God for Us (8:31–39)   295
33. The Doctrine of Election (9:1–5)   303
34. Jacob and Esau (9:6–13)   311
35. The Righteousness of God (9:14–16)   319
36. Predestination (9:17–20)   327
37. Vessels of Wrath and Mercy (9:20–24)   333
38. God's People (9:25–10:4)   339
39. True Confession (10:5–15)   349
40. The Obedience of Faith (10:16–21)   357
41. A Remnant (11:1–10)   365
42. Grafted In (11:11–24)   373
43. The Fullness of Time (11:25–26)   381
44. Out of Zion (11:26–35)   389
45. All Things (11:36)   397
46. Holy Sacrifices (12:1–2)   405
47. Communion of the Saints (12:3–8)   413
48. Brotherly Love (12:9–15)   421
49. Regard for Good Things (12:16–21)   429
50. Church and State (13:1–3)   439
51. The Power of the Sword (13:4–7)   447
52. For Conscience' Sake (13:5–8)   455
53. The Fulfillment of the Law (13:9–14)   463
54. The Weaker Brother (14:1–13)   471
55. Kingdom Life (14:14–23)   477
56. The Pursuit of Peace (14:19–15:13)   485
57. A Minister of God (15:14–33)   493
58. Final Greetings (16)   501
    For Further Study   511
    Index of Names   512

SERIES PREFACE

When God called me into full-time Christian ministry, he called me to the academy. I was trained and ordained to a ministry of teaching, and the majority of my adult life has been devoted to preparing young men for the Christian ministry and to trying to bridge the gap between seminary and Sunday school through various means under the aegis of Ligonier Ministries.

Then, in 1997, God did something I never anticipated: he placed me in the position of preaching weekly as a leader of a congregation of his people—St. Andrew's in Sanford, Florida. Over the past twelve years, as I have opened the Word of God on a weekly basis for these dear saints, I have come to love the task of the local minister. Though my role as a teacher continues, I am eternally grateful to God that he saw fit to place me in this new ministry, the ministry of a preacher.

Very early in my tenure with St. Andrew's, I determined that I should adopt the ancient Christian practice of *lectio continua*, "continuous expositions," in my preaching. This method of preaching verse-by-verse through books of the Bible (rather than choosing a new topic each week) has been attested throughout church history as the one approach that ensures that believers hear the full counsel of God. Therefore, I began preaching lengthy series of messages at St. Andrew's, eventually working my way through several biblical books in a practice that continues to the present day.

Previously, I had taught through books of the Bible in various settings, including Sunday school classes, Bible studies, and audio and video teaching series for Ligonier Ministries. But now I found myself appealing not so much to the minds of my hearers but to both their minds and their hearts.

I knew that I was responsible as a preacher to clearly explain God's Word *and* to show how we ought to live in light of it. I sought to fulfill both tasks as I ascended the St. Andrew's pulpit each week.

What you hold in your hand, then, is a written record of my preaching labors amidst my beloved Sanford congregation. The dear saints who sit under my preaching encouraged me to give my sermons a broader hearing. To that end, the chapters that follow have been adapted from a sermon series I preached at St. Andrew's.

Please be aware that this book is part of a broader series of books containing adaptations of my St. Andrew's sermons. The title of this series is *St. Andrew's Expositional Commentary*. As you can see, this is more than a convenient title—it is a description. This book, like all the others in the series, will not give you the fullest possible insight into each and every verse in this biblical book. Though I sought to at least touch on each verse, I focused on the key themes and ideas that comprise the "big picture" of each passage I covered. Therefore, I urge you to use this book as an overview and introduction, but if you desire to enhance your knowledge of this book of Scripture, you should turn to one or more of the many excellent exegetical commentaries (see my recommendations in the back).

I pray that you will be as blessed in reading this material as I was in preaching it.

—R. C. Sproul
Lake Mary, Florida
April 2009

PREFACE

On the first page of Romans in my Greek testament, I have scribbled at the top of the page a few significant dates. The first one is the year AD 386. In the latter part of the fourth century lived a young man whose father was a pagan and whose mother was a devout Christian. This young man had devoted himself to immorality. He had already sired one illegitimate son, yet his mother continued to pray for his soul and sought the counsel of her pastor, Bishop Ambrose of Milan.

This young man was pacing one day in a garden where a copy of the New Testament was chained to a lectern. As he was walking, he overheard children playing in the grass, singing a refrain to one of their childhood games: *Tolle lege, tolle lege*, which means "take up and read." So this young man, whose name was Aurelius Augustine, went to the Scriptures that were there. He allowed the volume of sacred writ to fall open where it would, and in the providence of God it fell open to Romans 13. Augustine's eyes fell on this passage:

> And do this, knowing the time, that now it is high time to awake out of sleep; for now our salvation is nearer than when we first believed. The night is far spent, the day is at hand. Therefore let us cast off the works of darkness, and let us put on the armor of light. Let us walk properly, as in the day, not in revelry and drunkenness, not in lewdness and lust, not in strife and envy. But put on the Lord Jesus Christ, and make no provision for the flesh, to fulfill its lusts. (Rom. 13:11–14)

As Augustine read these words, the Spirit of God took them and pierced between joint and sinew, bone and marrow, to the very depths of this young man's soul. By the power of the Word of God with the Spirit attending it, Augustine was converted to the Christian faith, and we know him today as Saint Augustine of Hippo.

Later in church history, in 1515, an Augustinian monk who had diligently pursued his doctoral studies in the works of Augustine was consigned to a university to be the professor of biblical studies. He had already delivered his first series of lectures on the book of Psalms, and now his task was to teach his students the book of Romans. As he was preparing his lectures on Romans and studying this epistle's first chapter, he found a notation from an ancient manuscript of Augustine defining the righteousness of Christ. Augustine said that when Paul speaks of the righteousness of God in Romans 1, it is not the righteousness by which God himself is righteous, but the righteousness that he freely gives to those who put their trust in Christ. For the first time in his life, Martin Luther, whose conscience had been wounded by the burden of the law of God that daily exposed his relentless guilt, understood the gospel of Christ. The doors of paradise swung open and he walked through, and it was from Paul's teaching on the doctrine of justification by faith alone that Luther stood against the whole world in the sixteenth-century Reformation.

Another date I have scribbled in my Greek testament is the year 1738, when a man who was already ordained to the ministry in the Anglican church in England was listening to a message being delivered outside in London at Aldersgate. He mentioned later that as he was listening to the words of Romans, he felt his heart was strangely warmed. He said that was the moment of his authentic conversion, and it defined the life and ministry of John Wesley for the rest of his days.

I could mention the impact of Romans on John Calvin, Jonathan Edwards, and a host of others throughout church history, but as we come to it now, I simply remind you that God has richly blessed those who have devoted themselves to the study of this book.

1

GREETINGS

Romans 1:1–7

Paul, a bondservant of Jesus Christ, called to be an apostle, separated to the gospel of God which He promised before through His prophets in the Holy Scriptures, concerning His Son Jesus Christ our Lord, who was born of the seed of David according to the flesh, and declared to be the Son of God with power according to the Spirit of holiness, by the resurrection from the dead. Through Him we have received grace and apostleship for obedience to the faith among all nations for His name, among whom you also are the called of Jesus Christ; To all who are in Rome, beloved of God, called to be saints: Grace to you and peace from God our Father and the Lord Jesus Christ.

The book of Romans begins with one word, **Paul** (v. 1). From the book of Acts we are familiar with the trials and missionary activity of the apostle Paul. He is well known to us. We consider him our mentor and friend. At the beginning of this letter he follows a custom practiced regularly in his day. In antiquity the author of an epistle usually identified himself by name at the beginning. Today we read "Dear Bill," or "Dear John," or "Dear Mary," then wait to the end of the letter to find out who wrote it. Paul does not depart from the old custom and identifies himself as the author of the epistle in the first word.

Who Was Paul?

Paul starts by giving his name, but he then seeks to define who he understands himself to be. This self-identification is not just Paul's introspection
or self-evaluation; the Holy Spirit superintends the apostle's writing, which
is how we know that this is a true and accurate description of the author
of the epistle.

Paul identifies himself as **a bondservant of Jesus Christ** (v. 1). I have
never been satisfied with that English translation of this second phrase. Some
translations have, "Paul, a servant of the Lord Jesus Christ." *Bondservant* is
an improvement, but I think the proper translation should read, "Paul, a
slave of Jesus Christ." The Greek word Paul used here is *doulos*. A *doulos* was
not a hired servant who could come and go as he pleased. A *doulos* was a
person who had been purchased, and once purchased he became his master's possession.

This idea of the *doulos* in Scripture is always connected to another
descriptive word, *kurios*. If you have a Roman Catholic background or if
you know something of sacred music in church history and high church
liturgy, you have heard of the Kyrie. "Kyrie eleison, Christus eleison,
Kyrie eleison." It means "Lord have mercy, Christ have mercy, Lord have
mercy," because the supreme title given to Jesus by the Father in the New
Testament is the title *Kurios*. *Kurios* translates the Old Testament *Adon* or
Adonai, which means "the sovereign one," a name in the Old Testament
that was reserved for God.

In the New Testament the title lord or *kurios* is used in three ways. There
is a simple, common usage, where calling someone *kurios* is like addressing
him as "sir," a polite form of address. The supreme use of *kurios* refers to
the sovereign God, who rules all things. *Kurios*, "the name which is above
every name" (Phil. 2:9), is the name given to Jesus, whom the Father calls
the King of kings and the Lord of lords. There is yet a middle usage of the
term *kurios* in the New Testament. It is used to describe a slave owner, which
is an apt description of Jesus, and it is from this that Paul describes himself.
He is not just a servant but a slave.

Paul, in addressing believers, said, "You are not your own. For you were
bought at a price" (1 Cor. 6:19). We have been purchased by the blood of
Jesus Christ (Acts 20:28). There is a paradox here: when the New Testament
describes our condition by nature, as fallen people, it describes us as slaves
to sin. We are by nature in bondage to sin, bondservants of the flesh, and
the only remedy for that, according to the New Testament, is to be liberated by the work of the Holy Spirit. For "where the Spirit of the Lord is,

there is liberty" (2 Cor. 3:17). Everyone born of the Spirit is set free from slavery to sin.

There is also irony here: when Christ sets us free from slavery to the flesh, he calls us to the royal liberty of slavery to him. That is why we call him Master. We acknowledge that it is from him that we get our marching orders. He is the Lord of our lives. We are not our own. We are not autonomous or independent. Unless people understand their relationship to Christ in these terms, they remain unconverted.

Paul makes a significant affirmation about himself and his mission: **called to be an apostle** (v. 1). In the early chapters of Acts, the church gathered to elect a new apostle, and it set forth the criteria for apostleship. The first criterion was having been a disciple of Jesus during his earthly ministry; the second was having been an eyewitness of the resurrection; and the third and most important criterion was having been directly and immediately called by Jesus (Acts 1:20–26).

On one occasion Jesus sent out seventy disciples. There were far more disciples than the Twelve. Not all those who were disciples became apostles. We tend to use these words interchangeably, as if *twelve disciples* and *twelve apostles* must mean the same thing, but a disciple is simply a learner or a student. Jesus was the Rabbi and enrolled in his school were many disciples. From out of that group he chose twelve to be elevated to the rank of apostle, those who were commissioned to speak for the Master. In the ancient world an apostle was like an ambassador who spoke on behalf of the king. The ambassador's message carried with it the authority of the one who sent him. The word *apostolos* in Greek means simply "one who is sent." "He who hears you hears Me, he who rejects you rejects Me, and he who rejects Me rejects Him who sent Me" (Luke 10:16).

People often say, "I like to know what Jesus says; it is Paul I do not want to listen to." Almost all we know about Jesus is that which comes through apostolic authority, so such remarks set Paul against Matthew, or Paul against John. That may not be done with impunity because all of the apostolic writings carry the delegated authority of Jesus himself. That is what it means to be an apostle. That is why the New Testament church is built on the foundation of the apostles.

In the three criteria for apostleship, Paul fails the first two tests: he had not been a disciple of Jesus during Jesus' tenure on earth, nor had he been an eyewitness of the resurrection of Christ. That is why there were some in the early church who seriously challenged the apostolic authority of Paul. The supreme qualification for apostolic authority was a direct and immediate call by Jesus. I believe that is why, in the book of Acts, the account of Paul's conversion on the road to Damascus, where Christ called him to be his apostle, is repeated three times. It is to remind the people that Paul is an authentic agent of revelation. He speaks with the authority of Jesus.

The next thing we learn about Paul is that he had been **separated to the gospel of God** (v. 1). In Latin *separated* means "segregated," set apart from the multitude to a specific, sacred, consecrated task. The phrase Paul uses involves a part of speech in the Greek language called the genitive, which indicates possession. He is not saying, "I have been commissioned to announce a message or good news about God." Rather, he is saying that the gospel he has been separated and called to proclaim is God's gospel. God is the author and owner of it. Paul is simply the messenger whom God has called and set apart to proclaim to people a message that comes from God himself.

If I said, "I have some great news for you," it would pique your interest. If I added, "This great news comes from God himself," you may think that I am unhinged, but if you thought for a moment that I was sober in such a statement and that I did have a message from God himself—some good news—you would want to hear it. That is what Paul is saying before he spells out the doctrines of grace. He says, "I have been commissioned to proclaim God's gospel, the gospel that belongs to him. It is his possession, and I am going to communicate it to you."

The Promised Gospel

Paul has been separated for the gospel **which He promised before through His prophets in the Holy Scriptures** (v. 2). Sometimes we make an artificial separation or distinction between the Old and New Testaments. We talk about the Old Testament as law and the New Testament as gospel, as if there were no law in the New Testament and no gospel in the Old Testament. Paul says at the very beginning that the gospel is not a novelty; it is the same gospel that was promised numerous times before.

The first time the gospel was promised in the Old Testament was in the context of a curse. As a result of the fall, God cursed Adam and Eve as well as the serpent. God said that the seed of the woman would crush the serpent's head, and in the process the seed of the serpent would bruise the man's heel. Centuries before Christ was delivered to the cross, where he crushed the head of Satan while being bruised for our iniquities, the gospel of Christ was given in the promise of the curse of the enemy. That is the *protoeuangelion*, the first proclamation of the gospel (Gen. 3:14–19).

Paul, an expert student of the Old Testament, was aware of that, which is why he said that this gospel is what God "promised before through His prophets in the holy Scriptures." The "sacred writings" is the actual phrase he uses here. Billy Graham successfully carried out crusades throughout the world in which he held up the Bible and said, "The Bible says . . ." He quoted the Bible and used it as the authority from which he called people to repent from their sins and to embrace Christ.

A few years ago I heard a professor say that the time is over when people can say, "The Bible says . . ." and expect to have any credibility, because the criticism of academicians has been so severe. People have lost confidence in the trustworthiness of sacred Scripture. God has not lost confidence in the power of the sacred Scriptures. He has invested the Scriptures with the power of the Holy Spirit. He declared to Isaiah, "My word . . . shall not return to Me void" (Isa. 55:11). When God utters words, the earth melts. One poet put it this way:

> Hammer away, ye hostile hands;
> your hammers fail, God's anvil stands.

Paul is not reticent about where his authority lies with respect to the gospel God "promised before through His prophets in the Holy Scriptures."

To my mind there is no greater source than the Word of God. No other source gives me more confidence or possesses more credibility. I am impressed by rational arguments on certain points and by the power of logic and the formal truth of mathematics. I am impressed when empirical science verifies hypotheses in amazing ways. However, nothing moves my soul and my mind to acquiesce in its certainty like finding it in the pages of sacred Scripture.

It annoys me when I see the bumper sticker that says: "God said it, I believe it, that settles it." We must get rid of that middle term. If God says it, it is settled, whether we believe it or not. There is no higher court of appeal than the voice of God. So it is perfectly appropriate for the apostle Paul, when defending the gospel he has been commissioned to proclaim, to say, "It is found in Scripture."

Our Lord himself, as he walked with people on the road to Emmaus after his resurrection, "beginning at Moses and all the Prophets" (Luke 24:27) opened up the Old Testament text to them, showing that they should not have been surprised by his resurrection. Jesus' identity was still hidden from these people. When they sat down to break bread together, Jesus left them, and they then realized who he was. Their response was, "Did not our heart burn within us while He talked with us on the road, and while He opened the Scriptures to us?" (Luke 24:32). It is good for our hearts to burn when we see the power of sacred Scripture authenticating God's truth.

Jesus Christ Our Lord

This gospel, Paul continues, is that **concerning His Son Jesus Christ our Lord** (v. 3). In this brief passage Paul calls Jesus the Son of God, and he calls him the Messiah of Israel, which is what the term *Christ* means. *Jesus Christ* is not his name. *Jesus* is his name. His full name would be Jesus bar Joseph or Jesus of Nazareth. The word *Christ* is his title, and the title Jesus Christ means "Jesus Christos," or "Jesus Messiah." God's Son is the Christ, **who was born of the seed of David according to the flesh** (v. 3). This is important to the Jew, because the Old Testament prophecies of the coming Messiah said he would be from the lineage of David. Luke spends much time on the nativity of Jesus, bringing us to Bethlehem, the city of David, because the Old Testament prophesied that the Messiah would be born from the loins of David. He was to be David's son yet at the same time David's Lord.

Paul reminds the recipients of this epistle that Jesus Christ was descended from David *kata sarka*, "according to the flesh." This is another important phrase in the New Testament. The Greek language uses two different words to refer to the physical nature of our humanity, words that are sometimes, but not always, used interchangeably. The more common word for *body*, or the physical makeup of people, is the word *sōma*. When psychiatrists and psychologists talk about psychosomatic illnesses, they are referring to illnesses that have their genesis in some aspect of one's psychology. It is not that the illnesses are not real—they are real, and they affect the *sōma*, the body.

In addition to the term *sōma*, there is the word *sarx*, which also refers to the physical dimension of human life. Paul says elsewhere that he did not meet Jesus in the flesh. He met him in the power of his resurrection on the road to Damascus, but he never met him personally during his incarnation in this world. That is what Paul is getting at here. Elsewhere the term *sarx* is loaded with theological content. It is used to describe our fallen, corrupt nature. When Jesus said, "That which is born of the flesh is flesh, and that which is born of the Spirit is spirit" (John 3:6), or, "The flesh profits nothing" (John 6:63), he was talking about our fallen condition, not about our skin and bones. He was talking about our corrupt nature, which Scripture frequently sets in contrast to the spirit.

There is a war in the Christian life between flesh and spirit. We still battle with the flesh, but the battle is not with our physical body. It may include that, but the battle between the flesh and the spirit is the battle between the old man, who is fallen and corrupt, and the regenerated person, who is now living by the Spirit of God. Paul will talk about that later in the epistle, but now he is saying that "according to the flesh," in his physical humanity, Jesus was "born of the seed of David."

Paul is not denying the virgin birth. Christ did not receive his deity from Mary or from Joseph. He brought his deity with him from heaven. The virgin birth bypassed the normal human reproductive process; nevertheless, concerning his human nature, he descended from David. With respect to his divine nature, of course, he came from the Logos of heaven. He was born of the seed of David according to the flesh and declared to be the Son of God. Paul summarizes the whole life and work of Jesus here: he is "born of the seed of David" and **declared to be the Son of God with power** (v. 4).

Paul makes clear in his next breath the way in which the declaration was made: **by the resurrection from the dead** (v. 4). When God the Holy Spirit raised the corpse of Jesus from the tomb, God was announcing to the world the sonship of Jesus. By what evidence do we believe that Jesus is the Son of God? By the testimony of God, who has declared him to be his Son through the power of the resurrection. Paul debated with the philosophers on Mars Hill at the Areopagus, where a monument was erected to an unknown god: "These times of ignorance God overlooked, but now commands all men everywhere to repent, because He has appointed a day on which He will judge the world in righteousness by the Man whom He has ordained. He has given assurance of this to all by raising Him from the dead" (Acts 17:30–31).

As we will see later in Romans 1, Paul labors the point that God has manifested himself so clearly to every human being that nobody has an excuse for denying him. When Jesus is declared to be God's Son through the power of the resurrection, that declaration may be all we ever get. We might be like Thomas and say, "Unless I see in His hands the print of the nails, and put my finger into the print of the nails, and put my hand into His side, I will not believe" (John 20:25). We do not want to say that to God on judgment day, because he has manifested the reality of Jesus through the power of the resurrection. That is the appeal Paul is making here. He is saying, "I'm not the one declaring to you that Jesus is the Son of God. God has declared that to you by the Holy Spirit in the power of the resurrection."

Called through Christ
Through Him we have received grace and apostleship (v. 5). Paul says that Jesus is the source of his apostleship, but he does not stop there: the

apostles had received grace and apostleship **for obedience to the faith among all nations for His name, among whom you also are the called of Jesus Christ** (vv. 5–6). Paul moves quickly from his own call as an apostle to the call shared by every Christian in the church at Rome and by every Christian in every church in every age. The Bible calls them elect, "the called out ones." The church is the *ekklesia*, a Greek word that comes from the verb *kaleo*, meaning "to call," and the prefix *ek-*, meaning "out of." Every Christian is called out of the world, out of bondage, out of death, and out of sin, and into Christ and into his body. Paul is not the only one who has been called. All who are truly part of the church have been called out, separated by the power of the Holy Spirit.

What are you called to be? **To all who are in Rome, beloved of God, called to be saints** (v. 7). That is your vocation.

"What are you studying?"

"I'm studying to be a saint. Do you think it will ever happen?"

"It has already happened if you are in Christ Jesus."

You are already numbered among the saints. The word for *saint* in the New Testament is the word that means "sanctified one," one who has been set apart by the Holy Spirit and called inwardly by Christ to himself. If you put your trust in Christ, you are right now a saint. You are set apart. You are part of the invisible church, which is beloved of God.

Finally in this section Paul expresses his traditional greeting: **grace to you and peace** (v. 7). In Old Testament times the Jews greeted one another the same way they do today: *Shalom aleichem*, "Peace be unto you." The response to the greeting was *Aleichem shalom*, "Peace also to you." Our Jewish friends say prayers for the peace of Jerusalem, and the Jewish benediction for centuries has been this: "The LORD bless you and keep you; the LORD make His face shine upon you, and be gracious to you; the LORD lift up His countenance upon you, and give you peace" (Num. 6:24–26). This peace is "not as the world gives," said Jesus in his final will and testament before leaving the world (John 14:27). He left us his peace, a peace that transcends earthly peace, a peace that is permanent and eternal, one in which the warfare between the sinner and God is over.

Isaiah was directed by God to say:

> "Comfort, yes, comfort My people!"
>> Says your God.
>> "Speak comfort to Jerusalem, and cry out to her,
>> That her warfare is ended,
>> That her iniquity is pardoned;

> For she has received from the LORD's hand
> Double for all her sins." (Isa. 40:1–2).

That cry is pronounced for every Christian, which is why Jesus is the consolation of Israel. He is our Paraclete because he is the one who comforts us; he gives us the peace of God that cannot be revoked. It is not an uneasy truce. God does not rattle the sword every time he is distressed with our behavior.

Having been reconciled, justified, we possess that peace right now—and forevermore—which is integral to the apostolic greeting, "Grace and peace." They go together because the peace of God is not something we can ever earn or merit or deserve. The peace that comes from God is by his grace. Paul wishes that his friends in the church at Rome would receive the grace of God.

It is my deepest prayer for each of you that you will know the grace of God and the power of the resurrection of Jesus, and that you will know his peace today and forevermore.

2

THE GOSPEL

Romans 1:8–17

First, I thank my God through Jesus Christ for you all, that your faith is spoken of throughout the whole world. For God is my witness, whom I serve with my spirit in the gospel of His Son, that without ceasing I make mention of you always in my prayers, making request if, by some means, now at last I may find a way in the will of God to come to you. For I long to see you, that I may impart to you some spiritual gift, so that you may be established—that is, that I may be encouraged together with you by the mutual faith both of you and me. Now I do not want you to be unaware, brethren, that I often planned to come to you (but was hindered until now), that I might have some fruit among you also, just as among the other Gentiles. I am a debtor both to Greeks and to barbarians, both to wise and to unwise. So, as much as is in me, I am ready to preach the gospel to you who are in Rome also. For I am not ashamed of the gospel of Christ, for it is the power of God to salvation for everyone who believes, for the Jew first and also for the Greek. For in it the righteousness of God is revealed from faith to faith; as it is written, "The just shall live by faith."

Paul continues his greetings and opening comments to the church at Rome with a thankful heart: **I thank my God through Jesus Christ for you all, that your faith is spoken of throughout**

the whole world (v. 8). The word Paul uses for "thanks" is *eucharisto*, from which the church gets the term *Eucharist*. The word was used to describe the celebration of the Lord's Supper. A profound spirit of thanksgiving lay at the heart of the Supper in the primitive Christian church, thanksgiving for what God had wrought in the work of Jesus Christ.

Paul conjoins the words *universe* and *cosmos* to say that the Roman Christians' reputation for faith has been broadcast throughout the cosmos, or universe. In a sense Paul is using hyperbole, but it is important to pause and pay attention to his use of the term *world*, one of many times in the Bible, particularly in the New Testament, where it occurs. When we think of the world, we typically have in mind the entire planet. We think of the continents and all the people who live in far-off places. However, when first-century people spoke of the world, they were speaking of the known world, which, in their case, was the Mediterranean world. Therefore, Paul is expressing joy that people throughout the Mediterranean world are talking about the faith of the Roman Christians; their faith had made an impact.

Paul's Vow

Paul follows this note of thanksgiving by swearing a vow—**for God is my witness** (v. 9). The fact that Paul swears a vow seems somewhat unusual. Jesus said:

> Do not swear at all: neither by heaven, for it is God's throne; nor by the earth, for it is His footstool; nor by Jerusalem, for it is the city of the great King. Nor shall you swear by your head, because you cannot make one hair white or black. But let your 'Yes' be 'Yes,' and your 'No,' 'No.' For whatever is more than these is from the evil one. (Matt. 5:34–37)

Similar instruction is found in the epistle of James: "Above all, my brethren, do not swear, either by heaven or by earth or with any other oath. But let your 'Yes' be 'Yes,' and your 'No,' 'No,' lest you fall into judgment" (James 5:12).

Some have concluded from these statements that there are never situations in which it is appropriate to take oaths or vows, yet the Westminster Confession of Faith contains a chapter titled, "Lawful Oaths and Vows." The Confession rehearses situations in which it is legitimate, and indeed delightful to God, for people to enter into covenant relationships and swear solemn oaths and vows. Such vows are exchanged when we contract marriages and when we join a church. The Bible shows us that there are appropriate times for the taking of oaths. From time to time the apostles swore an oath to guarantee the trustworthiness of what they were saying, just as we do in a courtroom when we say, "I swear to tell the truth, the whole truth, and nothing but the truth, so help me God." Paul does that here. He is eager that the recipients of his epistle understand the depth of passion he feels in his grateful heart for the remembrance that is being published throughout the known world concerning their faith, and he demonstrates his eagerness by swearing a vow. We will see later that this is not the only time in the epistle that the apostle takes such a vow to guarantee the truth of what he is saying.

For God is my witness, **whom I serve with my spirit in the gospel of His Son, that without ceasing I make mention of you always in my prayers, making request if, by some means, now at last I may find a way in the will of God to come to you** (vv. 9–10). The basic purpose of Paul's vow is to assure the Roman Christians that his desire to come visit them is not casual. He has made mention of them constantly in his prayers, and he has been hoping and planning that somehow, through the will of God, he will make it to Rome. He had no idea when he wrote those words that the manner in which he would finally make it to Rome would be in chains as a prisoner of the Roman government.

The Gospel of Jesus Christ

We noted in our last study that Paul identifies himself as one separated as an apostle and called by God to preach the gospel. I said that the phrase "the gospel of God" did not mean the gospel *about* God but, rather, the gospel that is *the possession* of God. God owns that gospel. He is the one who invented the gospel and commissioned Paul to teach it. The gospel did not originate with Paul; it originated with God. Here, Paul uses the same structure to refer not to the gospel of God but to the gospel of God's Son, Jesus Christ. The gospel is the possession of Jesus, but, even more, Jesus is the heart of the content of the gospel.

We use it so glibly in the church today. Preachers say they preach the gospel, but if we listen to them preach Sunday after Sunday, we hear very little gospel in what they are preaching. The term *gospel* has become a nickname for preaching anything rather than something with definitive content. The word for "gospel" is the word *euangelion*. It has that prefix *eu-*, which comes into English in a variety of words. We talk about euphonics or euphonious music, which refers to something that sounds good. We talk about a eulogy, which is a good word pronounced about someone at his funeral service. The prefix *eu-* refers to something good or pleasant. The word *angelos* or *angelion* is the word for "message." Angels are messengers, and an *angelos* is one who delivers a message.

This word *euangelion*, which means "good message" or "good news," has a rich background in the Old Testament. There, the basic meaning of the term *gospel* was simply an announcement of a good message. If a doctor came to examine a sick person and afterward declared that the problem was nothing serious, that was gospel or good news. In ancient days when soldiers went out to battle, people waited breathlessly for a report from the battlefield about the outcome. Once the outcome was known, marathon runners dashed back to give the report. That is why Isaiah wrote, "How beautiful upon the mountains are the feet of him who brings good news" (Isa. 52:7). The watchman in the watchtower would look as far as the eye could see into the distance. Finally, he would see the dust moving as the runner sped back to the city to give the report of the battle. The watchmen were trained to tell by the way the runner's legs were churning whether the news was good or bad. If the runner was doing the survival shuffle, it indicated a grim report, but if his legs were flying and the dust was kicking up, that meant good news. That is the concept of *gospel* in its most rudimentary sense.

When we come to the New Testament, we find three distinct ways in which the term *gospel* is used. First, we have four books in the New Testament that we call Gospels: Matthew, Mark, Luke, and John. These books are biographical portraits of Jesus. *Gospel* in this sense describes a particular form of literature. During the earthly ministry of Jesus, the term *gospel* was linked not particularly with the person of Jesus but with the kingdom of God. John the Baptist is introduced as one who comes preaching the gospel, and his message is "repent, for the kingdom of heaven is at hand!" (Matt. 3:2). Jesus did the same in his parables, proclaiming, "the kingdom of God is like . . ." On the lips of Jesus, the gospel was about the dramatic moment in history when, through the long-awaited Messiah, the kingdom of God had broken through in time and space. The good news was the good news of the kingdom. By the time the epistles were written, particularly the Pauline epistles, the term *gospel* had taken on a new shade of understanding. It had become the gospel of Jesus Christ. *Gospel* had a clear content to it. At the heart of this gospel was the announcement of who Jesus was and what he had accomplished in his lifetime.

If we give our testimony to our neighbors, saying, "I became a Christian last year. I gave my heart to Jesus," we are bearing witness about Jesus, but we are not telling them the gospel, because the gospel is not about us. The gospel is about Jesus—what he did, his life of perfect obedience, his atoning death on the cross, his resurrection from the dead, his ascension into heaven, and his outpouring of the Holy Spirit upon the church. We call those crucial elements the *objective aspects* of the New Testament gospel of Christ.

In addition to the person and work of Jesus, there is also in the New Testament use of the term *gospel* the question of how the benefits accomplished by the objective work of Jesus are subjectively appropriated to the believer. First, there is the question of who Jesus was and what he did. Second is the question of how that benefits you and me. That is why Paul conjoins the objective account of the person and work of Jesus (particularly to the Galatians) with the doctrine of justification by faith alone, which is essential to the gospel. In preaching the gospel we preach about Jesus, and we preach about how we are brought into a saving relationship with him.

The gospel is under attack in the church today. I cannot stress enough how important it is to get the gospel right and to understand both the objective aspect of the person and work of Jesus and the subjective dimension of how we benefit from that by faith alone.

Recently, a Protestant seminary professor, supposedly evangelical, was quoted to me as having said that the doctrine of imputation—by which our sins are transferred to Christ on the cross and his righteousness is transferred to us by faith—is of human invention and has nothing to do with the gospel. I wanted to weep when I heard that. It just underscored how delicate the preservation of the gospel is in our day and how careful the church has to be in every age to guard that precious good news that comes to us from God.

Paul's Longing

Paul has a deep yearning, a passion in his soul, to meet the Roman Christians face-to-face: **that I may impart to you some spiritual gift, so that you may be established** (v. 11). Paul is not referring to starting out in the Christian faith but to becoming confirmed, built up, and edified in it. Nor is he writing about charismatic gifts here but about establishing believers in confidence and maturity in their faith. This is why Paul wrote the letter to the Romans, and it is why, in the providence of God, his letter is given to us—that the faith that has taken root in our souls may be established so that we may grow to maturity and full conformity to the image of Christ.

Paul adds this reason to his desire to visit them: **that I may be encouraged together with you by the mutual faith both of you and me** (v. 12). He makes that comment in passing, so I do not want to labor it, but I do want to mention that Paul was such a tremendous pastor, as well as a theologian, a missionary, and an evangelist, because his heart was involved.

When he wrote to the church at Corinth recalling the experiences he had shared with the Corinthian Christians, he mentioned specifically that he had been with them in their trials and afflictions (1 Cor. 2:3). Paul did not just preach at or to people. He longed to be with the Roman Christians, not just so that he could encourage them but so that they could encourage him.

Every pastor needs to be encouraged. So often, the work of the pastorate in our day is an exercise in discouragement. The pastor is fair game for all criticism, and every Sunday afternoon people have roast pastor for dinner. When a pastor stands at the door at the end of the service and speaks to fifty people, forty-nine will say, "Thank you, pastor, for bringing the Word of God to us today. It ministered to me, and I appreciate that message I heard this morning." However, there is one who says, "I cannot believe that awful sermon you preached this morning." When the pastor goes home, is he going to remember the forty-nine words of encouragement or the one word of discouragement? If other pastors are like me, that one remark will eat away at them for the rest of the day. That is why pastors have to be encouraged. Paul needed that kind of encouragement.

Now I do not want you to be unaware, brethren, that I often planned to come to you (but was hindered until now), that I might have some fruit among you also, just as among the other Gentiles (v. 13). Paul refers to the Roman Christians as "Gentiles." I am sure there were Jewish converts mixed in among the Gentiles there, but the Christian Jews had been kicked out of Rome by the Emperor Claudius a short time before this epistle was written, and Gentiles were primarily the ones left.

I am a debtor both to Greeks and to barbarians, both to wise and to unwise (v. 14). He does not say he is a debtor to the Jew and the Greek but to the Greek and the barbarian. The Greeks were the highly cultured, civilized, intellectual elite of the ancient culture as distinguished from the rest of the Gentiles, who were pagan barbarians. Paul is in debt both to the high-minded Greek and to the barbarian, but he is not talking about a pecuniary obligation or debt; he does not owe them money. Paul is writing about a moral debt. He is burdened by an obligation that accompanied his office as an apostle.

He had been set apart as the apostle to the Gentiles, and he spends his life discharging that obligation. Ultimately, the debt Paul owes is owed to God and to Christ, but he transfers that indebtedness, that obligation, to the people who need to hear the gospel. To Paul's way of thinking, so long as he is alive he cannot pay that debt because he owes his life to every person he meets. Someone said to me, "R. C., I want you to know that I have decided to dedicate the rest of my life to serving Jesus." I have heard that many times from people, but it never gets stale. Such fervency of soul should be the heartbeat of every believer. Once again Paul reaches down into his soul to speak of the depth of his passion: **as much as is in me, I am ready to preach the gospel to you who are in Rome also** (v. 15). Paul is saying, "Every fiber of my being is ready to preach the gospel to you. I cannot wait to get there."

Unashamed

It should be for the pastor as it was for Paul: **for I am not ashamed of the gospel of Christ** (v. 16). If we think our culture is hostile to the gospel, the first-century culture Paul lived in was much more so. Yet Paul was not ashamed of the gospel; he gloried in it. "Let him who boasts boast in the Lord" (2 Cor. 10:17 NIV). Paul enjoyed nothing more than being known as a Christian. He had no shame.

Jesus warned us that if we are ashamed of him before men, he will be ashamed of us before his Father (Mark 8:38; Luke 9:26). That is the real crunch for many Christians. They want to be Secret Service Christians. They do not want to be known as "holier than thou." They know that if they say one word to their friends about Christ, they will be accused of trying to shove the gospel down their throats. If we get rebuffed enough times, pretty soon we find ourselves tempted to be embarrassed about our faith, but not the apostle. He could not wait to get to Rome because he was not ashamed of the gospel. The gospel is **the power of God to salvation for everyone who believes, for the Jew first and also for the Greek** (v. 16). This word *power* is the Greek word *dunamos*, from which we get the word *dynamite*. The power of the gospel is, literally, dynamite.

Martin Luther preached his last sermon on February 15, 1546, in his hometown of Eisleben, Germany. Luther had been summoned from Wittenberg, where he was a professor, to his hometown. A serious rift had developed between two nobles, and the townsmen hoped that if Luther came and mediated the dispute peace would come back to the city. Luther agreed to make the arduous journey to Eisleben, where he preached the sermon two days before his death. In that sermon Luther expressed concern about the gospel. He had warned people on prior occasions that any time the gospel is preached accurately and passionately, it will bring conflict, and since people flee from conflict, every generation will tend to water down or hide the gospel, allowing it to be eclipsed by darkness as it had been for centuries before the Reformation. At the time of Luther's death such an eclipse was already occurring in Germany.

Luther said that in times past, people would run to the ends of the world had they known of a place where they could hear God speak. Now that we hear and read God's Word every day, this does not happen. We hear the gospel in our homes, where father, mother, and children sing and speak of it. The preacher speaks of it in the parish church. We ought to lift up our hands and rejoice that we have been given the honor of hearing God speak to us through his Word. People say, "There is preaching every day, often many times every day, so that we soon grow weary of it. What do we get out of it? I go to church, but I don't get much out of it." The people who teach us how to grow churches tell us we have to be sensitive to what people want. We have to scratch people where they itch, or they will not come back. We are told that we have to cast our sermons and messages not on the basis of what the Word of God declares but on the felt needs of the people. That is not what people need. God's priority is that people understand his holy character. People may not feel their need of that, but there is nothing they need more than to have their minds exploded in their understanding of who God is. God forbid that we listen to Madison Avenue and those who tell us to become hucksters, which is what Luther was complaining about.

Luther said, "If you do not want God to speak to you every day in your house and in your parish church, then be wise. Look for something else. In Trier is our Lord God's coat; in Aachen are Joseph's britches and our Blessed Lady's chemise. Go there and squander your money; buy indulgences and the pope's second-hand junk." Luther said the people were crazy, blinded, and possessed by the Devil:

> There sits that decoy duck in Rome with his bag of tricks, luring to himself the whole world with its money and goods, and all the while anybody can go to baptism, the sacrament, and the preaching desk. But the people say, "What, baptism? The Lord's Supper? God's Word? Joseph's britches—that's what does it!"

In their madness people were going all over Germany to find the nearest collection of relics: a piece of straw from the crib of Jesus; milk from the breast of his mother, Mary; or part of the beard of John the Baptist. That is what the church was selling. Why did people buy it? What do people want today when they go to someone who promises healing and who slays them in the Spirit? They are looking for power. They want a powerful Christian experience. They want power to manipulate their environment, which is the great goal of the New Age movement.

Only one is omnipotent, and he is the Lord God, and the Lord God has power to spare. He does not need Joseph's pants. He does not even need the gospel, yet it has pleased the Lord God omnipotent to invest his power there. Power is not found in Joseph's pants or in the preacher's ability to slay somebody in the Spirit. God's power is invested in the gospel. God has promised that his Word will not return to him void (Isa. 55:11). The foolishness of preaching is the method God has chosen to save the world. That is why Paul said he was not ashamed. He wanted to preach the gospel because it is the power of God to salvation. It is not the power of the preacher's eloquence or the power of the preacher's education; it is the power of God.

Martin Luther's Text

We need the power of God to salvation, **for in it the righteousness of God is revealed from faith to faith; as it is written, "The just shall live by faith"** (v. 17). In the gospel the righteousness of God is revealed from faith to faith. I mentioned in the preface that this was the verse the Holy Spirit used to awaken Luther as he was preparing his lectures on the book of Romans. He glanced at a manuscript from Augustine and found where Augustine said that the righteousness here is not God's righteousness but that which he provides for people, who do not have any righteousness. It is the righteousness he makes available by free grace to all who believe. Luther called it "alien righteousness." This righteousness is not our own; it is Jesus' righteousness.

Luther sought every means he knew within the confines of the monastery to satisfy the demands of God's law, yet he had no peace. Luther was an expert in the law of God, and every day he was in terror as he looked in the mirror of the law and examined his life against God's righteousness. We are not in terror, because we have blocked out the view of God's righteousness. We judge ourselves on a curve, measuring ourselves against others. We never judge ourselves according to the standard of God's perfection. If we did, we would be tormented like Martin Luther was in the monastery. When Luther finally saw the doors of paradise swing open, he walked through, which is why he stood against kings and officials of the church. He refused to compromise. Once he had tasted the gospel of Jesus Christ and had been delivered from the pangs and torment of the law, nobody could take it from him.

I understand the sense of liberation that Luther experienced from reading that text. It is the thematic verse for the epistle. Everything that comes after

it will be an explanation of this one line: "For in it the righteousness of God
. . ." The Greek word *dikaiosune* is the word used in the New Testament for
"justification." We are going to see that word again and again as we pour
over this letter to the Romans.

The Life of Faith

"The just shall live by faith"—that phrase, which comes from the Old Testament book of the prophet Habakkuk, is quoted three times in the New
Testament: here in Romans 1:17, in Galatians 3:11, and in Hebrews 10:38.
In its original context, Habakkuk was deeply distressed. The people of God
were being invaded by pagans, the pagans were triumphing, and Habakkuk
was confused. He asked:

> You are of purer eyes than to behold evil,
> And cannot look on wickedness.
> Why do You look on those who deal treacherously,
> And hold Your tongue when the wicked devours
> A person more righteous than he? (Hab. 1:13)

Then Habakkuk stood in his watchtower and set himself on the rampart,
waiting to see what God would say to him. The Lord answered:

> Write the vision
> And make it plain on tablets,
> That he may run who reads it.
> For the vision is yet for an appointed time;
> But at the end it will speak, and it will not lie.
> Though it tarries, wait for it. (2:2–3)

Do you ever feel tension because the promises of God do not show up
when you want them to? You cry and say, "God, where are you in this?"
That was the complaint of Habakkuk, and yet the God we worship is a
promise-keeping God. He tells Habakkuk to be patient

> Because it will surely come,
> It will not tarry.
> Behold the proud,
> His Soul is not upright in Him;
> But the just shall live by his faith. (2:3–4)

One who lives by faith is a righteous person in the sight of God. The righteous live by trust. When Jesus was in the Judean wilderness under the unbridled assault of Satan, lonely and hungry, Satan told him to take stones and make them bread. Jesus said he would not do that: "It is written, 'Man shall not live by bread alone, but by every word that proceeds from the mouth of God'" (Matt. 4:4). Anybody can believe *in* God. What it means to be a Christian is to trust him when he speaks, which does not require a leap of faith or a crucifixion of the intellect. It requires a crucifixion of pride, because no one is more trustworthy than God.

When we do not trust God, it is because we transfer to him our own corrupt qualities, but God does not have any of those corrupt qualities. You can trust him with your life, and that is the theme of this epistle—the just shall live by faith—and from that vantage point, Paul opens up the depths and the riches of the whole gospel for the people of God.

3

THE WRATH OF GOD

Romans 1:18–25

For the wrath of God is revealed from heaven against all ungodliness and unrighteousness of men, who suppress the truth in unrighteousness, because what may be known of God is manifest in them, for God has shown it to them. For since the creation of the world His invisible attributes are clearly seen, being understood by the things that are made, even His eternal power and Godhead, so that they are without excuse, because, although they knew God, they did not glorify Him as God, nor were thankful, but became futile in their thoughts, and their foolish hearts were darkened. Professing to be wise, they became fools, and changed the glory of the incorruptible God into an image made like corruptible man—and birds and four-footed animals and creeping things. Therefore God also gave them up to uncleanness, in the lusts of their hearts, to dishonor their bodies among themselves, who exchanged the truth of God for the lie, and worshiped and served the creature rather than the Creator, who is blessed forever. Amen.

The text before us is foundational to our understanding of God's revelation of the gospel. Notice the abrupt change in the tone of the epistle from that which we looked at in our last study. Paul has just introduced us to the revelation of the righteousness of God, but no sooner does he mention it than he introduces another revelation—the wrath of God.

Wrath Revealed

I am sure that the apostle introduces the wrath of God at this point because no one can fully appreciate the good news as good except against the backdrop of our guilt before God. The good news is an announcement to people who universally are under the indictment of God and exposed to his wrath.

People today are not particularly concerned about the gospel because they do not know anything about the law of God, and they are not at all familiar with the revelation of his wrath. If people were sensitive to the manifestation of God's anger toward them, they would be so moved by enlightened self-interest that they would flee as fast as they could to hear the gospel, but their necks have become so hardened, their hearts so calcified, that they have no fear of God. People do not believe in God's wrath; they think he is incapable of it. They listen to preachers everywhere tell them that God loves them unconditionally, and when they hear that, they see no reason to fear his wrath.

Before Paul develops the theme of the gospel, he says that **the wrath of God is revealed from heaven against all unrighteousness and ungodliness of men** (v. 18). The Greek word Paul uses for "wrath" is *orgai*. The English word that derives from *orgai* is *orgy*. When we think of an orgy, we think of participation in unbridled sexual behavior, eroticism with reckless abandon. The point of contact between the English word *orgy* and the Greek word for *wrath* that Paul uses here is that God is not simply annoyed or irritated; God's anger is one of passion with paroxysms of rage and fury.

It is perfectly appropriate for a holy and righteous God to be moved to anger against evil. A judge with no distaste for evil would not be a good judge. God is angry with two distinct things: ungodliness, or irreverence or impiety (from the Latin word *impiatos*), and unrighteousness. When we think of those two terms, *ungodliness* and *unrighteousness*, we tend to think of ungodliness as a particularly religious transgression, such as blasphemy or irreverence, and unrighteousness as an immoral activity or behavioral pattern. We might look at this text, therefore, and deduce that God is mad at two things: he is angry at us for being irreverent, and he is angry at us for being immoral. I do not think that is the force of the text, because Paul uses a grammatical structure that we find sporadically throughout the Bible called a *hendiadys*, which literally means "two for one," two distinct things taken together to point to just one thing. I think it is proper to understand Paul as saying that

God is angry—furious—with a particular sin. When we examine that sin, it is seen to be both ungodly or irreverent and unrighteous or immoral.

Truth Suppressed

Ungodliness and *unrighteousness* are vast generic terms that cover a multitude of sins, but Paul is not talking about a multitude of sins here. He has in view one particular sin. It is a universal sin, one committed by every human being. It is the sin that most clearly expresses our Adamic nature, our corruption and fallenness in the flesh. Paul does not leave us to guess at the nature of this sin; God is provoked to an orgy of anger against the sin of those **who suppress the truth in unrighteousness** (v. 18). The single sin that provokes God's wrath against the whole human race is the sin of suppressing truth.

The root of the Greek word translated "suppress" is *katacain*, which can also be translated as "to hinder," "to stifle," "to incarcerate," "to put in detention," "to obscure," or "to repress." We might think of a gigantic spring or coil that would require all the strength in our body to push down or compress. While we are pushing it down, it is resisting our strength and seeking to spring back up and recoil into its original position. By nature we take the truth of God and press it down. We force it into our subconscious, as it were, to get it out of our mind; yet, despite all the strength we use to suppress it, we simply cannot eradicate it. We cannot get rid of it because it is always and everywhere pushing back up. The specific sin here is the suppression of truth.

What truth is being suppressed? Paul tells us: **because what may be known of God is manifest in them, for God has shown it to them** (v. 19). The truth that every human being suppresses is the truth of God, what God reveals of himself in nature to the whole human race. This is not the truth of God that we learn through the Bible. We suppress that too, but here Paul is writing of a truth that is known about God apart from the Bible, a knowledge of God that God makes manifest. The Greek word is *phoneros*, which means "to show plainly." We use the term *phenomenon*, which is derived from that Greek word. The Latin text translates it as *manifestum*. The knowledge God gives of himself is not obscure. It is not buried with hidden clues that only an intellectual, elite group of people are able to discover after a painful and tedious search of sifting through the evidence. The truth God gives of himself is manifest. It is clear—so plain that everybody gets it.

It is clear because God himself is the teacher, and we cannot say that the student did not learn because the teacher did not teach. That would impugn the ability and integrity of the Almighty. He shows it to everybody. The

Greek *agnosis* means "without knowledge." The agnostic portrays himself as a less militant form of atheist. The atheist boldly declares that there is no god, but the agnostic says, "I don't know if there is a God. I'm *agnosis*; I am without sufficient knowledge to make a firm judgment on this matter." (Incidentally, the Latin term for *agnosis* is *ignoramus*.)

Agnostics think they are not as militant as atheists, but they do not realize that their agnosticism exposes them to greater risk for the wrath of God than if they were militant atheists. Not only do they refuse to acknowledge the God who reveals himself plainly, but they blame God for their situation, saying he has not given them sufficient evidence.

I was invited to a university campus several years ago to speak to an atheists' club. They asked me to present the intellectual case for the existence of God. I did, and as I went through the arguments for the existence of God, I kept things on an intellectual plane. All things were safe and comfortable until I got to the end of my lecture. At that point I said, "I'm giving you arguments for the existence of God, but I feel like I'm carrying coals to Newcastle because I have to tell you that I do not have to prove to you that God exists, because I think you already know it. Your problem is not that you do not know that God exists; your problem is that you despise the God whom you know exists. Your problem is not intellectual; it is moral—you hate God."

Visibility of the Invisible God

God has plainly and clearly shown himself to everyone. **For since the creation of the world His invisible attributes are clearly seen** (v. 20). The Latin word used for "clearly seen" is the root for our English word *conspicuous*; God has made his self-revelation conspicuous to everyone since the creation of the world. God does not pop a clue into history about his existence every three thousand years or so. Every moment since the dawn of creation God has been manifesting himself through **the things that are made** (v. 20). God did not give us a world and just say, "Sit down and begin to think about where that world came from and reason from the cosmos back to God." We are to do that, but it is more than that. Every second, God is manifesting himself through the things that are made so that his testimony to his nature is plainly evident.

I am frequently asked, "What happens to the poor, innocent native in Africa who has never heard of Jesus?" That poor, innocent native in Africa goes straight to heaven when he dies. He has no need for a Savior. Jesus did not come in the world to save innocent people. There are no innocent natives in Africa or in Australia, South America, Europe, Asia, or anywhere else. People think that those who have not heard of Jesus are surely innocent, but Jesus came into a world already under the indictment of God the Father because it has rejected him. We must disavow ourselves of the idea that there are innocent people anywhere.

People also ask, "Will God send people to hell for rejecting Jesus, of whom they have never heard?" God is not going to punish someone for rejecting somebody he has never heard of, but their destination is hell for the rejection of the One they have heard of. Every human being knows of God and clearly perceives God but rejects that knowledge. For that, every person is exposed to the wrath of God. The only possible way someone can be rescued from that wrath is through the Savior. Paul is setting the foundation for the urgency of the gospel.

Immanuel Kant, the great philosopher of the eighteenth century and perhaps the greatest agnostic of all time, revolutionized the world of philosophy by giving a systematic and comprehensive critique of the traditional classic arguments for the existence of God. Kant argued that you cannot reason from the visible things of the world back to the invisible God. According to Kant, God is in a realm not known through theoretical reason or empirical investigation. If Kant was right, then the apostle Paul was wrong. If Paul was right, then Kant was wrong. It is time that the Christian church stopped rolling over and playing dead at the feet of Immanuel Kant and started showing the error of Kant's reasoning. In Romans Paul sets forth plainly that the invisible God, even though he cannot be seen because he is invisible, is clearly seen. God is not seen directly, but he is seen through the things that are made.

God reveals **His eternal power and Godhead** (v. 20) to the whole world. This revelation does not give us all the specific details about the character and nature of God, but it certainly gives us knowledge of God in general. This revelation includes God's eternal power. God's self-existent, eternal being has been revealed in every leaf, every page, every raindrop, and every inch of the cosmos since the beginning of time. The temporal world is the vehicle of divine revelation, and by it all people are able to know that God exists. God's eternal power and his inherent attributes—immutability, omniscience, omnipresence, and all that fits deity—are made clear through nature. God is also revealed by his moral perfection, holiness, righteousness, and sovereign right to impose obligations upon his creatures without their permission or ascent. God inherently has the right to command from his creatures what is pleasing to him. Paul says that all these things are made clear to us.

Without Excuse

Paul explains the rationale for the revelation of God's wrath: **they are without excuse** (v. 20). Man has no basis for an *apologia* to God's indictment. What answer will corrupt and fallen human beings try to give to God on the day of judgment? "God, I did not know you were there. If you had made your revelation clear to me, I would have been your obedient servant." People will be tempted to make a plea or excuse, but everyone stands without an excuse. There is no excuse of ignorance before God, not when he himself has given us the information. A plea of ignorance is an empty plea and will have no effect.

Although they knew God, they did not glorify Him as God, nor were thankful (v. 21). A well-known Dutch philosopher and theologian said about this text that although God has objectively revealed himself to the human race, this general revelation yields no natural theology; that is, the revelation does not penetrate man's consciousness. Those who hold to this view cite Calvin, who saw nature as a glorious theater that man cannot see because of his fallen condition. I think it is unfortunate that Calvin, the great Reformer, used that metaphor, because it was not consistent with everything else he taught about our response to general revelation.

To the Corinthians Paul writes that natural man does not know God, yet here in Romans 1 he says the natural man does know God. How are we to reconcile that apparent contradiction? I think the reconciliation is found in the language itself. The Greek word *gnosko* means "to know," but it can mean "to know intellectually," by *cognition* (the Latin term), or "to know intimately," as seen in Genesis 4:1: "Adam knew Eve his wife, and she conceived." The word here denotes an intimate knowledge, one the Bible uses to refer to those who, born of the Spirit, are born unto this intimate, salvific, personal knowledge of God that only the redeemed have.

When Paul writes to the Corinthians about the Spirit, who gives that kind of knowledge, he says that the natural man does not know God in that sense (2 Cor. 2:14). Here in Romans he says that man's problem is not that the knowledge fails to get through in the sense of a cognitive awareness of the reality of God. God is angry because that knowledge does get through. It is what we do with the knowledge that provokes the wrath of God. Knowing God, we refuse to honor him as God; neither are we grateful.

The most fundamental sin in our fallen, corrupt nature is the sin of idolatry, the sin of refusing to honor God as he is. We want to strip him of his attributes, turn him into a God made in our image, a God we can live with, a God that we can be comfortable with. People say God is a God of love, not a God of wrath, but that is not the God of Scripture. The God of love revealed in Scripture is also angry with sin. He is the God of justice, righteousness, and holiness. We cannot embrace the attributes of God that make us comfortable and reject the rest. When we do that, we join the throng of humanity that suppresses the truth of God and refuses to honor him as God or be thankful. The refusal to honor and worship God, and hearts that are not filled with joy and gratitude for what he gives, are what define our fallenness. There are few people who delight in the worship of God.

Each Sunday morning I go out to breakfast, and inevitably, after I have ordered my food, someone from our congregation sits at the table across from me, and we chat over breakfast. During one such breakfast I was asked, "R. C., what do you think about all the people that are in here eating? They are not going to church."

"I know," I replied. "People are everywhere but at church, because nothing is more displeasing to them than to worship God. They do not want to hear about God. That knowledge is suppressed. It is pushed down, and they have no desire to have God in their minds."

Darkened Hearts

Because men refused to glorify God as God, they **became futile in their thoughts, and their foolish hearts were darkened** (v. 21). Some of the most brilliant people come to very different conclusions about the nature of reality. Who was more brilliant than Thomas Aquinas or Aurelius Augustine? They were fiercely convinced of the reality of God, and their lives were driven by that conviction, which lay at the foundation of everything else they believed. Others of gifted intellect, such as Jean-Paul Sartre, John Stuart Mill, and Albert Camus, wound up on the other end of the spectrum, embracing nihilism à la Nietzsche, saying that there is no meaning or significance in human experience. How can such brilliant people end up so far away? If, at the very beginning of the pursuit of knowledge, people categorically deny what they know to be true—the reality of God—then, frankly, the farther away they will go from God. They have built their house on a lie so that their thinking becomes an exercise in futility, and their foolish hearts are darkened.

When Paul speaks of hearts that are dark, he uses the word *foolish*. To the Jew, the judgment of "foolish" is not an intellectual judgment; it is a moral judgment. That is why Jesus warned against calling people fools (Matt. 5:22). Don't say, "The fool has said in his heart, 'There is no God'" (Ps. 14:1). The fool is not only being stupid, he is also being wicked because he is denying what he knows to be true. The indictment on all people is this: they refuse to honor God as God. It is not that they fail to know God and therefore do not honor or thank him. They do know God but will not honor him or be grateful. That is the massive perdition in which we find ourselves as fallen human beings, and against that background the gospel comes.

Their foolish hearts were darkened and **professing to be wise, they became fools** (v. 22). There is an ongoing debate on television and in the newspapers between intelligent design and science. Intelligent design is not science. The word *science* means "knowledge." If you know that God is the author of all things, then you know that the affirmation of the existence of God is the purest scientific thought there is. To deny or exclude it is not to be scientific but to be foolish. It is ironic that those who refuse to acknowledge what they know to be true claim such activity in the name of wisdom. They call it "science" when actually it is foolishness—foolishness that betrays a heart of darkness. They do not become atheists, generally. They become idolaters. They become religious.

They **changed the glory of the incorruptible God into an image made like corruptible man—and birds and four-footed animals and creeping things** (v. 23). They exchange the truth of God—the majestic, self-existent, eternal God of heaven and earth—and begin to worship birds, bears, and totem poles. Can anything be more ridiculous than a religion that builds on a fundamental refusal to acknowledge what is known to be true? Can anything be more ridiculous than trading in the glory of God for the creature?

Therefore God also gave them up to uncleanness, in the lusts of their hearts, to dishonor their bodies among themselves, who exchanged the truth of God for the lie, and worshiped and served the creature rather than the Creator, who is blessed forever. Amen (vv. 24–25). (Even when Paul is talking about the wrath of God and the universal sin of fallen humanity he cannot help but break into doxology, speaking about the Creator.) The word "exchanged" is a critical term here. It is the Greek word *metallasso*. I cannot help but read this text through the eyes of modern psychiatry, which works in terms of repression and suppression. What kinds of ideas do we tend to suppress or repress? We do not push down pleasant thoughts; we push down frightening thoughts and bad memories. People go to see a psychiatrist because they have a nameless anxiety or dread. They do not know why they feel phobic, so the psychiatrist probes them with analytical questions. He checks their background and their childhood. He asks about their dreams and begins to probe their subconscious.

He knows that when people attempt to repress things, they do not destroy the memory; they exchange it for something they can live with, something that will not terrify their minds.

There is nothing more terrifying to a sinner than God. In trying to explain the universality of religion, Sigmund Freud asked why it is that people are so incurably religious. He claimed that we have invented God to deal with things in nature that we find frightening. He explained that by inventing God we personalize or sacralize nature. We feel deeply threatened by hurricanes, fires, tornadoes, pestilence, and armies, but we do not have the same terror concerning our personal relationships. If someone is hostile toward us, there are many ways we can try to defuse that anger. We can try to appease the angry person with words or gifts or flattery. We learn how to get around human anger, but how do we negotiate with a hurricane? How do we mollify an earthquake? How do we persuade cancer not to visit our house? Freud thought that we do it by personalizing nature, and we do that by inventing a god to put over the hurricane, the earthquake, and the disease, and then we talk to that god to try to appease him.

Terrible Consequences

Obviously, Freud was not on the Sea of Galilee when the storm arose and threatened to capsize the boat in which Jesus and his disciples were sitting. The disciples were afraid. Jesus was asleep, and so they went to him and shook him awake, and they said, "'Teacher, do You not care that we are perishing?' Then He arose and rebuked the wind, and said to the sea, 'Peace, be still!' And the wind ceased and there was a great calm" (Mark 4:38–39). There was not a zephyr in the air. You would think the disciples' gratitude would have led them to say, "Thank you, Jesus, for removing the cause of our fear." Instead, they became very much afraid. Their fears were intensified, and they said to one another, "Who can this be, that even the wind and the sea obey Him!" (v. 41). They were dealing with something transcendent.

What we see in the disciples is xenophobia, fear of the stranger. The holiness of Christ was made manifest in that boat, and suddenly the disciples' fear escalated. This is where Freud missed the point. If people are going to invent religion to protect them from the fear of nature, why would they invent a god who is more terrifying than nature itself? Why would they invent a holy god? Fallen creatures, when they make idols, do not make holy idols. We prefer the unholy, the profane, the secular—a god we can control.

Here in Romans the apostle brings us to the place where we have no excuse, where ignorance cannot be claimed, because God has so manifested himself to every creature that every last one of us knows that God exists and that he deserves our honor and thanks and is not to be traded in or swapped for the creature.

Paul outlines the dreadful consequences that fall on a race of people who live by refusing to acknowledge what they know to be true about the character of God. The result is a futile mind, a blackened heart, and a life of radical corruption. People are exposed to God's displeasure so that their only hope is the gospel of his dear Son. This portion of Paul's letter is preparatory; it is the groundwork. If he had stopped here, we would be without hope, lost forever in our guilt and sin.

4

JUDICIAL ABANDONMENT

Romans 1:22–32

Professing to be wise, they became fools, and changed the glory of the incorruptible God into an image made like corruptible man—and birds and four-footed animals and creeping things. Therefore God also gave them up to uncleanness, in the lusts of their hearts, to dishonor their bodies among themselves, who exchanged the truth of God for the lie, and worshiped and served the creature rather than the Creator, who is blessed forever. Amen. For this reason God gave them up to vile passions. For even their women exchanged the natural use for what is against nature. Likewise also the men, leaving the natural use of the woman, burned in their lust for one another, men with men committing what is shameful, and receiving in themselves the penalty of their error which was due.

And even as they did not like to retain God in their knowledge, God gave them over to a debased mind, to do those things which are not fitting; being filled with all unrighteousness, sexual immorality, wickedness, covetousness, maliciousness; full of envy, murder, strife, deceit, evil-mindedness; they are whisperers, backbiters, haters of God, violent, proud, boasters, inventors of evil things, disobedient to parents, undiscerning, untrustworthy, unloving, unforgiving, unmerciful; who, knowing the righteous judgment of God, that those who practice such things are deserving of death, not only do the same but also approve of those who practice them.

T he passage before us is one of the most grim that we find anywhere in sacred Scripture. Some regard these verses almost as a postscript to the main body of the text, and they move over them somewhat superficially, yet this assessment of our human condition is so radically different from what we hear every day that we need to hear it repeatedly so that we might be fully persuaded of our desperate condition apart from the mercy and grace of God.

Paul has already shown that humanity, universally, is guilty of suppressing and repressing the knowledge of God—knowledge that God makes clear in and through creation so that every person is without excuse. The fundamental sin of fallen humanity is the refusal to honor God as God or to be grateful (vv. 18–21). Now Paul describes a dreadful exchange. Fallen humanity trades the glory of Almighty God, the sweetness of his excellence, for a lie: **Professing to be wise, they became fools, and changed the glory of the incorruptible God into an image made like corruptible man—and birds and four-footed animals and creeping things. Therefore God also gave them up to uncleanness, in the lusts of their hearts, to dishonor their bodies among themselves, who exchanged the truth of God for the lie, and worshiped and served the creature rather than the Creator, who is blessed forever. Amen** (vv. 22–25).

Given Up

Three times in this section we read about human beings being given up by God. They are given up to their vile passions, the lust of the flesh, and their reprobate minds. When God judges people according to the standard of his righteousness, he is declaring that he will not strive with mankind forever. We hear all the time about God's infinite grace and mercy. I cringe when I hear it. God's mercy is infinite insofar as it is mercy bestowed upon us by a Being who is infinite, but when the term *infinite* is used to describe his mercy rather than his person, I have problems with it because the Bible makes very clear that there is a limit to God's mercy. There is a limit to his grace, and he is determined not to pour out his mercy on impenitent people forever. There is a time, as the Old Testament repeatedly reports, particularly in the book of the prophet Jeremiah, that God stops being gracious with people, and he gives them over to their sin.

The worst thing that can happen to sinners is to be allowed to go on sinning without any divine restraints. At the end of the New Testament, in the book of Revelation when the description of the last judgment is set forth,

God says, "He who is unjust, let him be unjust still; he who is filthy, let him be filthy still" (Rev. 22:11). God gives people over to what they want. He abandons them to their sinful impulses and removes his restraints, saying in essence, "If you want to sin, go ahead and sin." This is what theologians call "judicial abandonment." God, in dispensing his just judgment, abandons the impenitent sinner forever.

In biblical history we find people who experience a sense of being abandoned by God, an experience which provokes horrific darkness in their souls. In the Old Testament there is Job. He was never fully and finally abandoned by God, but for a season he was exposed to the evil one. In the first chapter of Job, Satan comes into the courts of heaven and brags to God that everybody on the planet belongs to him; all willingly follow his devices. God says, by way of rebuke, "Have you considered My servant Job, that there is none like him on the earth, a blameless and upright man, one who fears God and shuns evil?" (Job 1:8). Satan replies:

> "Does Job fear God for nothing? Have You not made a hedge around him, around his household, and around all that he has on every side? You have blessed the work of his hands, and his possessions have increased in the land. But now, stretch out Your hand and touch all that he has, and he will surely curse You to Your face!" (vv. 9–11).

For a season, God removes the hedge and lets Satan get at Job.

The worst expression of exposure to satanic seduction came to our Savior in the Judean wilderness where, after forty days of solitude and hunger, he was for a season exposed to the hostility of Satan. Our Lord withstood everything that Satan could throw at him. After the forty days Satan left him, and the Scriptures tell us that the angels came and ministered to Christ.

Later, when Christ began his public ministry and had called his disciples to himself, they came to him and said, "Lord, teach us to pray" (Luke 11:1). He gave them the model prayer, the Lord's Prayer, and he included in it the petition, "Do not lead us into temptation, but deliver us from the evil one" (v. 4). Jesus told them to pray for protection from Satan. They were to pray that the Father would never give them over to sin. The worst thing that could happen to anyone is judicial abandonment.

Throughout Christian history there has been a function that mirrors that very predicament, the discipline of excommunication. To be excommunicated from the body of Christ is the only thing worse than being sent to hell in the final judgment, yet there is only one sin for which a person is to be excommunicated—impenitence. There are many sins that can begin the process of church discipline such that the sinner may be censured and barred for a season from the Lord's Table. That and other prohibitions are intermediate steps of discipline designed to curb someone's sin, to bring that sinner to repentance, to restore him to fullness of fellowship in the church, and to guard his soul from utter ruin. However, if he remains consistently hardhearted and impenitent after all the intermediate steps are taken, the final step is excommunication.

We do not take that seriously today. Several years ago I knew a woman who left her husband for another man. She sought to divorce her husband so that she could be free to marry her lover. Church discipline was brought against her. During each consecutive stage of that discipline, she refused to repent. I went to see her on the eve of her excommunication and pleaded with her, saying "Please, do not go this last step. If you get excommunicated, the church is delivering you to Satan and abandoning you to your sin." She said, "I never thought about it like that. That is ghastly, and I hope you are wrong. But I am in love with my lover." She divorced her husband and married her lover, and later on she divorced him too. What so terrified me was how cavalier that woman was about excommunication. In our culture and in the church today church discipline does not mean much. Church discipline is one of the responsibilities that God gives to the church, as Paul makes clear in his first epistle to the Corinthians.

Here in Romans, God is, for a season at least, excommunicating the whole human race. He pronounces his judicial abandonment on all mankind for their refusal to respond to his clear revelation of himself. Since by nature we repress that truth, God delivers us to our sin.

Sin for Sin

Many times, if not most times, the sin we commit is a punishment for sin. When we sin, we are actually working out God's punishment for our sin. We are not committing a new transgression every time we sin; rather, the sinful impulses that we harbor, embrace, and experience in our actual transgressions are already the result of God's judgment for our sin. That is what happens in judicial abandonment. God gives us over to our sinful impulses. We become slaves to the things that we want to do.

Paul is not satisfied to speak in generalities, so he gives a detailed description of how those sinful passions are manifested in concrete human behavior: **For this reason God gave them up to vile passions. For even their women exchanged the natural use for what is against nature** (v. 26). This is a text that we will not hear often on television in this day and age. There are two things I need to say about it. First, when the apostle Paul describes the radical corruption of the human race, he sees the sin of homosexual behavior as the sin most representative of the radical nature of our fall. It is seen here not simply as a sin, nor even as a serious sin or a gross sin, but as the clearest expression of the depths of our perversity.

Second, when Paul introduces the sin of homosexual behavior, he first mentions females. Throughout human history man has been the gender that seems most brutish, most without conscience and godliness. The woman has been understood as the fairer sex, but when Paul wants to describe the depth of the fall of the human race, he says that even the women exchanged the natural use for what is *contra naturum*, against nature, not simply against culture, or societal convention. In other words, when we become involved in homosexual practices, we are not only sinning against God but against the nature of things. All the debates today about whether homosexual behavior is acquired or inherently genetic can be answered here in this text. The Word of God says that such behavior is not natural. It is against nature as God has created it.

Likewise also the men, leaving the natural use of the woman, burned in their lust for one another, men with men committing what is shameful, and receiving in themselves the penalty of their error which was due (v. 27). When men and women engage in this kind of behavior, there are necessary, divinely appointed consequences. A price must be paid when people go that far to defy the law of God. The word *due* has all but disappeared from our culture and vocabulary, but it is one that has a very rich history in ethics. It goes back to the Nicomachean Ethics of Aristotle and on down through Western civilization, throughout which justice has been defined not only in the church but also outside the church as giving people what is due them. When people so act against God's law and the law of nature, he gives them their due.

Homosexuality is just one sin that Paul describes in this section. If we can make it through Paul's entire list without feeling pangs of conscience, we are psychopaths. **And even as they did not like to retain God in their knowledge, God gave them over to a debased mind** (v. 28), a mind that does not focus attention on whatsoever things are true, pure, lovely, and just (see Phil. 4:8). A debased mind is one in which the thoughts are filled with impurities, the desires of the flesh, lust, jealousy, and hatred against people. Such a mind is in love with the lie and flees from the truth. Our basic nature as fallen human does not want to receive the knowledge of God, and when it does penetrate the mind, we do not want to keep it there.

We see again God's use of judicial abandonment. It is as if he is saying, "If you want a mind fixed on debauchery, you can have it."

It is rare that human beings have a taste for and a love of hearing the Word of God. If we have any affection in our hearts to hear the things of God, it is only possible because the Holy Spirit has already rescued us from the condition that Paul is describing, which is basic to all humanity. If we have a desire to learn the things of God, then something has happened to plant that desire in our hearts. At one time, we had the mind of a reprobate and did not want knowledge of God.

Filled with Unrighteousness

Because they did not want to retain God in their knowledge, God gave them over to debased minds **to do those things which are not fitting; being filled with all unrighteousness** (vv. 28–29). If we ask people whether they believe man is basically good, the majority answer yes. Due to the impact of humanism on our culture, people believe that man is basically good and simply makes mistakes on occasion. Such thinking leads people to believe they do not need Jesus. However, there is nothing we need more than Jesus. We tickle our imaginations if we say that we are basically good. The people who need to hear the gospel are not merely tainted by unrighteousness; they are filled with unrighteousness. That is how Paul describes us in our natural condition. No one is merely mildly affected by error or bad habits or mistakes; man is saturated with unrighteousness.

Unrighteousness is a general term, but Paul wants to get more specific, so he begins to elaborate on the kinds of unrighteousness that fill us as fallen creatures. First is **sexual immorality** (v. 29). Elsewhere the apostle writes, "Fornication and all uncleanness or covetousness, let it not even be named among you, as is fitting for saints" (Eph. 5:3). A recent Gallup poll reported that the incidence of fornication and adultery among born-again Christians is not measurably different from that of unconverted pagans. Truly regenerate Christians do fall into these sins, but it should be a radical exception to Christian behavior, not a generally accepted practice. Today people get their behavioral cues not from what God says is acceptable but from the culture.

Some argue that condemning immoral behavior is old-fashioned, but that sort of thinking is why we have Christian parents giving their daughters birth-control pills, something that sends a message that sexual immorality is okay. Paul, however, puts sexual immorality at the top of the list of what constitutes our corruption. Sex is a beautiful thing. God designed it and gave it to his people, but he gave a context for it—marriage—and he is jealous that it be reserved for that context.

To sexual immorality Paul adds **wickedness** and **covetousness** (v. 29). Covetousness is the sign of someone who does not want God in his thinking. When we covet someone else's property or prestige or job, we are saying, "God is not just in giving it to that person but not giving it to me." The minute we are envious and jealous of another, we have banished God from our minds.

I read a book on a new phenomenon called the "emergent church," which I hope is another fad that will go away as fast as it came. One of the gurus of the emergent church boasted that in the last ten years of his preaching, he has never once mentioned the word *sin*. He has not wanted to destroy people's identity and self-worth, their ego. I have mentioned the word *sin* more times in this study than that man has in his entire lifetime. You cannot read a page of sacred Scripture without dealing with the fundamental problem of our humanity.

John Calvin had the highest view of human beings of any theologian in history, as far as I know. Some think otherwise in light of all Calvin said about man's total depravity, but the reason Calvin takes sin so seriously is that he takes people so seriously. The reason God takes sin so seriously is not that he is a bully or a killjoy who does not want his creatures to have any fun. God takes sin seriously because he knows how destructive sin is to this world and to our friends, to family, and to marriage. God has a better idea for what humans are to experience, and in his ultimate plan of redemption he will banish sin from his world altogether.

Paul's list grows: **maliciousness; full of envy, murder, strife, deceit, evil-mindedness; they are whisperers** (v. 29). People whisper their plans because they cannot speak them aloud. Even in a fallen world our plans are so evil that others will reject them, so we whisper. Paul also includes **backbiters** (v. 30) on the list. Have people bitten us in the back? Have people slandered us? We must consider how many we have slandered and bitten in the back. This is not a problem only for pagans. As humans we are given to this sort of behavior.

Next on Paul's list are **haters of God**. Who will admit to that—to actually hating God? He also adds **violent, proud, boasters**, and **inventors of evil things** (v. 30). As if there were not enough temptations and sins to arouse our vile passions, we like to think up new ways to sin. Several years ago Random House commissioned a book series on the literary classics. Rod Serling from *The Twilight Zone* was commissioned to write the critical introduction to Augustine's classic, *Confessions*. Serling said he did not understand how *Confessions* had come to be regarded as a classic, because Augustine goes into great detail about the remorse he felt as the result of stealing pears from an orchard years before. He had no comprehension of what Augustine had experienced.

When I was a kid I used to go to Nick Green's orchard and watch Nick harvest rows of grapes. I moved along the rows with a big paper bag, stealing his grapes. I could afford to go to the store and buy the grapes, but it was more fun to steal them. I also stole pears and apples from Nick's trees. Once I was caught raiding a neighbor's garden, pulling up every onion from the onion patch, which made no sense, because I did not like onions. I am still paying the price for that; I understand why Augustine was so remorseful.

Paul adds to his list **disobedient to parents** (v. 30). When young people are disobedient to their parents, they are revealing their natural condition. Paul also includes those who are **undiscerning, untrustworthy, unloving, unforgiving, unmerciful** (v. 31). Despite the scope of his list, it is only partial. It is merely representative of our corruption. If Paul had enumerated all the sins that the Bible spells out, he could have filled the entire epistle and then some. He gives us a representative list that should be enough to stop every mouth and convict every conscience. Surely there is something on the list that we recognize as a part of our own experience. If we were to write down this list and compare it against the newspaper, we would see everything Paul mentions featured prominently in the news of the day.

Deserving of Death

The worst indictment is not found in this list of heinous crimes against God. It is found in the conclusion of the chapter: **those who practice such things are deserving of death** (v. 32). Paul says that fallen human beings not only do these things, but they know better. God has planted in the mind of every creature made in his image a conscience that can discern the difference between good and evil. Even Immanuel Kant understood the universal character of the categorical imperative. People without a conscience are called sociopaths or psychopaths; they are sick. A normal person—a fallen person whose normal behavior is the abnormality of sin—knows that people who do these things are worthy of death.

Young people, when you disobey your parents, do you think God would be just in taking away your life? God commands you to honor your parents, and if you dishonor them, you disobey God. God commands us not to covet, so if we covet, we are worthy of execution because we have committed an act of cosmic treason. Every time we sin, we challenge and defy God's right to reign over his creation and to impose obligations on us as creatures made in his image. Who are we to tell God that he has no right to restrain our behavior? Fallen humanity has declared independence, and the result is judicial abandonment.

It gets worse. Those who do those things **also approve of those who practice them** (v. 32). There is honor among thieves. Misery loves company. If we can entice others to join us in our sin, we can get rid of the taboos rather than repent of our guilt. We seek to establish a new ethic. If we are not convinced that Paul is describing how human beings function, we ought to watch television for the next three months and listen to all the rhetoric. I recall listening to a talk on television about a Supreme Court justice nominee. On the program was a woman from one of the organizations that favors abortion. She was concerned that the nominee would take away women's reproductive rights—the right to kill their offspring and to be involved sexually with no concern for the consequences. The word *right* has been redefined by our culture to mean that everybody has a right to do what they want with impunity. God does not give us that kind of right, but our culture seeks to lessen people's guilt in order to gain allies in the revolt against heaven.

Thanks be to God that Romans does not end here. The gospel, the good news, is coming. People who do not care about the good news might care if they digest the bad news first and realize what our Savior has done, what he has saved us from, what he has saved us for, and what he has saved us to. We are saved in order to be conformed to his image, to love the things he loves, and to hate the things he hates.

5

NO PARTIALITY

Romans 2:1–16

Therefore you are inexcusable, O man, whoever you are who judge, for in whatever you judge another you condemn yourself; for you who judge practice the same things. But we know that the judgment of God is according to truth against those who practice such things. And do you think this, O man, you who judge those practicing such things, and doing the same, that you will escape the judgment of God? Or do you despise the riches of His goodness, forbearance, and longsuffering, not knowing that the goodness of God leads you to repentance? But in accordance with your hardness and your impenitent heart you are treasuring up for yourself wrath in the day of wrath and revelation of the righteous judgment of God, who "will render to each one according to his deeds": eternal life to those who by patient continuance in doing good seek for glory, honor, and immortality; but to those who are self-seeking and do not obey the truth, but obey unrighteousness—indignation and wrath, tribulation and anguish, on every soul of man who does evil, of the Jew first and also of the Greek; but glory, honor, and peace to everyone who works what is good, to the Jew first and also to the Greek. For there is no partiality with God. For as many as have sinned without law will also perish without law, and as many as have sinned in the law will be judged by the law (for not the hearers of the law are just in the sight of God, but the doers of the law will be justified; for when Gentiles, who do not have the law, by nature do the things in the law, these, although not having the law, are a law to themselves, who show the work of the law written in their hearts, their conscience also bearing witness, and between themselves their thoughts accusing or else excusing them) in the day when God will judge the secrets of men by Jesus Christ, according to my gospel.

There was a brilliant Christian apologist who argued so compellingly during debates with his opponents that he reduced them to ashes, and afterward, it was said, he would dust off the spot where his adversaries had stood. I could not help but think of that description as I prepared this study of Romans 2.

Paul has just finished giving an indictment on all people. How long can he torment us with the oppressive character of the law and of our sin before he gives us some relief? After Jonathan Edwards preached one of his stirring sermons on the judgment of God and the threat of eternal damnation in hell, one of the parishioners cried out, "But, Mr. Edwards, is there no mercy with God?" Edwards reminded the people that they had to wait till the following Sabbath before they got that part of the message. The same is true here as we come to Romans 2. If we hope to get that good news now, our hopes are in vain, because the apostle is not finished with the bad news yet. Before we get to the gospel, the good news of justification by faith alone, we must be brought kicking and screaming, if necessary, before the holy standard of God's law so that we might be duly persuaded of our need for the gospel.

Paul continues his somewhat relentless indictment of our sinfulness: **Therefore you are inexcusable, O man** (v. 1). In light of all that he has just spread out before us of the universal rejection and suppression of God's manifest self-revelation, which everybody knows with clarity, and in light of God's eternal power, deity, and holiness, the sins people practice are worthy of death. People not only continue to practice these sins, but they encourage others to do so. Therefore, man is without excuse. We might think that the "O man" is a generic address to any human being, but it was a common form of address in antiquity used between Jews. When Paul uses "O man," he is clearly addressing Jewish people.

Hypocrisy

Whoever you are who judge, for in whatever you judge another you condemn yourself; for you who judge practice the same things (v. 1). The sin of hypocrisy is in view here. Paul is chastising his kinsmen according to the flesh, Israel, for their judgmental attitude toward the Gentiles. He is basically saying, "Who do you think you are? You condemn the

Gentiles yet practice the very same things they do." That is the essence of hypocrisy. It is the particular threat of doom to any preacher who dares to stand in a pulpit and correct sinners in the congregation, because he is himself a sinner and runs that very liability of condemning others for doing the very things that he does.

Even though these words are addressed specifically to Jews, there is a more universal application of the text. What was true for Israel is true for us—if we condemn other people for doing the very things that we do, then, by our condemning them, we are showing our awareness of the wrongness of certain activities, and we are in effect condemning ourselves.

According to Truth
But we know that the judgment of God is according to truth against those who practice such things (v. 2). We see judgments made and verdicts rendered in courtrooms, and we ask, "Was justice really done here, or was this simply a show of a titanic struggle between able attorneys, and to the victor go the spoils?" Somewhere, perhaps, in the midst of this combat between prosecution and defense, the pursuit of justice was lost. People are persuaded by clever arguments; as a result, justice is not always served in the courtroom or in the decisions we make in our community and church and even in our family.

The one thing we can be confident of is that the just judgment of God is always according to truth. As we noted earlier, Immanuel Kant criticized the traditional arguments for the existence of God, and as a result he arrived at agnosticism, believing that we cannot come to a knowledge of God through natural reason. He followed up that work of agnosticism with a critique of practical reason, and there he argued practically for theism. He said even though we cannot know for sure that God exists, we must affirm the existence of God in order for ethics to be possible. Kant pursued his investigation of human conscience, and he found that every person has some sense of *oughtness*, what he called the "categorical imperative." In other words, there seems to be an ineradicable moral duty in the human conscience. Behaviors may degenerate into all kinds of corruption, but there will always remain some vestige of light in the conscience, even in the most corrupt person. Kant concluded, from a practical basis, that if ethics is to be meaningful, then somehow, somewhere, justice has to prevail, because if in the final analysis the wicked prosper and the righteous suffer, why should anybody endeavor to be righteous? Justice is absolutely essential, Kant said, for a meaningful ethic.

Kant went on to speculate that for justice to occur certain things must follow. We must have life after death because we have to go someplace where the ultimate verdict can be rendered on our behavior. For that to happen, he said, we must have a judge who himself is perfect. A perfect judge must be omniscient in order not to overlook some exculpatory detail. He must know every imperfection, each aspect of all the extenuating circumstances for why people behave as they do. The perfect judge must also be righteous, not given to bribes or corruption, and render an impartial decision unmotivated by self-interests. Even that does not guarantee that justice will prevail, Kant said. To ensure justice, he said, the perfect judge must also be omnipotent. He must have the ability and the power to make certain that his decision is carried out. Kant argued that if our ethics are going to be meaningful and if society is going to be possible, we must affirm the existence of God.

That is what Paul is saying when he writes that the judgment of God is according to truth. Nobody can stand before the judgment seat of God and complain, "That's not fair." Our consciences tell us that every last person, at some point, will be held accountable before his Creator—believer and nonbeliever alike. Even though the believer passes from condemnation, he will still have to stand before God and be judged, and that judgment will harbor no secrets. It will be perfect and accurate, for it will be according to truth.

No Escape

Every time we read in the Scriptures descriptions of the judgment before the presence of God, we see that the human response is always silence. Every mouth will be stopped. We will see the futility of debate. The discussion is over when God renders his verdict, for we know that his judgment will be according to truth. **And do you think this, O man, you who judge those practicing such things, and doing the same, that you will escape the judgment of God?** (v. 3).

The deepest hope harbored in the hearts of corrupt humanity is that somehow we will escape. As W. C. Fields lay in his hospital room on his death bed, a friend came to see him and was shocked to find Fields reading the Bible. Fields was not known for his religious devotion. When Fields's friend asked him why he was reading the Bible, Fields's replied, "I'm looking for loopholes." Everyone thinks there is going to be a loophole, a way of escape from an omniscient, holy, righteous God, but there is no way to escape the judgment save through the way that that holy God has given to the world, which is the way of the cross. We do not want that way; we want to find a way to escape, yet there is none.

Or do you despise the riches of His goodness, forbearance, and longsuffering? (v. 4). Paul's rhetorical question is essentially asking, "Do you take the goodness of God lightly? Do you take it for granted? Do you assume that because God is good he will not judge?" That is the most pervasive religious myth in our culture today. God is viewed as a cosmic bellhop at our beck and call. He is a celestial Santa Claus. All we have to do is come and ask him for what we want, and he will provide it for us.

A judge who refuses to punish evil is not a good judge; he is an unjust judge. A corrupt judge is not good, but God in his goodness, the one who judges all and does what is right, promises judgment against evil. Do we so despise his goodness that we assume that there is no room in his goodness for justice? That is insanity. If God is good, then he will judge, and he will judge according to truth. We ought not to despise the riches of his goodness and forbearance. In his patience God is forbearing. He puts up with our rebellion and sin. He knows every sin we have ever committed, but he has not exposed them all. He has not visited his wrath on us for all those sins, but we wipe our foreheads and say, "God is good that he will never deal with my sins." Do you despise the riches of his goodness, Paul asks, **not knowing that the goodness of God leads you to repentance?** (v. 4). God's forbearance leads us not to repentance but to recalcitrance, to the hardened heart and the stiff neck.

Wrath Stored Up

What comes next is one of the scariest verses in the Bible: **in accordance with your hardness and your impenitent heart you are treasuring up for yourself wrath in the day of wrath and revelation of the righteous judgment of God** (v. 5). A friend once said to me, "I have been lusting after a woman, so I might as well go ahead and get on with the act because I am already guilty of the sin." I warned my friend to be very careful there. We have a tendency to think that come the judgment day, we are either in or out, innocent or guilty, but when somebody commits nine murders, they go on trial for nine counts of murder, not just one. Just so, God considers every sin we commit in thought, word, and deed. Each one is exposed to God's perfect judgment according to the truth.

In explaining our sin in relation to God's wrath, Paul uses a banking metaphor. If we begin to save our money, taking a small portion of each paycheck and putting it in the bank, we are building up, slowly but surely, a treasure; we are saving up for a rainy day. Just so, every time we sin, we add an indictment against ourselves, treasuring up wrath against the day of wrath. Do we really believe that? I do not think the world believes it. Every day that we sin without repenting, we are depositing future wrath into the account of God's judgment.

Some people think, "If you go to hell, you go to hell. What is the difference?" A professor of mine once said that the sinner in hell would give everything he owned and do anything he could to make one less the number of his sins during his lifetime, because he will be judged according to his deeds. There are various degrees of punishment in hell because hell is where God manifests his perfect justice, and the punishment always fits the crime. If someone commits thirty sins, he is going to be punished thirty ways. So long as our hearts remain hardened, we add to the indictment moment by moment.

Judged by Works

We are treasuring up for ourselves wrath for the day of wrath and for revelation of the righteous judgment of God. The judgment of God is rendered, first, according to truth and, second, according to righteousness. God **"will render to each one according to his deeds"** (v. 6). Our justification is by faith alone, but our rewards in heaven will be distributed according to our works. That is why our Lord told his followers, those who are justified by faith alone, to treasure up things in heaven (Matt. 6:20; Luke 12:33). Augustine said that in distributing rewards according to our levels of obedience, God is crowning his own works in us. On the day of judgment, we will be judged according to our works. God will subject our lives to the closest scrutiny.

Paul makes a distinction: God will give **eternal life to those who by patient continuance in doing good seek for glory, honor, and immortality** (v. 7). Those who gain eternal life are those who set their hearts on heaven, **but to those who are self-seeking and do not obey the truth, but obey unrighteousness—indignation and wrath** (v. 8). The Bible says that God is not just angry at our sin; he is indignant about it. It is an affront to God when we live our lives in constant defiance of and rebellion against his law. When we rebel against God, we attack his dignity, which makes him indignant. Who do we think we are, as his creatures, to do what we want to do rather than what God commands us? Those who are self-seeking and do not obey the truth but practice unrighteousness will know God's indignation and wrath, and there will be **tribulation and anguish, on every soul of man who does evil, of the Jew first and also of the Greek; but glory, honor, and peace to everyone who works what is good, to the Jew first and also to the Greek. For there is**

no partiality with God (vv. 9–11). We cannot come before God and say, "I was a member of a church," or, "I am a descendant of Abraham." That counts for nothing. God will render to every person according to his deeds; there is no partiality with God.

For as many as have sinned without law will also perish without law, and as many as have sinned in the law will be judged by the law (for not the hearers of the law are just in the sight of God, but the doers of the law will be justified; for when Gentiles, who do not have the law, by nature do the things in the law, these, although not having the law, are a law to themselves, who show the work of the law written in their hearts, their conscience also bearing witness, and between themselves their thoughts accusing or else excusing them) in the day when God will judge the secrets of men by Jesus Christ, according to my gospel (vv. 12–16). This is a vastly misunderstood text. Most people who read it think Paul is rebuking the Jews. Even though the Jews had the Ten Commandments and all the Old Testament, they were not keeping the law. Just knowing the law did not give them a way of escape. The Gentiles did not know anything about the Decalogue. They had never heard of Moses. They did not know the Old Testament. Nevertheless, the Gentiles were doing the things of the law.

The point is not that the Jews, who had the law, were sinning against God while the Gentile pagans, who did not have the law, were obeying the law. Paul is saying that those who have the law perish with the law, and those who do not have the law perish without the law. People demonstrate by their actions, by what the philosophers call the *ius gentium* (the law of nations), that even if they have never seen the Ten Commandments, God has written his law on their hearts. Their behavior reveals that they know in their hearts the difference between right and wrong. Both Jew and Greek have consistently defied God, and they will be judged according to the light they have been given. The Jews will have a greater judgment because they have greater light, but the Gentiles are not without light.

Full Revelation

We can tie Romans 1 and 2 together. In chapter 1 Paul develops the concept of mediate general revelation, which is revelation that God gives of himself through a medium. God communicates his eternal power and deity through the medium of the created order. "The heavens declare the glory of God; and the firmament shows His handiwork" (Ps. 19:1). Paul said the invisible things of God are clearly perceived through the things that are made (Rom. 1:20). The medium of nature reveals God to all people.

In addition to mediate general revelation, we also speak of immediate general revelation. Here, the term *immediate* is not used with respect to time; rather, immediate general revelation is that which God gives without some intervening medium. Simply, immediate general revelation is the knowledge of God that he plants in our souls. Before we ever took a breath, God planted in our soul an immediate knowledge and awareness of himself. This revelation is given apart from our reading the Bible or looking at nature.

Therefore, we know God both mediately, through nature, and immediately, through the sense of his deity that we have in our souls. God has revealed himself to the human heart such that everyone knows what is right and what is not right. We can practice our sins over and over again and get everybody in our community to think and agree that it is okay to do those things, but we know better. When did an adulterer not know that he was violating his wife, or she her husband, in that act? When did a murderer not realize that the wanton destruction of another human being was a sin against humanity and God? We all know. We know that it is evil to cheat, lie, slander, and covet, because God has given us a conscience. The conscience can be seared; we can become so hardened in our hearts that, as Jeremiah said about Israel (Jer. 3:3), we gain the forehead of a harlot. The Israelites had lost their ability to blush, and that can happen to us as we are delivered over to our sins, but even in that terrible corrupt state, we do not vanquish totally the light of God's revelation that is within our consciences. We show the work of the law written in our hearts because our consciences bear witness against us.

Our thoughts will accuse or excuse us in the day when God will judge the secrets of men by Jesus Christ, according to the gospel, because essential to the gospel is the announcement that Christ has been appointed the perfect judge of the earth. We will be judged by Christ on the day of judgment. The Father has delegated that role to his Son, and he will reveal the secrets of our hearts. Jesus himself warned his own generation that what they did in secret will be made manifest. All skeletons in all closets will be revealed. That is why we need to be covered. That is what redemption is all about—a divine cover-up. The last thing we would want to do is appear before God like Adam and Eve after they sinned, naked and uncovered.

It is absolutely essential that we gain the cloak of the righteousness of Christ so that when every secret is made manifest in the judgment we will be covered by the perfection of Christ's righteousness. Our righteousness will not do it. I want to cry when I hear people say, "I don't need Christ. My life is going along fine. I am happy. I am successful. My conscience does not bother me. What do I need with Jesus?" There is nothing we need more desperately than someone who will cover us when every secret is made manifest.

We are not yet to the good news. Paul is seeking to bring the whole guilty world before the tribunal of God so that we will stop giving excuses, shut our mouths, and go to the gospel. While we wait for the good news, we must tremble before the law of a just and holy God.

6

UNDER THE LAW

Romans 2:17–29

Indeed you are called a Jew, and rest on the law, and make your boast in God, and know His will, and approve the things that are excellent, being instructed out of the law, and are confident that you yourself are a guide to the blind, a light to those who are in darkness, an instructor of the foolish, a teacher of babes, having the form of knowledge and truth in the law. You, therefore, who teach another, do you not teach yourself? You who preach that a man should not steal, do you steal? You who say, "Do not commit adultery," do you commit adultery? You who abhor idols, do you rob temples? You who make your boast in the law, do you dishonor God through breaking the law? For "the name of God is blasphemed among the Gentiles because of you," as it is written. For circumcision is indeed profitable if you keep the law; but if you are a breaker of the law, your circumcision has become uncircumcision. Therefore, if an uncircumcised man keeps the righteous requirements of the law, will not his uncircumcision be counted as circumcision? And will not the physically uncircumcised, if he fulfills the law, judge you who, even with your written code and circumcision, are a transgressor of the law? For he is not a Jew who is one outwardly, nor is circumcision that which is outward in the flesh; but he is a Jew who is one inwardly; and circumcision is that of the heart, in the Spirit, not in the letter; whose praise is not from men but from God.

In our previous study, we found Paul addressing the hypocrisy of the Jews, who stood in special relationship to God and had been throughout the Old Testament God's chosen people. Despite their special distinction, the Jews were living in the same kind of godlessness that was found among pagans and Gentiles, strangers to the covenant. We noted the dreadful experience of sinners, who, every time they sin, are making a deposit in the account of their corruption, an account which mounts exponentially as they store up wrath against the day of judgment. We left that study hoping that soon we would get out from underneath the oppression of God's indictment so that we might hasten to the good news that comes in the declaration of the gospel.

The Weight of the Law

Before Paul brings us to the gospel, he examines our condition under the law. It is one of the reasons why, in classical Lutheran theology, there remains an important emphasis on both law and gospel. As we noted earlier, Martin Luther endured torment when he was in the monastery at Erfurt. Luther had come to the monastery from the university where he had already distinguished himself as a brilliant student of jurisprudence. To the monastery he brought a keen analytical ability to dissect law, and he used this ability to examine the law of God in great depth and detail. The more he studied the law, the more troubled he was in his conscience. Luther was terrified by the law of God, not because he was neurotic but because he was perceptive, as Paul himself was in his expert understanding of the righteous demands that God imposes upon his people.

Our problem is that we fail to feel the weight of the law. We are so hardened in our sin and so accustomed to our corruption that we give our attention not to the law of God but to the social customs of our culture, and we measure ourselves in conformity to those customs rather than against the standard of God's perfect righteousness. However, as Paul later wrote to the Corinthians, "We dare not class ourselves or compare ourselves with those who commend themselves. But they, measuring themselves by themselves, and comparing themselves among themselves, are not wise" (2 Cor. 10:12).

Jesus told a parable about two men who went up to the temple to pray. One was a Pharisee and the other was a publican. The Pharisee looked up to heaven and said, "God, I thank You that I am not like other men— extortioners, unjust, adulterers, or even as this tax collector. I fast twice a week; I give tithes of all that I possess" (Luke 18:11). He obviously had a highly exalted view of his performance, because he was judging himself by the curve of the culture. He had forgotten that God does not grade on a curve. He grades against an absolute standard of perfect holiness. The publican understood it. He could not even lift his eyes to heaven but simply cried out, "God, be merciful to me a sinner!" (v. 13). Jesus then turned to his audience and said, "I tell you, this man went down to his house justified rather than the other; for everyone who exalts himself will be humbled, and he who humbles himself will be exalted" (v. 14).

When we look in the mirror of the law, every one of our blemishes becomes instantly obvious. We cannot hide from what the law reveals about who we are. No wonder Paul speaks of the law as the schoolmaster that drives us to Christ.

Masters of Masquerading

Here in the second part of Romans 2 Paul continues addressing the issue of hypocrisy and the law. **Indeed you are called a Jew, and rest on the law, and make your boast in God, and know His will, and approve the things that are excellent, being instructed out of the law, and are confident that you yourself are a guide to the blind, a light to those who are in darkness, an instructor of the foolish, a teacher of babes, having the form of knowledge and truth in the law** (vv. 17–20). The Jews had the law of God, which was the glory of Israel. No other nation on the planet had such a clear manifestation of the law of God. We tend to think of Old Testament law as little more than the Ten Commandments, but the Ten Commandments are only the foundation of the law. After they were given, a whole host of laws were added to those ten and became what we call "the holiness code." In addition to the Ten Commandments we find the case law of the Old Testament, which further reveals the character of God and shows us how far short we fall from his standard. If we want to hide from the law, to escape that mirror, we can try to find somebody more sinful than we are and pat ourselves on the back. However, we cannot afford to do that, and God will not let us do it. He keeps coming to us with the law.

Can we not extrapolate the critique that Paul gives to his kinsmen, Israel, and apply it to today's church? We rely on the Word of God and on our doctrine. We are confident in our calling as guides to the blind, as lights to those who are perishing in darkness. We instruct the foolish; we are the teachers of infants. We have the form of knowledge and truth. Elsewhere Paul rebukes people for having a form of godliness but lacking the substance of it (2 Tim. 3:5). The outward form is there, but that form is an empty shell, and once God bores through that shell and examines the heart beneath the external form, there is no internal reality. That is the judgment that Paul is giving to Israel, but it also has application to us.

You, therefore, who teach another, do you not teach yourself? You who preach that a man should not steal, do you steal? (v. 21). These are not just empty questions. As Christians we stand up and say it is wrong to steal. The rule of thumb in ecclesiastical circles is this: do not ever count on receiving more than 80 percent of the pledges people make. People think nothing of not fulfilling their pledges. It is not just pagans who do not pay their bills; it is professing Christians too. The same people who shake their finger at the unbeliever for not being honest and forthright are practicing the very same things. They are stealing.

You who say, "Do not commit adultery," do you commit adultery? You who abhor idols, do you rob temples? You who make your boast in the law, do you dishonor God through breaking the law? (vv. 22–23). We have the law of God—what are we doing with it? We boast of it while we break it. Here is the clincher: **For "the name of God is blasphemed among the Gentiles because of you," as it is written** (v. 24). The Gentiles were blaspheming God for the way that the Jews were treating them. Non-churchgoers frequently complain that the church is full of hypocrites. We have heard that, and maybe we have even said it. I once heard a minister respond to that complaint saying, "Yes it is, and there is always room for one more." He went on to say, "If you ever find a perfect church, do not join it; you will ruin it."

Hypocrisy is a damnable thing, which is why our Lord was constantly rebuking the Pharisees, the masters of masquerading, who pretended to have a form of righteousness that they really did not possess. Christians do not pretend to be perfect. The church is filled with sinners, and being a sinner is the first qualification for joining a church. We have to be sinners to get in because it is not a place for perfect people. One reason people call us hypocrites is that they notice we are not perfect, but actually it is the hypocrite who claims to be more righteous than he is. That is a serious matter, and it is what Paul is talking about.

We claim more righteousness than we possess, which is destructive. We have set a high standard for behavior within the church, which can be a practical problem. We encourage people to grow in faith and sanctification, but at the same time we pressure them so that they feel they have to pretend to be more righteous than they actually are. I think we all feel that way, so we talk the talk but do not always walk the walk, and the world is watching that. How many times have we heard it said, "If that is what Christianity is, I do not want any part of it"? It is true that unbelievers blaspheme because of the horrible example and witness that we often give to them, but if we treated them perfectly, they would blaspheme still. The fact that we add to their impulse of blasphemy does not get them off the hook in the final analysis.

One of my favorite stories was told to me by a Christian participating in the PGA golf tour. A non-Christian friend of his, also on the tour, had been voted golfer of the year. As such he was given the honor of playing golf with the president of the United States, Jack Nicklaus, and Billy Graham. It made for a high-powered foursome. At the end of the round, the champion walked off the golf course with a red face because he had played poorly. He walked over to the practice tee and began hammering drives down the green to get rid of his frustrations. My friend sat down near him and watched him for a few minutes and then asked him what was bothering him.

The champion replied, "I do not need to have Billy Graham trying to shove religion down my throat all day." Then he went back to beating the balls.

After a few minutes, my friend asked, "Did Billy really put it to you today?"

The golfer turned to my friend and said, "No; actually, Billy did not say a word about religion. I just had a bad day."

Why would he say that Billy Graham was trying to shove religion down his throat, when Billy Graham did not? Billy Graham did not have to say a word to him. The champion knew who Billy Graham was and what he represented, so he felt crowded all day. He was uncomfortable in the presence of such a man. That is what happens. When I used to play golf, I did not want anybody to know I was a minister. As soon as other players found out, they would start apologizing to me for their language. I would say, "God is hearing everything you say; I am not the one you need to apologize to." The Gentiles will blaspheme God at every opportunity, but we must not aid and abet their blasphemy by being less than kind, loving, or sensitive to them.

Signs of the Covenant

For circumcision is indeed profitable if you keep the law; but if you are a breaker of the law, your circumcision has become uncircumcision. Therefore, if an uncircumcised man keeps the righteous requirements of the law, will not his uncircumcision be counted as circumcision? (vv. 25–26). Paul explains the difference between outward circumcision and inward circumcision: **he is not a Jew**

who is one outwardly, nor is circumcision that which is outward in the flesh; but he is a Jew who is one inwardly; and circumcision is that of the heart, in the Spirit, not in the letter; whose praise is not from men but from God (vv. 28–29). In other words, Paul is saying, those on the outside might be more sensitive to the spirit of the law than the Jews were, even though the outsiders did not know the letter of the law.

Paul uses circumcision as his illustration. Circumcision is very important to Paul's understanding of redemption and of the law and the gospel. In the Old Testament, circumcision was the sign that God gave to his people of his covenant promise. When God called Abraham out of Mesopotamian paganism, God promised to be Abraham's God and to make him the father of a great nation. God told Abraham that his descendants would be as the stars of the sky and as the sands of the seashore (Gen. 22:17). What God required of Abraham in the covenant was circumcision, which was the cutting off of the foreskin of his flesh. The requirement was put on Abraham and his children. Throughout the Old Testament this sign of the covenant, circumcision, was given to adults and to their children. That is the basic reason why the sign of the new covenant is also given to the children of the covenant. When God gives his covenant promises, he gives them to those who receive them and to their children.

God appeared to Abraham and told him that he would be his shield and his very great reward (Gen. 15:1). Abraham replied, "Lord GOD, what will You give me, seeing I go childless, and the heir of my house is Eliezer of Damascus? Look, You have given me no offspring; indeed one born in my house is my heir!" (vv. 2–3). God said, "This one shall not be your heir, but one who will come from your own body shall be your heir" (v. 4), and this son would be the child of promise. Then we read that Abraham "believed in the LORD, and He accounted it to him for righteousness (v. 6).

There we have the first clear teaching of justification by faith alone, but no sooner did Abraham say he believed God than he staggered at God's promise of making him a great nation. How could Abraham know for sure that God would give him these things? Abraham was an old man at that point, and his wife was barren; how could he know that God would give him a child? That was his question. God said to Abraham, "Bring Me a three-year-old heifer, a three-year-old female goat, a three-year-old ram, a turtledove, and a young pigeon" (v. 9). Abraham "brought all these to Him and cut them in two, down the middle, and placed each piece opposite the other" (v. 10). After this God put Abraham to sleep, and in the middle of that sleep the terror of the presence of God was manifested to him. In his sleep Abraham saw a burning pot and a smoking furnace move down the aisle between the animal pieces, and in that vision God assured him that he would keep his covenant (vv. 12–13).

At conferences and similar events people bring Bibles to me and ask me to sign them and to include my life verse. Jesus said we are supposed to live by every word that proceeds from the mouth of God, so I struggle with the idea of using one verse to define my life. Nevertheless, I have provided one for folks, and over my many years of doing so, I have used a host of different verses. The one I like best to sign is Genesis 15:17: "It came to pass, when the sun went down and it was dark, that behold, there appeared a smoking oven and a burning torch that passed between those pieces." They think I am joking, but I am not. The verse contains a theophany. The fire represents God, and God moves between the pieces that have been torn asunder.

God is essentially saying to Abraham, "If I do not keep this promise, may I be cut in half. I am promising by my very character; my eternal Godhead is on the line." We see something similar in Hebrews. When God could swear by nothing higher, he swore by himself (6:13).

There was a cutting rite involved in setting up the covenant. God commanded Abraham to have the foreskin of his flesh cut off, a very crass thing. Many years ago I was in Philadelphia speaking about the relationship between the old covenant and the new covenant, and I talked about how the Old Testament covenant sign of circumcision had both a positive and a negative side. The cutting in the rite of circumcision signified that God was consecrating—cutting—Israel out of the mass of nations in the world, separating it to himself, distinguishing the Israelites in an act of grace. The Israelites bore a sign in their skin that they had been chosen by God's grace to receive the greatest benefit that any nation could have. The negative side of the sign was that the Israelites bore in their bodies the sign of a covenant that had not only promises, benefits, and blessings but also curses. In Deuteronomy we find God saying:

> If you diligently obey the voice of the LORD your God, to observe carefully all His commandments which I command you today, . . . the LORD your God will set you high above all nations of the earth. And all these blessings shall come upon you and overtake you, because you obey the voice of the LORD your God: Blessed shall you be in the city, and blessed shall you be in the country. Blessed shall be the fruit of your body, the produce of your ground and the increase of your herds, the increase of your cattle and the offspring of your flocks. Blessed shall be your basket and your kneading bowl. Blessed

shall you be when you come in, and blessed shall you be when you go out. (Deut. 28:1–6)

But what would happen if the covenant was broken?

Cursed shall you be in the city, and cursed shall you be in the country. Cursed shall be your basket and your kneading bowl. Cursed shall be the fruit of your body and the produce of your land, the increase of your cattle and the offspring of your flocks. Cursed shall you be when you come in, and cursed shall you be when you go out. (vv. 16–19)

Breaking the covenant would cut off God's people from blessings and bring the curse of judgment.

While I was giving that explanation of circumcision, somebody yelled out from the crowd, "That is primitive and obscene." I stopped and said, "What did you say?" I knew what he had said, but I wanted a moment to gather my thoughts and to see whether he really had the boldness to say it again. He did. "That is primitive and obscene." I replied that I liked his choice of words to describe it. I cannot imagine a more crass or primitive religious rite than the cutting off of the foreskin of the man's flesh. It is primitive. However, the promise that God made was not for the benefit of only a gnostic, elite group of intellectuals. He was communicating his promise in a sign so base, so primitive, that the least of the people in the nation could grasp it in its graphicness.

Signs Do Not Save

I also like the word *obscene* to describe circumcision because there is no better word to describe what sin is. When we look to the New Testament, we see that Christ received the curse of God when he hung on the tree, when he took upon himself the corporate sins of his people. That is the greatest obscenity that the world has ever beheld. Primitive and obscene—that is the significance of this external sign of circumcision. Paul reminds the Christians at Rome that the fact that they are circumcised does not guarantee the blessing. If they would remember Deuteronomy, the second giving of the law (Deut. 29–30), they would know that the sign of which they were boasting was the very sign that condemned them and marked them as covenant breakers.

The same could be said for us and our sign of the new covenant, baptism. Baptism does not save anybody (nor does joining the church). Baptism is an outward sign of what God promises to do inwardly. The final analysis is not whether we are baptized outwardly but whether we are baptized inwardly. Do we possess the spiritual reality that the sign points to? That is what Paul is saying to the Jew, who was circumcised. All the people who crucified Jesus were circumcised. The Pharisees thought that because they had biological roots to Abraham, they were guaranteed salvation. Just so, there are people today who think they are guaranteed salvation because they grew up in a Christian home, were baptized, went to catechism, joined the church, and enjoy the Lord's Supper.

Some time ago an old friend, a Christian leader, dropped in to visit me. He told me that one of his daughters is not a believer. She is hostile to Christianity and will not take her daughter, my friend's granddaughter, to church. He told me, "R. C., I baptized my granddaughter in my swimming pool. I wanted to make sure she was covered." Then we started talking about whether one has to be a minister in order to administer baptism or the Lord's Supper. There is nothing in the Bible that says only clergy can baptize or administer the sacraments. That tradition developed in church history to protect people from an abuse of these sacred signs.

I was reared in a very liberal church but nonetheless we were required to go through catechism class. There were about thirty of us in the class, and when it was over, we had to be examined in front of the whole congregation. We all passed the test, and on Maundy Thursday we were confirmed. After our confirmation we had our first Communion. I remember afterward standing in the foyer of the church, and one of my buddies asked what I had thought about it. They had given us paper-thin wafers, and I said, "The stuff tasted like fish food," and we all laughed. A woman turned to me and said, "How can you talk about Communion like that?" I thought, *What's the big deal?* I had obviously tramped on something sacred to her. Despite three months of catechism, of giving a credible profession of faith before the elders, and taking my first Communion, I did not have the slightest understanding of what the Lord's Supper is all about.

I have kept in touch with some who were in that class with me, and I know of only two who are professing Christians today. It is assumed we are in the kingdom of God just because we were baptized, joined a church, or got confirmed. We look on outward appearances; God looks on the heart. In the final analysis, the only circumcision or baptism that matters is that of the heart. I am not saying that we should do away with the external—Jesus made it clear that we are to use the signs of the covenant for the world to see. But we must always remember that they do not save us. Our justification, as we will see, is by faith alone. My mother's faith cannot save me, nor can my father's or my sister's or my wife's. I have to have it, and it has to be in the heart.

Paul continues to drag us before the law. The beginning of Romans 3 continues the bad news, but the good news is within striking distance. Law and gospel both have their place in the Christian life. By the deeds of the flesh, by the law, nobody is saved. Salvation comes only through the gospel, but if we ignore the law, we will never feel the weight of our need for the gospel.

7

A GREAT ADVANTAGE

Romans 3:1–8

What advantage then has the Jew, or what is the profit of circumcision? Much in every way! Chiefly because to them were committed the oracles of God. For what if some did not believe? Will their unbelief make the faithfulness of God without effect? Certainly not! Indeed, let God be true but every man a liar. As it is written:

> "That You may be justified in Your words,
> And may overcome when You are judged."

But if our unrighteousness demonstrates the righteousness of God, what shall we say? Is God unjust who inflicts wrath? (I speak as a man.) Certainly not! For then how will God judge the world? For if the truth of God has increased through my lie to His glory, why am I also still judged as a sinner? And why not say, "Let us do evil that good may come"?—as we are slanderously reported and as some affirm that we say. Their condemnation is just.

We have been following the apostle Paul as he sets before us the wrath of God, which is revealed from heaven against all unrighteousness and ungodliness of men who suppress that truth of God, truth that God so plainly makes clear to every person in the world

(Rom. 1:18–20). Paul has told us the consequence for rejecting the knowledge of God is being given over to sin (1:24–32). Paul has also exposed the hypocrisy of his kinsmen, Israel. The Jews boasted in their possession of the law and in the fact that they are God's chosen people, demonstrated through circumcision (2:1–24). Paul has argued that outward circumcision gets no one into the kingdom of God; it is inward circumcision that marks the children of promise (2:25–29). Afterward Paul anticipates the response of his listener, as he does so many times in his epistles, which is where we resume.

What advantage then has the Jew, or what is the profit of circumcision? (v. 1). If being Jewish does not save them and circumcision is no guarantee, then where is the advantage? If Paul were writing today, he might mention church membership or baptism as that which does not guarantee salvation. Many place their confidence in the fact that they have been baptized or have joined a church, but our Lord gave weighty, ominous warnings about that. The church is a community where there are always tares growing along with the wheat (Matt. 13:24–30). Jesus warned that people honor him with their lips, but their hearts are far from him (Matt. 15:8). Making a verbal confession of faith is no guarantee. What is in the heart determines our redemption.

So what advantage has the Jew? Paul has downplayed circumcision, so we would expect him to answer his question by saying that there is no advantage. Instead he answers, **Much in every way!** (v. 2). Just so, there is advantage to us in receiving baptism and being a member of a Christian church. There are a multitude of advantages to that in every conceivable manner.

The Oracles of God

What is the advantage to the Jew? Much in every way, Paul writes. **Chiefly because to them were committed the oracles of God** (v. 2). There is a technical point here. The actual word Paul uses is "first," not "chiefly"— "First, to them were committed the oracles of God." Some who stand against the authority of Scripture have said that the fact that Paul uses "first" shows that he could not possibly have been inspired by the Holy Spirit since it suggests there will be a long list of advantages, but he gives only one. The word translated "chiefly" is a form of the word *protos*, which in Greek means "first"—not necessarily in sequence but in the order of importance. It is the word Jesus used when he said, "Seek first the kingdom of God and His righteousness, and all these things shall be added to you" (Matt. 6:33). The translator has it right when he renders the word "chiefly." There are many advantages to being a Jew, but the main advantage is that Jews were given the oracles of God. The apostle is pointing out the tremendous advantage that Jews had over the Philistines, the Syrians, and the Babylonians—the Word of God.

There is no greater advantage for anyone than to be within earshot of the Word of God. I have mentioned that I was reared in a liberal church. The minister did not believe in the resurrection of Jesus. He denied the miracles of the New Testament, and his sermons exhibited that skepticism. However, part of the liturgy in that church every Sunday was the reading of the text of the Bible. Everything that went before the reading of the Bible and everything that went after it was distortion and heresy. Still, in spite of the minister—not because of him—I was sitting under the Word of God. That was the advantage to me. When I became a Christian, it was through the testimony of the Word of God. In preparation for my call to conversion, the Word of God was at work in my life.

God has chosen the foolishness of preaching as his method of saving his people, and he has invested his power in the Word. The power is not in the preacher. The power is not in the program. The power is not in the liturgy. The power is in the Word because it is attended by the Holy Spirit. The Word can cut through our minds and hardened hearts; it can pierce our souls and bring us to Christ. There is much advantage where the Word of God is preached, just as there was advantage to the Israelites in possessing the oracles of God.

God used Jonathan Edwards mightily during the eighteenth-century Great Awakening in New England. Edwards was a firm believer in the doctrine of election. He believed that unless God had chosen a person, elected him to salvation, that person would never come to faith. Nevertheless, he pled, cajoled, and scared people half to death, telling them to repent and come to faith, because he did not know who was numbered among the elect. I share Edwards's perspective, assuming the election of every person I meet. I cannot read others' hearts, and I do not know the hidden decrees of God, which are none of my business.

Some heard Edwards and asked, "What if I am not elect? What should I do?" Edwards said, "Be in church every Sunday morning because you do not know that you are not elect, and you should do everything you can do in your fallen condition." Edwards said there is nothing people can do to incline themselves to the things of God. They cannot muster from their hearts true repentance unless the Holy Spirit changes their souls, but they can hear the Word of God and know that they are going to be judged at the end of their lives. Edwards recommended that people be seekers.

We have to be careful here; Edwards's doctrine of seeking has caused much consternation among Reformed people. Edwards was not advocating a salvation by seeking. False repentance—repenting to get a ticket out of hell but not really being convicted of sin—will not move God to save anybody. Such repentance is like a little child caught with his hand in the cookie jar who says, "Mommy, I'm sorry; please do not spank me." It is a repentance motivated not by a broken and contrite heart but by a fear of punishment. We call that *attrition* rather than *contrition*. Edwards said that even if all we have is attrition, bring it to church and listen to the Word of God, and maybe God will save us. That was sound advice. Some people are reached by the gospel even though they have never darkened the door of a church, but the church is where the means of God's saving grace is most heavily concentrated.

The wisest thing you can do, even if you are not a believer, is to listen to the Word of God every chance you have because, if nothing else, it will exercise a restraint on your sinful desires and tendencies. Many churches today are moving away from a serious exposition of the Word of God, yet the Word is where the power and advantage lie. The church that moves away from the Word disadvantages its people. Hearing the Word of God is a tremendous advantage to you, even if you do not like it or believe it. I urge you to take advantage of that advantage, which is what Paul is saying to his kinsmen, the Jews.

The Integrity of God

For what if some did not believe? Will their unbelief make the faithfulness of God without effect? (v. 3). If a majority of those baptized never come to faith, does that mean we should do away with baptism? Do we say that since baptism does not guarantee salvation, there is no advantage to it? Baptism is simply a visible expression of God's promise to all who believe. Those who do not believe in no way diminish the value of the promise that God makes to those who do believe. If everyone is a covenant breaker, that does not destroy the integrity of God in his part of the covenant.

Paul exposes the Jews' thinking. If people do not believe in the significance of circumcision or in the oracles of God, does not that unbelief destroy the faithfulness of God? Will such unbelief make the faithfulness of God without effect? **Certainly not! Indeed, let God be true but every man a liar** (v. 4). The Bible makes that condemnation—all men are liars. We are all promise breakers. God is the only perfect promise keeper. That is how we live as Christians: we trust that God is not like us. We break our promises and lie to each other, but God cannot lie because his eternal being and character are truth. It is impossible for God to lie. Just because we lie does not mean that God does. Because we ignore his Word does not mean that his Word becomes worthless. Paul warns against ever allowing such thinking into our heads.

Paul cites a passage from Psalm 51, the great penitential psalm of David that he composed after being confronted by Nathan for his adulterous relationship with Bathsheba: **As it is written: "That You may be justified in Your words, and may overcome when You are judged"** (v. 4). David was driven to his knees, and he wrote the greatest psalm of repentance ever penned.

> Have mercy upon me, O God,
>> According to Your lovingkindness;
>> According to the multitude of Your tender mercies,
>> Blot out my transgressions. (Ps. 51:1)

David utters the most powerful point of the whole prayer:

> For I acknowledge my transgressions,
>> And my sin is always before me. (v. 3)

That is true confession. David is saying, "O God, I am a haunted man. I am like Lady Macbeth scrubbing her hands to get the blood out, saying, 'Out, out, damned spot,' and I cannot get rid of it. It is always there. I know it. I cannot hide from it." Then he says to God:

> Against You, You only, have I sinned,
>> And done this evil in Your sight. (v. 4a)

In one sense, David's words are hyperbole. David had sinned against his wives, his children, Bathsheba, her husband, and all his subjects in Israel, who looked to their king as a moral exemplar. He had let them down. He had disappointed them. It does not seem that he is making much sense when he says that he has sinned against God alone. David understood that he had violated Bathsheba, his wives, his family, and the whole nation, but he is speaking in the ultimate sense. The wickedness of sin does violence to the perfection, the majesty, and the holiness of God.

In the final analysis, David says that God is the one against whom he has committed his evil. David's next words show what real repentance is:

That You may be found just when You speak,
And blameless when You judge. (v. 4b)

A Just Judge

In true repentance there is no rationalization. There is no attempt to minimize guilt. There is no attempt at self-justification, which is the human tendency. Even when we confess our sins, we always hold back something, some of the gravity of it, but not so with David.

David understands that if God responds to his actions according to the law and his own character of righteousness, he has every right to do it and to punish David in whatever way he chooses, so David throws himself on the mercy of the court. That is why David asked God to deal with him not according to his justice but according to his tender mercy. That was David's only hope, and that is our only hope in the presence of a holy God.

An illustration of what Paul is saying here, and what David was saying in Psalm 51, is found in the time when Eli was judging Israel. One night God awakened the young student Samuel from his sleep by Eli's side. Samuel went over and tugged at Eli and said, "Here I am, for you called me."

Eli said, "I did not call; lie down again." So Samuel went back to sleep.

A few minutes later, God called again, "Samuel!" And again Samuel jumped up, ran over to Eli, and said, "Here I am, for you called me." Eli answered, "I did not call, my son; lie down again."

Eli was beginning to put two and two together, so he said, "Go, lie down; and it shall be, if He calls you, that you must say, 'Speak, Lord, for Your servant hears.'" And again God called, "Samuel! Samuel!" And Samuel responded, saying, "Speak, for your servant hears." Then God revealed to Samuel his plan to judge the house of Eli. God was going to kill Eli and his wayward sons, and the ark of the covenant was going to be taken away from the nation.

In the morning Eli asked Samuel, "What is the word that the Lord spoke to you? Please do not hide it from me. God do so to you, and more also, if you hide anything from me of all the things that He said to you." Then Samuel told him everything, and hid nothing from him. And Eli said, "It is the Lord. Let Him do what seems good to Him" (1 Sam. 3:1–18).

Most who hear that indictment would consider that a bit harsh, but when Eli hears it, his response is, "It is the Lord." Eli recognizes the word of God, and he acknowledges that he has been wrong and God has every right to do to with him what he wills.

Every one of us has been a victim of injustice. Every one of us has been falsely accused of things we have never done and been subjected to slander and jealousy, and every one of us has inflicted that kind of damage on other people. When we are treated unfairly, we have the right, according to the Word of God, to seek redress, to confront people, to go to the church and even to the law; however, when we are unfairly treated, we also have to look to heaven and say, "Lord, what do you have in mind?" We can never say that it is unfair for God to allow us to be treated unfairly by people. No matter what we have to suffer at the hands of people, it is not worth comparing to the grace by which we are covered by God in the forgiveness of our sins.

When God calls us to account for our lives, he will be perfectly justified in sending us to hell forever. If we do not realize that, then we have never really dealt with our sin, nor do we really know who God is, or his holiness. If we were to die tonight and wake up in hell tomorrow morning, we would be most unhappy, but we would know that the fact that we are there is just. That is what Paul is saying here.

But if our unrighteousness demonstrates the righteousness of God, what shall we say? Is God unjust who inflicts wrath? (I speak as a man.) Certainly not! For then how will God judge the world? (vv. 5–6). Even when we sin, our unrighteousness indirectly bears witness to the righteousness of God. How would we ever recognize sin for what it is if we did not have a standard by which to judge it? Nobody is really a relativist. The culture claims to be morally relative, yet the person who says that there is no morality is the first one to scream foul when somebody steals his wallet. We know better than that, but we excuse our sinfulness and say, "After all, boys will be boys; to err is human, and to forgive is divine. Everybody is entitled to one mistake." We have this moral entitlement program in our culture, but God does not entitle us to any mistakes, not to one sin.

We begin to think that God is glorified in our sinfulness, so we might as well continue in sin that grace may abound. This is how distorted we are. We say, "Let God be God. I will be who I am. I am just being myself. At least I am honest about it; at least I am an honest sinner." There is no such thing, and Paul warns against that sort of thinking. It is silly too, for then how would God judge the world? If God is unjust for inflicting wrath, he would never be able to judge the world. Nothing could be more obvious than that, yet nothing is more repugnant to the culture and, in many cases, to the church than the idea that God is capable of judging people by pouring out his wrath.

The Bible says that salvation is being saved from the wrath to come. No preacher in the history of the world spoke more ominously about the certainty of the wrath of God than Jesus. God will not hold back his wrath forever. Every person is going to have to face the judgment of God. We will either face it on our own or we will face it with God's appointed defense attorney, Jesus. If it is not right for God to have wrath, how can we be judged? How could he judge the world?

Paul is astonished here with the thinking of his contemporaries, and if he were around today he would say, "Have you people lost your mind, that you have no room in your theology for the wrath of God? Do you think there is no judgment—that everybody gets a free pass?" That is the secret hope of every impenitent person in this world. "I'm fifteen . . . I'm eighteen . . . I'm twenty-five . . . I'm forty-five . . . I'm seventy-five, and I have not been judged thus far. I have not experienced the wrath of God yet. All that stuff about the wrath of God is just scare tactics that the preachers use to keep us in line and manipulate us with guilt. I do not have anything to fear from the judgment of God because a good judge, a loving judge, would never punish anybody. He hates the sin, but he loves the sinner, and he loves him unconditionally." God does not send sin to hell; he sends sinners there as their just judgment.

No one, says Paul, should forget the righteousness of God. It is because God is righteous that he is wrathful. His wrath is not a manifestation of a lack of righteousness; rather, it is a manifestation of the fullness of the righteousness in him. **For if the truth of God has increased through my lie to His glory, why am I also still judged as a sinner?** (v. 7). That will be the cry of Judas on the last day: "Why are you picking on me? The best thing that ever happened to the world was the crucifixion of Jesus. If it were not for me, you would have no atonement. You people should be thanking me that I fulfilled the Scripture and delivered him into the hands of the Gentiles. Why am I judged as a sinner?"

And why not say, "Let us do evil that good may come"?—as we are slanderously reported and as some affirm that we say (v. 8). Paul was accused of antinomianism, of so despising the law of the Old Testament and being so intoxicated by the primacy of grace and the sweetness of the gospel that he had completely dispensed with the law of God. Such slander went around the community, where people said this Jewish teacher was denying the law of God. Paul never denied God's law. He always understood the proper relationship between the law of God and the gospel of God. Paul is not saying:

> Free from the law,
> O blessed condition;
> We can sin all we want
> And still have remission.

There is no room in Paul's theology for the carnal Christian, one who takes Christ as Savior but does not take him as Lord. That would be nonsense to the apostle. We cannot put that slander at his feet. He never said, "Let us do evil that good may come." Paul never entertained the idea that the end justifies the means. Rather, he said, **their condemnation is just** (v. 8). Those who twist his teaching, the apostolic word, and accuse him of teaching antinomianism will be condemned, and justly so.

Paul is about to develop the universal guilt of the human race. Jew and Gentile—every last one of us—is under the weight and condemnation of sin. He will turn to the Old Testament to spell that out in detail before he reaches the crescendo, where he brings every human being before the divine tribunal, showing that all need the gospel.

8

UNDER SIN

Romans 3:9-20

What then? Are we better than they? Not at all. For we have previously charged both Jews and Greeks that they are all under sin. As it is written:

> "There is none righteous, no, not one;
> There is none who understands;
> There is none who seeks after God.
> They have all turned aside;
> They have together become unprofitable;
> There is none who does good, no, not one."
> "Their throat is an open tomb;
> With their tongues they have practiced deceit";
>
> "The poison of asps is under their lips";
> "Whose mouth is full of cursing and bitterness."
> "Their feet are swift to shed blood;
> Destruction and misery are in their ways;
> And the way of peace they have not known."
> "There is no fear of God before their eyes."

Now we know that whatever the law says, it says to those who are under the law, that every mouth may be stopped, and all the world may become guilty before God. Therefore by the deeds of the law no flesh will be justified in His sight, for by the law is the knowledge of sin.

W e are not ready to hear the gospel until we first understand the indictment against humanity that comes down to us from God himself. The view of humanity that we see in Romans 3:10–20 is on a collision course with everything our culture tells us about our natural condition. People today profoundly disagree with the apostle Paul's assessment of our condition, but we must not be caught up in what we as fallen people think of ourselves. What matters is God's assessment of our condition.

What then? Are we better than they? Not at all. For we have previously charged both Jews and Greeks that they are all under sin (v. 9). When the apostle Paul says that we are all under sin, he means that sin is not something that just scratches us on the surface. Sin is not tangential to our lives. The weight of sin is so heavy that it presses down upon us. We are under a weighty burden of guilt as a result of our sin. The force of what Paul is saying in verse 9 is that because of our sin, each one of us, under the verdict of the law, is exposed to the judgment of God.

When we are succeeding, we say that we are "on top" of things. With respect to our performance of obedience before God, we are not on top; we are underneath it, and the law hangs like the Sword of Damocles over our necks. We are under an awesome weight of sin and a burden of guilt before God. I desire that we come to a greater capacity to feel the weight of that burden, because we have become experts at denying it. We dodge it so that we do not feel the burden. Not one person in a thousand has a complete comprehension of the weightiness of this matter.

Paul, in order to buttress his claim and defend this grim assessment of our condition, rests not on his own insights or experience but goes back into the pages of the Old Testament. The quotations that follow are not found in one particular place. Paul is giving us an amalgamation of several texts, most of which are from the Psalms and some from the prophet Isaiah. Everything that Paul quotes here in verses 10 through 18 is taken from the sacred Scriptures of the Old Testament. Paul sets it before us in a kind of chronological order. The Old Testament references are not just loosely laid together; rather, the second judgment follows from the first, and the third from the second, and so on throughout the indictment.

None Righteous

If we were in God's court right now, the charges would sound like this: **As it is written: "There is none righteous, no, not one"** (v. 10). Not one person, when judged against the standard of God's righteousness, can be seen to be righteous, yet our self-description of righteousness leads us to suppose that we can pass the judgment of God on judgment day based on our own performance.

When we evangelize, we sometimes ask, "If you were to die tonight and stand before God, and God were to say to you, 'Why should I let you into my heaven?' what would you say?" Ninety percent of those asked give a works-righteousness answer: "I would say to God, 'I tried to live a good life. I belonged to a church. I gave to charity. I never did anything really bad.'" That is a pretense of righteousness that has no substance to it. There is none righteous, and in case we do not get it, the emphasis follows: "no, not one." There is no exception to this universal judgment.

Since there is none righteous, it follows irresistibly that **"there is none who understands"** (v. 11). In view here is a failure to understand the things of God. If we as fallen creatures do not want to have God in our thinking, and if we dismiss him and develop a worldview that fits our performance, how can we not end up with complete inability to grasp the truths of God? Who among us understands the sweetness of God? Who among us, even in a converted state (if indeed we are converted) hungers and thirsts to understand the deep things of God? How many professing Christians have you heard say, "I do not need to study the Scriptures; I do not want to get involved with theology?"

"There is none who seeks after God" (v. 11). No one in his natural condition seeks after God. Seeking after God is the business of the believer. The moment we become a Christian is the moment when our quest for God begins. Prior to our conversion we were fugitives from God; we fled from him. Churches today structure worship, teaching, and preaching toward the pagan to help him find what he is desperately searching for but just cannot seem to uncover, but it is foolish to structure worship for unbelievers who are seeking after God when the Bible tells us there aren't any seekers. It manifests a failure to understand the things of God. If we understood the things of God, we would know that there is no such thing as unconverted seekers.

Thomas Aquinas was asked on one occasion why there seem to be non-Christians who are searching for God, when the Bible says no one seeks after God in an unconverted state. Aquinas replied that we see people all around us who are feverishly seeking for purpose in their lives, pursuing happiness, and looking for relief from guilt to silence the pangs of conscience. We see people searching for the things that we know can be found only in Christ, but we make the gratuitous assumption that because they are seeking the benefits of God, they must therefore be seeking God. That is the very dilemma of fallen creatures: we want the things that only God can give us, but we do not want him. We want peace but not the Prince of Peace. We want purpose but not the sovereign purposes decreed by God. We want meaning found in ourselves but not in his rule over us. We see desperate people, and we assume they are seeking for God, but they are not seeking for God. I know that because God says so. No one seeks after God.

How desperately was Paul searching for God while on his way to Damascus to destroy the followers of Jesus? He was no more searching for God than I was when God stopped me in my path one night and brought me sovereignly to himself. I knew then that I did not come to Christ because I was seeking him. I came to Christ because he sought me. No one seeks after Christ until he has first been found by Christ—that begins the seeking of the kingdom. That is why Jesus says to those who come to him, "Seek first the kingdom of God and His righteousness, and all these things shall be added to you" (Matt. 6:33). That is meaningful only to the believer.

Evangelists often say, "If you open up the door, Jesus will come into your life. If you will just seek him a little bit, you will find him." However, those words—"knock, and it will be opened to you" (Luke 11:9); "Seek the LORD while He may be found" (Isa. 55:6); "Seek, and you will find" (Matt. 7:7); "Behold, I stand at the door and knock" (Rev. 3:20)—are addressed to the church. Jesus seeks believers, so it is believers who are called to seek the Lord. While we are living in unbelief, we do not seek God. If we do seek God, it is a clear indication that we are already in the kingdom. If we do not seek him, it is a good indication that we are not in the kingdom. There is none who seeks after God.

"They have all turned aside" (v. 12). Those in the Christian community were called people of the Way before they were called Christians (a term of derision used for them at Antioch) because Jesus identified himself as the way: "I am the way, the truth, and the life. No one comes to the Father except through me" (John 14:6). Do we believe that? Do we believe there is only one way? The culture tells us there are many ways. God says there is only one. If there are none righteous and no one understands and no one seeks after God, where would we expect people to go except out of the way? If they have turned aside, if they have no understanding of the things of God, if they are not searching after God, and if there is no righteousness, the net result is this: **"They have together become unprofitable"** (v. 12).

I had just finished writing about one hundred pages of a book when my computer crashed. The file was not backed up. You might know how a writer feels when he has produced a hundred pages and then loses them. A friend of mine had worked for five years on his doctoral dissertation and was in the last days of completing it when a fire burned his office to the ground. He lost it all; he had to start again. Nothing seems more tragic than to labor as hard as we can and see the fruit of our labor destroyed. God says that is the bottom line for the richest and most successful people in the world who do not know Christ and the gospel. They have become futile, unprofitable in all they do.

Paul concludes this section of the indictment: **"There is none who does good, no, not one"** (v. 12). Some argue, "It is one thing to say people are not righteous, but surely you are not going to say that no pagan ever does anything good? We have seen pagan soldiers lay down their lives for their brothers on the battlefield and pagan mothers sacrifice themselves to save their children." Calvin called this "civic righteousness."

God's Standard

From our perspective, there are good deeds, but if we define goodness the way God does, the verdict comes out a little differently. From a biblical standpoint, there are two aspects to a good deed. When God weighs our actions, he weighs whether they correspond outwardly to his law. God requires honesty, and we are honest if we do not cheat on our income taxes or steal. It is good that we do not steal; it is good that we do not cheat—so far, so good. We have that external conformity to the law of God. However, when God evaluates our behavior not only does he judge the outward action, but he also considers the work, the inward motivation. Therefore, for people to do good in God's sight, they not only have to do something that externally conforms to his law, but they also must be motivated in that action by a heart that is trying to please God, a heart that loves him completely, with the whole mind.

If that is the standard of a good deed, then even after our conversion there is a pound of flesh in everything we do. We have never in our lives loved God with our whole heart. I am somebody who has never loved God with his whole mind. I have loved him with part of my mind, but not all of it. If loving God supremely is the Great Commandment, to fail in this is the great transgression. Nobody has loved God with his whole heart and mind, even for five seconds.

If that is the standard by which God is going to judge our deeds, then we see why Paul would say that nobody does good. The rich young ruler who approached Jesus was very enthusiastic. He interrupted Jesus and said, "Good Teacher, what good thing shall I do that I may have eternal life?"

Jesus didn't reply, "You have to make a decision to follow me." He said, "Why do you call Me good?" Jesus was not denying his sinlessness or perfect obedience, but he knew that the young man had no idea who Jesus really was. So Jesus continued, "No one is good but One, that is, God. But if you want to enter into life, keep the commandments," and Jesus named some of the Ten Commandments.

The rich young ruler thought he had it made: "All these things I have kept from my youth," he told Jesus.

Jesus didn't say, "That is remarkable. You are the first person I have met who has done that, who has kept all these commandments from your youth. You do not need me." Jesus said, "'If you want to be perfect, go, sell what you have and give to the poor, and you will have treasure in heaven; and come, follow Me.' But when the young man heard that saying, he went away sorrowful, for he had great possessions" (Matt. 19:16–22).

The saddest thing about that encounter is that Jesus met a man who really thought he was good. Obviously, the rich young ruler had not been present for the Sermon on the Mount in which Jesus explained the depth of the import of the Ten Commandments. The young man had a superficial understanding of goodness and of the law of God.

All Corrupt

To bring his point to practical application, Paul gives a list of metaphors to describe the extent to which we are not righteous but have gone astray and the extent to which we do not understand the things of God. In this relentless indictment, he begins to use parts of the body, principally the throat, the mouth, and the tongue, to show our corruption. **"Their throat is an open tomb"** (v. 13). Jesus had said to the Pharisees, "You are like whitewashed tombs which indeed appear beautiful outwardly, but inside are full of dead men's bones and all uncleanness" (Matt. 23:27); in other words, "If I open your mouth and look down your throat, I see corruption and death."

Paul moves from the throat to the tongue: **"With their tongues they have practiced deceit"** (v. 13). The Bible says that all men are liars. We are deceitful. By nature we do not love truth. We use truth only when it advances our self-interest. Apart from that our lips are full of deceit: **"The poison of asps is under their lips; whose mouth is full of cursing and bitterness"** (vv. 13–14). The adder, or asp, is one of the deadliest reptiles in the world. Not only is its bite fatal, as was the case with Cleopatra, but it is exceedingly painful. The Bible describes our tongues as sacs of venom; we are like pit vipers. The words we use destroy, maim, and poison; they are vituperative.

I rarely heard my father curse. If he hit his thumb with a hammer he might have said a bad word. Today I live in a world where lots of people I know cannot speak a sentence without vulgarity or blasphemy. On television or at the movies we are given symbols to represent which rating a program or movie has been assigned, such as PG or R. Alongside the rating we find letters: AC for adult content or AL for adult language. When we see the symbol AL, we know we are going to get an earful. Gratuitous language is so much a part of the warp and woof of our society that we wonder how people who made movies before 1950 were able to communicate anything in those films. We take for granted that we are people whose mouths are full of cursing and blasphemy and filthy talk. That is who we are; it is our nature. It is not just that we let a bad word slip every now and then; our mouths are filled with such talk. Mouths filled with cursing and bitterness demonstrate sheer paganism.

Paul moves from the throat, the mouth, the lips, and the tongue to the feet: **"Their feet are swift to shed blood"** (v. 15). In our bitterness and propensity for violence, we run toward it; we cannot wait to spill blood. What kind of being would be worthy of a description like this: **"Destruction and misery are in their ways"** (v. 16)? Many think that Paul is quoting nothing more than antiquated texts from the Old Testament that seem to depict God as vengeful. Such thinking predominates in our sophisticated world, where we are more civilized.

Somebody did a calculation of the violence in warfare during the last two thousand years of Western civilization, measuring the number of wars and the magnitude of violence in each. The most peaceful century in the history of Western civilization was the first century, which was the century that witnessed the coming of the Prince of Peace. The second most peaceful century in history was the nineteenth century, which is why people became so optimistic at the end of it. They thought that through science and education, warfare was over. They did not anticipate that there would be more violence and warfare in the first quarter of the twentieth century than in any full century before it. This was before World War II, before the slaughter of millions in the Soviet Union or Red China, before Vietnam, before Korea, and before the world wars that have broken out across every aspect of the globe in the last twenty-five years. Far and away the most violent century in recorded human history was the twentieth century because the way of peace we have not known.

The conclusion of this biblical rehearsal of God's assessment comes down to the bottom line: **"There is no fear of God before their eyes"** (v. 18). The scariest thing of all is that the pagan is not afraid of God. Of course, inherent in the fear Paul mentions is a sense of reverence. We are by nature irreverent people. We have no sense of awe, no desire to honor God or to glorify him as God. We are not naturally afraid of God. God scares me to death. I know I am redeemed; I know that now there is no condemnation for those who are in Christ Jesus, but I know that God is holy, so even though I am covered by the Savior, I am still frightened at times by the character of God, and with good reason. Old Testament wisdom literature says, "The fear of the LORD is the beginning of wisdom" (Prov. 9:10). This is the incredible thing: people who do not fear God think they are smart. They think they are wise. People who have no fear of God have not an ounce of wisdom in their head or heart. "The fool has said in his heart, 'There is no God'" (Pss. 14:1; 53:1).

All Guilty
Now we know that whatever the law says, it says to those who are under the law, that every mouth may be stopped, and all the world may become guilty before God (v. 19). Every time the New Testament describes with vivid imagery the scene of the final judgment where God's verdict comes down in his courtroom, the response of those on trial is silence.

I had a friend who did his PhD at Harvard in neurological studies—advanced studies on the function of the brain—and he once said that the brain is more incredible than the most vast computer system in the world. Every experience we have and every word we speak is recorded in our brains. Concerning the judgment day he said, "I think that in the last day God is going to take our brain out of our head, put it on a table there in his courtroom, plug in a recorder, and punch rewind. We are going to have to sit there and listen to our brain replay everything we have ever done, said, and thought. The prosecuting attorney doesn't have to say a word."

After such a recitation, what would there be to say? What use is there in arguing with God, when God says he has weighed us in the balance and found us wanting? God will say, "I cannot find any goodness. I search your soul, and I do not see righteousness. I see the poison of snakes in your mouth. I give you my law, and you break it at every point."

Here is the conclusion of this segment of the epistle, a conclusion that no sane person dare miss: **Therefore by the deeds of the law no flesh will be justified in His sight, for by the law is the knowledge of sin** (v. 20). If we are paying attention to the law, we know it will not justify us. We know we will never be able to get into heaven on the basis of our works, because the law reveals to us our filthiness. The law teaches us that by the works of the law, no flesh, no human being, will ever be justified in God's sight. Why then do people continue to hope that their good deeds are going to be good enough to satisfy the demands of God? We must despair of that. We must not rest on our works as grounds for our justification because by the works of the law no flesh will be justified in his sight.

Verse 21 begins with my favorite word in the New Testament—*but*. It makes all the difference in the world. Those three letters, b-u-t, are the difference between heaven and hell. Finally, after this relentless indictment that we have had to endure, we are coming to where Paul finally says, "But now the righteousness of God apart from the law is revealed" (v. 21). It is time for the gospel. We have listened to the bad news so that we might hear the goodness of the good news, which we will begin to examine next.

9

RIGHTEOUSNESS REVEALED

Romans 3:21–26

But now the righteousness of God apart from the law is revealed, being witnessed by the Law and the Prophets, even the righteousness of God, through faith in Jesus Christ, to all and on all who believe. For there is no difference; for all have sinned and fall short of the glory of God, being justified freely by His grace through the redemption that is in Christ Jesus, whom God set forth as a propitiation by His blood, through faith, to demonstrate His righteousness, because in His forbearance God had passed over the sins that were previously committed, to demonstrate at the present time His righteousness, that He might be just and the justifier of the one who has faith in Jesus.

We come now to the doctrine of justification by faith alone, a doctrine that has provoked the most serious controversy in the history of the Christian church. The controversy resulted in the sixteenth-century Protestant Reformation, which focused on the material cause of the doctrine of justification. The controversy involved this simple question: how can an unjust person ever hope to stand before the just judgment of God? In other words, how are we saved? This is a matter of eternal consideration. The Reformation was not a tempest in a teapot or a question of theological shadowboxing. At stake in the controversy, in which many paid with their lives, was this doctrine that is central to the New Testament gospel. However, in this day and age there are few professing Christians who can even define the meaning of the term *justification*.

Justification

Luther insisted that justification by faith alone is the article upon which the church stands or falls, and if the church does not get this right, the church ceases to be an authentic church. If the church denies or obscures the doctrine of justification by faith alone, it is no longer a Christian body. To Luther's sentiment Calvin added that the doctrine of justification is the hinge by which everything else turns. J. I. Packer used another metaphor. He said that the doctrine of justification by faith alone is the Atlas that carries the whole of the Christian faith on its shoulders. If justification by faith alone stumbles, the whole Christian faith comes crashing to the ground. We need to be clear as to what the word *justification* means and what the doctrine is all about.

Let me explain what justification does not mean. When we are justified in the sight of God, it is not an act of divine pardon. In justification, God does not pardon the sinner. When a governor or president exercises executive clemency and pardons a convicted criminal, he more or less forgives the criminal of his crime and sets him free. Certainly justification involves forgiveness, as I hope we will see at some point, but let us not confuse the act of divine justification with an act of pardon.

In justification God makes a legal declaration, what we call a forensic declaration. We see in television programs such as *Numbers* or *CSI* that there are people who gather what is called forensic evidence, which is used at trials in criminal cases. Forensics has to do with judicial judgment or declaration. The New Testament shows us that in the act of justification God makes a judicial declaration about a person's status before he makes his judgment. Again, what happens in justification is not a pardon; it is an act whereby God declares a person to be just. Justification is that act by which God judicially declares a person to be righteous in his sight.

In the sixteenth century both Roman Catholics and Protestants agreed that, in the final analysis, the act of justification is something God does, and it is a judicial declaration. Both sides, Catholic and Protestant, agreed that justification does not happen until God declares a person righteous. The issue then and now is this: on what grounds does God make that declaration? Why would God look at us, when he sees one who is dead in sin and trespasses, and say, "You are a just person," when manifestly we are not just people? The good news of the gospel is that God pronounces people just, astonishingly enough, while they are still sinners.

That was the debate with Rome. Rome set forth their doctrine—and still does—that God will never declare a person just until that person actually, under divine scrutiny, is found to be just. In the sixth session of the Council of Trent, in the middle of the sixteenth century at the heart of the Counter-Reformation, the Roman Catholic Church defined her doctrine of justification, which it has continued to echo through the centuries, declaring without equivocation that before God will ever declare a person just, righteousness must inhere in that person. The Latin word is *inherens*. In other words, when God looks at us, he will not say that we are just until he sees that we really are just.

Rome teaches that we cannot be just without grace, that we will never become just without faith, and that we will never become just without the assistance of Christ. We need faith, we need grace, and we need Jesus. We need the righteousness of Christ infused or poured into our soul, but you must cooperate with that grace to such a degree that we will in fact become righteous. If we die with any impurity in our soul, thereby lacking complete righteousness, we will not go to heaven. If no mortal sin is present in our life, we will go to purgatory, which is the place of purging. The point of the purging is to get rid of the dross so that we become completely pure. It may take three years or three million years, but the object of purgatory is to make us righteous so that we can be admitted into God's heaven.

Declared Righteous

Part of the reason for this belief, that justification is rooted in an inherent righteousness in the sinner, comes from something unfortunate in church history. In the early centuries, when the Greek language passed away from the central attention of the church fathers and Latin became the dominant language, many scholars read only the Latin Bible, not the Greek Bible, and they borrowed the Roman or Latin word for justification, *iustificare*, from which we get the English word *justification*. The Latin verb *ficare* means "to make" or "to shape" or "to do." *Iustus* means "righteousness" or "justice," so *iustificare* literally means "to make righteous," which we believe is what happens in sanctification, not in justification.

The Greek word that we are dealing with here in the Romans text is the word *dikaioo, dikaiosune*, which does not mean "to make righteous" but rather "to declare righteous." In the Roman Catholic view, God will never pronounce a person just or righteous until, by the help of God's grace and Christ, that person actually becomes righteous. If God were to judge us tonight, what would he find? Would he find sin in our lives? Could he possibly declare us just if he considers only the righteousness that he finds in us today? Remember what the apostle Paul said: "By the deeds of the law no flesh will be justified in His sight" (3:20). That is precisely why the ground for our justification cannot be found in us or in any righteousness inherent in our souls. That is why we need so desperately what Luther called a *iustia alienum*, an alien righteousness, a righteousness that comes from outside of ourselves. Luther called this righteousness *extranos*, outside of or apart from us.

In simple terms, this means that the only righteousness sufficient for us to stand before the judgment of God is the righteousness of Christ. The doctrine of justification by faith alone is only theological shorthand for the affirmation that justification is by Christ alone, by his righteousness, which is received by faith. When Paul speaks here about justification, he is not talking about pardon, and he is not talking about God's declaration of what he finds in us and in our behavior. He is talking about something else altogether.

One of the slogans formulated by Luther and widely repeated in the sixteenth century was a little Latin phrase: *simul iustus et peccator. Simul* is the root from which we get the word *simultaneously*, which means "at the same time." *Iustus* means "just" or "righteous." When we put the words together, we get "at the same time righteous." *Et* means "and," and *peccator* is the word for "sinner." If somebody is without sin we say that he is impeccable. We use the term *peccadillo* to describe a little sin. The point of Luther's slogan was this: the Christian is someone who is at the very same time righteous and sinner. How can that be? While we are sinners, we are also righteous in God's sight by virtue of the legal transfer God made by assigning to us the righteousness of Jesus, if we put our trust in Christ. By virtue of this transfer, or the imputation of the righteousness of Christ to us, we are declared to be righteous while still sinners.

That is the good news—we can be declared just by God while we are still sinners. That is the heart of the gospel. We do not have to wait to become perfectly righteous before we are acceptable to God. This is the point that the apostle is laboring to make in this section of the epistle. **But now the righteousness of God apart from the law is revealed, being witnessed by the Law and the Prophets** (v. 21).

When we get to Romans 4, Paul is going to show that the doctrine of justification by faith alone is not a novelty. It is not a new doctrine announced by Jesus during his incarnation, nor is it one that the apostle Paul dreamed up in his ministry. This doctrine of the gospel is rooted in the testimony of the Old Testament. The whole point of the law is to drive us to this One who possesses the righteousness that we do not have. We find it in the teaching of the prophets. Paul will show us in Romans 4 that we are justified today on this side of the cross the same way that people in the Old Testament were justified. To give us a heads-up of what is to come, Paul mentions here in Romans 3 that this is **even the righteousness of God, through faith in Jesus Christ, to all and on all who believe** (v. 22).

When we claim justification is "by faith" or "through faith," we have to be careful that we do not misunderstand that. To be justified by faith is not to be justified because we have faith, in the sense that our faith now is the supreme work that makes us righteous. The language here of being justified by faith or through faith simply means that faith is the means by which we lay hold of Christ. It is the means by which the righteousness of Christ is bestowed upon us.

Rome and the Reformation

The Roman Catholic Church defines faith as important and indeed essential to justification. Faith is the foundation for justification, but the instrumental cause of justification, according to Rome, is the sacrament of baptism. To understand the idea of an instrumental cause, we have to go back before Jesus to the philosopher Aristotle, who examined different ways that change is brought about. He said the word *cause*, in and of itself, is too vague. We need to be more specific if we are going to be scientific in discerning various types of causes.

Aristotle used a piece of sculpture as an illustration. A piece of sculpture starts out as a block of stone; it has no beautiful shape. How does the block of stone change into a gorgeous statue, such as one created by Michelangelo? Aristotle said there is a *material cause*, the stuff out of which something is brought to pass; the material cause in the case of the sculpture is the block of stone. Then there is the *formal cause*, which is the idea that the sculptor or artist has before he creates his piece of art. An artist has a sketch, or even just an idea in his head, and he follows that blueprint in order to produce the sculpture. That is the formal cause. The *efficient cause* is the one whose work brings about the change. In the case of the sculpture, the efficient cause is the sculptor. The *final cause* is the purpose for which something is made. In the case of the sculpture, the final cause might be to beautify an emperor's garden. Aristotle also spoke of the *instrumental cause*, which is the means by which the sculptor shapes that stone into a beautiful statue. The instruments the sculptor uses are the chisel and the hammer. The instrumental cause of

Rembrandt's paintings was his brushes. The instruments are the means by which the change takes place.

Rome says the instrumental cause of justification is baptism, in the first instance, and the sacrament of penance, in the second instance. If someone loses his justification through mortal sin, he can have it restored through the sacrament of penance, which includes doing works of satisfaction. In the sixteenth century Rome declared that the sacraments are the means by which a person is made righteous, but the Reformers said that the instrumental cause of our justification is not the sacraments. Faith is the only instrument by which one is linked to Christ and receives his righteousness.

The Double Transfer

It is vitally important for us to understand what faith is—why we call people to faith and why the New Testament calls us to faith. Faith means that we place our trust in Christ and his righteousness. We do not trust our own righteousness because we do not have any. When we trust Christ's righteousness on our behalf and embrace him, then God transfers legally his righteousness to us. A double transfer is involved in salvation. Christ dies for our salvation, but he also lives for our salvation. Our sins are transferred to Jesus, and he died on the cross for us to bear those sins.

This is a legal transfer. God did not reach down into our souls and grab a hunk of sin and place it on the back of Jesus. God assigned our guilt to his Son. He transferred it from us to Christ, but that is only half the transaction. The other half is that he took Christ's righteousness and assigned it to us when we believed so that now when God looks at us, knowing all of our righteousness is as filthy rags, we will not perish. He has given us the cloak of the righteousness of Jesus. That is the righteousness of God that Paul introduced in Romans 1, the righteousness not by which God himself is righteous but that which he makes available to all who put their trust in Christ. **For there is no difference; for all have sinned and fall short of the glory of God, being justified freely by His grace through the redemption that is in Christ Jesus** (vv. 22–24).

Paul is talking about the grace by which God freely gives the righteousness of Christ to a sinner, one who is at the same time just and sinner, through the redemption that is in Christ Jesus, **whom God set forth as a propitiation by His blood, through faith, to demonstrate His righteousness, because in His forbearance God had passed over the sins that were previously committed, to demonstrate at the present time His righteousness** (vv. 25–26). A storm of controversy arose when the

Revised Standard Version appeared in English. The words *expiation* and *propitiation* were removed from the English text based on the reasoning that people in this day and age do not use words like that, and if people are going to understand the New Testament such strange terms must be eliminated. We must never get rid of the words *propitiation* and *expiation*. Those are two of the most glorious words that we find anywhere in the New Testament.

Propitiation means to satisfy the demands of justice. In biblical terms it means to satisfy the demands of God's wrath. God places sin and evil under his judgment and decrees that he is going to pour out his wrath upon it. In New Testament terms, what we are saved from is God. We are saved by God from God, from the wrath that is to come. Propitiation satisfies completely the demands of God's wrath and justice, which is what the cross was all about. Christ as our substitute took upon himself the wrath that we deserve, to pay the penalty that was due for our guilt to satisfy the demands of God's justice. In his work of propitiation, Jesus did something on a vertical level, something with respect to the Father, satisfying the justice of God for us.

Expiation has to do directly with us. The prefix *ex-* means "away from" or "out of." One of the benefits of justification is the remission of sin, our sin being removed from us. Our sin goes away. After a close friend's wife had fought cancer for several years, he told me, "She is in her fourth remission." For the time being, at least, the cancer had gone away. It had been removed. If we buy something on our credit card, a bill will come requesting us to remit payment. When we send in the payment, the money is transferred from our account to the merchant. When the New Testament speaks about expiation, it is referring to the sense in which Christ removes our sin from us and takes it away. The psalmist tells us, "As far as the east is from the west, so far has He removed our transgressions from us" (Ps. 103:12).

In the work of Christ, there is propitiation and expiation. The sanctuary at St. Andrew's is in the form of a cross, a cruciform. The center beam of the cross, the vertical beam, comes down the middle, and the side bars are the various transepts. I have told my congregation that every time they come into church on Sunday morning and walk down that aisle, the vertical bar, they should think of the vertical dimension of their justification, which is the propitiation, the satisfaction, that Christ has accomplished for them before the Father. The horizontal bar of the cross represents their expiation, whereby Christ not only satisfied the justice of the Father but also removed their sins from them. We must not lose these words, *propitiation* and *expiation*. They so richly capture the essence of the gospel that stands upon what Christ did on the cross in paying for our guilt and in his life of perfect obedience in earning the righteousness that he freely gives to us.

God set forth Christ as a propitiation by his blood through faith **that He might be just and the justifier of the one who has faith in Jesus** (v. 26). There is no such thing as cheap grace. The gospel is not simply an announcement of pardon. In justification God does not merely decide unilaterally to forgive us our sins. That is the prevailing idea, that what happens in the gospel is that God freely forgives us of sin because he is such a loving, dear, wonderful God, and it does not disturb him that we violate everything that is holy. God never negotiates his righteousness. God will never lay aside his holiness to save us. God demands and requires that sin be punished. That is why the cross is the universal symbol of Christianity. Christ had to die because, according to God, the propitiation had to be made; sin had to be punished. Our sin has to be punished.

In the drama of justification, God remains just. He does not set aside his justice. He does not waive his righteousness; he insists upon it. We cannot be justified without righteousness, but the glory of his grace is that his justice is served vicariously by a substitute that he appointed. God's mercy is shown in that what saves us is not our righteousness. It is someone else's. We get in on someone else's coattails—that is grace. That somebody, our Redeemer, is perfectly righteous and has fulfilled the justice of God for us perfectly. That is the glory of justification. God demonstrates that he is both just and justifier. If all he did was maintain his righteousness without extending the imputation of that righteousness to us, he would not be the justifier. He is both just and justifier, which is the marvel of the gospel.

10

FAITH AND WORKS

Romans 4:1–8

What then shall we say that Abraham our father has found according to the flesh? For if Abraham was justified by works, he has something to boast about, but not before God. For what does the Scripture say? "Abraham believed God, and it was accounted to him for righteousness." Now to him who works, the wages are not counted as grace but as debt.

But to him who does not work but believes on Him who justifies the ungodly, his faith is accounted for righteousness, just as David also describes the blessedness of the man to whom God imputes righteousness apart from works:

"Blessed are those whose lawless deeds are forgiven,
And whose sins are covered;
Blessed is the man to whom the LORD shall not impute sin."

Since righteousness comes only through faith in Christ Jesus, Paul asks, "Where is boasting then?" (3:27). Paul answers his question emphatically—boasting is excluded. Since our justification is by faith alone, by no merit in us or endeavors of our works, there is no room whatsoever for boasting, save in Christ. In this section of the epistle, Paul is going to bring forth exhibit A to prove his case. He does not do it by an abstract exposition of doctrine but by a historical reconnaissance. He reaches back to the Old Testament to the person of Abraham, who was known to the Jews as the father of the faithful. Paul looks to Abraham as the supreme example of how a person is justified by faith and not by works.

Before we get into the exposition of Romans 4:1–8, it is important to understand that salvation occurred in the Old Testament in the same manner that it occurs in the New Testament. When Paul speaks of Abraham's justification as being by faith, that is shorthand for saying that Abraham was justified by the righteousness of Christ. The only difference between our justification and Abraham's is that Abraham looked forward to the promised one. He trusted in the promise of the Redeemer, whereas we look backward to the work of Jesus. The only difference is the timeframe of where the object of faith is. Abraham's faith looked forward and our faith looks backward, but the ground of Abraham's justification was exactly the same as ours, namely, the person and work of Jesus.

That is very important to understand, because the dominant theology in our country today tends to see a strong disjunction between salvation in the Old Testament and salvation in the New Testament. The Old Testament is viewed as the age of law and the New Testament is viewed as the age of grace; therefore, God's way of salvation differed in the two covenants. Paul refutes that idea right here when he brings forward as his example of the doctrine of justification by faith not someone from the New Testament but someone from the Old Testament, Father Abraham.

Abraham Believed God

What then shall we say that Abraham our father has found according to the flesh? For if Abraham was justified by works, he has something to boast about, but not before God (vv. 1–2). Abraham was excluded from boasting because he was not justified by works, anymore than we are. **For what does the Scripture say? "Abraham believed God, and it was accounted to him for righteousness." Now to him who works, the wages are not counted as grace but as debt** (vv. 3–4). Here Paul cites a statement found in Genesis 15, where God appeared to Abraham and told him that he would be his shield and his very great reward (v. 1). Abraham was staggered by that announcement because he was one of the wealthiest men on earth. What do you give a man who has everything? To the Jew you give progeny. You give him sons. Abraham had plenty of cattle, livestock, and property, but he had no son, so he said, "Lord GOD, what will You give me, seeing I go childless, and the heir of my house is Eliezer of

Damascus?" (v. 2). God told him, "This one shall not be your heir, but one who will come from your own body shall be your heir" (v. 4).

This staggering promise that God gave to Abraham in his old age resulted in Abraham's believing God (v. 6). He trusted the promise of God. Abraham's faith was not without some admixture of wavering or doubt—"Lord GOD, how shall I know that I will inherit it?" (v. 8)—but God put him to sleep and gave him a magnificent theophany. God, because he could swear by nothing greater, swore by himself in the drama of that vision (vv. 12–21).

What we are mainly concerned about in Genesis 15 is that Abraham believed God, and it was counted to him as righteousness. That is, Abraham was reckoned or considered by God to be righteous, not because of any righteous deeds that Abraham had performed but simply because he believed the promise.

Faith *and* Works*?*

Paul's argument in Romans 4 is somewhat problematic because of the way in which the apostle James deals with the issue in his epistle:

> What does it profit, my brethren, if someone says he has faith but does not have works? Can faith save him? If a brother or sister is naked and destitute of daily food, and one of you says to them, "Depart in peace, be warmed and filled," but you do not give them the things which are needed for the body, what does it profit? Thus also faith by itself, if it does not have works, is dead. But someone will say, "You have faith, and I have works." Show me your faith without your works, and I will show you my faith by my works. You believe that there is one God. You do well. Even the demons believe—and tremble! But do you want to know, O foolish man, that faith without works is dead? (James 2:14–20)

Here is where the plot thickens:

> Was not Abraham our father justified by works when he offered Isaac his son on the altar? Do you see that faith was working together with his works, and by works faith was made perfect? And the Scripture was fulfilled which says, "Abraham believed God, and it was accounted to him for righteousness." And he was called the friend of God. You see then that a man is justified by works, and not by faith only. Likewise, was not Rahab the harlot also justified by works. . . . (vv. 21–25)

In the middle of the sixteenth century, after the Protestant Reformation was in full swing, the Roman Catholic Church held its ecumenical council in the city of Trent in Italy, known later as the Council of Trent. During the sixth session of that council, Rome set forth her doctrine of justification along with several canons condemning the Protestant understanding. At the Council of Trent footnotes were affixed to biblical texts that would support the Roman Catholic decrees, and two or three times in the sixth session they quoted from James 2, particularly this verse: "You see then that a man is justified by works, and not by faith only" (v. 24). On the surface it would seem that there could be no clearer repudiation of the doctrine of justification by faith alone.

Many look at that and say, "I guess Luther was wrong and the Protestant church has been wrong ever since, and we need to return to Rome and say, 'Fathers, we have sinned.'" What makes the plot more difficult is that when James makes his case—"a man is justified by works, and not by faith only"—his primary exhibit in the court of theological debate is none other than Father Abraham. It would be nice if we could resolve this conundrum by saying that James, when he refers to justification, uses a different Greek word from the word Paul uses in Romans 4, but James and Paul used exactly the same Greek term, *dikiaiōsune*.

Some scholars have argued that Romans was written before the book of James and that James wrote to correct Paul's error of justification by faith alone. Others argue that James was written first and Paul gave this lengthy exposition in Romans to correct the error that James was disseminating among early Christians. Others have argued that neither one knew about the other's writing so what we have here is a plain contradiction in the Bible between the teaching of Paul and the teaching of James. When I come to a text such as this, I come as one already persuaded that it is nothing less than the Word of God, and I am also persuaded that God does not speak with a forked tongue. Therefore, as problematic as it seems on the surface, we must dig deeper into the text and see if there is a genuine basis for resolution.

Luther's Catholic adversaries kept rubbing his nose, as it were, into the second chapter of James until Luther, in frustration, declared James to be an epistle of straw. Luther said that it did not belong in the canon of the New Testament, but he repented of that later in his life and finally acknowledged that James was indeed part of the canon.

Works Prove Faith

In order to reach a resolution, we must first examine the context in which the statements were made and ask, "What question is the author trying to answer?" Many of my philosophy students found the subject matter difficult to deal with because of its abstract content. As they struggled to grasp the ideas bandied about by various philosophers, I tried to help them, and I asked them to consider what problem confronted Descartes, for example, and the people of his time that provoked him to undertake a deep analysis of how we know what we know. Once the students could understand the problem that the philosopher was trying to unravel, they were better able to follow his reasoning process. In the same manner we do well to ask that question with respect to James.

James tells us what question he is trying to answer: "What does it profit, my brethren, if someone says he has faith but does not have works? Can faith save him?" (v. 14). That was one of the most critical questions of the sixteenth-century Reformation. When Luther insisted that justification is by faith alone, people took that to mean that all one has to do is give intellectual assent that Jesus was the Savior of the world. However, that is no different from believing that George Washington was the first president of the United States. We may grant that it is a true proposition, but it is not the same thing as trusting our eternal life to George Washington. We do not have personal faith and trust in George Washington. Luther was never an apostle of what we call "easy believism."

If, before I was a Christian, you had asked me if I believed in God and that Jesus was his Son, I would have said yes, but I had no personal relationship with Christ; I had no saving faith whatsoever. It was merely an intellectual assent to an abstract proposition. James writes here in this text, "You believe that there is one God. You do well. Even the demons believe—and tremble!" (v. 19). Believing in God—big deal. All that does is qualify us to be demons. Anybody can believe in the existence of God. Satan believes. The demons know that God exists and they tremble before him, but they do not put their trust in God for salvation. Luther had to spell out the ingredients of saving faith, which include not only the data, the content to believe, but also the intellectual assent to the propositions. If we have the content and the assent but if that is all we have, we are not going to be justified.

The third and most critical element that Luther delineated was what he called *faducia*, personal trust in Christ. *Faducia* is necessary for salvation. In his Evangelism Explosion program D. James Kennedy would use the illustration of a chair. He would point to a chair and ask people, "Do you believe that is a chair?"

They would say yes.

"Do you believe that if you sit in that chair it will hold you up?"

They would look at the chair. It seemed firm and well constructed so they would say, "Yes, I believe that the chair will hold me up."

Then Kennedy would ask, "Is it holding you up now?"

They had to say no because they were not sitting in it. We can believe that Jesus can save us without having saving faith. We have to trust that he does save us, and we put our trust in him alone.

The Reformers added a footnote to the formula of justification by faith alone. The full phrase was this: "Justification is by faith alone but not by a faith that is alone." The point is that if we have true faith, it will immediately and necessarily be manifested in a changed life. If no change follows from our profession of faith, all we have is a profession of faith. We do not possess the real thing, because real faith always issues in some degree of obedience. Works flow necessarily from faith, but the point of the gospel is that the works that flow from faith are in no way the grounds of justification. God declares us just in his sight the moment true faith is present, before a single work flows from our faith.

James is addressing this question: "If I say I have faith but have no works, will that faith save me?" Nobody has ever been saved by a profession of faith. We were not saved by raising our hand in an evangelistic meeting or walking down an aisle. The possession of faith justifies us, not the profession of it.

If we possess it, we should profess it, but Jesus makes clear that people can profess it without possessing it. "This people honors Me with their lips, but their heart is far from Me" (Mark 7:6). They call him Lord, but they are workers of evil, and Jesus does not even know their name. True faith must always be manifested in obedience, to some degree, so James asks, "What does it profit, my brethren, if someone says he has faith but does not have works? Can faith save him?" (v. 14). He then gives an illustration:

> If a brother or sister is naked and destitute of daily food, and one of you says to them, "Depart in peace, be warmed and filled," but you do not give them the things which are needed for the body, what does it profit? (v. 15–16)

Here is his conclusion: "Thus also faith by itself, if it does not have works, is dead" (v. 17). James's point is that a dead faith cannot save anyone. Luther said the faith that justifies is a *fides viva*, a vital faith, a living faith. It is healthy. It brings forth the fruit of true faith. A profession of faith that produces nothing is useless. It has no life in it.

James continues, "But someone will say, 'You have faith, and I have works. Show me your faith without your works, and I will show you my faith by my works'" (v. 18). It is show-and-tell time. This is very important to understand.

James is saying that the only way to know if we have genuine faith is by our works. That is how faith is demonstrated or made manifest.

Counted Righteous

I mentioned earlier that both Paul and James use the same Greek word for justification, *dikaiōsune*. That Greek word has more than one use. It can mean "to be declared righteous by God" or it can mean "the demonstration of the truth of an affirmation." Jesus used this very word in a metaphorical way when he said, "Wisdom is justified by her children" (Matt. 11:19). Jesus was saying that if we want to know if a plan is wise, we have to wait until we see the outcome.

We must remember what James is wrestling with—the nature of saving faith. If someone claims to have faith, the proof of it is obedience. God does not have to wait to see our behavior before he knows if the faith we profess is authentic. We may need to see the works, but God does not. When James references Abraham, he quotes from Genesis 22 where Abraham offers up Isaac on the altar: "Was not Abraham our father justified by works when he offered Isaac his son on the altar? Do you see that faith was working together with his works, and by works faith was made perfect [or complete]?" (James 2:21–22).

When Paul references Abraham, he quotes from Genesis 15. Paul's point is that God did not have to wait until Mount Moriah (Genesis 22) to know whether Abraham's faith was authentic. The moment Abraham believed, God counted him righteous. We are the ones who do not know that his faith was authentic until we see how he responds to the test that God gives him in Genesis 22, which is what James means. James is speaking about vindicating or demonstrating the truth of a profession of faith. James concludes, "The Scripture was fulfilled which says, 'Abraham believed God, and it was accounted to him for righteousness.' And he was called the friend of God. You see then that a man is justified by works, and not by faith only" (vv. 23–24). There is nothing in James about merit attending the obedience of Abraham; James is describing Abraham's obedience as proof that his profession of faith is real and valid. This is difficult, but it resolves the problem between these two writers of sacred Scripture.

If the ground of Abraham's justification was his works, then Abraham's justification would not be by grace. If his works had been good enough to make him just in the sight of God, if Abraham had brought merit to the table—whether *meritum de congruo* or *de condigno*—then his justification would not have been reckoned as grace but as debt. In other words, God would owe him justification, which is what Paul is demolishing here in verses 3 and 4.

But to him who does not work but believes on Him who justifies the ungodly, his faith is accounted for righteousness (v. 5). This does not mean your faith itself is the righteousness that is the grounds for our salvation. Faith only lays hold of Christ. Faith is the instrument by which we are linked to Jesus. Only Christ's righteousness is the grounds of our justification. When God declares his legal judgment of our status in his sight, when he sees faith, he counts us righteous—even when we are still sinners. This is *simul justus et peccator*.

Blessed

Paul then argues his point from David: **just as David also describes the blessedness of the man to whom God imputes righteousness apart from works** (v. 6). In our day, the doctrine of justification has been battled afresh within certain so-called evangelical circles, which shows that they are not truly evangelical. Anyone who challenges *sola fide* cannot do that and legitimately be counted as an evangelical, because justification by faith alone is at the very heart of historic evangelicalism. Be that as it may, there are many who call themselves evangelicals but their profession of evangelicalism is a false profession because they deny the *evangel* that defines evangelicalism.

At the center of the current debate is whether the aspect of imputation is crucial to justification by faith alone. About fifteen years ago some leading evangelicals in our country declared to the world that they had a unity of faith in the gospel with their Roman Catholic friends. The movement was called Evangelicals and Catholics Together (ECT). In discussions with its proponents I raised the question of imputation. How can we have unity with those who deny that doctrine? So much controversy arose out of the ECT initiative that the first document they forged was put aside, and they came out with a second document, which, in my judgment, was far worse than the first. In the second document they declared that justification *requires* faith, which, they said, was the same thing that the Reformers were saying in the sixteenth century. They decided to "leave the question of imputation for later discussion," but as Michael Horton has said, if we are making chocolate chip cookies and we get flour and milk and sugar and mix it all together, we have the stuff that makes up chocolate chip cookies, but there is one critical ingredient missing—chocolate chips. Without the chocolate chips we do not have chocolate chip cookies, and without *sola fide* we do not have justification by faith alone.

The issue historically is how the righteousness of Christ becomes ours. Is it poured into us through the sacrament of baptism and later again through the sacrament of penance? Or is the righteousness of Christ imputed to us, transferred to our account? Here is the whole debate in a nutshell: is the righteousness by which we are justified an inherent righteousness? If so, it is not gospel; it is bad news. It would leave us without hope. The gospel is that we are righteous on the basis of the righteousness of Jesus, which is transferred to our account—what Luther called a *justitium alienum,* an alien righteousness, one that is *extra nos,* outside of us. It is Christ's righteousness that justifies us. All we bring to the table is our trust in him and his righteousness. If we add one ounce of our own righteousness as our confidence, we repudiate the gospel. That is why Paul cites David: **"Blessed are those whose lawless deeds are forgiven, and whose sins are covered; blessed is the man to whom the LORD shall not impute sin"** (vv. 7–8). There is no greater blessedness under heaven than to have God in his mercy and grace transfer the righteousness of Jesus to our account.

When we stand before God, he knows everything we have ever done wrong—every evil thought, every wicked deed. When he looks at us *inherently,* all he sees are filthy rags, but that is not how he looks at us. He looks at us and sees Christ. He sees the covering of the righteousness of Christ, the cloak of righteousness. That is why the New Testament says that Christ is our righteousness. The only righteousness we possess is the righteousness of Christ, and we possess it by transfer, by reckoning, by imputation.

I tell my friends in the theological world that if they negotiate imputation, they give it all away. It is the article upon which *sola fide* stands or falls, and *sola fide* is the article upon which the gospel stands or falls, and the gospel is the article upon which the church stands or falls.

11

BLESSED

Romans 4:5–12

But to him who does not work but believes on Him who justifies the ungodly, his faith is accounted for righteousness, just as David also describes the blessedness of the man to whom God imputes righteousness apart from works:

> Blessed are those whose lawless deeds are forgiven,
>> And whose sins are covered.
> Blessed is the man to whom the LORD shall not impute sin.

Does this blessedness then come upon the circumcised only, or upon the uncircumcised also? For we say that faith was accounted to Abraham for righteousness. How then was it accounted? While he was circumcised, or uncircumcised? Not while circumcised, but while uncircumcised. And he received the sign of circumcision, a seal of the righteousness of the faith which he had while still uncircumcised, that he might be the father of all those who believe, though they are uncircumcised, that righteousness might be imputed to them also, and the father of circumcision to those who not only are of the circumcision but who also walk in the steps of the faith which our father Abraham had while still uncircumcised.

L ast time we focused our attention on Paul's appeal to Abraham as the supreme example in the Scripture of one who was justified by faith. Paul, for a moment, interspersed with his appeal to Abraham another Old Testament example, David. Although Abraham is Paul's primary witness, Paul calls upon David as another example, par excellence, of justification by faith: **But to him who does not work but believes on Him who justifies the ungodly, his faith is accounted for righteousness, just as David also describes the blessedness of the man to whom God imputes righteousness apart from works** (vv. 5–6).

Blessedness

It disturbs me not a little bit that modern commentators, seeking to be relevant to the culture, prefer to translate the word *blessed* as the word *happy*. If any word would cheapen the concept that is before us, I can think of no word that would cheapen it more than *happy*. The terms *happy* and *happiness* have been used to such a superficial degree that they have lost the force of their import. We say that "happiness is a warm puppy," but the kind of happiness in view in such adages is miles away from the happiness contained in the biblical word *blessed*.

When Old Testament prophets were anointed by the Spirit of God to proclaim the Word of God and to be agents of revelation, the favorite device used by those prophets to communicate God's message was the oracle. Oracles were uttered by prophets, even in the secular world. Those oracles, such as those uttered by the Oracle of Delphi, were of two types: the oracle of woe and the oracle of weal. The former was that by which the announcement of God's wrath was communicated, and the latter pronounced God's good news upon his people. I want to tie that in to the context of what Paul is saying about justification. A benediction found in the Old Testament was an integral part of the religious life of the people of Israel:

> The LORD bless you and keep you;
> The LORD make His face shine upon you,
>   And be gracious to you;
> The LORD lift up His countenance upon you,
>   And give you peace. (Num. 6:24–26)

That great Hebrew benediction is expressed in a literary form called parallelism, in which there are three stanzas. In this case each stanza is saying the same thing only with different words. The first segment of those three lines is the one we are most concerned with. The two lines "The LORD bless you" and

"The LORD make his face shine upon you" are called *synonymous parallelism*. The second line has the same idea as that contained in the first line. To be blessed of God is to have God make his face shine upon us. The idea is reinforced even more strongly in the third line: "The LORD lift up His countenance upon you and give you peace." The Jew understood blessedness always in terms of the proximity that one had to the presence of God.

In the garden before the fall, Adam and Eve rejoiced when God came in the cool of the day. They rushed to be in his presence and enjoy the light of his countenance, but once sin marred that relationship, they, and we, were expelled from the presence of God. The mandate came from God: "You cannot see My face; for no man shall see Me, and live" (Ex. 33:20). In fact, in the Bible the imagery of hell is the place of outer darkness where not the slightest glimmer of light penetrates from the countenance of God. To be cursed by God is to have God turn his back upon someone and remove his grace and take away all hope of peace. The curse of God is communicated through the oracle of woe. Jesus said, "Woe to you, scribes and Pharisees, hypocrites! For you travel land and sea to win one proselyte, and when he is won, you make him twice as much a son of hell as yourselves" (Matt. 23:15). Elsewhere Jesus pronounces the oracle of doom with the expression of woe and a curse upon those who were moved from the presence of God.

In bold contrast to the oracle of woe is the oracle of weal that is pronounced by God with the oracular expression *blessed*. In Psalm 1 David declares:

> Blessed is the man
>> Who walks not in the counsel of the ungodly,
>> Nor stands in the path of sinners,
>> Nor sits in the seat of the scornful;
> But his delight is in the law of the LORD,
>> And in His law he meditates day and night. (vv. 1–2)

What will be his laud? "He shall be like a tree planted by the rivers of water, that brings forth its fruit in its season (v. 3). Notice the pronouncement of the blessing: "Blessed is that man." David adds, "The ungodly are not so, but are like the chaff which the wind drives away" (v. 4).

In the New Testament, in the Sermon on the Mount, Jesus, the prophet par excellence, uses the same device, the oracle, to pronounce the joy that God gives to his people:

Blessed are the poor in spirit,
For theirs is the kingdom of heaven.
Blessed are those who mourn,
For they shall be comforted.
Blessed are the meek,
For they shall inherit the earth.
Blessed are those who hunger and thirst for righteousness,
For they shall be filled.
Blessed are the merciful,
For they shall obtain mercy.
Blessed are the pure in heart,
For they shall see God.
Blessed are the peacemakers,
For they shall be called sons of God.
Blessed are those who are persecuted for righteousness' sake,
For theirs is the kingdom of heaven. (Matt. 5:3–10)

We tend to cheapen the word *blessed* by saying, "Bless you, my friend" or "God bless you." Yet the highest experience and joy of the human soul is to experience that blessedness that only God can give. So when Paul is talking here about the gospel, about justification by faith alone, he calls attention to this great beatitude, to the supreme state of blessedness, by calling attention to David. If we transformed that into the oracular form, David could be saying, "How blessed is the one who receives the imputation of the righteousness of Christ."

What do we give a man who has everything? We give him righteousness. The greatest gift we could ever receive from the hand of God is the blessed gift of the righteousness of Christ. How can we put our arms around the fact that, in God's eyes, God counts us as righteous as Jesus? Rome protests this vociferously, saying that the Protestant doctrine of justification by faith alone, based on this concept of imputation, is a doctrine that involves a legal fiction and makes God a liar because it has God counting people as righteous who are not righteous. This is not a legal fiction but a legal declaration. There is absolutely nothing fictional about God's act of imputation. The righteousness of Jesus is real righteousness, and the imputation of that righteousness to our account in Christ is a real imputation. If it were only a fiction we would despair, but the reality of that imputation is to us the reality of blessedness, something that all who receive such imputed righteousness enjoy.

Paul quotes David: **"Blessed are those whose lawless deeds are forgiven, and whose sins are covered"** (v. 7). We do not read, "Blessed are those who have obeyed the law, whose meritorious, lawful deeds have justified them." We read that the blessed ones are those whose law*less* deeds are forgiven.

Lawlessness

One of the scariest titles in the New Testament for the antichrist is "man of lawlessness" (2 Thess. 2:3 NIV). Sin is lawlessness. We are a nation of scofflaws. We have become immunized against obedience, even to the civil law. There are so many laws that we tend to discount their significance. It is one thing to scoff at the laws made by men, but to scoff at the law of God is the deepest kind of evil. That is why the antichrist himself is described as "the man of lawlessness."

Jesus concluded the Sermon on the Mount by stating that many will come to him on the last day and say to him, "Lord, Lord, have we not prophesied in Your name, cast out demons in Your name, and done many wonders in Your name?" Jesus will tell them, "I never knew you; depart from Me, you who practice lawlessness!" (Matt. 7:22–23). It is scary to think that people will claim to know Jesus intimately and yet he will say, "Please leave; I do not know your name." He will say it because those people are characterized by lives of lawlessness. Such are unrepentant sinners who profess to be Christians but have never trusted in Christ's righteousness alone.

That is what we are by nature. That is *who* we are—lawless people before God. To be a lawless person is to earn, merit, and deserve the wrath of God, but instead of God's wrath we get his blessing, which is why David cries out, "Blessed are those whose lawless deeds are forgiven." At the heart of our justification is the fact that God forgives our sins. He removes our sins as far as the east is from the west (Ps. 103:12).

When our daughter, Sherrie, was about six years old, I was serving on the staff of a church in Cincinnati, Ohio. Every year we held what is called a "preaching mission week." We brought in a minister to proclaim the gospel, and we actually had altar calls every night during that week. As I was going to the service one evening, I dropped off Sherrie in the nursery; then I went over to the sanctuary and introduced the speaker. He gave a powerful message on the cross of Christ and afterward called those who wanted to give their lives to Christ to come forward and commit to Jesus. I watched people coming forward, and to my horror I saw Sherrie walking down the middle aisle. I thought, *This is an emotional thing. She does not understand what she is doing. I am going to have a talk with her afterward about this commitment.*

On the way home I asked her, "Honey, why did you do that?"

She said, "Daddy, I did not want to. I was embarrassed to go down there, but something just compelled me to get up and go, and so I went. Now, Daddy, I feel clean. I feel like a newborn baby."

So I told her, "I think you have it there, honey."

She did understand the simple message of the forgiveness of sins, and she was a blessed little girl to understand it.

Before I had ever heard the word *justification*, I found myself on my knees confessing my sins to God. It was September 13, 1957, in a dormitory room, alone, at eleven o'clock at night. When I got up off the floor, I was a Christian. The experience I had that night was an experience of forgiveness of sin—the greatest blessedness I had ever known, the most life-transforming event of my entire experience. I can relate to David's words, "Blessed are those whose lawless deeds are forgiven and whose sins are covered."

When Adam and Eve committed their first transgression, shame and guilt were experienced for the first time in human history. We notice in the creation account that "they were both naked, the man and his wife, and were not ashamed" (Gen. 2:25). That was their condition until the first transgression. As soon as they sinned the first sin, the Bible tells us their eyes were opened, they realized that they were naked, and they were embarrassed about it.

New Clothes

We are unlikely to see naked people walking around, but if we observe the rest of the animals in the universe we do not see them wearing shirts or dresses or coats or trousers. Occasionally we will see an animal with a hat or a dog wearing a sweater, but Mother Nature does not make clothes for the creatures of this world except for human beings. We are what Desmond Morris called "the naked ape." We are the only ones that go about with artificial covering, something that started in the garden with the first sin. The first experience of sin was an experience of guilt, and it was manifested in a profound sense of shame and embarrassment. From that moment on, the human species became fugitive—headed for cover and darkness.

Men love the darkness rather than light. John tells us that is because "their deeds were evil" (John 3:19). Adam and Eve went to the bushes to hide from God, and when God came to them, he said, "Where are you?" (Gen. 3:9). Adam replied, "I heard Your voice in the garden, and I was afraid because I was naked; and I hid myself" (v. 10). Then God asked, "Who told you that you were naked? Have you eaten from the tree of which I commanded you that you should not eat?" (v. 11). And Adam answered, "The woman whom You gave to be with me, she gave me of the tree, and I ate" (v. 12).

There are the creatures trembling before the Creator, guilty of sin, debtors who cannot possibly pay their debt. This is our universal condition, and everybody, Christian or non-Christian, knows that they carry a burden of guilt that they cannot fix themselves. The very first act of redemption occurred when God condescended to make clothes for his embarrassed creatures and cover their nakedness. He could have said, "Go ahead; stay embarrassed; stay ashamed." Instead, he covered them.

We, whose righteousness is as filthy rags, receive a new set of clothes, the clothing of the righteousness of Jesus, which is given to us as a covering. That is the gospel. This was dramatized constantly in the tabernacle and then in the temple of Israel. On the Day of Atonement when the animal was slain and his blood was carried into the Holy of Holies, the blood was sprinkled on the mercy seat. The blood was a covering on the throne of God. Habakkuk tells us that God is too righteous to even look at evil (Hab. 1:13), so unless we are covered, he will avert his glance from us. He will never make his face to shine upon us. He will never lift up the light of his countenance on us unless we are covered, and the only adequate covering that enables us to stand in his presence is the covering of the righteousness of Christ.

After quoting David in a positive fashion, Paul repeats it, poetically, in a negative way: **"Blessed is the man to whom the LORD shall not impute sin"** (v. 8). The opposite expression would be this: "Cursed is the man to whom the LORD imputes sin." Does that ring a bell? In Galatians Paul says that on the cross our sin was transferred to one who was sinless, to one who was perfectly righteous. God imputed our sin to him and then cursed him. That is why Paul says that Christ on the cross became a curse for us by imputation, by the transfer of sin from our account to his. Again, the opposite of the curse is the blessing, and the blessing is stated here: "Blessed is the man to whom the LORD does not impute sin." That is us.

Circumcision

Does this blessedness then come upon the circumcised only, or upon the uncircumcised also? (v. 9). This blessedness of which David spoke is not for Jews only. It is not tied to the Old Testament sign of the covenant, which is circumcision. Paul comes back again to Abraham: **For we say that faith was accounted to Abraham for righteousness. How then**

was it accounted? While he was circumcised, or uncircumcised? Not while circumcised, but while uncircumcised (vv. 9–10).

In our last study I mentioned that both James and Paul appealed to Abraham to make their case. The difference is that Paul goes to Genesis 15, whereas James goes to Genesis 22 where we have the record of Abraham offering up Isaac on the altar. Paul is making the point that Abraham was justified before he offered up Isaac on the altar and even before he was circumcised. The sign of the covenant, circumcision, was not the ground of Abraham's justification; it was the imputed righteousness of Christ. When Abraham believed the promise of God, God counted him righteous, so Paul is arguing that Abraham was not justified by works, nor was he justified by circumcision.

Many believers question the biblical basis for infant baptism. Baptism is the sign of the new covenant, and the sign of the covenant has always been given to the believer and to his seed. Baptism is not the same as circumcision, but both circumcision and baptism are signs and seals of God's promise. The promises are realized only by faith, which is true in both the New and the Old Testaments.

Abraham had faith before he was circumcised. His son Isaac had faith after he was circumcised. The faith to which circumcision pointed was not tied to the time in which circumcision was rendered. The point is that the sign of the covenant is the sign of all the benefits that God promises to his people who believe. Circumcision did not justify anybody. Baptism does not justify anybody. The sole instrument of justification is faith. Baptism and circumcision have this in common: not only are they both signs of the covenant—circumcision the sign of the old covenant, baptism the sign of the new covenant—but both are also seals. **And he received the sign of circumcision, a seal of the righteousness of the faith which he had while still uncircumcised, that he might be the father of all those who believe** (v. 11). This is what baptism has in common with circumcision—both are a sign and a seal.

If we are on our way to downtown Orlando and we come to a sign that says *City Limits of Orlando* or *Welcome to Orlando*, the sign itself is not Orlando. A sign points beyond itself. The sign of circumcision pointed beyond itself to the covenant promise that God had made with his people. God destroyed the world by flood, the waters receded, and Noah and his family emerged from the ark safely. Then God put his bow in the sky and promised Noah and his progeny that he would never again destroy the world by water. That is the promise—another deluge will never wipe out the world. Every time it rains and the sun shines behind the raindrops, we see the bow in the sky, for God said that the bow is his sign, and every time he sees it, it is a reminder of his promise (Gen. 9:8–17). Circumcision was a sign of the promise of justification by faith alone. So is baptism. It does not confer what it signifies, which is the promise of God to all who believe.

But it is not only a sign; it is also a seal. That term *sealing* in the Scriptures is very important. The New Testament Greek word for seal goes back to the idea of the signet ring of the king. When the king issued a decree at the end of a document, he put wax on the paper and then took his ring and pressed it down into the wax, and it became the seal that identified the promise of the king. Scriptures tell us that those who are in Christ are sealed by the Holy Spirit. We are not just saved; we are sealed. God has put his indelible mark upon us. In the sacraments, God guarantees the consequences of justification to all who believe, not to all who receive the sign.

Abraham received the sign of circumcision, a seal of the righteousness of faith, that he might be **the father of circumcision to those who not only are of the circumcision, but who also walk in the steps of the faith which our father Abraham had while still uncircumcised** (v. 12). The circumcised Jew is justified by faith alone. Those who are uncircumcised are justified the same way—through the imputation of the righteousness of Christ.

Understanding justification by faith alone is not hard. Anyone can grasp it intellectually, but to get it in the bloodstream is extremely difficult because the voices all around us are saying, "No, that is too easy. You have to earn it. You have to deserve it." Our righteousness accomplishes nothing. The only thing we can ever merit is eternal damnation. If God were to give us what we earn, what we deserve, we would perish from his wrath, but thanks be to God that he gives to us what was earned by his Son. Jesus got what he did not deserve; we got what he did deserve—the righteousness that is by faith.

12

THE RIGHTEOUSNESS OF FAITH

Romans 4:13–23

For the promise that he would be the heir of the world was not to Abraham or to his seed through the law, but through the righteousness of faith. For if those who are of the law are heirs, faith is made void and the promise made of no effect, because the law brings about wrath; for where there is no law there is no transgression. Therefore it is of faith that it might be according to grace, so that the promise might be sure to all the seed, not only to those who are of the law, but also to those who are of the faith of Abraham, who is the father of us all (as it is written, "I have made you a father of many nations") in the presence of Him whom he believed—God, who gives life to the dead and calls those things which do not exist as though they did; who, contrary to hope, in hope believed, so that he became the father of many nations, according to what was spoken, "So shall your descendants be." And not being weak in faith, he did not consider his own body, already dead (since he was about a hundred years old), and the deadness of Sarah's womb. He did not waver at the promise of God through unbelief, but was strengthened in faith, giving glory to God, and being fully convinced that what He had promised He was also able to perform. And therefore "it was accounted to him for righteousness." Now it was not written for his sake alone that it was imputed to him.

Paul is so caught up in the doctrine of justification by faith alone that he just cannot seem to let go of it. He labors it all through Romans 3 and 4. Sadly, in light of church history perhaps the apostle did not labor it enough, because in every generation there are those who stand up and oppose this essential truth of the gospel. Paul already appealed to Abraham to prove the point that in every economy of divine redemption there is only one way of salvation, that which is through justification by faith. Paul argued that before Abraham had done any works of the law, before he had offered Isaac on the altar, even before he was circumcised—as early as Genesis 15—God counted him as righteous because Abraham believed the promise.

Received through Faith

Paul continues to press home his example of Abraham: **For the promise that he would be the heir of the world was not to Abraham or to his seed through the law** (v. 13). Abraham and his seed are the heirs of God, joint heirs with Christ.

Actually, the only proper heir of God the Father is God the Son. God the Son alone is worthy to inherit the kingdom that his Father promised, but through the gift of faith and through that righteousness that is by faith, those who are adopted into the family of God become his heirs also. Later in the epistle Paul will give more details about what it means to be an heir of God, but here he introduces the concept to us and reminds us that the heirs of Abraham and his seed do not receive the promised inheritance through the law but through faith: **For if those who are of the law are heirs, faith is made void and the promise made of no effect** (v. 14). If we could receive the kingdom of God through the law, it would vitiate the primary importance of faith. If we could receive the gifts of God apart from faith—through our works and striving and attempts at merit—then we would, in effect, empty the significance of faith, which is indeed the solitary instrumental cause of our justification. The promise of God to Abraham and his seed has no effect apart from faith.

Why does Paul come to such a grim conclusion about those who think that justification comes through the works of the law rather than through faith alone? He answers that question for us: **because the law brings about wrath** (v. 15). What the law effects is not salvation, justification, or forgiveness; it is the wrath of God. If we put our confidence in the law, the only thing we can hope to gain by it is the wrath of God. If we seek to base our salvation on our merit, the only thing we will ever merit is God's wrath.

For where there is no law there is no transgression (v. 15). If God had not set any standards or imposed obligations on us, then we would be autonomous. We would be free to do whatever we want to do. As Russian novelist Fyodor Dostoyevsky said, "If there is no God, all things are permissible." We live in a society that seeks to banish the very concept of sin from human consciousness, but in order to do that we must first banish God from the equation.

In setting forth the shorter catechism, the Westminster divines provided a simple definition of sin. The question in the catechism asks, "What is sin?" The answer given is, "Sin is any want of conformity there unto or transgression of the law of God." That gets at it succinctly. The somewhat archaic language in this phrase simply means "a lack of conformity to the law of God." If God imposes a law or a rule for our behavior, saying, "You shall do this" or "You shall not do that," we fail to conform to his standard of righteousness if we don't conform to that law or if we disobey that commandment. In one sense, this failure to conform calls attention (not always but sometimes) to what we call "sins of omission." We commit sins of omission when we fail to do those things that we ought to have done, things that God commands us to do. Not only are there negative failures or omissions, but there are also sins of commission, actual transgressions of the law of God.

When we pray the Lord's Prayer, some people say, "Forgive us our debts as we forgive our debtors," but others say, "Forgive us our trespasses as we forgive those who trespass against us." We have all seen signs in certain places that say "No Trespassing." Such signs indicate that there is a border over which we are not allowed to step. If we do, we are liable to prosecution because we have violated the law that prohibits us from stepping across that boundary. God has also established boundaries by the law, and when we transgress those boundaries, we trespass; we step over the line and break his law. As soon as we do, it exposes us justly to his wrath—his punitive wrath, not merely his corrective wrath, which he gives as a means of disciplining his children whom he loves and has forgiven. His punitive wrath is manifested when his judgment falls upon impenitent sinners who have failed to conform to or have transgressed his law.

Paul will labor this point a little more fully in chapter 5, and it is one that needs to be labored. Our culture lives in such a spirit of lawlessness that even Christians do not spend much time thinking about the law of God, sometimes going so far as to think that even having laws is beneath the dignity of God's love or his goodness. He is the one who made us, the one who rules us, and the one who is sovereign over us, and there is nothing more perfectly rational than that a just and holy God should declare what is his will. There is nothing at all unjust or irrational about a God who imposes standards and obligations upon his creatures. That is what we learn in the law—what God requires of us.

If God had never given any law, there would be no transgression. Without the law there is no sin, which is what the apostle is saying here. However, there is a law, and it manifestly reveals our sin. The law of God is what demonstrates our falling short of his glory. When we break the law of God—something we do, have done, and continue to do—the problem is not simply that we have violated some moral, abstract standard that we call "law." The law of God is a personal matter. When we sin, we do not just sin against some abstract norm or piece of legislation. We sin against the one whose law it is. We do violence to him, to the Author of our very life. That is why sin is such an egregious matter in his sight. If we seek to find our salvation through the law, we are on a fool's errand, because the only consequence of that law for us is exposure to his wrath. We must banish from our minds forever any thought of justifying ourselves by our behavior, good deeds, merits, or work. Just as Dante posted above the entrance to hell the words "Abandon hope, all ye who enter here," so we should abandon all hope of entering the kingdom of God by virtue of our obedience to the law.

According to Grace

Therefore it is of faith that it might be according to grace, so that the promise might be sure to all the seed (v. 16). This is a complicated sentence. On the cover of our bulletin each Sunday we have the image of the Celtic cross and around it are named the *solas* of the Reformation: *sola fide, sola gratia,* and *solus Christus.* These three *solas*—faith alone, grace alone, Christ alone—capture the essence of the doctrine of justification, which the Reformers recovered after it was obscured in the Middle Ages. Our justification is by grace through faith because of Christ. Paul emphasizes our justification when he says, "Therefore it is of faith."

Next we have a purpose clause, something that gives us a reason. Why is it by faith? "It is of faith that it might be according to grace." When we really grasp this doctrine of justification by faith alone, we grasp with it the sole graciousness of our redemption. When Luther wrote his book *The Bondage of the Will* (which I believe was Luther's most important work) in response to the diatribe of Erasmus of Rotterdam, he argued against the great humanist scholar that the real issue underlying the debate over justification was not *sola fide* but *sola gratia*—salvation by grace alone.

Elsewhere Paul writes that we "should no longer be children, tossed to and fro and carried about with every wind of doctrine" (Eph. 4:14). We are not to be double-minded people, leaning this way then that way, never coming to a point of conviction or assurance of salvation. When I was a seminary student, one of my classmates took a poll of the students and asked this simple question: do you know for sure that you are saved? He was probing what we call "the doctrine of the assurance of salvation." The vast majority answered that question in the negative, saying that they were not sure. Most significant was that they considered assurance to be an indicator of arrogance. They held the opinion that there is something wrong with people who think they could know for sure that they are in a state of grace and salvation. That is amazing, since the New Testament gives us the exhortation to make our election sure. We are called not to vacillate, not to waver in our confidence, but to be sure of our status before God and of our receiving the promises of God.

Suppose our salvation depended on our obedience to the law of God. How sure would we be of our salvation? How sure *could* we be of our salvation? If we had to look at the law of God and then look honestly at our own life, any assurance that we had scraped hold of would be demolished in an instant. That is why, in the sixteenth century, Agricola said, "To the gallows with Moses." Every time Agricola looked at the law he saw his unrighteousness, and he lost hope because he had no assurance. If justification were according to law, we would have no certainty whatsoever.

The apostle says that justification is by faith so that it might be of grace so that all the seed of Abraham—all those who come after him and follow in his way—may be sure. The surety belongs to **those who are of the faith of Abraham, who is the father of us all (as it is written, "I have made you a father of many nations")** (vv. 16–17). Abraham is not simply the father of Isaac and his progeny or the father of the Jews, but he is also the father of the Gentiles who trust in the same promise that he embraced by which he was counted righteous before God. So Paul labors to show that we too are the seed of Abraham, not only the Jews, and that we are the seed of Abraham by faith, not by the law.

Faith That Justifies

. . . In the presence of Him whom he believed—God, who gives life to the dead and calls those things which do not exist as though they did; who, contrary to hope, in hope believed, so that he became the father of many nations, according to what was spoken,

"So shall your descendants be" (vv. 17–18). There is a goldmine in that lengthy clause. When we talk about faith that justifies, such faith has content to it. There is information that must be understood. Historically we call that the data or the *indicia* that we believe. We must believe it in the sense of intellectual assent, what the Reformers called *assensus*. However, belief and intellectual assent, although necessary to saving faith, do not make up saving faith. The critical element of saving faith is *faducia*, personal trust. We are justified by faith by trusting in Christ alone for our salvation. That is the nature of the faith of Abraham. He did not just believe in God; anybody can believe *in* God. Satan believes in God. The demons believe in God and tremble (James 2:19). Saving faith is all about believing God, putting our trust in him for our life and death, and living by trusting his promises even when we cannot see the fulfillment of those promises.

Sometimes people get this all mixed up and think that saving faith is a leap into the dark. People are told, "Just close your eyes, take a deep breath, make a leap of faith, jump into the darkness, and pray that Jesus will be there to catch you." Jesus never calls people to jump into the darkness. He calls them to jump out of the darkness. He never asks us to crucify our intellect to become Christians. Faith is not believing the absurd or the foolish. Faith is ultimately trusting what is preeminently trustworthy. There is tension when it comes to staking our life on God, which is why Paul writes that Abraham believed "God, who gives life to the dead and calls those things which do not exist as though they did; who, contrary to hope [or against all hope], in hope believed." That would seem to give some credence to the idea that true faith is faith that believes against the evidence and against all reason. Here is Abraham, who, against all hope, hoped. Is that a leap of faith, or did he have a reason for it, against all earthly indicators?

Abraham's body was for all intents and purposes dead: **not being weak in faith, he did not consider his own body, already dead (since he was about a hundred years old), and the deadness of Sarah's womb. He did not waver at the promise of God through unbelief, but was strengthened in faith, giving glory to God** (vv. 19–20). Abraham was one hundred years old, and his wife was barren, but God said that Sarah would have a child. Eliezer of Damascus would not be Abraham's heir; one from Abraham's loins would be his heir (see Gen. 15:2). Abraham looked at himself and his wife and saw a hopeless situation. "How can I possibly believe that promise?" Then he looked at the One who made the promise and realized instantly that there was nothing hopeless about it. The only thing hopeless was the idea that the promise would *not* come to pass, because it is impossible for God to lie. It is impossible for God to break a promise.

In our sin, we project onto the character of God our own character. We break promises, and we live in the midst of people who break promises routinely. Therefore, we question how, since we are so accustomed to broken promises, we can trust this One who promises us things against all earthly evidence. How could Mary believe the announcement of the angel Gabriel, who told her that she would bring forth a child? She asked, "How can this be, since I do not know a man?" (Luke 1:34). Gabriel said, "The Holy Spirit will come upon you, and the power of the Highest will overshadow you; therefore, also, that Holy One who is to be born will be called the Son of God" (v. 35). The angel was not talking about the power of men here. He was talking about the author of the universe. With him all things in this world are possible, and Mary said, "Let it be to me according to your word" (v. 38).

Satan has never performed a miracle in his life. He does not have the power to perform miracles. All his attempts at miracles are counterfeits because he does not have the power that God alone possesses. The one whom Abraham believed is the God who can create *ex nihilo*, who can bring something out of nothing, who can bring life out of death. Satan could have gone to the tomb of Lazarus and cried, "Come forth" until he lost his voice, but not a grain of life would have stirred in that corpse because Satan does not have the power to bring life out of death. Satan could speak into the void and with all his energy say, "Let there be light," but not a candle-watt of light would appear. He cannot bring something out of nothing.

Fully Convinced

Abraham was dealing with God, and the God he was dealing with can say, "Let there be . . ." Abraham put his trust in the promise of God. That is what it means to be a Christian. Our only hope in life and death is trusting in the Word of God. There is nothing else to trust in. Everything this world offers passes away. Abraham did not waver at the promise of God through unbelief, but was strengthened in faith, giving glory to God, **and being fully convinced that what He had promised He was also able to perform** (v. 21).

When Vesta and I were offered our second teaching appointment at a Christian college in Boston, we sought a realtor to help us secure a home. A woman who was connected to the college was also a real estate agent, and she took us around Hamilton, Massachusetts, so we could look for a place to live. At the end of that day we went back to her house, and I met her husband, who was sitting on the couch watching a Boston Celtics game. There were all kinds of medicine bottles in front of him, and he explained that he had not been feeling well. I talked to him that evening and watched the game with him. After we returned to Pennsylvania to prepare for the move to Boston, I got word that the man I had met that night had been diagnosed with cancer of the pancreas, and his condition was terminal. God gave me an enormous burden for him, and not a night went by, even before we moved to Boston, that I did not wrestle with God for that man's life.

After we moved to Boston, I went every day to Massachusetts General Hospital to visit him. The only thing I could do was read the Bible to him and put ice on his lips. When he could no longer talk, he would just point at the Bible, and I would read to him from Hebrews: "Because God could promise by nothing greater he swore by himself." Through his last breath that man trusted the promises of God. When he died, I saw the valiant death of a Christian who believed God, and it was counted to him for righteousness. He was like Abraham, who did not waver. His faith was strengthened, he gave glory to God, and he became fully convinced that what God promised he was able to perform.

13

JUSTIFIED

Romans 4:23–25

Now it was not written for his sake alone that it was imputed to him, but also for us. It shall be imputed to us who believe in Him who raised up Jesus our Lord from the dead, who was delivered up because of our offenses, and was raised because of our justification.

We have been looking at the central importance of the doctrine of imputation. The merit of Christ—his righteousness to our account—lies at the very heart of the gospel. Without that imputation we lose everything. It is only by his righteousness that we have any standing in the presence of God. I mentioned earlier that there is a double imputation in our salvation. God reckoned or imputed our sin to Christ in his work for us and in his atoning death upon the cross. When we say that Jesus died for us, we mean that his death was vicarious, he did something for us in our place as our substitute, and that God accepted the transfer of our guilt to his Son. The imputation is dual in the sense that while our sin is reckoned to Christ, his righteousness is imputed to us. He gets our guilt; we get his merit. This double imputation is the great benefit of redemption that Christ won for us.

Resurrection

It would seem that once we have that double imputation by virtue of the life and death of Jesus, our justification would be secure, but there is one more element that we have not yet addressed, and that is the resurrection of Christ, which Paul introduces at the end of chapter 4: **It shall be imputed to us who believe in Him who raised up Jesus our Lord from the dead, who was delivered up because of our offenses**, and was **raised because of our justification** (vv. 24–25). We could understand how the apostle would say that Jesus was raised for his own vindication, to declare to the world that his conviction by an earthly court of accusers was fraudulent and that death could not hold him. That Jesus was raised for his own vindication is an essential element of the resurrection of Jesus, but here Paul is saying that Christ was raised for our justification. To understand that, we want to revisit what happened on the cross for our redemption.

With respect to our condition of guilt before God, the language of the New Testament is often expressed in the category of indebtedness. What is the nature of the debt that we owe God because of our sin? I go back to an illustration I used before to demonstrate a very important distinction in our situation as sinners before a righteous God, as debtors who cannot pay their debt. I make the distinction, as the church fathers did, between a moral debt and a pecuniary debt. A pecuniary debt is a monetary or financial debt, which is not the same thing as a moral debt.

Imagine that you see a young boy come into an ice cream parlor and order an ice cream cone from the waitress. He wants two scoops of ice cream on the cone, so the waitress scoops the two scoops onto the cone, hands it to the little boy, and tells him, "That will be two dollars." Then you see the lip start to quiver on the face of the little boy, and he says to the woman, "My mommy only gave me a dollar." He has a problem. He now owes two dollars for the ice cream cone, but he has only one dollar. As you watch this unfold, what do you do? You do the same thing that anyone would do in that situation. You say to the waitress, "Excuse me, ma'am. If it would be all right with you, I would be happy to make up the difference between what the little boy has and what he needs." Is the waitress under any obligation to accept the dollar that you offer her? Yes, she is, because the debt is a pecuniary debt, and you are offering her legal tender, which means she must accept it in payment of the debt.

Let us change the story just a bit: you are standing in line at the ice cream counter and the young boy runs in, runs behind the counter, scoops up two scoops of ice cream onto a cone, and runs out the door with the waitress in pursuit, calling for the police, "Stop, thief!" The policeman on the corner sees what happens, grabs the urchin by the scruff of his neck, brings him back into the store, and says, "Is this the boy? Did he do something?"

"Yes, he just stole two scoops of ice cream, not to mention the cone."

You say, "Wait a minute. Wait a minute. Take it easy, Officer," and you reach in your pocket and take out two dollars and hand the money to the waitress, saying, "Now the boy's debt is paid. Can we just all go home and forget about this?"

The policeman says, "Ma'am, you do not have to accept that money. This boy has broken the law. He is guilty of petty larceny, at least. Would you like to press charges?"

The woman has every right under the law to press charges. She is under no obligation whatsoever to accept your vicarious payment of the little boy's debt. If she is a merciful person she might accept it, but she is not bound by the offer.

When a moral transgression has taken place, the offended person is under no obligation to accept the payment of a substitute on behalf of the guilty. Christ laid down his life for his sheep on the cross. He offered himself in his perfect righteousness and took upon himself the sin of his people. If Jesus had stayed dead, we would have no justification, but when the Father raised the Son from the dead, he said to the world, "I accept this payment for the debtors who cannot pay." The resurrection of Jesus is not simply for his vindication; it is for our justification, because it is God's demonstration to his unjust people that he accepts the payment in full for the moral debt they have incurred.

Active and Passive Obedience

We make a distinction in theology between Jesus' active obedience and his passive obedience. We have been looking at the active obedience. Jesus' perfect obedience to the law of God was such that he earned by his own merit eternal felicity with the Father in the Father's kingdom. He fulfilled all the terms of God's covenant with man, the promise for which was blessedness. By his perfect obedience, eternal blessedness was Jesus' reward. It is that reward that he trades for our sin. His perfect active obedience is followed by his perfect passive obedience, submitting himself to the curse of the law and the wrath of the Father by willingly bearing our sins upon the cross. In his life he shows his active obedience; in his death he manifests his passive obedience. Both active and passive obedience are essential for our justification.

We are called not only to profess our faith in Christ but also to defend the faith of Christ to the world around us. Beyond the responsibility of professing and defending the faith, we are called to contend for the faith. That is where many Christians get off the boat. "I will profess my faith and even

defend it, but do not ask me to contend for it. I will not get in the arena and
fight for the truths of the gospel." We are not to have a contentious spirit,
where we fight over every point of doctrine and engage in battle at the drop
of a hat, but where the gospel is under siege in any generation, where the
controversy is hot and the truth of the gospel is at stake, every Christian is
called to contend with all his might.

In John Piper's book *Contending for Our All* he points out that every Christian
is called to profess faith in Christ. Piper gives a cameo examination of three
great contenders for the faith beginning with Athanasius, whose tombstone
reads *Athanasius, contra mundum*.[1] No individual in church history fought longer
and harder for the church's affirmation of the full deity of Christ than did
Athanasius, who was exiled time after time because Arian heretics sought to
destroy him. They could not silence him, however, because he was contending for the whole of the gospel in the person of Christ.

The second person Piper examines is John Owen, the seventeenth-century
English Puritan whom many believe was the most brilliant English-language
writer of Christian truth ever to grace the world. Owen's closest friend in
ministry was perhaps John Bunyan. Owen was a brilliant scholar and an
academician, the head of Oxford and then the chief lieutenant to Oliver
Cromwell, and he had the ear of all those in high places, including Charles
II at the time of the Restoration. Bunyan was an uneducated tinker, totally committed to the truths of the gospel. When Bunyan was imprisoned,
Owen sought his release, and King Charles II asked why Owen would do
that for a lowly tinker. John Owen replied, "May it please your Majesty, if
I could possess the tinker's abilities to grip men's hearts, I would gladly give
in exchange all my learning." All Owen's efforts to secure Bunyan's release
failed. He put his reputation on the line to get Bunyan out of jail, but nothing worked. Finally Bunyan was released from prison, and he came out with
a manuscript he had written while in isolation entitled *The Pilgrim's Progress*.
The all-time best-selling book in the English language is the Bible; the second
is *The Pilgrim's Progress*. Owen was glad that, in the providence of God, his
efforts to get Bunyan released prematurely ended in failure.

The third person John Piper examines is J. Gresham Machen, who brought
the theological elite from Princeton Seminary to found a new seminary
in Philadelphia, Westminster Theological Seminary, in order to keep the
Reformed faith alive in America. At the age of fifty-five, during a Christmas break in December 1936, Machen was invited to travel by train from

---

1. John Piper, *Contending for Our All: Defending Truth and Treasuring Christ in the Lives of Athanasius, John
Owen, and J. Gresham Machen* (Wheaton, IL: Crossway, 2006).

Philadelphia to Bismarck, North Dakota, to preach. His friends on the faculty at Westminster knew that his health was frail, and they profoundly urged him not to make such an arduous journey. They told him to use the Christmas holidays to get some rest, but he would not listen. He got on the train, and he traveled all the way to North Dakota. When he arrived there, he became ill with pneumonia, an illness which proved to be fatal. He died on January 1, 1937, at seven-thirty in the evening. Before Machen died he wrote a telegram—the last thing he ever wrote—to his good friend and fellow faculty member John Murray.

Murray married at the age of seventy, became the father of two children, and then returned to his native Scotland. Machen knew he was dying when he composed his telegram to Murray, and this is what he wrote: "John, am so thankful for active obedience of Jesus. Stop. No hope without it." On his deathbed Machen was thinking of the perfect active obedience of Jesus, the sole ground for the justification of J. Gresham Machen and the sole ground for our justification.

It is one thing to study theology in the abstract, but to find joy in the perfect active obedience of Jesus when the end of your life comes is the mark of a true saint. Oh, that God would raise up more contenders for the faith in our day like these men from the past.

14

PEACE

Romans 5:1–5, Part 1

Therefore, having been justified by faith, we have peace with God through our Lord Jesus Christ, through whom also we have access by faith into this grace in which we stand, and rejoice in hope of the glory of God. And not only that, but we also glory in tribulations, knowing that tribulation produces perseverance; and perseverance, character; and character, hope. Now hope does not disappoint, because the love of God has been poured out in our hearts by the Holy Spirit who was given to us.

Paul is looking at the doctrine of justification as something that has already taken place: **Therefore, having been justified by faith** (v. 1). The great truth of the "therefore" is that we can be justified now, contrary to what the Roman Catholic Church claims. Those who put their faith in Jesus Christ do not have a prolonged wait for their justification. The moment they believe in Jesus and put their trust in him, God declares them just, once and for all. "Having been justified" refers to an action in the past, to something that has been accomplished. The work of Christ is finished. Justification is a past action. We received it the moment we believed.

Sometimes we look at concepts or doctrines such as justification by faith alone, and we shrug and ask, "So what?" The *so what?* is set forth for us here by Paul. We see that our justification is a *fait accompli*. It took place the

139

moment we believed—it is not something that we must wait to accomplish in purgatory—and there are consequences to it.

Peace with God

The first consequence is that, having been justified by faith, **we have peace with God through our Lord Jesus Christ** (v. 1). Peace comes through our peace agent, the peacemaker, the Prince of Peace. He is the medium, the means, through which this peace is given to us.

When I was about six years old, my family was living temporarily in an apartment in Chicago. One summer afternoon I was playing stickball in front of our apartment. Home plate was a manhole cover in the middle of the street. I was delighted to be up at bat until my turn was rudely interrupted by a spontaneous outcry of great noise and carrying on. I was completely amazed to see people running out of buildings and aproned ladies pounding on pots and pans with wooden spoons. They were screaming and yelling in unrestrained jubilation. I had no idea what was going on except for the fact that my stickball game had just been ruined. I was not happy about it until my mother came out of the apartment building and rushed over to me with tears streaming down her face, crying, "It's over! It's over!" She grabbed me and hugged me. This was the joy of VJ Day, the end of World War II. That meant, of course, in our home, that my father's tenure in the service was over and that he would be restored to our family.

A couple of years after that, several of my buddies in our new hometown outside Pittsburgh had planned to sleep out one summer evening. We pitched a tent and roasted marshmallows, and then one of the boys began to talk about the atomic bomb and the events occurring in Berlin. When the boys began to describe what would happen if the bomb fell in our community, I became so terrified that I got sick at my stomach and fled the sanctuary of the tent and went home.

When we have peace in this world, we can rejoice for a season, but peace is something that never lasts. One of the most infamous photographs from the early days of the World War II was that of Neville Chamberlain, prime minister of England. After he negotiated a peace arrangement with Hitler, he had his photograph taken while leaning over a balcony, and he uttered the words, "We have achieved peace in our time." Right then, however, Hitler was mobilizing the Blitzkrieg into Eastern Europe.

Peace in this world is fragile. It quickly gives way to new hostilities. World War II was followed for many years by the Cold War, the conflict in Korea, and the tremendous war that broke out in Vietnam. It seems that our nation is engaged in some kind of war at most times. Hostilities end, but once again people begin to rattle the sword; we never know when the next conflagration will break out.

There is a strong contrast between the peace we experience during conflicts in this world and the peace about which Paul is writing in Romans 5. Paul is writing about the end of the worst of all possible wars. The vast majority in our country today are engaged in a war of cosmic proportion. The New Testament repeatedly describes the natural condition of fallen people as one of enmity with God. By nature we regard God as our enemy, but few people will own up to that. They feign a kind of indifference about all things religious, yet the heart of man is recalcitrant. It has become hardened to the point that it no longer pulsates with any spiritual life whatsoever. The Scriptures tell us that in our natural condition we do not want to have God in our thinking.

That is why the central motif of the gospel in the New Testament is reconciliation. What is a necessary condition for reconciliation to take place? The most important—and necessary—ingredient for reconciliation is estrangement. Where there is no estrangement, there is no need for reconciliation. The New Testament repeatedly describes the ministry of Jesus as a work of mediation, because the God-Man came into a hostile world estranged from God. The work of Christ is that of mediator to bring the estranged parties together. He is the Prince of Peace, who came to end the warfare that is so real.

We can understand this if we look at all the biblical texts that speak of our estrangement. We are children of wrath, so it would seem that the only antagonist in this conflict between God and man is us. Surely God is a God of love, patience, and mercy. Certainly he does not regard us as enemies, does he? The Scriptures tell us that not only are we at war with God, but God is at war with us. The imagery of God in the Old Testament is the soldier whose bow is bent. His chariots come to trample out the vintage where the grapes of wrath are stored.

The book of Romans begins with Paul giving a lengthy exposition of the reality of the wrath of God, anger that is directed against sinful people, who refuse to honor him as God, who refuse to manifest gratitude to him, and whose basic penchant is to exchange the truth of God for a lie and to engage in idolatry by serving and worshiping the creature rather than the Creator. When God looks at our idolatry, he is not at peace; he is at war with us. We might be so hardened in our hearts, so stiff in our necks, that we think, "Surely God could not be at war with us."

That is the legacy of nineteenth-century liberal theology, which captured the church in Europe. It was then exported to the United States. As a result, we have been born and raised in a country where we hear that all are God's children, and that God is a God of love who has no capacity for wrath or judgment. The god you hear of every day in the marketplace is an idol. That god simply does not exist. God is a holy God—so holy that he cannot bear to look at iniquity. There is a basic revulsion in the very character of God for those engaged in cosmic treason every day of their lives.

We need reconciliation. We need the end to the estrangement, and what brings it is the good news of the gospel, the good news that publishes peace and says the war is over. Being justified, we have peace with God, and God has taken the initiative to bring about that peace. We did not surrender and sue for peace; God conquered us, and in his gracious mercy he enabled us to be reconciled to him through the work of his Son. When God enters into a peace treaty with his people, it is a permanent peace. He may be displeased with us, and we may grieve him, but once we have peace with God through the work of Jesus Christ, that peace is ours forever.

When Jesus was about to go to his death, he gathered his frightened disciples in the upper room the night on which they celebrated the Lord's Supper, and he gave them his last will and testament. He did not have any worldly goods to bequeath to his friends, so what was his legacy? He said to his disciples, "Peace I leave with you, My peace I give to you; not as the world gives do I give to you. Let not your heart be troubled, neither let it be afraid" (John 14:27). It is peace with God that settles the soul and gives the assurance of forgiveness. "Speak comfort to Jerusalem, and cry out to her, that her warfare is ended, that her iniquity is pardoned; for she has received from the LORD's hand double for all her sins" (Isa. 40:2). That is the gospel in advance. Once we are justified, the Holy Spirit testifies to us, speaking comfort.

Our consciences are not always at peace. We sin, and when we sin, our consciences are troubled. Sometimes we tend to look over our shoulder to see if God has bent the bow again and pointed it at us, but he has not. When he looks at us he sees us covered by the righteousness of Christ. We have the peace of Christ. Christ is our peace, so for us there is no more war with God. That is only the first benefit that Paul mentions.

Access to God

The second consequence or benefit is another that we should never take lightly: **we have access by faith into this grace in which we stand,**

and rejoice in hope of the glory of God (v. 2). We have access to the Father. Jews looked back on the whole scope of redemptive history, back to the dawn of creation where God made human beings in his image to be a little lower than the angels, and saw that the best thing Adam and Eve experienced was unlimited access to God. They rushed to commune with him until that communion was ruined by the first transgression. After that, instead of rushing to their creator when he entered the garden, they fled from his presence and hid themselves because they had become aware of their nakedness and were overcome with a sense of shame. If our sin is not covered, if our shame has not been removed, there is no way we can be anything but fugitives.

Despite that unbelievable work of condescension, of mercy and grace, still there were penalties that had to be paid: "In the day that you eat of it you shall surely die" (Gen. 2:17). They suffered spiritual death immediately, but the judgment of physical death was postponed. God let his creatures live, covered, in his presence but with no further access to the garden of Eden. They were expelled, driven out of Paradise into the darkness. After that earthly governments were established. The very essence of government is legal force, which we will examine in more detail when we get to Romans 13. The first appearance in sacred Scripture of the power of the sword is found with the sentinel that God placed at the entrance to the garden of Eden. God put an angel by the garden with a flaming sword, which was meant to be an instrument of coercion to prevent creatures tainted by sin from entering back in. The significance of that loss is reiterated through the Old Testament Scriptures.

A critical moment in the history of Israel occurred when God summoned Moses to Mount Sinai. Moses was to go up on the mountain to receive the law by which God was to constitute the Israelites as a nation of his people. Only Moses was allowed to go up the mountain. If others so much as put one finger or foot on that holy mountain, they were to be executed. Even those who would simply witness the mountain shaking with thunder, lightning, earthquake, volcanic eruption, and cloud when God appeared would be required to go through days of cleansing and purification.

Likewise, when the nomadic tribes of Israel encamped, they set up the camp in a circle, according to the tribes, and at the very center of that circle was the tabernacle. The point of the circle was to ensure that no one tribe had greater access to the presence of God than any other tribe. The glory of the people of Israel was in the tabernacle because it manifested the presence of God. The people were comforted because God was in their midst. In this gracious condescension God dwelt with his people, but even in that grace there was a limit. At the core of the tabernacle in the center of the camp was the *sanctus sanctorum*, the Holy of Holies. Contained in the Holy of Holies was the ark of the covenant, a chest, on which was the mercy seat, and in the chest were copies of the Decalogue, some manna from the wilderness, and Aaron's rod that had blossomed. It was on top of the mercy seat, the *kapporeth*, where the blood of the offering was sprinkled on the Day of Atonement. From among the whole nation of Israel only one person, the high priest, was allowed inside the Holy of Holies. Others could stand in the holy place or in the outer court; they could come that close to God but no farther. Even the high priest could go in only after going through elaborate ablutions and rites of purification, and even then he entered the Holy of Holies in a spirit of fear and trembling. One tradition says (we don't know whether it's accurate) that the great high priest would have a rope tied around one of his legs and bells strung on his cassock so that if he had a heart attack and fell over while inside, the bells would ring, and he could be dragged out by the rope. No one else was allowed to go in, even to save the great high priest's life.

We see the same picture over and over again, the picture of no access. One of the most intricately designed parts of the tabernacle was the curtain, or the veil, which later became the veil of the temple that separated the Holy Place from the Holy of Holies. The veil was composed of very thick drapes that could not be broken. Nothing could break through that barrier that separated the people from the immediate presence of God until Golgotha, until that day in Jerusalem when the sun was blotted out of the sky in the middle of the day and it became pitch black as night. On that day, when Christ was the curse on the cross, there was an earthquake, and in that earthquake the veil of the temple was ripped like tissue paper (Matt. 27:51).

Concerning the earthquake, I heard a missionary say that it was as if God the Father, in the midst of the crucifixion, took the earth by his hand and shook it for what had been done to his Son. During that earthquake the wall of separation came crashing down through the work of the Mediator, the Savior. When he rose from the dead, he entered into the heavenly sanctuary, into the heavenly Holy of Holies, where he gives us access.

When we come together for worship on Sundays, we no longer come to that mountain that was shaking with thunder and lightning and hidden in clouds:

> But you have come to Mount Zion and to the city of the living God, the heavenly Jerusalem, to an innumerable company of angels, to the general assembly and church of the firstborn *who are* registered in heaven, to God the Judge of all, to the spirits of just men made perfect, to Jesus the Mediator of the new covenant. (Heb. 12:22–24)

We come to the presence of God. We have access to his presence. There is no more veil. The angel's sword of flame has been doused with the blood of Christ, and God welcomes us into his presence.

There is no greater human experience than to have an overwhelming sense of being in the presence of God. The greatest of Christians testify that the times they recall of having an acute sense of being in the presence of God can be numbered on one hand. If we have tasted it, we have had a taste of heaven, a taste of the presence of divine glory that Christ opened up for us.

Our justification is not just about forgiveness or the imputation of the righteousness of Christ. It is not just about escaping the judgment of divine wrath, though it includes all that. In our justification we have peace that passes all human understanding. While once we were barred admittance into the immediate presence of God, now we are called to enter into his presence boldly. However, there is a difference between boldness and arrogance; we are never to enter into the presence of God arrogantly. Many speak flippantly about their relationship to Christ or God as that of pal or peer, but if Jesus Christ walked into our presence, everyone would be on his face in a posture of submission and adoration, overwhelmed by Christ's glory.

"We have access by faith into this grace." Faith and grace are inseparably related. The most unmerited favor that any creature, any sinner, can experience is the grace of being allowed into the presence of God. How would we feel if we received a written invitation for a personal audience with God? What would we wear? What would we say? That engraved invitation comes to all who are justified. It is a fruit of our justification. That is the grace in which we stand in Christ Jesus and in which we rejoice in the hope of the glory of God.

Hope

The third consequence or benefit of justification that Paul mentions in the beginning of chapter 5 is the "hope of the glory of God" (v. 2). Elsewhere Paul tells us that the triad of Christian virtues consists of faith, hope, and love, and the greatest of these is love (1 Cor. 13:13). The word *hope*, *elpis* in the Greek, is one of the richest terms we find anywhere in the New Testament.

It is the gift that God gives to every person justified by faith. It is a hope that radically differs from our normal understanding of hope.

If we are asked, "Do you think the Steelers are going to win?" we might reply, "I don't know, but I hope so." Such a use of the word *hope* expresses the desire that certain things will come to pass, but we have no assurance that they will. Not so with the biblical concept of hope. The Bible describes hope with a metaphor: hope is the anchor of our souls. Our souls are not tossed to and fro by every wind of doctrine. We have stability in our lives because, in the midst of the tempest, there is an anchor, and that anchor is the hope that God the Holy Spirit has shed abroad in our hearts. It is a hope that cannot possibly be ashamed, as we will consider more in the next study. It is a hope that carries with it God's assurance; it is a hope that cannot fail. In one sense our faith looks backward so that we put our trust in what Christ has done for us. In another sense our hope looks forward with the same assurance to what he will do when he completes his work of redemption in us, a work that cannot fail.

Those are the three things Paul tells us are the fruit of our justification—peace with God, access to his presence, and the hope of his glory, which is shed abroad in our hearts.

15

HOPE

Romans 5:1–5, Part 2

Therefore, having been justified by faith, we have peace with God through our Lord Jesus Christ, through whom also we have access by faith into this grace in which we stand, and rejoice in hope of the glory of God. And not only that, but we also glory in tribulations, knowing that tribulation produces perseverance; and perseverance, character; and character, hope. Now hope does not disappoint, because the love of God has been poured out in our hearts by the Holy Spirit who was given to us.

Paul's epistle to the Romans was his *magnum opus*. In it we have the most extensive exposition of the New Testament gospel anywhere in the Bible. In our last study we considered three benefits we derive from our justification: peace, access into God's presence, and hope. It is important to note that these benefits come to us **through our Lord Jesus Christ** (v. 1). Just as our justification is by faith and grace because of Christ, the benefits of peace we enjoy come through his ministry to us. He is the Prince of Peace. He has effected our reconciliation with the Father, and we receive the legacy of his peace. The access we have and the benefits we gain through Christ are things **in which we stand** (v. 2). Our standing before God is as those covered with the righteousness of Christ and declared just in his sight; we have had our sins remitted and our guilt satisfied by Christ's atoning death.

Rejoicing

Here we will look more fully at that third benefit: **we . . . rejoice in hope of the glory of God** (v. 2). There are three words in this little phrase that are vitally important to understand properly. The first is the word "rejoice." That translation, "rejoice," does not quite get it; the meaning is more than simply "rejoicing." The actual word Paul used is not the normal word for joy or rejoicing; it is the word more often translated "boasting." In both the Greek and Latin texts we see a play on words: we "glory now in glory." We have a sense of celebration and ecstasy beyond normal levels of joy, and the target of our joy is the hope directed toward the manifestation of the glory of God.

The second word, "glory," comes from the Greek noun *doka* or *doxa*. From it we get the word *doxology*. When we sing the Doxology, we sing praises to the majesty of God; we glorify God. We are in the activity of glorifying the one who possesses glory, which is the play on words in both the Latin and the Greek. Paul is saying that once we are justified, one of the things that delights us and causes joy to fill our souls is to contemplate who God is. Our greatest delight is in his character and glory.

The Old Testament frequently speaks about the nature of God. He manifests his glory. The word for *glory* in the Old Testament is *kabod*, sometimes rendered *kavod*. In the original Semitic language, the word meant "weightiness" or "heaviness." When we speak about the glory of God, we speak about one whose very being is not light or insignificant; it is substantive and heavy. We use similar language in everyday situations. When someone says something we think is profound, we might shake our heads and say, "That was heavy." We also use the term to indicate something that should be taken seriously. There is a link in the original languages between the weightiness or dignity of God and his august nature. God's glory is tied to his dignity or gravity.

The purpose of worship is to ascribe glory to God, to honor and revere him, to adore him in the excellence of his being. Augustine was not narrow in his selection of the sort of music that is fitting for worship. He pointed out that there are different music strains and styles, but no matter what type of music we use in the celebration of God's glory, there ought to be some connection between the glory of God and what Augustine called the *gravitas*, gravity, or weightiness in the means by which we worship him. Sometimes we get too familiar in the way we worship God, forgetting who he is, the weightiness of his very being. Part of this particular benefit of justification is the delight we take in glorifying God, for once faith has taken hold of our hearts we perceive the things of God in a way totally different from how we did in our natural state. Something is created in our souls the moment we come to faith that involves the dimension of hope.

Hope Misunderstood

In the last study I mentioned the triad of Christian virtues—faith, hope, and love. As important as love is (1 Cor. 13:13), we know that faith is not unimportant. We have been working closely on the significance of faith, and we understand the importance of love, but so often that third element in this triad of virtues, hope, gets overlooked in Christian experience.

If there is any word in Romans 5 that we might radically misunderstand, it is "hope." There is always an element of doubt that clouds our understanding of Paul's use of the word. When we use the word *hope*, typically we use it to describe a wish or a desire that something would take place, something we are not sure will actually happen. That is not the way the word functions in the New Testament. When we are regenerated by the Holy Spirit, we are born anew to a hope that forms the basis for our confidence in living out the Christian life. The only difference between hope and faith is that faith looks to what has already taken place, and we put our trust in it. Hope is merely faith looking forward.

I mentioned earlier that the metaphor used in the New Testament to describe the nature of hope is that of an anchor. Hope, we are told, is the anchor of the soul. We frequently find this nautical image in the New Testament. The unstable are compared to boats that have no anchor, tossed to and fro with every wind of doctrine. Such people are characterized by vacillation and uncertainty, but the hope planted in the soul by the Holy Spirit is not like that. This hope gives a foundation and stability and assurance. Hope is the anchor that keeps us from being blown all over the place. It is the hope that God is going to do in the future every single thing he has said he will do.

The fruit of justification is that kind of hope. Justification, in a sense, is the down payment for all that God promises us in his work of redemption. Hope is created by the Holy Spirit within us. Elsewhere Paul will speak about the Holy Spirit giving to us the "earnest" or down payment of the Holy Spirit, which gives us total assurance for the future. Hope is not taking a deep breath and hoping things are going to turn out all right. It is assurance that God is going to do what he says he will do.

The great Princeton theologian Charles Hodge made a contrast between the metaphor of an anchor and that of a spiderweb. He said that hope is not a spiderweb because we can see a spider weave its web. We might be amazed at the glory of that work of nature, amazed to see how effective the web can be in trapping flies or bugs to provide meals for the spider, but we can take a pebble and throw it against the spiderweb and the pebble goes right through it. There is no weighty substance to a spiderweb. It is wispy. We cannot do that with an anchor. Hope is not a spiderweb. It is the solid stability that anchors the soul.

Glory in Tribulations

Not only that, but we also glory in tribulations (v. 3). There is nothing more unnatural than to enjoy afflictions or tribulation. Tribulation is something we desperately seek to avoid. However, once we have been justified, we have a whole new perspective on tribulations. We no longer see suffering as an exercise in futility, something that takes away our hope. Once we have the anchor on our soul, it holds when tribulation comes. It is not that we have the capacity of a Stoic to grin and bear it; it goes beyond endurance to rejoicing in tribulations.

Paul was not a masochist. He is not saying that tribulation is a joyful, pleasant, pleasurable experience. Rather, he is saying that because we have been justified, even the tribulations and afflictions we experience can be an occasion for joy. Above all, the fruit of justification is the presence of joy in the Christian's life. We have found the pearl of great price, and no matter how much pain we have to go through, as bad as things may be, these things are not worthy to be compared with the joy that God has set before us in Christ. If we lose everything the world can give us, we still possess that priceless pearl of our justification. Because God has redeemed us, we are able to rejoice no matter what life brings.

Once we are reconciled and justified we can rejoice even when people slander us and wound us deeply. We can glory in it because of Christ and our justification. We glory in tribulation because we know what tribulation does. Paul understood, because he believed in the sovereignty and providence of God. There are no accidents in this world. No matter how many injustices are heaped upon us this side of heaven, they do not mean anything compared to the crown of glory that God has prepared for his people. Paul is saying that when we go through afflictions and tribulations we can glory in them, not because we enjoy pain but because we know what tribulation yields. For most people, tribulation breaks the spirit, leads them to despair, and causes them to abandon all hope. Not so for the Christian.

The Fruit of Tribulation

Tribulation produces perseverance (v. 3). Tribulation puts muscle on our souls. Tribulation makes it possible for the people of God to persevere rather than to give up. Tribulation produces perseverance; **and perseverance, character** (v. 4). An easy life does nothing to produce character. Character is forged in the crucible of pain. Character is built when we have no alternative but to persevere in tribulation. Those who come out on the other side are those in whose souls God has built character. The result of character is **hope** (v. 4)—there it is again. Authentically joyful people are those who know where their hope is. They have been through the crucible. They have been through afflictions, persecution, and rejection from their friends. They have been through pain. They have identified with the humiliation of Christ. They have been crucified with Christ and raised in his resurrection and now participate in his exultation. That is the hope that Christian character produces.

What about the result of that hope? Here is the best part: **Now hope does not disappoint** (v. 5). Other translations say that hope "does not make us ashamed." It is embarrassing that the world's idea of hope is to invest it in some particular enterprise only to see that enterprise fail. When it fails we are dashed to pieces, but the hope that we have from God will never disappoint. It will never embarrass us. We will never have to be ashamed for putting our confidence and trust in Christ. If you put your trust in anything else but Christ you are destined for disappointment and embarrassment. Hope in Christ is the only hope that never shames us. The New Testament tells us that if we are not in the faith, if we do not believe, we are without hope and destined ultimately to disappointment.

All of us struggle with the weaknesses of the flesh and sin. One of the many things I am ashamed of is that I still have a hard time dealing with disappointments and unrealized expectations. When I travel across the country and arrive at my destination, tired and just wanting to get to the hotel room to take a nap, and I find that the hotel has mislaid my reservation, I find myself in a fit of "hotel rage." Infants are quick to cry and scream, and almost every time it is because they are disappointed. They did not get what they wanted. They were looking forward to something that did not happen, and they cannot handle it. That tendency does not leave us as we grow older. One of the hardest things to deal with in life is disappointment when our hopes have been dashed into pieces. Yet the hope we have of the glory of God and for the ultimate victory of his kingdom will never let us down. Nobody is going to cancel that reservation or let it fall between the cracks. We can rely absolutely on God. That is what we learn when we understand the gospel and our justification. This is just one more fruit.

Love Poured Out

Paul gives another reason for hope: **the love of God has been poured out in our hearts by the Holy Spirit who was given to us** (v. 5). Paul is not saying that affection for God will prevent us from experiencing disappointment or shame, even though such affection is one of the most important fruits of salvation that the Holy Spirit kindles within our hearts. Here Paul is not talking about our love for God; he is talking about God's love for us. The love of God is a love that the Holy Spirit sheds abroad. God's love for the justified is no mere feeling; neither are the gifts that God gives us or the benefits that he pours upon us. It is God's affection that God puts inside of us, his love for us. That is what fuels our hope and gives us confidence that we will not be ashamed. It is what enables us to persevere and endure tribulations and afflictions. The love God pours out is no small portion; it is an outpouring of divine love, lavished upon us. He pours his love for us into our souls to such a degree that even if the rest of the world hates us we can know that he loves us and has given us hope that we will never be ashamed. It is one of the works of the Holy Spirit.

Salvation is not like receiving just one gift under the Christmas tree but gift after gift all wrapped up together. The first package we find is our justification, and when we open that package, we find inside it another—peace with God. Inside that package is access into his presence, and inside that gift is the ability to rejoice in glorifying the glory of God. Inside that package we find there is joy in the midst of tribulation, and that very tribulation gives us another gift—perseverance. Tear off the ribbon from that gift, and there is another one, which is the character that perseverance gives us, and within that gift is hope that will never embarrass or disappoint us. Finally we open one more present, and it is the love of God poured profusely into our hearts by the grace of God. All these are the gift of our justification. Do we wonder, then, at that doxological writing of the apostle Paul, who rejoices in these things over and over again? For Paul, Christmas never ends.

16

THE ATONEMENT

Romans 5:6–11

For when we were still without strength, in due time Christ died for the ungodly. For scarcely for a righteous man will one die; yet perhaps for a good man someone would even dare to die. But God demonstrates His own love toward us, in that while we were still sinners, Christ died for us. Much more then, having now been justified by His blood, we shall be saved from wrath through Him. For if when we were enemies we were reconciled to God through the death of His Son, much more, having been reconciled, we shall be saved by His life. And not only *that,* but we also rejoice in God through our Lord Jesus Christ, through whom we have now received the reconciliation.

After showing us the benefits that accompany justification—peace with God, access to God's presence, and hope—Paul turns his attention to the atonement of Christ: **For when we were still without strength, in due time Christ died for the ungodly** (v. 6). At this point Paul discusses the *when* of our atonement, the point in history at which the redemption of the people of God was accomplished. Paul speaks of the *when* of this accomplishment in two ways. The first is with respect to us. At what point in our personal history did Christ offer himself on the cross? Paul tells us first that Christ offered himself "when we were still without strength."

Let's look at that before we look at the second way, the temporal aspect of the atonement.

Original Sin

One of the cardinal doctrines of biblical Christianity has to do with original sin and its impact on our spiritual strength. This issue has provoked a battle in every generation throughout church history. Virtually every church confesses some doctrine of original sin, but, as we have seen, this original sin does not refer to the first sin committed by Adam and Eve but to the consequences of that sin by which God visited corruption upon the entire human race. All the progeny of Adam and Eve are born in a state of spiritual death and moral corruption. The debate comes in with regard to the degree of that corruption. To what extent have we fallen from our original righteousness?

Augustine waged this battle in antiquity against the heretic Pelagius, who denied the fall altogether. The cardinal point Augustine taught was that the ravages of sin are so great and penetrate so deeply within our souls that we are left in a state of spiritual death. Spiritual death means that even though we are still alive biologically, even though we have faculties that remain intact—a brain, a mind, affections, a will—our humanity has been so damaged by the fall that our state, by nature, is one of moral inability.

The idea of moral inability is this: we have been plunged so deeply into sin that we do not have the moral capacity to incline ourselves in any way to the things of God. If God in his mercy and grace were to offer us complete forgiveness and salvation in Jesus Christ but do nothing to work in our hearts, we would never exercise that option. We simply do not have the moral capacity. We have the volitional power to choose what we want in any circumstance, but sin is so deep that we no longer have any desire for God or any want for the gospel or for Christ.

The overwhelming report in America today among professing evangelicals is that God offers the gospel to everybody, and that those who exercise their will to receive Jesus, to make a decision for Christ, are the ones who are saved. Although God does 99 percent, the 1 percent that decides our fate for eternity rests in our cooperating and *choosing* Jesus freely. The minute I am persuaded of that will be the minute I climb down from my pulpit, because I would have no hope whatsoever that the work of evangelism would be successful or that preaching would bring any fruit. It would be like a preacher preaching the resurrection with great eloquence, power, and rhetorical skills in the middle of a cemetery, calling the corpses to come to life. They are not going to come. Unless the Holy Spirit empowers the word of preaching and the outreach of evangelism, no one will come to Christ. That is the point that Jesus made when he said, "No one can come to Me unless the Father who sent Me draws him" (John 6:44). Paul is teaching this same principle. He is saying that Christ died for the ungodly while we were still without strength. The strength that Paul has in view is clearly spiritual strength. We have no strength in and of ourselves to effect our salvation.

In Due Time

God did not wait for us to exercise our wills, incline ourselves to him, repent of our sins, or get ourselves in such a state that it would be appropriate to provide an atonement for us. No, while we were still in this state, which Paul later, in his letter to the Ephesians, describes as spiritual death, while we were dead in trespasses and sin (Eph. 2:1), Christ died. That is the *when* with respect to our human condition.

Concerning the historical *when*: "A decree went out from Caesar Augustus that all the world should be registered. This census first took place while Quirinius was governing Syria" (Luke 2:1–2). It is an integral part of the Christmas narrative in Luke, but the point here is that Christ came into the world in real time in real history. It did not happen outside of space and time. Christ came in the fullness of time. He was born on the exact date and in the exact place that the Father had decreed. Throughout the whole Old Testament—in the activity of God ministering to his people, in creating a nation for himself out of Israel, in giving them the Law and the Prophets, in ministering to them through their entire sojourn—God was ripening history for the moment that Christ would come. He came "in due time."

There is great joy in a household when Mama reveals to the rest of the family that she is pregnant. When we hear such news, we ask, "When is the baby due?" The doctor gives us a due date, and we circle it on the calendar, but we know that the baby will not necessarily come on that date. I remember the birth of our first child, Sherrie. The due date came, and Vesta and I were waiting and ready, but she did not deliver for ten more days. Once a birth takes place, the day is marked as "birthday." It is a day to celebrate. The time leading up to the birth date is forgotten. Who cares about the due date after the real date occurs? Well, God is never late. When he appoints a day for something to happen, it happens that very day.

When we read in the Gospel narratives about the death of Christ, we find political machinations going on behind the scenes. Caiaphas, Pilate, and Herod all give their advice. The soldiers conspire. The Sanhedrin gets involved; they pay money to Judas to make sure that all would take place.

God knew from the foundation of the world that this was the day because he had ordained it. All these things came together in the concurrence of divine providence so that on a specific date Christ would die.

For the Ungodly

Whenever Paul mentions the death of Christ, he speaks of its purpose. Paul does not see the death of Christ as a tragedy in the history of human affairs. He does not see it as the great destruction of an innocent man through a corrupt clergy and political body in Jerusalem. There is a reason why Christ died in due time. Christ's death was not simply to demonstrate the love of God or to display some kind of moral influence to the universe, but to die "for the ungodly."

It is easy to come to the conclusion, even if we are in the category of the ungodly, that Christ died for us—but not so fast. It is true that Christ died for the ungodly—all for whom Christ died are numbered among the ungodly. Once again we are confronted with one of the most volatile controversies that abides in every generation of Christians: did Christ die for all the ungodly? I do not hesitate to answer that question: I do not believe for one moment that Christ died for all the ungodly. The Bible does not teach that everybody goes to heaven. Only believers go to heaven, those who belong to Christ. Every saved believer was at one time completely ungodly. Christ certainly died for the ungodly in the sense that he died for those who come to faith in him, but the controversy is whether Christ died for everybody. We know that everybody is ungodly and that Christ died for the ungodly, so the conclusion many make is that he died for everybody, but if everybody's sins are paid for, who is in hell?

Do we have the idea that in order to satisfy the righteousness of God, Christ had to die *and* we have to repent and come to him? In that case, his death would not cover every sin, because the sin of unbelief would be excluded. If we really believe that Christ died for all the sins of all people and that his atonement was effective, then we would have to come to the conclusion that he died for everybody equally and that everybody is in heaven. The Bible gives little reason to believe that. The Bible does not teach that Christ died to make salvation possible. Christ died for his sheep. He laid down his life for them, and when he did, there was never a doubt in heaven that all for whom he died had their sins covered and will spend eternity in heaven. To his disciples Jesus said, "This is the will of the Father who sent Me, that of all He has given Me I should lose nothing, but should raise it up at the last day" (John 6:39). He died for those whom the Father has given to him.

When young men are examined for ordination, they are asked, "Do you believe in limited atonement?" In other words, do they believe that Christ did not die for everybody? The standard answer they give is that Christ's death is sufficient for all but efficient only for some. It is valuable enough to cover the sins of all, and in that sense it is universally sufficient, but it is efficient, that is, it effects salvation only for those who believe. I have no quarrel with that, but it is not limited atonement. Every Arminian believes that Christ's atonement is sufficient for all and efficient only for believers.

The question about the scope of the atonement is this: what was God's eternal purpose in designing the death of his Son? From all eternity God had a plan of salvation. Did he plan to save everybody? If God is God and if God is sovereign and if saving everybody was his eternal plan, then nothing could defeat that plan, and every human being would be saved, but manifestly the Scriptures teach that not everybody is saved. Do we doubt that God has the power and the right to save everybody? If God had determined to save everybody in the world, everybody would be saved.

A friend of mine says, "God saves as many people as he possibly can." I say to him, "Shame on you. Do you mean that God cannot save the unbeliever?" He believes that God cannot intervene in the life of one of his creatures and work faith in the heart of that believer because doing so would somehow violate the sinner's freedom, but every sinner in hell would do anything he could to have God intervene in his life. God can do it, certainly, and he has the right to do with the clay what he wills, but God has not decreed from all eternity to save everybody. He has decreed to do more than make salvation possible.

There is in Scripture, from Genesis to Revelation, a doctrine of election. We may not like the doctrine, and if we do not, it is because we do not understand it. I do not know how people could have affection for Christ in their hearts and not rejoice at the unspeakable grace of God to include them in salvation and make certain that they would be saved.

The idea of limited atonement deals with the question of God's design. Did God intend to save a remnant of the world and send his Son to die for those people to ensure their salvation? That is what "limited atonement" means. It means "definite atonement." The atonement of Christ was not just to make salvation possible. If that were the case, Christ could have died and never have seen the travail of his soul and been satisfied. If the efficacy of Christ's death depends on us, Christ would have no fruit from his death; but while we were powerless in our souls to incline ourselves to the things of God, in due time Christ died for the ungodly.

For scarcely for a righteous man will one die; yet perhaps for a good man someone would even dare to die (v. 7). The words Paul uses are translated "righteous" and "good," but Calvin believed that since there is no distinction between a righteous person and a good person that Paul was using a *hendiadys*. A hendiadys is the name given to two different words used to refer to the same thing. Luther, on the other hand, was convinced that Paul was making a distinction. Although a good man would necessarily have to be a righteous man, the idea here is that "righteous" is somewhat formal. A righteous person might be somebody who obeys the law and does what is right so that his behavior provokes a certain measure of respect. Although we can respect people we think are morally upright, it is rare that we would lay down our lives just because we respect their character.

When we talk about "good" people, we are speaking about more than their moral activity, more than their conformity to principles of righteousness. A good person is the sort who produces in us a certain love and concern. When we say, "He is a good fellow," we mean that he is a nice guy. He is a kind person. He is the sort of person for whom we would be willing to go the extra mile to reciprocate his affection and kindness toward us. Paul is saying that rarely will anybody die for a righteous man, although maybe someone will die for a loved one or for someone who has shown personal kindnesses. Even pagans, on occasion, might be willing to jump on a hand grenade for such a person, but in the case of the atonement, Jesus did not die for righteous people or for good people; he died for godless people.

In the heart of every corrupt human being, even in one who is partially sanctified, there remains a little buzz that seeks to persuade, "I was not that bad." Rarely do we come to a full conviction of our helplessness and wickedness. All the power of our psychology is at work every minute to suppress full admission of our guilt and hopelessness. When people repeatedly give me reasons as to why they are Christian while their friends are not, I begin to wonder if they are in the kingdom at all, because they certainly have not yet been convinced of their helplessness and sin.

God's Love for Sinners

But God demonstrates His own love toward us, in that while we were still sinners, Christ died for us (v. 8). There is a shift in language here from the generic "ungodly" to the specific "for us." While we were in a state of sin, God set forth *for us*. Again and again in his epistles Paul speaks of the specific work of grace that Christ does for the believer. When he talks about "us," he is talking about those who are in Christ Jesus. He is talking about Christians.

What about the love of God? "God demonstrates His own love toward us." There are two aspects to consider concerning this clause. The first is how theology distinguishes among three distinct types of God's love. The first type of divine love is the *love of benevolence*. The word *bene* means "good" or "well." The word *volens* has to do with the will. The Bible tells us that God's basic attitude toward the world, toward fallen humanity, is one of goodwill. God is not unkind or mean-spirited; the basic posture of the Creator toward the world is one of goodwill, and every person in the world experiences it in one way or another. The fact that people are alive is an indication of God's goodwill. Every moment a sinner continues to exist in this world, he does so only by virtue of the goodwill of God, by God's forbearance and patience. God loves everybody in the sense that his goodwill flows toward all.

The second sense of divine love is God's *beneficence*. His benevolence refers to his goodwill, whereas his beneficence refers to his good acts. The Bible tells us that God's rain falls on the just and the unjust (Matt. 5:45). All people, repentant or not, believers or not, receive certain kind acts from the hand of God. In that sense, they all experience God's beneficent love.

When ministers preach that God loves unconditionally, the pagan thinks that God loves him no matter what he does or does not do. He thinks he can depend on the love of God even if he rejects Jesus Christ and never repents of his sins, but that's not the biblical message. When we talk about the unconditional love of God, the love that never fails, we are talking about his *complacent* love, the third type of divine love. The concept of complacent love is a bit difficult to grasp, because it is not used in the sense in which we use the word *complacent* today. When we say that people are complacent, we mean they are smug and satisfied with all they have achieved. They have no desire to go beyond where they are. When we talk about God's complacent love, we are talking about the delight he takes, supremely, in his Son. God's love for his Son is without measure or qualification; he loves his Son fully and perfectly. The love the Father has for his Son extends beyond his Son to those who belong to his Son. Therefore, only believers receive God's complacent love. They do not receive it because of anything in them but only because God gives gifts to his Son. From all eternity he has loved his Son and planned to give him a portion of humanity so that his Son might be the firstborn among many brothers. God loves his Son with the love of complacency, and he demonstrates that complacent love for us in that "while we were still sinners Christ died for us."

Wrath Satisfied

The second aspect of God's "demonstrating his own love toward us" is quite technical, so I will mention it briefly. A debate emerged in the twentieth-century German theology about the atonement. Some theologians were opposed to the classic doctrine of the atonement as the Son's satisfying the wrath of the Father. Old creeds present God's anger, *ira Dei*, as something that needs to be assuaged so that sin is repaid through the satisfaction offered by his Son. Some theologians scoff at any idea of an atonement that provides satisfaction for our sins. They say God does not need satisfying and his love is so great that it cancels his wrath. However, this is more like *Mr. Rogers' Neighborhood* than the kingdom of God. This attack on the classical and biblical doctrine of the atonement was called the *Ömpstemung Controversy* among some of the German theologians. According to this view, God is at odds with God. God the Father is angry at sinners and pours out his wrath upon the ungodly, but God the Son arrives on the scene and rescues poor humanity from the wrath of the Father. God the Son persuades God the Father to set aside his wrath.

That whole idea posits an internal conflict in the Godhead among the Trinity. The biblical view is that although the Son comes and satisfies the righteousness of God by taking the wrath of God upon himself, he comes because the Father sends him. It is the Father's idea from all eternity, an idea to which the Son gives his total agreement, as does the Spirit. This is called the *covenant of redemption*. From all eternity there is one purpose and one mind in the Godhead, and it is out of love.

Several years ago at a Christian booksellers' convention, I was asked to give the keynote address to six thousand people, and I decided to speak on the urgency of the gospel. I had to steer my ship between two issues. I did not want to speak above the intelligence of those gathered, nor did I want to dumb down my talk to such a degree that I would be insulting them. Titling my talk "Saved from What?" I went back to the rudimentary concept of salvation, and I told them that if we look at the concept of salvation in the Bible, we see that the most rudimentary meaning of salvation is to be rescued from some calamity. If we are restored from sickness, we are saved from the effects of that illness. If we experience victory in battle, we are saved from the ignominy of defeat. That is the way the Greek word for salvation is used in the New Testament; for example, any time someone is rescued from catastrophe, he experiences salvation, but then there is the grand doctrine of salvation that speaks of salvation in the ultimate sense, in which we are rescued from the worst of all possible catastrophes—God's wrath.

The church does not believe that anymore. Many believe in a god who has no wrath, but if God has no wrath, there is no need for Christ. Unbelievers say, "That's fine for you, but I do not need Jesus," yet there is nothing in heaven or on earth they need more than Jesus. As long as people are unconcerned about the wrath of God, they feel no need to come to Jesus. If God is real, so is his wrath, and the biblical view of salvation is rescue from wrath.

In my address at the booksellers' convention I said, "Do you want to know what you are saved from? In a word, you are saved from God." They just gasped, and to this day when I attend that convention people come up to me and say, "I had never thought of that until I heard your message." It is God who saves people from God because his wrath is stored up against the day of wrath, and he most certainly will demonstrate, as he has demonstrated, his love toward us "in that while we were still sinners, Christ died for us."

17

RECONCILIATION

Romans 5:10−14

For if when we were enemies we were reconciled to God through the death of His Son, much more, having been reconciled, we shall be saved by His life. And not only that, but we also rejoice in God through our Lord Jesus Christ, through whom we have now received the reconciliation. Therefore, just as through one man sin entered the world, and death through sin, and thus death spread to all men, because all sinned—(For until the law sin was in the world, but sin is not imputed when there is no law. Nevertheless death reigned from Adam to Moses, even over those who had not sinned according to the likeness of the transgression of Adam, who is a type of Him who was to come. . . .

Paul begins this section with a comparison: **For if when we were enemies we were reconciled to God through the death of His Son, much more, having been reconciled, we shall be saved by His life** (v. 10). The theme of this verse has to do with reconciliation. I mentioned earlier that the one absolute, essential precondition for reconciliation is estrangement, because without estrangement there is no need for reconciliation. The fact that through Christ we have been reconciled to God is one of the central motifs of the New Testament.

Enemies of God

Sinclair Ferguson has said that there is almost a universal repudiation of the idea that human beings have a natural enmity toward God. I can think of nothing that provokes more anger from unbelievers than when we tell them that they hate God. They deny it emphatically. "I might be indifferent to God, but I do not hate God," they say. However, if people are indifferent to the Lord God Almighty, the one who created them and has given them every blessing they receive, what is that except hatred? We do not sense the weight of our natural hostility toward God. The New Testament speaks about reconciliation because reconciliation to God is so greatly and earnestly needed. We are estranged from him. Not only are we at enmity with God, but God is at enmity with us. God is the natural enemy of corrupt sinners.

There is a love that God displays to creatures indiscriminately, but at the same time the Scripture is replete with descriptive terms that tell us how God's face is set steadfastly against the wicked. He is too holy to even look at us, so great is that gulf of estrangement. There is a big difference in the driving force of the estranged parties. Driving our opposition toward God is evil. His estrangement from us is founded on a holy opposition to sin. We must understand that difference and not project onto God's character the same unjust grounds for enmity that we are guilty of ourselves. It is not right for the creature to be estranged from the Creator, but if the creature is sinful it is right and proper for the Creator to be estranged. He is holy and we are not. Paul is declaring here the glorious work of redemption in which God takes the initiative for our reconciliation.

On the cross by his work of propitiation Jesus reconciled the Father to the Father's people. On Good Friday when Christ paid for our sin and made atonement for his people with the perfect sacrifice and satisfied God's wrath completely, that was the end of the estrangement on God's part. We were reconciled in the sense that God, the injured party, was satisfied. God was reconciled toward us while we were still estranged from him. In this drama of reconciliation, Christ satisfied the righteousness and holiness of his Father. On the day that God became satisfied and was no longer in opposition to his people, we did not automatically change. We do not experience that reconciliation until our opposition and hostility toward him end—when we are regenerated by the Holy Spirit, our hardened hearts are broken, and we are brought joyfully into a loving relationship with the Father through the Son.

It is one thing to experience the reconciliation that comes through the death of Christ, but how much greater is the reconciliation that occurs through the life of Christ. We can look at that in two ways. Christ's life of perfect obedience to the law, by which his righteousness was merited and earned, is now given to us who have no righteousness of our own. We can say it is the life of Christ even more than the death of Christ that is the ground of our justification. That is true, but I am not sure it is what Paul is talking about here when he says, "How much more are we reconciled through the life of Christ." Paul has already introduced the idea that not only are we justified by the death of Christ but also that Christ was raised for our justification. We are reconciled because we have a Mediator who not only died for us but also was raised from the dead and continues to make intercession. He is our peacemaker. He lives forever, continuing in that role representing us before the Father. As wonderful as was that once-for-all death on the cross, how much greater is that reconciliation that we realize and experience because he lives and ever intercedes for us.

Reconciled

I want to explore just a little bit more the meaning of this term *reconciliation*. Paul said in Romans 1 that the substance of our universal guilt and corruption before God is this: our proclivity for idolatry, the sin of exchanging the truth of God for the lie, serving and worshiping the creature rather than the Creator. When we first looked at that, I made mention of a word Paul used, *metallassō*, which indicates an exchange or a swap. We trade the glory of the eternal, immortal, everlasting God for the glory of contemptible things, creeping things, bugs and snakes and idols of all sorts. The word *metallassō* has the prefix *meta-*, which means "with." One thing is traded for something else. The same root is found in the word *reconciliation*. There, it is not *metallassō* but *katallassō*, a verb (the noun form is *katallagē*). That is the word Paul is using here when he says, "We were reconciled to God through the death of His Son, much more, having been reconciled [again, the form of *katallassō*] we shall be saved by His life." **And not only that, but we also rejoice in God through our Lord Jesus Christ, through whom we have now received the reconciliation** (v. 11). Reconciliation is a substantive reality. It is a gift that God has given to his people through the death and resurrection of Christ.

Rejoicing in Reconciliation

The result of reconciliation is unspeakable joy. The Christian life from beginning to end is meant to be a life of joy. We have much to be happy about. There is no room for the sourpuss in the kingdom of God. There is nothing dour about our redemption. If we suffer to a degree that nobody else has ever been called to suffer—a modern-day Job sitting on the dung heap—we would have no right to say anything different from what Job declared: "Though He slay me, yet will I trust Him" (Job 13:15). No affliction so dire, no sorrow so deep, no pain so intense, is worthy to be compared to the glory of that *katallagē*, that reconciliation, that we have received in the Beloved.

We contemplate our state of affairs in this world and we see our bank accounts slipping away, our homes destroyed, our jobs lost, and our bodies torn by disease, and we have every reason to complain, whine, and weep, but if we lift our eyes for one second to the cross and the resurrection, we see that the Lord God omnipotent, who is too holy even to look at us, now looks at us and embraces us and adopts us as his children because he has been reconciled to us.

Joy is another benefit that flows from our justification. Verse 11 is just an expansion of what Paul said at the beginning of Romans 5, that, having been justified, we have peace with God and access into his presence, and we can now glory in tribulation because it works perseverance; and perseverance, character; and character, hope, which is never put to shame.

Death through Adam

In verse 12 Paul introduces a most difficult concept: **Therefore, just as through one man sin entered the world, and death through sin, and thus death spread to all men, because all sinned—(For until the law sin was in the world, but sin is not imputed when there is no law. Nevertheless death reigned from Adam to Moses, even over those who had not sinned according to the likeness of the transgression of Adam, who is a type of Him who was to come . . .** (vv. 12–14). There is so much in that text that it keeps the theologians busy studying and arguing. It is one of the most important texts in the Bible because it talks about the fall of the entire human race through Adam.

One man, Adam, brought sin. With that sin came death, which came on the whole human race because all have sinned, but not up to the similitude of Adam's sin. Even babies sometimes live only a few hours. Death is the penalty for sin. Without sin there can be no death, and without the law there can be no sin. Death was in the world before God gave his law through Moses. Since Adam's fall all creatures have died because all have sinned, and they sinned before the Law of Moses was given.

There can be no sin unless there is law, because sin is defined as the transgression of God's law. If there is no law, there can be no foul, but if there is a law, then a penalty is incurred when we break the law. Since the penalty for sin is death, and since death reigned from Adam to Moses, there is a sense in which everybody in the world somehow broke the law in Adam. That is the point here in Romans 5. Through one man sin and death came into the whole world. Somehow we are related to Adam.

Realism

People ask, "How can God blame me for sinning when all I am doing is what comes naturally? I was born in sin, and when I sin, I am just acting according to the nature I was born with. How can God hold me responsible for acting out a nature he gave me before I was even born?" The answer is that they sinned in Adam. They reply, "How can God hold people responsible for what Adam did when they were not even there in the garden?" Several answers have been given through the ages.

A common explanation is the doctrine called "realism." Realism operates on the premise that the only way God could justly and morally condemn us for what Adam did was if we were really there participating in the act. We were really there in terms of our preexistent souls before we were actually born with bodies; our souls existed with Adam, so that when he sinned, we sinned, because we were really there. The favorite text used to defend this kind of realism is found in Hebrews, where the author compares and contrasts Jesus with the people of the past—with Moses, angels, and others along the way—and talks about the superiority of Christ's high priesthood (Hebrews 1–2).

A first-century complaint waged against the Christian confession of faith in Jesus concerned his priesthood. Jesus, from the tribe of Judah, was the long-awaited king descended from David, and he was proclaimed as the Great High Priest. The critics of Jesus said, "He cannot be our high priest because one of the necessary qualifications for the high priest is that he be from the tribe of Levi. The priesthood was given to Aaron and his family, the Levites, but Jesus was from the tribe of Judah." The author of Hebrews addresses that charge by reminding his readers of an episode recorded in the book of Genesis. A mysterious figure named Melchizedek met Abraham, and Abraham paid tithes to Melchizedek and received a blessing from him. The author of Hebrews labors the point that the greater receives tithes from the lesser. The priesthood exercised by Melchizedek was a higher order of priesthood than that found in Aaron and his descendants among the Levites, so even though Jesus was not a Levite, his priesthood was of a higher order of priesthood. As the Scriptures say, going back to Psalm 110, Christ is a priest after the order of Melchizedek.

Those who argue for realism, who say we were really there in preexistent souls in the garden, argue from that text in Hebrews about Abraham paying tithes to Melchizedek. Abraham was the father of Isaac, and the father is greater than the son, so since Isaac was Abraham's son, then Abraham was greater than Isaac. If Melchizedek was greater than Abraham, and Abraham was greater than Isaac, then Melchizedek was greater than Isaac. The plot thickens: Isaac had a son, Jacob. Isaac was greater than Jacob, Abraham was greater than Isaac, Melchizedek was greater than Abraham; therefore, Melchizedek was greater than Jacob. Then Jacob had sons, including Levi. Jacob was greater than Levi, Isaac was greater than Jacob and, therefore, greater than Levi. Abraham was greater than Isaac, who was greater than Jacob, who was greater than Levi. We put it all together and conclude that Melchizedek was greater than Abraham, who was greater than Isaac, who was greater than Jacob, who was greater than Levi. So who was greater: Levi or Melchizedek? The author of Hebrews says that "even Levi, who receives tithes, paid tithes through Abraham, so to speak, for he was still in the loins of his father when Melchizedek met him" (Heb. 7:9–10). Some jump on that passage and say that when Abraham paid tithes to Melchizedek, Levi was really there in the loins of his father, but to claim that is to squeeze something out of the text that just is not there.

Federalism

Classic Reformed theology refers to "federalism" as distinguished from realism. Adam was the federal head of the whole human race. The name Adam, *adam*, means "mankind." What Adam did in the garden was not simply for himself but for all those whom he represented. God appointed him during his probation in Eden to act for himself and for all his progeny. People do not like that. They say, "No damnation without representation," but, indeed, there was representation, which is the whole point here. People squirm under this and say, "I did not choose my representative."

According to the American legal system, if I hire somebody from Murder Incorporated to kill someone, and I establish an alibi for myself so at the time of the crime I place myself in another city and am witnessed there by lots of people, and my hired gunman kills my appointed victim, can I be charged with first-degree murder? Yes, because my hired killer was carrying out my will, and I am held accountable for the conspiracy to commit murder. We see the clear justice of that. In a similar fashion, Adam represented us in the garden. Some argue that the analogy breaks down because the accused will-fully hired someone to commit that heinous act of murder, whereas people have nothing to do with selecting Adam as their representative.

When Parliament changed the rules of the game and imposed taxes on the colonists without giving them representation in Parliament, the colonists protested because it was a violation of British law. The colonists were not just rebelling against the crown; they were calling the crown to obey the law. We can have no confidence that our interests will be represented by someone chosen for us by someone else. That is why we want to be able to elect our governing representatives. In the American electorate, we listen to the candidates and their positions on the issues. We hear their campaign promises. We become persuaded that candidate X is the one who can most accurately represent us, and we cast our vote. Later we are annoyed that the elected candidate does not do what he said he was going to do, but he is our representative because we put him there.

How could it be just for God to appoint one man to represent all kinds of people when the people do not even have a voice in the election? There is a big difference between King George, our congressmen or senators, and God. When God selects our representative, he makes that selection infallibly and impeccably. Nowhere in time and space have we been more perfectly represented than we were in the garden of Eden by the representative that God selected to act in our place. Since that is true, we can never curse God and say it is not fair. When we complain about being misrepresented by Adam, all we do is prove the perfection of that representation. Those who do not like that say, "It is not appropriate for God to accept the representa-tion of one person for another," but if they want to hold to that principle consistently, then they must also reject their representation by Christ. The principle of representation is at the very heart and soul of our salvation. We must be careful not to reject that principle because if we do, we have rejected our only hope of salvation.

Edwards's Identity Theory

There is perhaps a deeper combination of realism and federalism expressed in the profound thinking of the Puritan divine Jonathan Edwards. He put forth the identity theory. We would need to have some idea of Platonic philosophy to really understand this. The idea is that in the garden we were present, not because our souls were there but because we were there in the mind of God and what is present in the mind of God is present in reality. In Edwards's great treatise on original sin he said that if the Bible never taught a universal plunge of the human race into ruin at the beginning, in Adam, and if there was no such account of the fall in the Scripture, reason would require that we posit such an event. How else could we explain the universality of sin in the human race? Our culture is schizophrenic on this point. People do not want to acknowledge the reality of sin but of mistakes. They want to say that the origin of sin is environment and that people become corrupt because they are reared in a flawed culture.

Jean-Jacques Rousseau thought that man was born free and now is everywhere in chains. The idea behind his thinking is that we are born neutral and innocent and we sin because we are overwhelmed by the corrupting influences all around. Edwards said that if this were the case, we would expect at least 50 percent of the population to stay in that state of innocence. We have to look beyond the external influence of fallen society and cultural inducements to sin to explain the universality of it. The question, therefore, is this: if we were all born innocent, how did society become so corrupt? Society is comprised of people. It is not as if 5 percent are evil and they seduce the other 95 percent. One hundred percent are evil because we are born in that fallen state. In Adam, sin and death and destruction came into the whole world.

That is Paul's premise here when he turns our attention away from Adam to the new Adam, the new representative. The new Adam did not succumb to the enticements of the serpent but lived a life of perfect obedience, not just for his own sake but for the sake of the people whom he came to represent, to reconcile, and to save.

18

IMPUTATION

Romans 5:12–17

Therefore, just as through one man sin entered the world, and death through sin, and thus death spread to all men, because all sinned—(For until the law sin was in the world, but sin is not imputed when there is no law. Nevertheless death reigned from Adam to Moses, even over those who had not sinned according to the likeness of the transgression of Adam, who is a type of Him who was to come. But the free gift is not like the offense. For if by the one man's offense many died, much more the grace of God and the gift by the grace of the one Man, Jesus Christ, abounded to many. And the gift is not like that which came through the one who sinned. For the judgment which came from one offense resulted in condemnation, but the free gift which came from many offenses resulted in justification. For if by the one man's offense death reigned through the one, much more those who receive abundance of grace and of the gift of righteousness will reign in life through the One, Jesus Christ.)

Forty years ago I was teaching a college course in theology at a Christian school in Massachusetts, and we came to the section of theology called *soteriology*, which focuses attention on salvation and how it is acquired. Part of that course involved covering the so-called famous five points of Calvinism, summarized by the popular acrostic T-U-L-I-P. The acrostic stands for the fairest flower in God's garden.

I began teaching at the beginning of TULIP, with T, which stands for total depravity. There were about thirty students in my class, and I explained the doctrine of total depravity, showing them that sin is not simply tangential to our existence. Sin is not the blemish on our exterior; sin penetrates to the very core of our humanity, despoiling us in body, mind, and will and rendering us in a state of moral inability. So much are we captivated by this bondage to sin that we no longer have within us the moral capacity to incline ourselves to the things of God. I labored through all of that for the college students, and at the end of the discussion about total depravity, I asked for a show of hands as to how many were persuaded of this doctrine.

There was no hesitation; every hand went up. On the top left corner of the blackboard I wrote the number 30, and then I wrote a message to the janitor: "Please do not erase."

Class resumed the following Monday, at which time I started on the U of TULIP, unconditional election. When I got through and asked how many agreed with it, there was quite a bit of attrition. Once we got to L, limited atonement, there was wholesale abandonment of their convictions. I said to them, "It's QED (*quod erat demonstrandum*); it is automatic. If you understand the doctrine of total depravity, you would have to believe in unconditional election or limited atonement even if the Bible didn't teach it. If you do not believe in irresistible grace, you would have to assume it once you understood the nature of our fallen condition."

As I mentioned in the last study, virtually every church in history has confessed belief in original sin; however, when we begin to define the contents— the depths—of original sin, the controversies emerge. In my book *Willing to Believe* I examine the positions of Pelagius, Luther, and Calvin, as well as semi-Pelagianism, Augustinianism, dispensationalism, and Arminiansm.[1] I have already explained the competing theories of how we are related to Adam's fall. We have explored the doctrine of realism, which argues that the reason the Bible says we all sinned in Adam is that we were actually present back in the garden, and we sinned there together with Adam. I rejected that doctrine in favor of the doctrine of federalism, but we can so intently focus our attention on our relationship to the fall of Adam and Eve and to the nature with which we enter the world that we can miss the context of what Paul is talking about here in Romans 5.

1. R. C. Sproul, *Willing to Believe: The Controversy over Free Will* (Grand Rapids, MI: Baker, 1997).

Romans 5 is not a dangling participle, having no relationship to what comes before and after. Paul is laboring over further critical implications of the doctrine of justification. In a real sense, the whole epistle of Romans is Paul's explanation of the full-orbed significance of the doctrine of justification by faith alone, but in chapter 5 he is giving us the contrast between our state of ruin brought about through Adam and our state of justification brought about by the obedience of another. The contrast here is between Adam and Christ, and it all has to do with justification.

A Hill to Die On

As I mentioned earlier, the evangelical world was shocked by an initiative some years ago called Evangelicals and Catholics Together (ECT). Very well-known members of the Christian evangelical community joined forces with representatives of the Roman Catholic community to declare their joint effort in combating what we call common-grace issues: the issue of relativism in the culture, the issue of the destruction of marriage and the family, the issue of abortion, and so on. Historically, Protestants have argued for the legitimacy of joining hands with people of any theological persuasion in arenas of what we call common grace—ministering to the very basic human needs of people. However, the ECT document went beyond this joint activity and declared to the world that its signers shared a common faith in the gospel.

I along with several other evangelical leaders publicly protested the document because we saw in it the compromise of the gospel of justification by faith alone. This was a very painful time for me because it involved breaking ranks with some very close friends and comrades. The protest provoked a second ECT article in which people agreed that faith is necessary for justification but said there are other matters that still need to be discussed, such as imputation. I responded to the architects of that particular document and said, "If you do not have justification by faith alone, you do not have the gospel, and if you do not have imputation, you do not have justification by faith alone."

"You keep raising the bar, moving the goal post," they responded.

I had not moved anything. Since the time Paul wrote Romans and Galatians and the time of the sixteenth-century Reformation, it has been clear that if we do not have *sola fide*, we do not have the gospel. Absolutely essential to justification by faith alone is the doctrine of imputation.

Many say, "It is fine for you theologians to worry about dotting the i's and crossing the t's, but why can't we just all get along?" This minor detail of imputation is the article upon which we live or die, upon which our eternal life is at stake. That is why theologians get exercised about it, and woe to the theologian who does not. It is just too important.

I have been asked, "Do you find it easier to tolerate error in the church more now than when you were young?" I reply that I have learned over the years that the more we study the things of God and the more theology we are engaged in, the more we begin to realize the difference between essential things and errors that we can get along with. I am not ready to give up on the deity of Christ or to negotiate it, and God forbid that I would ever negotiate *sola fide*, justification by faith alone. If I am not going to negotiate that, I am not going to negotiate imputation.

After the first two editions of ECT appeared, those of us opposed to the initiative met with those involved in it. A proposal for another document was brought forth, *Evangelicals and Evangelicals Together*, to assure the evangelical community of what we believe and to make clear that we had not negotiated the gospel. Several of us, including members of the original ECT committee, met for over a year and wrote another document called *The Celebration of the Gospel*, which contained about thirty affirmations and denials pertaining to beliefs about the gospel. It was interesting to watch what happened in the theological community, particularly in the evangelical world, in response to it. Contained in the affirmations and denials is the statement that imputation is essential to the gospel. Many were willing to say they believe in all the articles of affirmation and denial except for the one containing the term *imputation*. A growing movement called the "new perspective on Paul" has been pervasive in the Christian community, even among evangelicals. It denies the imputation of the righteousness of Christ as the grounds for our justification. We may not all be aware of the movement, but the church is in flames over the issue of imputation. It has not been this big an issue since the sixteenth century.

I have labored this point for a reason: there is no place in the Bible where the doctrine of imputation is set forth more clearly and centrally than here in Romans 5. I can find no other way to make sense of the way in which Paul says that we sinned in Adam than to understand this assertion putatively, i.e., we sinned in Adam by imputation. Paul labors the point that Adam's sin is reckoned and transferred, that is, imputed, to the entire human race. We know he is talking about imputation here because he spends time drawing the remarkable contrast that just as one man's offense and sin were reckoned to the entire human race, so another man's righteousness, in a similar manner, was imputed to all who believe.

Universal Death

Even though there is an ongoing controversy between Arminians and Calvinists about the extent of original sin, one thing these groups agree on is that Adam's sin produced a ruinous effect for the entire human race. There is no way we can avoid the thrust of what Paul is teaching in Romans 5 about the consequences of the fall of Adam and Eve. Paul ties the universal extent of the sin of Adam to the universality of death: **Therefore, just as through one man sin entered the world, and death through sin, and thus death spread to all men, because all sinned** (v. 12). This is where it is important to make another distinction, that between original sin and actual sin.

Actual sin occurs when we do something that transgresses the law of God. We looked at this briefly during our last study, but here we are looking at it from a slightly different perspective. Actual sin occurs when we violate the law of God. A baby in the crib, though it bears the weight of original sin, does not bear the weight of the guilt of actual sin because actual sin requires a conscious awareness of right and wrong and an actual violation of law. An infant in the crib does not know anything about the law of God. Has not God planted in the human heart the law of nature (*lex naturalis*) so that we learn from nature itself without ever hearing about the Ten Commandments? Yes, that is true. God does reveal his law in ways and places other than the Ten Commandments. Nevertheless, for sin to be involved, one must have some kind of discernment, a conscious understanding, of the prohibition, which we are saying an infant does not have. Until people reach an age of accountability, they have not yet committed actual sin even though by nature they are sinners.

If that is the case, if there is a period of time between birth and accountability before a person commits actual sin, why is it that people die? How do we account for babies dying in infancy? Since death is the punishment for sin, and if an infant is incapable of actual sin, how is it possible for the infant to die in his crib? Again, it makes sense only in the way Paul argues here—that death reigned from Adam to Moses. Before there was any law in the world, there was still sin as a result of the imputation of Adam's sin.

Posse non Peccare

At an earlier point I looked briefly at Augustine's treatment of original sin. In Augustine's debate with Pelagius he argued that at creation, before the fall, Adam had two abilities. He had what Augustine called the *posse peccare*, the possibility of sinning and the ability to sin. The word *peccare* means "to sin." We use the word *impeccable* for someone who is without any stain or blemish. We talk about little sins or peccadilloes, a word that comes from the Latin root *peccare*. Augustine said that in creation Adam and Eve were made with the ability to sin, the *posse peccare*, but they also had the ability not to sin. They were not fallen or corrupt. Adam and Eve had the power to resist temptation and not fall into sin; they had the *posse non peccare*, the power or the ability not to sin.

Looking at it from the perspective of mortality and death, Augustine argued that just as Adam and Eve, in creation, had the *posse peccare* and the *posse non peccare*, they also had the *posse mori* and the *posse non mori*; that is, they had the ability to die and the ability not to die. They were not created immortal. They could die under certain circumstances. Death was not necessary to our original parents; had they obeyed the command of God they would not have died. They had the ability to live forever, the *posse non mori*. We see that they had twin abilities: the ability to sin and not to sin, and the ability to die and not to die.

After the fall Adam's progeny lost the *posse non peccare*, the ability not to sin. Since the fall no human being has had inherent power to live a perfect life. Nobody can live without sinning, just as nobody can live without dying. Augustine said the curse of the fall is this: we are now in a state of *non posse non peccare*; it is not possible not to sin. Likewise, we have the *non posse non mori*, which is the inability not to die. What Augustine is explaining here is our basic humanity. In heaven, after we are fully glorified, we will have the *non posse peccare* and the *non posse mori*: we will not be able to sin and we will not be able to die, which is what we look forward to.

Paul is arguing that because of Adam's sin, both sin and death are universal because the guilt of Adam is reckoned to the whole race. We are dealing unassailably with the doctrine of imputation in its worst possible manifestation. The imputation of guilt from one person to all whom he represents leads us to ruination, our present estate as fallen and corrupt sinners.

In contrast is imputation in its best possible manifestation, the imputation of someone else's righteousness to us. We must not dismiss this as a theological technicality. The very essence of the gospel is that someone else's righteousness counts for us. If we get rid of imputation, we have no basis for any hope in standing before the judgment seat of God. Either we stand before God's judgment with our righteousness or with someone else's. If we have to stand before God with our righteousness, which righteousness the Bible says is nothing but filthy rags (Isa. 64:6), we have no hope. Take away the imputation of the Savior's righteousness, and there is no good news left to the gospel. We are on our own. Nothing we can bring to the table is enough to escape the wrath of a holy God. Give me the imputation of Christ or give me death. I'd be happy, proud, and honored to die on that hill.

Imputation and Works

There is another issue in the ongoing controversy of our time that is tightly related to the issue of imputation. It has to do with the covenant of works. Historic Reformed theology often goes by the name of "covenant theology," which stands in counter-distinction from the modern theology called "dispensationalism." Dispensationalism divides redemptive history into seven timeframes, seven ways in which God judges people. Dispensationalists want to "rightly divide" the Word of truth, so they divide up the Bible into these seven time frames instead of looking at the structure in which the Bible itself is written, which is covenant.

In the Old Testament God made a covenant with Noah (Gen. 6:18). After God destroyed the world by flood, he promised never to do it again; he put his rainbow in the sky. Then God called Abraham out of the land of paganism, and he said, "I am the LORD, who brought you out of Ur of the Chaldeans, to give you this land to inherit it" (Gen. 15:7). In the framework of that promise is a covenant that God made with Abraham. God called a people for himself after Abraham's covenant was passed on to Isaac and Jacob. Then Jacob's descendants were called into bondage, and God brought the descendants of Abraham together and added to the covenant he had made with Abraham by giving them the Decalogue and the blessings and the curses that follow the law. God also made a covenant with David and his house, the promise to restore his kingship forever.

Over and over again we see God establishing covenants in the Old Testament, but the first covenant we encounter is the covenant of works. God made that covenant with Adam and Eve on behalf of the whole world. In it he set before them the promise of blessedness: they could eat of the tree of life and live forever if they were obedient. They were told that they must not eat from the tree of the knowledge of good and evil lest they die. What happened to Adam and Eve in the garden is surrounded with the structure of an agreement, a promise of either destruction or blessing, depending on how they performed. That is why it is called a covenant of works. Those who worked righteousness would live, but those who worked disobedience would perish along with all their progeny.

In recent years people have raised a protest against that: "God does not owe his creatures any promise of redemption whatsoever, so the fact that he enters into a covenant with Adam and Eve is a matter of grace." That is true, but it is not the point of the distinction between the covenant of works and the covenant of grace. The point of the distinction is this: Adam and Eve failed the covenant of works, and when that failure took place, God did not destroy the human race but added a promise to the original covenant of redemption, which would come through the seed of the woman. The promise pertained to one who would crush the head of the serpent even while his heel would be injured in the process. God's promises to Abraham, Isaac, and Jacob, to Moses, to David, and to all the rest were promises to pour out his blessing upon people on the basis of his preserving, redeeming, saving grace.

The Bible teaches that justification is by faith alone, yet ultimately there is only one way anybody is ever saved in the presence of God, and that is through works. The question is not *whether* we are going to be saved through works; the question is *whose* works. We are saved through the works of the one who alone fulfilled the terms of the covenant of works. That is why it is not just the death of Christ that redeems us, but it is also the life of Christ.

By one man's disobedience we were plunged into ruin, but by the obedience of one man, the new Adam, we are justified. Saying that we are justified by faith alone is simply shorthand for saying that we are justified by Christ alone. Justification by faith alone means that we cannot make it on the basis of our works but by trusting in someone else's works. Our works will never save us, but Christ's works are perfect, and they meet all the requirements of the covenant of works.

There is a connection between the covenant of works and imputation. If we take away the covenant of works and imputation, we take away the significance of the perfect act of obedience of Jesus. Without the imputation of the righteousness of Christ, there is no justification, and without justification, there is no gospel. Paul shows the centrality of Christ's perfectly obedient life as the only possible ground for our salvation, which comes by imputation.

19

THE REIGN OF GRACE

Romans 5:20–6:4

Moreover the law entered that the offense might abound. But where sin abounded, grace abounded much more, so that as sin reigned in death, even so grace might reign through righteousness to eternal life through Jesus Christ our Lord. What shall we say then? Shall we continue in sin that grace may abound? Certainly not! How shall we who died to sin live any longer in it? Or do you not know that as many of us as were baptized into Christ Jesus were baptized into His death? Therefore we were buried with Him through baptism into death, that just as Christ was raised from the dead by the glory of the Father, even so we also should walk in newness of life.

Moreover the law entered that the offense might abound (v. 20). This is a purpose clause, which is one that gives a reason why a certain action takes place. The purpose of this clause is to show why the law became part of the equation of justification. Death reigned from Adam to Moses, but then God added to the covenant he had made with Adam and Noah. To Abraham, Isaac, and Jacob he added the whole of the Old Testament law. God added the law so that sin might abound.

Why the Law?

Why would God want sin to abound? We would think he would want it to abate, to see it ebb and disappear from his creation. The law comes and

179

reveals to us our helpless condition; the law reveals the reality of sin. We must remember the principle that the Scriptures set forth: where there is no law, there is no sin. By definition, sin is a transgression of the law of God, yet we have this inherited corruption from our father Adam, and God gives law that we may see the extent of our sin. There is also a true sense in which the added laws incite us to sin. So desperately wicked are we in our hearts that every time God adds a new law we take it as an occasion to further our rebellion and disobedience. We see that happen with our children. The more rules we give them, the more determined they are to break them.

A story is told of a preacher who spent an entire sermon giving nothing but a litany of sins. He designated some sixty-five specific human acts that the Bible regards as sinful. After the service he got a letter from one of his parishioners: "Thank you, pastor, for teaching us about all those sins. There were several I did not know about and have not tried yet." Where the law was added, sin abounded.

Paul makes a contrast: **But where sin abounded, grace abounded much more** (v. 20). This is not just a comparison. It is not like an equation with sin and grace on either side of it. Paul might have said, "Where sin abounded, grace abounded, so five pounds of sin, five pounds of grace." It is not a comparative; it is a superlative. There really is no comparison. Where sin abounds, Paul says, grace does much more abound. The scales are not equal. Sin is far outweighed by the grace that God gives. That is true in our lives. We live in the presence of a superabundance of grace that is far greater than the depths of our disobedience.

The Reign of Sin

Paul adds parenthetically: **so that as sin reigned in death, even so grace might reign through righteousness to eternal life through Jesus Christ our Lord** (v. 21). Paul is not saying that sin reigned unto death so that wherever sin is in power it results in death. He has already told us that death is one of the consequences of sin. Where there is no sin, there is no death. He is not talking about the mere presence of sin; he is talking about its reign, about sin exerting its power and authority. The reign of sin may be found in the face of death because in death we see the exultation of sin, the empowering of it, into this world.

Before my son was born, my mother longed for a grandson so that the Sproul name could continue. On the day my son was born, my mother was so excited. I took her to the hospital so that she could look at him through the nursery glass. Afterward we went out to dinner and then we went home.

When we got to the door there was a package awaiting my mother from her favorite dress shop. She was thrilled because it was the dress she had ordered for my ordination, which was to take place about two weeks later. Before she went to bed she told me she was tired, and she added, "Son, this is the happiest day of my life." She had seen her grandson and gotten her dress. Then she went to bed. A little later I went to bed. The next morning I heard our daughter, Sherrie, who was just three years old at the time, shouting at my mother in an attempt to wake her up. I walked into the room, and as soon as I did, I knew that my mother was dead. I walked over and touched her; she was cold. Rigormortis had set in; obviously she had died several hours before.

Upon awakening in the morning it sometimes seems that only a minute or two has transpired since we fell asleep, when in fact it has been eight hours. I stood there by my mother's bed. The day before I had witnessed the entrance into the world of my son, a new life, and it seemed like only a few moments since my mother was a living, breathing, warm human being. That is not right. Death is the final enemy.

The Reign of Grace

One of Paul's favorite contrasts in his writing is the suffering and pain we experience as not being worthy of comparison to the glory that awaits us when we pass from this world. Our destiny is not to become citizens in the realm of sin under the power of death. The power of that enemy has been vanquished, and by God's grace he has much more poured upon us the gift of righteousness, which gives us the ultimate benefit of justification—eternal life through Jesus Christ our Lord.

We can see now why the gospel is so important, why the doctrine of justification by faith alone can never be negotiated. In it the glory of the grace of God is made manifest. While we were still sinners Christ took upon himself the curse of that reigning death and defeated the grave by his righteousness, which is imputed to us by faith if indeed we put our trust in him. Sin reigns in death, but Christ triumphs over death. Death is but a moment; the triumph lasts forever.

As we come to Romans 6, Paul is still in the midst of this contrast, but the basic theme now sounds a new note. Here we find a theological distinction between justification and sanctification. We can see the transition. That is likely why those who divided the epistle into chapters made a division at the beginning of Romans 6—the attention turns toward another consequence of justification, which is sanctification.

Sanctification

What shall we say then? (6:1). Paul interrupts his discourse; there is a pregnant pause here. He has just developed all these fantastic benefits that flow from our justification, the rich fruits that accrue to us as a result of the gospel, and after explaining all of that he comes to the *so what?* How are we to respond to it? What shall we say to this supremacy and triumph of grace over sin and death?

Paul knows how sinful people think. He has just given the argument that where sin abounds, grace much more abounds, so the logic seems simple: if we want more grace, then we should commit more sin. Therefore, he says, **Shall we continue in sin that grace may abound?** (v. 1). He asks the question rhetorically and then supplies the answer, and we cannot miss the impact it makes: **Certainly not!** (v. 2). My translation (NKJV) is weak here. Some translations are even weaker, supplying simply, "No." My favorite is this one: "Shall we continue in sin that grace may abound? God forbid" (ASV). In other words, we must not even think about it. Paul is not simply expressing a denial of that premise; the force of his language signals apostolic abhorrence. Paul would be appalled if he heard any true Christian say, "If I keep getting grace when I sin, I am just going to keep on sinning that grace may abound." God forbid.

At the time of the Reformation in the sixteenth century, Luther was charged with antinomianism. *Anti* means "against" or "opposed to," and *nomos* is the Greek word for "law." *Antinomian*, therefore, means "being opposed to the law of God" or "against the law of God." The Roman Catholic Church feared that people would take the doctrine of *sola fide*, justification by faith alone, as a license for sin. If justification is by faith alone without any works, the layperson is going to understand it simply to mean that he is saved by grace, by faith alone, so he can live however he wants to live. It was critical to the sixteenth-century Reformers to answer that charge because they had the same concern. They reminded their friends in the Roman Catholic Church that Paul addresses this question in Romans 6.

Luther responded to the charge by explaining that we are justified by faith alone but not by a faith that is alone. Justification by faith alone, as we have seen, is shorthand for justification by Christ alone and by his righteousness, but justification by faith alone was never intended by God as a license for sin.

Every time the gospel is preached, the demon of antinomianism knocks at the door and says that if we are justified by faith, then works do not count, and if works do not count then works do not matter. No work we do will ever contribute to our justification; in that sense, our works do not count. However, that is not the same thing as saying they do not matter, because we are justified *unto* good works. We are not justified by our sanctification, but we are justified *unto* sanctification. The fruit of true faith, the fruit of true justification, will always be conformity to the image of Christ. That is what Paul is beginning to spell out for us.

Rome believes that faith is necessary and indispensable to justification. An orthodox Roman Catholic can say, "Yes, I believe that justification is by faith," but he must choke to death on the word *alone*, because his communion teaches that justification is by faith plus works. The Roman Catholic formula is faith + works = justification. You have to have the works or there is no justification, because the works are part of the ground for that justification. The Reformation view, the biblical view, is justification + works = faith. The works are there, but they are on the other side of the equation. The antinomian formula is justification – works = faith, which is the heresy that Paul abhors here at the beginning of Romans 6.

Carnal Christians?

Earlier in our study of Romans, I made mention of a controversy that broke out in the United States several years ago within dispensational circles that became known as the lordship-salvation controversy. Some classic dispensationalists were saying that if we claim that true justification must result in good works, then we are denying the free grace of the gospel. They were saying a person can receive Jesus as Savior and not as Lord and still be saved.

A division arose between Zane Hodges and Charles Ryrie. Hodges said and taught emphatically that people could be converted to Christ, put their trust in him as their Savior, and never produce a single work of obedience, yet still be saved. He insisted that if we argue for producing the fruit of righteousness, we are mixing work with faith and thereby destroying the gospel. Ryrie was less militant. He said that if we have true faith, eventually we will begin to show some change in our pattern of living. Distinct from Hodges, Ryrie said that if we have true faith, good works are inevitable at some point. That is a less militant form of antinomianism.

The gospel teaches us that if we have true faith in Jesus Christ, works of obedience are not only inevitable but immediate, because a justified person is a changed person. Justification is the fruit of faith, and faith is the fruit of regeneration. We cannot have saving faith unless the Holy Spirit has changed the disposition of our souls. Therefore, only the regenerate have faith. All the regenerate are changed. We cannot have the Holy Spirit changing the disposition of our hearts and bringing us to faith but then leaving us hanging there with no change in our lives.

The doctrine of the carnal Christian went like wildfire through the Christian community. Used to represent this view is an analogy of a chair and a circle. Concerning an unconverted person, self is on the chair or throne and Christ is outside the circle. Concerning the converted person, Christ is now inside the circle but self is still on the throne. For the Spirit-filled person, Christ is on the throne and the self has been removed. The metaphor teaches that we can have Christ in our lives—we can be converted—without having Christ on the throne of our lives.

I am grateful to John MacArthur for his indefatigable labor in correcting that biblical error. We cannot receive Christ as Savior without at the same time bending our knees to his lordship. This does not mean we believe we are perfect, but it does mean that at the moment we believe, we are changed. Our lives are turned around, and the beginning of the process of sanctification has taken place. Justification does not produce the fullness of sanctification, but it initiates it immediately. If we have made a profession of faith but there is absolutely no evidence of change in our hearts and lives, then we need to ask whether that profession of faith was genuine. True faith always and immediately produces change.

Yes, indeed, the battle with sin goes on for our whole lifetime. We do not believe in instantaneous sanctification. Justification is instantaneous. The second we believe, we are fully justified. We will never be any more justified than we are at the moment we believe, but sanctification is a process that begins at our justification and is completed in our glorification in heaven. If we are believers, we are in that process of sanctification.

Luther said that in terms of our justification, we are justified solely on the grounds of the righteousness of Jesus, but when God pronounces us just by imputation he gives us the medicine by the indwelling power of the Holy Spirit through which we are becoming righteous, not only by imputation but by sanctification. The medicine of the indwelling Holy Spirit will effect our full sanctification. What shall we say then? Shall we continue in sin that grace may abound? Certainly not!

Baptized into Christ

How shall we who died to sin live any longer in it? (v. 2). When we come to Christ, when we are born anew, the old man is put to death. Nevertheless the old man keeps kicking and screaming. In a very real sense, we are crucified with Christ, so the new life in Christ is just that—new. "If anyone is in Christ, he is a new creation; old things have passed away; behold, all things have become new" (2 Cor. 5:17).

Paul continues in a metaphorical way: **Do you not know that as many of us as were baptized into Christ Jesus were baptized into His death?** (v. 3). We have lost touch with the riches of the sacraments that God has given to his people. Luther used to say, when the Devil would tempt him, "Get away from me! I'm baptized!" Baptism is not what saves us, but in our baptism God gives us a tangible sign of his promise of redemption. All the processes that are wrought through the redeeming work of Christ are contained in that sign. Baptism is a sign of our being regenerated by the Holy Spirit. It does not effect regeneration, but it is a sign of it. It is the sign of God's promise that all who believe will, in fact, be justified. It is a sign of our sanctification. It is the sign of our being indwelt by the Holy Spirit. It is a sign of our glorification. It is a sign of our identification with Christ. We are in Christ and he is our champion.

I differ from my Baptist friends on whether babies should be baptized. Of all the doctrines we wrestle with in the church, there is none I am more certain of than that we ought to baptize our babies. The one thing I concede to my Baptist friends is the existential benefit of waiting for baptism until a later point at which one is aware of his faith and of being immersed. There is powerful symbolism in going under the water and being brought up out of it.

Even Calvin, a great advocate of infant baptism, said that where possible the preferred—although not required—method of baptism is immersion, because it carries so brilliantly that symbol of burial and resurrection. Paul says that if we are believers, if we have received the grace of justification, baptism is a reminder of our union in the death and burial of Christ. We are not only baptized into his death and burial, but also we are baptized into his resurrection. All these things are part of what is being communicated graphically with the sign of baptism.

We baptize babies and see them fuss or giggle sometimes, but it is a precious thing. One of the people I want to meet when I get to heaven is the minister who baptized me in the Methodist church. He was a beloved pastor to my family when I was a small boy, and I long to have the opportunity to sit down and tell him that during the first seventeen years of my life I looked like a child of hell, but then God quickened my soul. All the promises that were communicated to me in baptism were realized the moment I believed and understood my burial and resurrection in Christ.

A motif throughout the Pauline literature is people's being ashamed of Jesus. People do not want to be counted as Christians. Paul says that if we are not willing to identify with Jesus' humiliation, with his death and burial, then we cannot expect to participate in his exaltation. Jesus himself said, "For whoever is ashamed of Me and My words in this adulterous and sinful generation, of him the Son of Man also will be ashamed when He comes in the glory of His Father with the holy angels" (Mark 8:38).

In a very real sense we have already died and been buried, and we are already participating in the resurrection of Christ. **Do you not know that as many of us as were baptized into Christ Jesus were baptized into His death? Therefore we were buried with Him through baptism into death, that just as Christ was raised from the dead by the glory of the Father, even so we also should walk in newness of life** (vv. 3–4). We are resurrected people. We already have the down payment of eternal life in our souls by having been given the sealing of the Holy Spirit. How can someone in Christ Jesus, someone who participates in the power of his resurrection, continue in sin that grace may abound? It is not possible.

20

DEAD TO SIN

Romans 6:4–11

Therefore we were buried with Him through baptism into death, that just as Christ was raised from the dead by the glory of the Father, even so we also should walk in newness of life. For if we have been united together in the likeness of His death, certainly we also shall be in the likeness of His resurrection, knowing this, that our old man was crucified with Him, that the body of sin might be done away with, that we should no longer be slaves of sin. For he who has died has been freed from sin. Now if we died with Christ, we believe that we shall also live with Him, knowing that Christ, having been raised from the dead, dies no more. Death no longer has dominion over Him. For *the death* that He died, He died to sin once for all; but the life that He lives, He lives to God. Likewise you also, reckon yourselves to be dead indeed to sin, but alive to God in Christ Jesus our Lord.

No matter how many times I have lectured on Romans, every time I get to this section of chapter 6 I really want to race to the end of it so that I can turn my attention to the next chapter. Romans 6 is difficult because of the language Paul uses. It is hard to discern whether he is speaking physically or mystically. Because of this difficulty, I sometimes find myself changing views in the middle of my study. One of the advantages of doing expository preaching is that we have to deal with what comes next, and since this is what comes next, we cannot detour around it.

Chapter 6 begins, as we have seen, with a rhetorical question: "Shall we continue in sin that grace may abound?" Paul answered not only with denial but with abhorrence, saying, "God forbid." Paul's great concern is that those who have been justified have been justified *unto* holiness. We have not been justified *by* our holiness or *through* our holiness but *unto* it so that we might grow in conformity to the image of Christ.

Newness of Life

To make sense of what Paul is teaching here, it is important to look again at how strongly he articulates the idea of our mystical union with Christ. By the Holy Spirit every person who believes in Christ is joined to Christ spiritually. If we are believers, we are in Christ and Christ is in us. The invisible church is made up of all who are in Christ Jesus, all who participate in this mystical union with him. In this text Paul takes the idea of our mystical union further. He tells us that not only are our sins imputed to Christ in his death on the cross, the benefits of his resurrection transferred to us, and the benefits of his righteousness imputed to us by legal transaction, but also there is a real spiritual union with our Savior. In a spiritual sense we died with him on Calvary. When he went to the cross, he went not for himself but for his sheep. He did a work that we could not possibly do for ourselves. It was our sin that he was carrying in his death, so when he died, he did not simply die for us; we, by virtue of this spiritual union, died with him.

Therefore we were buried with Him through baptism into death, that just as Christ was raised from the dead by the glory of the Father, even so we also should walk in newness of life (v. 4). In a very real sense, we who are in Christ share in the power of his resurrection not merely after we die and go to heaven but right now, because everyone who believes savingly in Jesus Christ has been raised already from spiritual death.

When we considered in an earlier study our condition of original sin, we used the biblical metaphors of death and slavery. By nature we are born into this world DOA, dead on arrival, spiritually although alive biologically. We have no inclination whatsoever in our souls toward the things of God—no interest, no passion, no love. We are dead. Because we are spiritually dead, we are slaves to the sinful impulses and lusts that drive our behavior. We are not just participants in sin; such a description is far too weak. The Bible teaches us again and again that we are slaves to sin. Sin is not only in our nature, but it is our master.

The great Augustine on occasion used the metaphor of Satan riding a horse. Prior to conversion we, the horse, have one rider—Satan. He has the bit in our teeth. He is in control of the reins. When he turns our head in a certain direction, that is the direction we go. When he says "Whoa," we stop, and when he says, "Giddyup," we go, because he is our master, and we are his slave. Augustine went on to say that once we are converted by the power of the Holy Spirit, it is not as if Satan is sent back to the stables so that the only one riding us now is Jesus. Satan gives up the reins reluctantly. He will do everything he can to get that bit back in our mouth and to recover us as a slave. He hates to lose a slave. We have to fight against the enticements of Satan throughout our whole Christian life because he is furious that we have left his design, but something radically new has happened—we have gone through a spiritual resurrection. What does the Bible say? "If anyone is in Christ, he is a new creation; old things have passed away; behold, all things have become new" (2 Cor. 5:17). The Spirit of God has raised our souls from the dead.

Paul elaborates on this idea in his letter to the Ephesians, particularly in chapter 2: "You He made alive, who were dead in trespasses and sins, in which you once walked according to the course of this world, according to the prince of the power of the air, the spirit who now works in the sons of disobedience, among whom also we all once conducted ourselves in the lusts of our flesh" (Eph. 2:1–3). That is Paul's description of spiritual death and slavery. He is referring to regeneration, and the idea of regeneration lies beneath everything Paul is teaching here in Romans 6. The justified are people who have been changed, and they have been changed supernaturally.

Luther, in extolling the wonders of spiritual rebirth or regeneration, said that regeneration is the greatest miracle of all. I quibble with the Reformer there. I do not think regeneration is a miracle, because regeneration is invisible. A tight definition of *miracle* in the biblical sense is "something that happens in the external, perceivable world that only God can bring to pass, such as bringing life out of death or something out of nothing." Regeneration is hidden. It takes place in the soul of a human being so that we cannot see it. However, regeneration is every bit as supernatural as any outward miracle, and that is what Luther was getting at. Regeneration is not something we can do for ourselves.

We had no influence in our physical birth or conception. When it comes to spiritual rebirth we have even less influence. We might have kicked in our mother's womb so that we hurried up the day of our birth, but we cannot even do that much in terms of our spiritual rebirth. Only God has the power to raise a human soul from spiritual death to spiritual life, so we define *regeneration* as "that supernatural work of God the Holy Spirit that happens supernaturally and immediately in the soul of a human being." By "immediately" we mean without the use of any means, without intermediary devices. The Spirit works directly, and he works monergistically, which is to say he is the only one operating in this endeavor. Regeneration is not a joint venture between us and God. The flesh, which is all we are before conversion, can do nothing.

Jesus had a conversation one night with a man named Nicodemus. Nicodemus came with his flattering comments: "Rabbi, we know that You are a teacher come from God; for no one can do these signs that You do unless God is with him" (John 3:2). He showed sound thinking up to that point. Then Jesus stopped him short and said to this teacher of Israel, "Most assuredly, I say to you, unless one is born again, he cannot see the kingdom of God. . . . Unless one is born of water and the Spirit, he cannot enter the kingdom of God" (vv. 3, 5). He cannot see it. He cannot enter it. Jesus said, "That which is born of the flesh is flesh" (v. 6). The flesh cannot produce the spirit. As Jesus later said, "The flesh profits nothing" (John 6:63). Luther had to remind Erasmus in their debate that "*nothing* is not a little something."

We are born 100 percent flesh, and the flesh is at enmity with God. The flesh is spiritually dead. The flesh is enslaved. Unless God the Holy Spirit changes our flesh and gives us spirit, we will stay flesh forever. Of course that baffled Nicodemus, so he asked, "How can a man be born when he is old? Can he enter a second time into his mother's womb and be born? . . . How can these things be?" (John 3:4, 9). Jesus said to him, "Are you the teacher of Israel, and do not know these things?" (v. 10). For Nicodemus this should have been Theology 101. He should have known ages ago of his helpless condition in the flesh apart from the supernatural intervention of God.

You cannot cause yourself to be born again. A book was written called *How to Be Born Again*.[1] This how-to manual was a waste of words, because there is nothing we can do to be born again. God does it all, not 99 percent but 100 percent. Only God can raise somebody from the dead, both physically and spiritually, so here in Romans 6 Paul is saying that we have been raised from the dead. We have a new genesis. *Gennaō* means "to be," "to become," or "to happen," and *regeneration* refers to a new or a second of the original genesis. We had a genesis when we were born; then we have a new genesis,

1. (Billy Graham, *How to Be Born Again* (Nashville, TN: Nelson, 1989).

a rebirth, only this time it is a spiritual birth wrought by the supernatural work of God the Holy Spirit.

Think of the blessings that we have received in our lifetimes. Think of how many times we have grumbled about what we did not get. Think of how many times we have lacked contentment and been dissatisfied with the hand God has dealt us, and then look around the world and see the vast multitudes who have no idea what it means to be born of the Spirit. If we are living in a hovel or are living through constant chronic pain and illness but have received the supernatural work of regeneration in our souls, we have no reason to do anything but praise God for the rest of eternity because we have received the pearl of great price. We have been raised from the dead already. We are already going to live into eternity because the sting of death has been removed. Death cannot destroy what God has regenerated.

We have newness of life. Our lives have been changed. That is why I spend time explaining the pernicious doctrine of the lordship-salvation controversy, that people can have Jesus as Savior and not as Lord. How can somebody dead be made alive yet not be different? How can somebody in slavery be released from bondage yet not be changed? The biggest change we will ever go through in life takes place when we are reborn. We have changed from spiritual death to spiritual life, from bondage to freedom. "Where the Spirit of the Lord is, there is liberty" (2 Cor. 3:17).

Paul is asking us to consider what has happened. We died with Christ; we were raised in the power of his resurrection. In a sense there is a strange combination of the imperative and the indicative. Since this is the way we are, then we must behave that way. We must live as people who have a new life, because if we are regenerate we do have new lives, and if we are justified, we are new creations. Now that God has rescued us from death, he expects us to live for him the rest of our days.

The Old Man

For if we have been united together in the likeness of His death, certainly we also shall be in the likeness of His resurrection, knowing this, that our old man was crucified with Him (vv. 5–6). By "old man," Paul is talking about the former human nature, the nature that we brought into this world where our humanity was dead in sin. That person, the old person with a singular disposition toward sin whose heart was a heart of stone, is the one who was crucified with Christ. Christ did not just die for our sins; he died for our sinfulness. He did not just die for our sin legally, bearing our guilt; he died to kill our original sin, our moral inability. Our dead, corrupt, fallen nature was crucified with Christ on the cross. My old man received the curse of God on Calvary.

I put question marks in my Bible, and I have one after these words: "knowing this, that our old man was crucified with Him, that the body of sin might be done away with." By saying "body of sin," Paul is describing our physical body. He uses the Greek word *sōma*, which is not the usual term used to describe our corrupt nature, our flesh, which, as I have already indicated, is *sarx*. Here he is talking about our physical body, the body of sin.

Let me tell you what Paul does not mean. Paul does not equate sin with physicality. We have a tendency to cling to our Greek roots. We tend to think of sins simply in terms of physical appetites and acts of disobedience that immediately involve our body—gluttony, sex, drunkenness. We have a mind of flesh. Sin is something in our thoughts. Sin is something deeply rooted in our souls. Some try to bifurcate the human person and say the physical part is sinful and the spiritual part is good, the way Plato did, but that is not the way. Paul may be using the expression "body of sin" similarly to the way we talk about a body of literature comprised of several volumes. The mass of sin that describes our fallen condition, what Augustine called a mass of perdition, is crucified with Christ and done away with. Later in Romans 7 Paul cries out, "O wretched man that I am! Who will deliver me from this body of death?" (v. 24); here in chapter 6 he uses a similar expression, "body of sin."

I have been told that one of the penalties for murder in some sectors of the ancient world was to tie the murdered, decaying corpse onto the murderer who had to drag it everywhere on his person while it was rotting. Can you imagine anything more ghastly than being tied to a dead body? Some think this is what Paul is speaking of here when he refers to the body of sin. The sin nature we brought into this world is like a putrid, decaying, corrupted corpse, a body of death that we still have to carry around with us until we go to heaven. Even though we have been reborn, even though we have been let out of prison and set free from slavery, we still sin and fall. However, that does not mean we are unchanged. We are changed, and the old man is dying daily. He dies the death by inches, but each day that we live in the grace of God, the new man, which has been raised with Christ, is being strengthened and is growing, and the old man is dying more and more. In a very spiritual way, it died already on the cross, but at the same time it is still kicking and screaming, and we have to deal with it to our life's end.

I am still not sure what Paul means by the "body of sin." It is likely that he is just talking about the mass of sin we have to deal with; however, his intent is clear: **that we should no longer be slaves of sin** (v. 6). It is one thing to be a sinner; it is another to be a slave of sin. We all sin, but if we have been born of the Spirit, we are no longer slaves to that sin. We can no longer say to God, "I cannot help it. I am dominated by the power of sin." If we are still in a condition of slavery to sin, then we are not regenerate. Of course, we have besetting sins, those that cause us to fail over and over again, but we are called to resist those sins. The greatest Christians fight against such all of their spiritual lives, yet in the final analysis we have been set free, and we now have the power of God at our disposal so that we can have victory over every sin.

I believe it is possible for a Christian after conversion to live a perfect life, but let me qualify that. I think it is hypothetically possible that we can live the rest of our days without sin, but it is virtually certain that we will continue to struggle with sin. There is so much weakness left in us, and we are bombarded with so many opportunities for sin. However, the God who raised us from spiritual death has given us the grace to resist. No longer do we sin under compulsion as slaves. We have been set free, but our liberty is extremely weak. We are not accustomed to the power of the resurrection. Our comfort zone is still back in the graveyard of spiritual death even though we really have been set free by the power of the Holy Spirit.

Reckoned Dead

Corpses in the cemetery are not struggling with temptation. The battle is over. Saints in heaven are not exposed to sin. Once we die, the battle is over. That's why Paul says, **For he who has died has been freed from sin. Now if we died with Christ, we believe that we shall also live with Him, knowing that Christ, having been raised from the dead, dies no more** (vv. 7–9). Jesus died once, and he would not have died even that once had he not been willing to receive in his own person the imputation of our sin. Death had no claim over him because he was sinless, but he died one time, "once for all." The work of Christ was finished on the cross.

Death no longer has dominion over Him (v. 9). Death did not have dominion over Christ for very long. He was vulnerable to death only because of the imputation of sin, but after he paid the price for our sin, death became powerless. The dominion of death was gone. People say that the resurrection of Christ is impossible because they determine possibilities on the basis of probabilities based on what they observe. We have never seen anybody come out of the grave. People die and stay dead, so people come to the conclusion that the resurrection could not have happened, but that is not the way the

Bible looks at it. The Bible says that death could not maintain dominion over Christ. For God, raising his Son from the dead was easy.

Christ's resurrection from the dead is no greater in power and scope than was our conception as a human soul in the womb of our mother. Both occurred by the power of God and only by the power of God. **For the death that He died, He died to sin once for all; but the life that He lives, He lives to God** (v. 10). The life he lived and the life he gives are not like vapor that passes away. The Christ who is alive lives forever. Death is no longer a threat to him. **Likewise you also, reckon yourselves to be dead indeed to sin, but alive to God in Christ Jesus our Lord** (v. 11). Here Paul is making application of our union with Christ and his death and resurrection. Just as our Savior defeated death and sin, not just for himself but for us, we are to reckon ourselves dead to sin but alive to God.

In old Western movies we hear, "You think it is going to rain today, partner?" and "I reckon" is a common reply. It means "I think so." It has to do with thinking or judging or esteeming. Paul is saying to think of ourselves as being dead to sin. We are to reckon to ourselves the life that is ours in the power of the gospel and in the Spirit of God. We have been made alive by Christ and for Christ and unto Christ. Our life belongs to him. We are to consider the old man dead, as ancient history. It is a bit like D-Day—the war was over but nobody knew it. There was still the Battle of the Bulge to come. We have been made alive in Christ Jesus, and we need to think of ourselves in those terms.

21

SLAVES OF RIGHTEOUSNESS

Romans 6:12–23

Therefore do not let sin reign in your mortal body, that you should obey it in its lusts. And do not present your members as instruments of unrighteousness to sin, but present yourselves to God as being alive from the dead, and your members as instruments of righteousness to God. For sin shall not have dominion over you, for you are not under law but under grace. What then? Shall we sin because we are not under law but under grace? Certainly not! Do you not know that to whom you present yourselves slaves to obey, you are that one's slaves whom you obey, whether of sin leading to death, or of obedience leading to righteousness? But God be thanked that though you were slaves of sin, yet you obeyed from the heart that form of doctrine to which you were delivered. And having been set free from sin, you became slaves of righteousness. I speak in human terms because of the weakness of your flesh. For just as you presented your members as slaves of uncleanness, and of lawlessness leading to more lawlessness, so now present your members as slaves of righteousness for holiness. For when you were slaves of sin, you were free in regard to righteousness. What fruit did you have then in the things of which you are now ashamed? For the end of those things is death. But now having been set free from sin, and having become slaves of God, you have your fruit to holiness, and the end, everlasting life. For the wages of sin is death, but the gift of God is eternal life in Christ Jesus our Lord.

We have looked at the fact that we ought to consider ourselves dead to sin because we have been crucified with Christ, and in the passage before us now, Paul brings that to a conclusion: **Therefore do not let sin reign in your mortal body, that you should obey it in its lusts** (v. 12). We reckon ourselves dead with Christ in his crucifixion and do not allow ourselves to be under the dominion of sin. The conclusion is that we are called to guard against allowing sin to rule over us.

Slavery and Bondage

Paul has set forth more than once in the epistle our natural condition of original sin. By way of review, original sin is described by two basic metaphors in the New Testament. One is the metaphor of death. By nature we are spiritually dead in our sins. In our natural condition, we have no life with respect to the things of God, no vitality whatsoever. The second metaphor is the one Paul is developing here in Romans 6, the metaphor of slavery and bondage. We are by nature in bondage to sin.

We have to be very careful when we read the New Testament to try to read it with virgin ears. We do not want to bring to the text all the baggage from the secular culture around us. One of the most destructive ideas we tend to bring is the pagan notion of free will, which holds that every time we have a moral option before us, we have the power to say yes or no; the will is basically in a state of indifference. That idea is as American as apple pie and Chevrolet and baseball, and it is as heretical as can be. It is not just unbiblical; it is anti-biblical. The notion of freedom cannot be found anywhere in sacred Scripture.

We are free in the sense that we have a will and the power of volition; by nature we have the capacity to make choices according to our desires. The problem is that the desires of our hearts by nature are only wicked continually. By nature we have no inclination toward the things of God. Therefore, as Augustine argued against Pelagius, we are in a state of moral inability. We have no ability to do the things of God.

This was the essence of Luther's most important work. He responded to the diatribe of Erasmus of Rotterdam with a book entitled *De Servo Arbitrio*, or *The Bondage of the Will*. It is a Christian classic, and I urge everyone to read it. After that you can read Jonathan Edwards's *Freedom of the Will*.

We must not think that we have the moral power to incline ourselves to the things of God. Jesus made it clear to Nicodemus that unless a man is born again he cannot even see the kingdom of God, let alone take steps to enter it (John 3). Prior to our rebirth by the work of the Holy Spirit, we are in prison through our sinful impulses. The Bible is not the only place we learn that. We can know it just by looking at the world around us as well as our own hearts.

Made Alive

And do not present your members as instruments of unrighteousness to sin, but present yourselves to God as being alive from the dead, and your members as instruments of righteousness to God (v. 13). We have been made alive. Paul is addressing believers, those no longer in their original state of sin but raised from the dead and set free from bondage and slavery. That is our condition now. When we sin now, even though the freedom we have from sin and bondage is real and the power of the Holy Spirit is there, we still struggle. We will experience this conflict until the day we die. In fact, Paul speaks in other places about the intense warfare that continues between the old man, which was completely flesh, and the new man, which now has the power of the Holy Spirit indwelling him and enabling him to move toward the things of God. As Christians we still sin, but we do not have to. Every time we are presented with a temptation, God gives us a way out. He promises us the present power of the Holy Spirit if we will simply cooperate.

The work of the Christian life is synergistic, not monergistic. Our regeneration, our rebirth, was the work of one Person, God. It was not a joint venture; but from the moment we take our first breath of regenerated spiritual life, it becomes a joint effort. That is why the apostle elsewhere says, "Work out your own salvation with fear and trembling; for it is God who works in you both to will and to do for His good pleasure" (Phil. 2:12b–13). God is working, and we have to work.

Paul is speaking here to free people, to those whom God has regenerated, but still we are tempted and have weaknesses. We bring a lot of baggage into the Christian life, sinful patterns of behavior, and they do not disappear overnight. What disappears is the bondage. Now we have the responsibility to cooperate with the grace that God makes available to us. We are to make diligent use of the means of grace and make sure our souls are being fed regularly by the Word of God. We have responsibility to be on our faces before God earnestly on a regular basis and never to miss the corporate worship of the people of God unless we are absolutely indisposed.

All these means of grace God has given us to help us in our pilgrimage. We are to feed the new man and starve the old man. If, as a Christian, sin is reigning in our mortal body, it is because we let it reign. We do not have to let it reign. We can no longer use the excuse that the Devil made us do it unless, indeed, we are unregenerate. Even then, it is no excuse. "Therefore do not let sin reign in your mortal body, that you should obey it in its lusts." We are not to obey sin anymore. Paul personifies sin as if it has an individual existence, as if it were a tyrant that would try to enslave us again. We are not to let that happen.

Set Free for Righteousness

Paul is not referring simply to sexual sin in verse 13. He is referring to every aspect of our human life. We are not to let our minds be instruments of sin. We are not to let our legs be instruments of sin; we must not be swift to shed blood. We are not to let our lips be instruments of sin; we must guard our tongues. We must not allow ourselves to be enslaved once again to sinful patterns. Instead, Paul says, we are to offer ourselves to God. We are to present ourselves to God as resurrected people. Our minds, mouths, ears, eyes, and feet are to be used as tools in our toolkit for offering our whole person to God.

Later in the epistle Paul will say, "I beseech you therefore, brethren, by the mercies of God, that you present your bodies a living sacrifice . . . which is your reasonable service" (Rom. 12:1). Instruments, or tools, are means by which certain works are accomplished. The sculptor has a chisel by which he creates a statue. The painter has his brushes and the paint, and the brushes are the instruments he uses to create the painting. The pool player has the cue stick. The baseball player has a bat. All these tools or instruments are used to bring about a desired effect. We can use such tools for good or for evil. We can use our minds for sin or for righteousness. We can use our speech to blaspheme or to praise. We can use our legs to walk in sin or to walk in righteousness.

Paul says the whole person has been raised from spiritual death and is called to a new kind of slavery. He continues this metaphor of slavery when he calls us to be slaves of righteousness—not servants of Satan, but servants of Christ. That is the difference between the old life and the new life, **for sin shall not have dominion over you, for you are not under law but under grace** (v. 14). That is a promise. The phrase is written in the indicative, not the imperative. Earlier it was written in the imperative: "Do not let sin reign" (v. 12). Now Paul is writing in the indicative. He is describing our state of affairs now. Sin's dominion is gone. It is history. We cannot be brought back again into absolute bondage to sin as we once were.

Under Grace

I said earlier that one of the hardest things to understand about Paul is how he uses references to the law. He does not always refer to the law in the same way, which has vexed the best minds of Christendom for two thousand years. When Paul says, "You are not under law," some people take this as a license to sin, as if we are no longer under any obligation to keep the law of God. They believe we passed from law to grace; the law was Moses but grace is Jesus, so we are free from the law. I do not think that is what Paul means here, nor do I think Paul is referring simply to the Law of Moses. Earlier, in Romans 5, he pointed out that the law was in the world even before Sinai. God reveals his law in nature and in the conscience of human beings. We cannot just restrict law to the laws of Moses. From the beginning of our sinfulness we have been under the dreadful burden of the law, because the law condemns us. The law reveals our disobedience, and the law cannot possibly be the means by which we will be saved because, as debtors to the law, we can never pay our debt.

I think he means that we are no longer under the law in the sense of being underneath the awesome, weighty burden of the law. Paul says we are no longer in the condition of being crushed under the weight of the law, no longer oppressed by its burden of guilt and judgment. We are now under grace. "For by grace you have been saved through faith, and that not of your-selves; it is the gift of God" (Eph. 2:8)—a truth of which Paul was continually reminding Christians. Now that we have been freed from the burden of the law, are we going to go back? Now that we know we have been justified by faith alone, are we going to try to return to justifying ourselves through our works? No. We move from grace to grace, from faith to faith. Grace does not end at our justification; grace is ever present in the process and progress. We are as much sanctified by grace as we are justified by grace.

I recall a moment that took place in my life years ago. I was walking down the hall of the lecture house at the Ligonier study center in Western Pennsylvania, and I had one of those sudden moments of self-awareness. An idea came into my head: *R.C., what if you are not really saved? What if your destiny is hell?* Instantly a chill went from the top of my head all the way down my spine to my feet, and I was frozen in that spot in absolute terror. I realized that I can fool myself. I can pass an exam in theology and think that I am in a state of grace when perhaps I am really not. It is in moments like this that Satan comes to us and says, "If you are a Christian, then why do you keep failing?" I felt more and more shame and uncertainty, so I ran to my study and picked up my Bible, and I was reading the gospel again with all my might. I got on my face before God and said, "Lord, I have nothing else to hold on to but the gospel. I have nothing to bring to you except Christ and his righteousness." The only way we can have any assurance of salvation is by looking at grace, not at our performance or achievements.

That is why we have to get justification by faith in our bloodstream every minute of every day. We must continually return to the ground of our justification, which is Christ's righteousness alone. It is grace. It is *sola gratia*, by grace alone. The law slays us. It is a mirror of our sin, so it drives us to the cross. That is what Paul is talking about here. We are not under law; we are under grace.

Then Paul comes at us with another rhetorical question: **What then? Shall we sin because we are not under law but under grace? Certainly not! Do you not know that to whom you present yourselves slaves to obey, you are that one's slaves whom you obey?** (v.v 15–16). To fully grasp Paul's meaning we have to understand something about indentured servitude. When we think of slaves, we tend to think of the slave trade in the West in more recent centuries—man stealing. We think of slavery as kidnapping young people from Africa, bringing them across the ocean to the auction block, and selling them to other men. In the ancient world slavery was primarily voluntary servitude. When someone had a debt he could not pay, he would offer his services to fulfill the debt. That is the context in which Paul asks, "Do you not know that to whom you present yourselves slaves to obey, you are that one's slaves whom you obey?" He is saying that if we present ourselves again to sin as slaves to sin, it will lead to death. If we obey sin as a slave, the only outcome is death, but if we present ourselves as slaves of obedience, the end is righteousness.

Slaves of Righteousness
But God be thanked that though you were slaves of sin, yet you obeyed from the heart that form of doctrine to which you were delivered. And having been set free from sin, you became slaves of righteousness (vv. 17–18). Paul uses a word here that has almost disappeared from Christian vocabulary—*righteousness*. If I give a seminar on spiritual growth, people will flock to it. If I give them five keys to spirituality, they will sign up. If I give a seminar on how to become righteous, no one will come because it is no longer the goal of the Christian. Today's Christian wants to be spiritual or pious or moral, but not righteous. Righteousness is so closely linked to the idea of self-righteousness that we want to distance ourselves as far as we can from the very idea.

We know we cannot be saved by our righteousness, so we do not think that righteousness has any part in our quest for sanctification. Never mind that Jesus said, "Seek first the kingdom of God and His righteousness, and all these things shall be added to you" (Matt. 6:33). The primary business of the Christian life is the quest for righteousness. Jesus also said, "Unless your righteousness exceeds the righteousness of the scribes and Pharisees, you will by no means enter the kingdom of heaven" (Matt. 5:20). Jesus might simply have been saying that the only righteousness that will get someone into the kingdom of God is a righteousness greater than that of the Pharisees, namely his own. Jesus might have been giving a cryptic, thinly veiled lesson on justification by faith alone, but I do not think so. I think he really meant what he said—that unless our righteousness exceeds the righteousness of the Pharisees we will never make it. We are not going to make it on the basis of our righteousness, but only on the basis of faith. If the faith is genuine, the fruit of that faith will be real righteousness.

We might not think that exceeding the Pharisees is that difficult. After all, they were the worst criminals of all time. They were the ones who killed Jesus. They were the hypocrites, the ones who provoked Jesus' wrath. "Woe to you, scribes and Pharisees, hypocrites," Jesus said (Matt. 23:13; Luke 11:44). Oh, he did come down hard on them. The Pharisees were tired of the secularism of the Jews. They were the conservatives. They were the "evangelicals" and wanted to restore covenant purity to Israel. So they called themselves the "set apart ones," set apart for the singular pursuit of righteousness.

Although Jesus roundly and soundly condemned them, he threw them a bone from time to time: "You tithe mint and rue and all manner of herbs, and pass by justice and the love of God. These you ought to have done, without leaving the others undone" (Luke 11:42). They did not care about justice or mercy, but at least they tithed. The polls show that 4 percent of professing evangelical Christians tithe their goods and services to the Lord; the other 96 percent systematically, routinely, day after day rob God of what he calls us to give him for the building of his kingdom. That is a very serious matter. At least the Pharisees were tithers.

Jesus said to Pharisees, "You search the Scriptures, for in them you think you have eternal life; and these are they which testify of Me. But you are not willing to come to Me that you may have life" (John 5:39–40). They did search the Scriptures, but they did not have life. The majority of those who have been Christians for at least ten years have never read the whole Bible, so the Pharisees beat us there. Their prayers were motivated by pomp and outward displays of piety when they prayed in the marketplace, but at least they prayed.

Jesus said to them, "Woe to you, scribes and Pharisees, hypocrites! For you travel land and sea to win one proselyte, and when he is won, you make him twice as much a son of hell as yourselves" (Matt. 23:15). Calling them "children of hell" was not complimentary, but they were committed to evangelism and missions. They went over land and sea for one convert. It was hard to travel in those days. When I am asked to travel somewhere to speak, I have a speaking committee to make those decisions for me; they are not going to send me over land and sea to make one convert. The scribes and Pharisees beat us like drums on many points. Jesus says unless our righteousness exceeds that, we will never enter into the kingdom of God.

I speak in human terms because of the weakness of your flesh. For just as you presented your members as slaves of uncleanness, and of lawlessness leading to more lawlessness, so now present your members as slaves of righteousness for holiness. For when you were slaves of sin, you were free in regard to righteousness (vv. 19–20). We did not have any righteousness. When we were under slavery to the dominion of sin, we were completely free from righteousness. **What fruit did you have then in the things of which you are now ashamed? For the end of those things is death. But now having been set free from sin, and having become slaves of God, you have your fruit to holiness, and the end, everlasting life** (vv. 21–22). Freedom from sin means freedom for righteousness, freedom for eternal life.

The Gift of God

Paul closes this section with a well-known passage: **For the wages of sin is death, but the gift of God is eternal life in Christ Jesus our Lord** (v. 23). The wages of sin—what does sin earn? What is its basic wage? The more we sin, the more we earn, and what we earn is death. There is always a payoff. Remember what God said: "'Vengeance is Mine, I will repay,' says the Lord" (Rom. 12:19). If we are slaves to sin, we earn demerits; we earn wrath. If God did not pay what we earn, he would be unjust. "The wages of sin is death."

In stark contrast to that is the good news, the gift of God. Wages are something we earn; a gift is something we cannot possibly earn. Wages are something we merit; the gift, on the other hand, is free. It is gratuitous. The wages of sin is death; the gift of God is eternal life in Christ Jesus our Lord. All the way through this section Paul has been dealing with contrasts:

slavery to sin versus slavery to righteousness; wages of death versus the gift of eternal life. We now have experienced grace.

G. C. Berkouwer once said, "The essence of Christian theology is grace, and the essence of Christian ethics is gratitude." What draws us to obedience and righteousness is not duty but love. It is gratitude. Once we have received this grace of eternal life in Jesus Christ, we should be willing to crawl over broken glass to honor and praise him for that grace.

22

DELIVERED

Romans 7:1–6

Or do you not know, brethren (for I speak to those who know the law), that the law has dominion over a man as long as he lives? For the woman who has a husband is bound by the law to her husband as long as he lives. But if the husband dies, she is released from the law of her husband. So then if, while her husband lives, she marries another man, she will be called an adulteress; but if her husband dies, she is free from that law, so that she is no adulteress, though she has married another man. Therefore, my brethren, you also have become dead to the law through the body of Christ, that you may be married to another—to Him who was raised from the dead, that we should bear fruit to God. For when we were in the flesh, the sinful passions which were aroused by the law were at work in our members to bear fruit to death. But now we have been delivered from the law, having died to what we were held by, so that we should serve in the newness of the Spirit and not in the oldness of the letter.

We have come to Romans 7, which means we are sailing into uncharted waters. Before we look at the beginning of chapter 7, we do well to recall that when Paul wrote this epistle he did not divide it into chapters or verses. Such divisions are advantageous, however, because they facilitate our study. The disadvantage is the tendency they create to look at each chapter as a self-standing unit and to forget its interconnectedness to what has gone before and what comes after. There is no great break in subject matter between the end of Romans 6 and the beginning of Romans 7, just as everything we looked at in Romans 6 was an extension of what Paul had written before it on the gospel and its consequences.

Married to Another

Paul continues the application of our having been crucified with Christ: **Or do you not know, brethren (for I speak to those who know the law), that the law has dominion over a man as long as he lives? For the woman who has a husband is bound by the law to her husband as long as he lives** (vv. 1–2). Here Paul gives an extended analogy from marriage. It is very simple: we get married; we take our vows. We promise to honor and cherish each other as long as we both shall live. We understand that if one partner in the marriage covenant should die, then all the obligations incumbent upon the one remaining are now set aside, and the widow or widower is completely free in the eyes of God to be married again. The law that binds us and regulates our marriage is in effect only as long as our partner remains alive.

    Therefore, my brethren, you also have become dead to the law through the body of Christ, that you may be married to another (v. 4). There is a shift here: our spouse has not died, but we have died. Paul does not say that the law has died. We have died and therefore our marriage to the law is over. The law no longer has dominion over us the way it did before we died. We died in Christ, and in Christ the law was fulfilled.

    Is Paul talking about the ceremonial law or is he talking about the Law of Moses given at Sinai? Or is he talking about law in an even broader sense? I am persuaded that he is talking about the whole of God's moral law, not just that given by Moses or that found in the ceremonies of the Old Testament. Paul goes all the way back to creation. In Romans 5 Paul labored the point that death reigned from Adam to Moses to prove that apart from the law there is no sin, and apart from sin there is no death.

    Since death entered into the world with Adam and Eve, and people after Adam and Eve all died before the Law of Moses was given, sin was in the world before the law. The only way sin could be in the world before the Law of Moses is if another law preceded the Law of Moses, namely, the moral law of God, which he reveals in nature and in our conscience. Therefore, from the very beginning the law of God has had dominion over us. Since the fall the consequences of God's law have issued in our death. The law of

God has exposed us to the judgment and condemnation of the holiness of God. Since the fall, we have been under the relentless burden of the law that weighs us down and exposed moment by moment to the full curse of that law. The law has not been removed but in Christ we have died, and Christ has taken the full weight of the curse of the law upon himself so that we no longer carry that burden on our backs.

The Covenant of Works

The original covenant that God made with man is sometimes called "the creation covenant." In it Adam and Eve were on probation. They were made good, in the image of God, and God set before them a test and told them that they were not to eat the fruit of the tree. If they did, they would die. If they were obedient, theirs was the tree of life. We know how things fell apart. The original relationship all human beings had with God is what Reformed theologians call the "covenant of works." Of course, the very fact that God entered into any kind of a covenant with his creatures is pure grace. The gracious covenant he entered into with Adam and Eve is called a "covenant of works" because the terms and conditions for blessedness are related to obedience.

We saw earlier the stark contrast between the first Adam—the calamitous response to the whole race because of his disobedience (see Rom. 5:18)—and the Second Adam, the Lord Jesus Christ, who, like the first Adam, was put to the test and subjected to a probation. He was exposed to the complete, unbridled assault of Satan in the wilderness for forty days, and yet he resisted to the end, saying that his meat and drink was to do the will of the Father (John 4:34) and that he lived by every word that proceeds from the mouth of God (Matt. 4:4; Luke 4:4).

His perfection endured not simply for forty days in the wilderness; it endured from the day he was born until the moment he expired on the cross. At no time in that interim did Christ violate the law of God. His perfect act of obedience is as much the grounds of our salvation as is his punishment on the cross as he satisfied the wrath of God for our guilt. He died for our sin; he lived for our righteousness. As the new Adam, Jesus kept the covenant of works. He did what no other human being has ever accomplished. He remained absolutely faithful and obedient to every law of God from the beginning.

The Covenant of Grace

The "covenant of grace" refers to the promise God gave immediately after the fall of Adam and Eve. He did not annihilate the human race but promised redemption that would come through the seed of the woman. The promise of the covenant of grace is that we will be redeemed not because we keep the law. We cannot keep the law. We will be redeemed through the ministry of the one who does keep the law. In the final analysis, as much as we talk about justification by faith alone, it is really just shorthand for justification by Christ alone, because our justification is ultimately through works alone. The only way anyone can be justified in the sight of God is through real righteousness, and real righteousness is achieved only through real obedience to the law of God.

We are justified through the works of Jesus alone, who alone kept the terms of the covenant of works. Since he died for us as our substitute in a vicarious manner, the apostle sees that, in a very real sense, we died with him, and because we died with him, we died to the law as a way of salvation. We never look again to obeying the law in order to receive the blessing of God. As Paul will say later, this does not mean we have a license to sin. Additionally, just because we have been freed from the dominion and curse of the law does not mean the law is a bad thing, something to be despised.

The two magisterial Reformers of the sixteenth century, Martin Luther and John Calvin, had a great disagreement over the use of the law in the life of the Christian. Luther stressed what he called the *elenchticus* use of the law, the *usus elenchticus*, which simply means the teaching or pedagogical purpose of the law. The law's main function, according to Luther, is to serve as the schoolmaster to drive us to Christ. The law exposes our sinful condition and strips away all pretense to our moral ability to reach heaven by our works.

Every one of us is a sinner. Even if we have experienced what the Bible describes as the conviction of sin, we have not begun to feel the weight of that conviction. We have not begun to understand how far short we have fallen of the glory of God. We are at ease in Zion. We live in the most narcissistic age in Christian history, where the chief virtue of religion is to guarantee self-esteem, to make sure we are not brought low by a sinister and neurotic sense of guilt, yet we have not touched the guilt that is ours.

Luther and the Law

A psychological theologian, Erik H. Erikson, once attempted an analysis of Martin Luther—five hundred years after Luther lived—and he came to the conclusion that Luther was at least seriously neurotic and probably psychotic. Krister Stendhal from Harvard gave an address at the American Psychologists Convention in which he talked about Martin Luther's distorted, neurotic introspection that caused him to interpret the gospel in such a way as to give relief to his troubled state of mind and that the church has been suffering from that distortion ever since.

Luther's father, who owned mines in Germany, was very pleased to send his son to the best law school. He wanted to be able to boast about his son the attorney. Luther went to the university and distinguished himself and was considered by many to be the most brilliant young student of jurisprudence in all of Germany. On his way home for a school break, Luther encountered a severe thunderstorm and a lightning bolt struck right next to him. He fell to the ground and in utter terror cried out, "Help me, St. Anne! I'll become a monk."

To his father's unvarnished chagrin, Luther entered the monastery in Erfurt and sought to become a monk of the Augustinian order. If anybody ever tried to get to heaven through monkery, it was Martin Luther. He was zealous for godliness, totally committed to the disciplines of the Augustinian order. He awoke early in the morning for many hours of prayer. He buffeted his body and engaged in self-flagellation to punish himself for his sins. He studied the Scriptures in great depth, and he went to daily confession, where he would drive his father confessor to apoplexy. The typical monk's confession went something like this:

"Father, I have sinned."

"How long has it been since your last confession?"

"Twenty-four hours."

"What did you do?"

"Last night I stayed up with a candle to read an extra chapter of Romans, and yesterday afternoon I coveted the lamb chop on Brother Philip's plate."

After five minutes of confession, the priestly absolution would come: "Say a few 'Hail Marys' and 'Our Fathers' and be on your way."

Luther handled it differently. He would come into the confessional and spend an hour or two (or more) confessing his sins from the preceding twenty-four hours. He would receive absolution, and peace would flood his soul, but on the walk back to the cell he would think of a sin he had failed to confess, and he would be in misery once again. All he could see was Christ the angry judge and the Law of Moses hanging over his head. "You ask me if I love God," said Luther; "sometimes I hate him." His father confessor would come to him and say, "Brother Martin, you are taking yourself too seriously. Do not come to me and belabor these peccadilloes."

That is why Erikson looked at the life of Luther and said he was crazy. Maybe he was. They say there is a thin line between genius and insanity. It may be that Luther was skating back and forth across that line through his entire life. I would not be surprised about that, because it would take a madman to stand against the whole world the way Luther did at the Diet of Worms. However, I do not think we can understand Luther's misery simply in terms of defective psychology. We have to look deeper. Whatever else we say about Luther, we must say that he transferred his training in the law to the law of God.

What is the worst sin a person could commit? The logic is simple. If the greatest commandment is to love the Lord your God with all our heart, strength, and soul and our neighbor as ourselves, it would seem to me that breaking that commandment is the worst thing we could do. Yet have we ever lost sleep because we failed to keep the Great Commandment? I have not. Luther would examine himself and say in his prayers, "God, I did not love you with my whole heart today. How can I get relief from your judgment?" That does not bother us, but it was killing Luther. If he was crazy, I thank God that he gave us a crazy man to open our eyes to the gospel. The craziest thing we could ever do is to try to work our way into heaven.

The Function of the Law
The apostle Paul has already told us, "By the deeds of the law no flesh will be justified in His sight" (3:20). We still try to do it. It is the ladder we try to climb—the ladder of our own righteousness—so that we can come to God at the last day with something in our hand other than the cross. Nobody understood this better than Augustus Toplady:

> Rock of Ages, cleft for me,
> Let me hide myself in Thee.
> . . . .
> Nothing in my hand I bring.
> Simply to the cross I cling;
> Naked, come to Thee for dress; . . .
> Foul, I to the fountain fly;
> Wash me, Savior, or I die.

Preachers today do not preach sin. Does my congregation feel Sunday after Sunday that they are getting a relentless barrage of guilt over their sinfulness? I do not think so. The reality is that we do not feel our sinfulness. We do not feel the weight of it. When we do feel the weight of it, we know how to get rid of it. When Satan comes with his accusations—"It's me again with the law"—that liar tells me the truth in a distorted way: "You are helpless, Sproul. Look at the law; look at your life. What do you see?" I see my helplessness, and I see the cross. I see the gospel, which is the thing Satan hates more than anything in the world. This is what Paul is unpacking for us here at the end of chapter 6 and into chapter 7.

The dead man is not capable of obedience or disobedience. The will has ceased functioning. When we are dead, there is no more sin. Dead people do not sin. The law does not reign over corpses, and in Jesus Christ we are corpses. We are dead. The law cannot touch us with the scourge of its curse.

Luther said that the basic function of the law is to lead us to Christ, whereas Calvin held to what became famously known as his threefold function of the law. The first function of the law is to reveal the character of God. That is what we have to understand first: whose law it is. The moral law is not simply a list of abstract duties, a list of do's and don'ts. The law first reveals the lawgiver. In the final analysis laws are not grounded in the nature of things; the law is grounded in the character of God. It flows from his very being. As the author of human life and the creator of our souls, God has every right to impose upon us whatever obligations he wants.

God has the right to say, "Thou shalt do this" and "Thou shalt not do that." Who are we to defy the Lord God omnipotent, to say that he does not have any right to tell us what to do and what not to do? "I'm a woman, and I have an inalienable right over my own body." No, you do not. The God who made our bodies rules our bodies, and he tells us what we may do with them. Therefore, the first use of the law is to express the character of God. It reveals his holiness. That is why we distance ourselves from it. We are not zealous to pursue a deeper knowledge of the law. When we get involved with the study of the knowledge of God, we are drawn irresistibly close to that ultimate standard of righteousness found in God's character. At the same instant the law reveals the holiness of God it reveals to us our unholiness. The law is a mirror.

When I joined Weight Watchers twenty years ago and successfully completed it, I became a lifetime member. It took me five years to put back on the weight that I had taken off. While attending a Weight Watchers meeting, the instructor asked us, "What made you finally come and join this group and decide to really get serious about losing weight?" When she called on me, I explained that I had decided to join because when I walked past store windows I could see the image of my rotund middle reflected in the glass. Also, one day while I was shopping, the store proprietor came over and said, "There is a telephone call for you from your wife." I said to him, "How did you know that I am her husband?" He replied, "She said she was calling for a short, chubby guy."

I did not like the mirror. I did not like what it showed me about my shape. Our blemishes are revealed to us by honest mirrors, but they do not make mirrors for the soul. Such a mirror is found in the law of God, and when I look in that mirror, it never lies; it drives me to my knees because the law of God reveals my pollution. As Calvin once said, the law reveals to us our corruption. As Luther said, it serves as the pedagogue that teaches us of the gospel and drives us to Christ.

There are two other functions or uses of the law. The law serves as a restraint upon our sin. We live in a lawless culture, and yet some sociologists are saying we are an over-governed culture. Every year Congress adds hundreds of new laws—new ways to make us guilty before the state and to get into trouble. We have to have law enforcement to keep a civil society because every day people violate the law and other people. Can we imagine what society would be like if we did not have any law? We have laws that post the speed limit at 65 mph, but we go 75 or 80 mph. If speed limits were removed we would be driving 90 or 95 mph. There is some restraint, which is why no government is worse than bad government. The worst of all possible societies are those marked by anarchy, because law, as much as we hate it, still exercises some restraint upon us. As sinful as we are, we would be even more sinful if the restraints were removed.

Finally, the third use of the law, which in Latin is called the *tertius usus* of the law, is one of the most important insights of Swiss theology. Even though we are freed from the burden and destruction of the law, it continues to reveal to us what is pleasing to God.

A long time ago I was invited to give a series of lectures on the holiness of God at a large church in New York State. I gave the first lecture, and afterward about twenty attendees went to a mansion of great grandeur for dessert and prayer. Once at the house the group turned out the lights, got down on their knees, and began to pray. To my utter shock, they began to pray to their departed relatives. I was in the middle of a séance.

They told me, "We are channeling. We are communicating with our departed relatives."

I said, "Do you know what the Word of God says about that? In the old covenant God made this activity a capital offense. He considers it an abomination. Not only would he punish its practitioners, but if the nation tolerated it, he also would curse the whole country."

They said, "We know that, but that was the Old Testament. Now the Spirit has led us and we are free from the law."

I asked, "What in the history of redemption has changed so that an activity that was utterly repugnant to God is now all of a sudden pleasing to him?"

The law, in its continual revelatory value, makes it very clear to me that no Christian should ever be involved with such an activity. In that case, the law served as a guide for me. It likewise serves as a guide for all believers. We are not under its curse or weight, but the beauty of the law is still available to us, as Paul begins to deal with in verse 7.

We have become dead to the law through Christ. We have been married to another—**to Him who was raised from the dead, that we should bear fruit to God. For when we were in the flesh, the sinful passions which were aroused by the law were at work in our members to bear fruit to death. But now we have been delivered from the law, having died to what we were held by, so that we should serve in the newness of the Spirit and not in the oldness of the letter** (vv. 4–6).

23

THE FUNCTION OF THE LAW

Romans 7:7–14

What shall we say then? Is the law sin? Certainly not! On the contrary, I would not have known sin except through the law. For I would not have known covetousness unless the law had said, "You shall not covet." But sin, taking opportunity by the commandment, produced in me all manner of evil desire. For apart from the law sin was dead. I was alive once without the law, but when the commandment came, sin revived and I died. And the commandment, which was to bring life, I found to bring death. For sin, taking occasion by the commandment, deceived me, and by it killed me. Therefore the law is holy, and the commandment holy and just and good. Has then what is good become death to me? Certainly not! But sin, that it might appear sin, was producing death in me through what is good, so that sin through the commandment might become exceedingly sinful. For we know that the law is spiritual, but I am carnal, sold under sin.

Throughout this section, Romans 6 and 7, Paul is dealing with the consequences of our justification and the fact that sanctification necessarily follows immediately upon our justification. In the midst of it he sets forth a rather lengthy discussion of the use of the law. In our last study we considered some aspects of how the moral law works in our lives, most importantly how it drives us to the gospel.

The Law as Mirror

Paul has already asked a series of rhetorical questions and then responded to them with great strength, indicating his abhorrence at the idea of misconceptions that might follow from the things he is teaching. He continues that here: **What shall we say then? Is the law sin? Certainly not!** (v. 7). Again we find him giving an emphatic response. Just because the law may stir up hostile feelings toward God's righteous law—that by hearing and understanding the law we may be provoked to greater sinning than we would had we not known the law—we cannot come to the conclusion that something is wrong with the law, that it is evil or sinful. Paul is saying that we need to keep in front of our eyes a clear distinction between the righteousness of the law and the sinfulness of our response to it. The law is not the culprit; it is our fallen corruption.

Is the law sin? **On the contrary, I would not have known sin except through the law. For I would not have known covetousness unless the law had said, "You shall not covet"** (v. 7). Paul is again making the point that the revelatory character of God's law is a mirror by which we see not only the glory and radiance of God's perfection but also ourselves, warts and all. The law is not sin, but the law makes known to us our sin. We will not come to the gospel or beg for the mercy of God until the Holy Spirit convicts us of sin, and the instrument that the Spirit uses to bring us to the cross is the revelation of law.

We are at ease in Zion. We are inured to the power of the law. The pagan walks around virtually oblivious to the radical disobedience he exhibits every hour of his life. He may be willing to admit that he is not perfect, but he does not feel the weight of that. He just takes for granted that we are doing what comes naturally. To err is human; to forgive is divine, so the fact that we covet and lust is no major matter. We are comfortable in our sin.

Paul uses repeatedly the image of someone spiritually dead to any awareness of the gravity of sin. It is the testimony of the greatest saints in the history of the church that the more deeply they have come to know the character of God, the more acutely conscious they have become of the severity of their sin. One of the sweet characteristics of God's mercy is that he does not reveal all our sin to us at once or in all its fullness. If God were to reveal to me this moment the degree of abiding sin that continues in my life, even since I have come to the cross, I could not bear it, nor could you. The downside is that when God withholds his judgment from us and the anguish of conviction, we can begin to think that he does not care. The world has lost its fear of God. There is no sense of judgment.

This was never clearer to me than in the days following the catastrophe of 9/11. For a short period the idea of evil made a comeback in the news. With the repeated images of the towers crumbling to the ground and people jumping out of windows, people said, "There is such a thing as evil, and we have just experienced it." At the same time we all saw the ubiquitous bumper sticker "God Bless America." Yet when commentators from the church were saying that the events of 9/11 were a reflection of God's judgment on our nation, it was received as pure heresy. If we are going to ask God to bless the nation, we must understand that we are praying to one who has every right and power to withhold that blessing. God has the capacity to bless a nation, but he also has the capacity to judge it. That is the state of mind that Paul is describing here.

The Law and Sin

But sin, taking opportunity by the commandment, produced in me all manner of evil desire (v. 8). Rather than the commandment turning us from sin, restraining us from covetousness, our sin, in response to the law of God, was stirred to even greater sinfulness and covetousness. Sin took opportunity by the commandment, and it produced in us all manner of evil desire.

The little phrase "evil desire" is translated in a variety of ways. The Latin text uses the word from which the English term *concupiscence* comes. This word was involved in one of the great disputes between the Reformers of the sixteenth century and the Roman Catholic Church. Rome said that man was created with concupiscence, not with evil. They defined concupiscence as being *of* sin; it *inclines* to sin, but it is not sin. The Reformers replied that an evil desire that gives birth to evil action is already sin. Our sinful deeds flow out of our sinful desires, so we cannot excuse those evil desires as being less than sin. The Greek word used here is *epathumia*, which is the word for "passion" or "desire" with a prefix that intensifies it. Our specific sins make plain the root of those sins, which is our fallen nature.

I learned some time ago that I was quoted in a vampire movie put out by Hollywood. One of the vampires in the movie quoted me as saying that we are not sinners because we sin, but we sin because we are sinners. I am glad that if Hollywood was going to quote me, at least they quoted me accurately on that point. That is the same point Paul is making. Actual sin, specific violations of the law of God, is rooted in a passion of sin, a sinful inclination or disposition. We have to understand that there is something wrong with the root of the tree, and nothing can change it short of the divine and supernatural intervention of the Holy Spirit.

For apart from the law sin was dead (v. 8). Throughout chapter 6 and into chapter 7 Paul uses images of death and life. Until the law came, sin was dead. It was not active. It was dormant until it was awakened by the presence of the law.

In 1970 the film *Tora! Tora! Tora!* portrayed the events surrounding the attack on Pearl Harbor. The film was based on archives from the imperial navy in Japan and the American military headquarters. After the attack was successfully made, Admiral Yamamoto of the Japanese imperial navy said, "I am afraid that all we have accomplished here was to awaken a sleeping giant and fill him with a terrible resolve." That is what Paul is talking about. Sin, for the most part, was sleeping until the law came along and awoke that sleeping giant and filled us with the horrible resolve of wickedness.

Apart from the law sin was dead. **I was alive once without the law, but when the commandment came, sin revived and I died** (v. 9). We were at peace. We were happy. We were getting along fine without the law. "I was being one of the guys. I did not go to sleep at night wallowing in guilt. I was happy"—that is the language used today to describe the difficult metaphors Paul is using here. Paul says he was feeling great, without guilt, and then he died when the law revived sin in him. If we think back to our pre-Christian days, were we overburdened by a sense of sin and guilt? Not until the Holy Spirit brought his conviction on us, quickened our consciences, and made us alive to the law did we feel for the first time the weight of our guilt. That is what drove us to Christ and gave us a new life.

The Deceit of Sin

And the commandment, which was to bring life, I found to bring death. For sin, taking occasion by the commandment, deceived me, and by it killed me (vv. 10–11). In the Scriptures Satan is called "the great deceiver" or "the slanderer." What is so attractive about sin? Why would any creature made in the image of God be tempted by sin? Why would we be inclined to steal what belongs to somebody else? Why would we bear false witness against our neighbor? We are tempted because in the temptation is the offer of happiness, and the pursuit of happiness is given to us as a constitutional guarantee. The Devil never says, "Do this and suffer" or "Do this and die." The passions are so excited by sin that we come to believe that unless we act on our passion, we will be denying ourselves fundamental happiness.

Sin is attractive because it brings us pleasure. It brings pleasure but never happiness. That is the monstrous lie of the father of lies: "Do this, and you will be happy." It is impossible for sin to bring happiness to a child of God, yet we do not believe it. "I will not be happy unless I do this" and "I will not be happy unless I have that"—this is how sin deceives us. The serpent told Eve, "You will not surely die. For God knows that in the day you eat of it your eyes will be opened, and you will be like God, knowing good and evil" (Gen. 3:4–5). In other words, "You do not know what happiness is, Adam, and you do not know what pleasure is, Eve, until you taste the fruit." Satan tells us that God is withholding happiness and that we have a right to be happy.

The biggest moral justification in the secular culture for all kinds of monstrous evil is that we have the right. "I have the right to do what I prefer to do. I have the right to destroy my baby." Where did you get that right? "I have a right over my own body." Says who? Does God give us the right to do those things? We know better. Every person in the world knows better than that, but they say, "If I do not do this, I will not be happy." If we do evil things, we destroy all hope of happiness. We cannot get in our minds the difference between pleasure and happiness.

The Holiness of the Law

Paul gives his conclusion to this section: **Therefore the law is holy** (v. 12). A woman I know left her husband and five children to live with another man. Another minister and I went to talk to her, understanding the fear and trembling involved in Jesus' words, "Where two or three are gathered together in My name, I am there in the midst of them" (Matt. 18:20). There, Jesus was promising to be in the midst of those gathered to fulfill the biblical mandate of calling a brother or sister back from sin, what we call church discipline. If there is ever a time when we need to know the presence of Christ, it is when we are calling someone back from sin.

During our visit we were not angry or harsh. We pleaded with her, "You are a Christian, a married woman, and the mother of five children. You have to end this relationship and come home."

She responded, "I do not have to listen to legalism."

I said to her, "Legalism has many faces. We invent laws where God has left us free, we major in minors, and we obey the letter and destroy the spirit. You have to understand it is never legalism to obey the law of God, because God's law is holy, and what you are doing is unholy."

Thanks be to God, she did repent and come back, but it does not always work out that way. People harden their hearts and make all manner of excuses.

Therefore the law is holy, and the commandment holy and just and good (v. 12). So the law of God is holy, just, and good, but what happens when a holy and just law is delivered to unholy creatures? They do not think it is very just. When God puts a restraint upon our desires, we say it is not fair, as if there were some hint of injustice in the character of God, but the law of God is good because he is good. The law of God was designed to bring life, but we turn it into an occasion of death.

The Great Battle

This brings us to one of the most controversial sections in the entire epistle. If the teaching of predestination were not so strong in chapter 9, chapter 7 would be the most controversial. What follows from here is Paul's description of the battle that goes on between the spirit and the flesh, between obedience and disobedience. A large portion of Christendom believes that what Paul describes is his own pre-conversion era; in other words, he is describing the struggles he had with sin prior to his conversion. Not for one minute do I believe that. When the apostle speaks autobiographically in Romans 7 of the struggle that continues between the flesh and the spirit, he is talking about the struggle that characterizes every Christian's life. This dashes to the dust all false doctrines of sanctification that promise perfection this side of heaven. It debunks the idea of some kind of higher Christian life that only an elite group can experience.

Has then what is good become death to me? Certainly not! (v. 13). Again, God forbid. **But sin, that it might appear sin, was producing death in me through what is good, so that sin through the commandment might become exceedingly sinful** (v. 13). Paul cannot get loose from the idea of the weight of our sin, yet we just do not feel it.

I once read an essay by a psychiatrist about a patient with agoraphobia, the fear of going outside. A case in point was Howard Hughes. He lived as a recluse and let his fingernails grow several inches long. He lived out his days as a madman, using antiseptic on his doorknob, forbidding visitors entry to his home for fear they would bring in germs. Those who have this phobia are afraid of all the dangers that lurk outside. They will not go on a picnic because they might be bitten by a poisonous snake. They will not go to the store or down the street because they might get hit by a car. They will not go visit their children because the airplane might crash. Such people justify their fears by pointing to the newspapers, which contain daily reports of snake bites, fatal automobile accidents, and plane crashes. These things do happen; there are clear and present dangers. In his essay the psychiatrist wrote that agoraphobics have a neurotic response to real dangers, which moves to the level of psychosis. It happens to those who have lost their capacity to shield themselves from real danger. He explained that a normal human being is aware of dangers, but he sublimates that awareness; normal people are able to function in a world with blood on tooth and claw. In other words, normal people deaden their awareness to the perils of life in this world.

That is what happens to us with respect to sin, but the law breaks down the calluses. The law breaks down the normal defense mechanisms we use to deny our guilt. Every time we sin and know that we sin, we try to rationalize it. We do not say, "I sinned." We say, "I made a mistake, a bad choice." We do not acknowledge that we have offended the holiness of God.

An Ongoing Struggle

Paul takes it to the next level: **For we know that the law is spiritual, but I am carnal, sold under sin** (v. 14). This is the biblical basis, the biblical proof-text, for the doctrine of the carnal Christian. The idea of the carnal Christian was invented to deal with the problems inherent with mass evangelism. Many come forward and make a decision for Christ, but the next day most are living just as they were the day before. Rather than attribute this to a false profession of faith, some say, "Oh, they were converted. It just has not taken yet. They are carnal Christians." A true Christian believer, one born again of the Holy Spirit, cannot have self on the throne of his or her life. It is an impossibility, as we noted previously. Defining a carnal Christian as someone still in the flesh altogether is a contradiction in terms. There is no such thing as a carnal Christian by that definition.

Someone I knew who had made a profession of faith in Christ was co-habitating with his girlfriend. The couple was involved with both the use and sale of drugs. He was happy as a clam. His life was not going to change. He believed he did not need to change so long as he simply believed. He felt safe in the arms of Jesus while living in abject sin.

When we are born again of the Spirit, the carnal disposition of our original nature is not destroyed. We have to fight against it from the day we are converted until the day we enter the gates of heaven. We all have a residual force of the flesh, the *sarx*, and we have to fight against it. In that sense, every Christian is a carnal Christian, but there is no such thing as a completely carnal Christian. The completely carnal are not Christians. On the other hand, there is no such a thing as a Christian who is carnal-less, one who is so Spirit filled that he does not have to struggle with the remnants of his own carnality. Such is the Christian life. Paul does not make all this clear here in his initial affirmation, but the remainder of chapter 7 will make it as clear as could possibly be.

24

THE CONFLICT

Romans 7:14–25, Part 1

For we know that the law is spiritual, but I am carnal, sold under sin. For what I am doing, I do not understand. For what I will to do, that I do not practice; but what I hate, that I do. If, then, I do what I will not to do, I agree with the law that it is good. But now, it is no longer I who do it, but sin that dwells in me. For I know that in me (that is, in my flesh) nothing good dwells; for to will is present with me, but how to perform what is good I do not find. For the good that I will to do, I do not do; but the evil I will not to do, that I practice. Now if I do what I will not to do, it is no longer I who do it, but sin that dwells in me. I find then a law, that evil is present with me, the one who wills to do good. For I delight in the law of God according to the inward man. But I see another law in my members, warring against the law of my mind, and bringing me into captivity to the law of sin which is in my members. O wretched man that I am! Who will deliver me from this body of death? I thank God—through Jesus Christ our Lord! So then, with the mind I myself serve the law of God, but with the flesh the law of sin.

I mentioned before that Romans 7 has been the focal point of very serious theological controversy. The focus of that controversy has to do with whether it is possible—and, indeed, important—for the Christian to achieve a state of moral perfection in this life prior to entering into glory.

Several movements throughout church history have taught the idea that in addition to the singular moment of regeneration, there is a second work of grace that effects instant, complete sanctification.

The Perfectionist View

The most important biblical text that speaks against this doctrine of a second work of grace is the text before us now, Romans 7:14–25. The apostle Paul, writing in the present tense, talks of a painful, ongoing struggle in his life, which is that between walking according to the Spirit and surrendering to the vestigial remnants of the flesh.

The advocates of the perfectionist view have argued that although Paul writes in the present tense he is not referring to his present situation but is recollecting the state in which he lived prior to his regeneration. This passage has been worked over by the best Greek interpreters of history. I can say dogmatically that I find absolutely no justification whatsoever for seeing here anything other than the contemporary struggle that the apostle was having with respect to his own progress in sanctification.

In the nineteenth century several churches, particularly in America, following some ideas set forth by John Wesley, developed Holiness churches. Contained in their doctrine is the idea of a second work of grace available to all Christians by which they can experience instantaneous holiness. The beginnings of modern Pentecostalism were also tied in with this perfectionist idea. Speaking in tongues was considered to be evidence of this second work of grace. Only in recent times with the advent of neo-Pentecostalism have adjustments been made to that doctrine. Now the thinking is that the baptism of the Holy Spirit empowers Christians for ministry but does not necessarily produce in them an immediate victory over all sin.

In my entire life and experience as a teacher and preacher, I have encountered only two people who believed they had received this second work of grace and were therefore sinless. The first was a woman who, in all honesty, you would probably not want to spend much time with. Indeed, she was nasty, but she was so filled with the conviction of her perfection that she did not want to hear anything to the contrary. My discussions with her from the Bible were of no avail. She strongly asserted that Paul in Romans 7 was talking about his pre-conversion condition.

The second was a young student, seventeen years old, whom I met when I was doing my graduate work in the Netherlands. He was an American student from Texas studying as an exchange student in Holland. I was involved coaching baseball there, and since he was playing baseball I had a chance to step beside him. He had come from a Holiness church, and he told me he had arrived at perfection. When I began to discuss with him the teaching of Romans 7, he was quick to use the standard response, that Paul was not speaking in the present tense. I bullied this poor soul by bringing out the Greek New Testament and pointing out passage upon passage where Paul clearly was speaking in the present tense about his present condition. I told him that the sentiments that the apostle expresses in Romans 7 are those that we do not find in unregenerate people, such as his love for the law and his great desire to please God. After lengthy discussion I was finally able to convince him that, in fact, Paul was talking about his present condition. I assumed the debate with the young man was over, and I asked, "What do you think now about your assessment that you have reached a level of perfection?"

He said, "I am sad to hear that the apostle had not made it."

I said, "Do you really believe that at age seventeen you have achieved a higher level of sanctification than Paul had reached at the time that he wrote his magnum opus to the church at Rome?"

He looked me straight in the eye and said, "Yes, I am more sanctified at my age than Paul was when he wrote to Rome."

We hear doctrine from a pastor or Christian mentor for whom we have great affection and admiration, and we accept it. If we later hear his teaching challenged, no argument in the world will cause us to leave our dedication to him. We all struggle with that, but I hope that in such cases when we look at the clear biblical teaching we would be able to snip those love-lines of dedication wherever necessary. The young man did not realize how far someone must discount the law of God and exaggerate his own achievement to come to the conclusion that he lives without sin. I pray that by now he has abandoned his idea. The conviction of the Holy Spirit is powerful enough to destroy such illusions and visions of grandeur. The testimony of the greatest saints in history is that the longer they are Christians and the more deeply immersed they become in the Word of God, the more acutely conscious they become of their shortcomings. As we grow in grace, we grow in our understanding of our ongoing need for that grace.

No Shortcuts

It is important that we not be deceived into thinking there are shortcuts to Christian maturity, to growing up into the fullness of conformity to the image of Christ. It is a lifelong pursuit. None will achieve that perfection until we enter into glory and all the remnants of sin and the flesh are removed from us. In one sense, it is comforting to know that even Paul had to struggle against the temptations of the flesh, because there has probably never been another more dedicated to the pursuit of holiness and obedience to his Lord Jesus Christ than the apostle Paul. If Paul had struggles like this, I take comfort in it, not because I want to rejoice in evil or in somebody else's weakness but because I am not left hopeless when I consider my own weaknesses.

In the early days of my conversion, I longed for that second work. Some of my close friends came from Holiness churches. Even though they did not think they had reached a level of total perfection, they still believed in a second work of grace as the means to sanctification. I sought earnestly for that second work of grace. I had good reason to because I brought much baggage into my Christian life. I knew the power of the flesh, and I knew I had no ability to overcome it. On the day of my conversion my behavior underwent a radical change. My language cleaned up and other areas of my life changed dramatically. For the first time I had a thirst and a passionate hunger to learn the truths of the Scripture. I enjoyed prayer and going to church to sing hymns of praise to the Lord God, but I struggled with besetting sins.

Within the first few months of my conversion I remember sitting in the local college grill, smoking, and our math professor, a Christian, was sitting across from me. He took a straw and held it as if it were a cigarette and put it to his lips and pretended to inhale and exhale. He said, "Let me tell you about my experiences with the Holy Spirit." Of course, that was his way of rebuking me for my failure to clean up my life as a new Christian. Because of my smoking I was on the lookout for instant sanctification. I tried everything.

One evangelist gave me an idea: "If you want to stop smoking, put a picture of Jesus in your cigarette package. Every time you want to smoke, take that pack of cigarettes out and look at the picture of Jesus and say, 'I love you, Jesus,' and then you will not be tempted to smoke." I tried it. By three o'clock in the afternoon nothing was more repugnant to me than that picture of Jesus, and I had to remove it. I cannot tell you how serious that struggle was in my soul. I would come to the text of Scripture, "I can do all things through Christ who strengthens me" (Phil. 4:13), and I would think, *I can't say that. I cannot do all things through Christ who strengthens me.* I asked people to lay hands on me. I had a Holiness minister pray for the second work of grace and my instant sanctification. It did not work. Somebody prayed in tongues. Another minister gave me a nail and told me to put it in my pocket, which I did. He said, "Every time you think about smoking, think of the death of Jesus. Pull out that nail and think of what Jesus did for you." That lasted a few hours until I threw away the nail.

It took twenty-five years from the day I became a Christian till the first time I went twenty-four hours without smoking, and it took another ten years to go a month without smoking, and it was at least another ten years after that to get rid of it altogether. All that time I listened to the accusation of Satan. I struggled with my spiritual state because I had an addiction to the flesh that I simply could not get rid of. I know I am not alone. In a sense, although it should not be the case, it becomes a normal dimension of the Christian life. We all are faced with some besetting sin that we bring before God and seek to get rid of. Sooner or later we have to hear the words, "My grace is sufficient for you" (2 Cor. 12:9).

I can feel the anguish. I do not mean to cheapen that oft-used expression, "I feel your pain," but I can feel the anguish of the apostle in this text and elsewhere in his letters as he talks about the war that goes on in the soul of the Christian between the spirit and the flesh, between the old man, who does not want to die, and the new man, who is working for inward renewal and maturity in Christ. I cannot tell you why sometimes the Lord allows us to struggle for years before liberation comes, but he does. However, at every moment the grace is there to overcome, no matter what the sin problem is.

The Spirit-filled Life

John Wesley first successfully taught the idea that the Spirit does a work of grace that, while not rendering someone morally perfect, nevertheless enables him to achieve a "perfect love." For Wesley this was the second work of grace. Out of that has come broad attention to the idea of a higher sanctification that results in two tiers of Christians. First is the ordinary Christian. He seeks spiritual growth by reading his Bible and going to church, and he is diligent about using the means of grace; nevertheless, he never reaches that plateau called "the higher life" or "the deeper life." The Christian in the second tier has supposedly reached a greater level of victory. At the end of the nineteenth century and into the twentieth in England and the United States, Deeper Life movements were spawned that taught this higher plateau of spiritual victory.

In more recent times similar movements have advocated what is called the "Spirit-filled life." Here again are two levels of Christians. First are those regenerated by the power of the Holy Spirit and assisted in their quest for sanctification by the Spirit's help but who have not yet been filled with the

Spirit to the level of the second plateau. Advocates of the Spirit-filled life do not claim total perfection but a much greater level of sanctification than that achieved by other Christians.

I once heard a leader in this movement say, "From time to time I will pray a prayer of confession for my sins, if I have any." Time would not allow me to confess all the transgressions I have been guilty of in the last twenty-four hours. If I were to think I could go a day or a week or a month without sin, I would be just like that seventeen-year-old boy from Texas. If I were to think I could go without sin for an hour, I would have to pull God down or raise myself up. The apostle Paul tells us that the law is spiritual, and when we look at ourselves through the lens of the law, we do not have to look very far or very long to find out that there is no *if* about the abiding sins that mar our lives.

Duality

In Christian circles is also a view of anthropology called *tripartitism*, which teaches that that we are made up of a triune nature—body, soul, and spirit. We see such wording in Paul's Thessalonican benediction: "Now may the God of peace Himself sanctify you completely; and may your whole spirit, soul, and body be preserved blameless at the coming of our Lord Jesus Christ" (1 Thess. 5:23). Elsewhere Paul talks about the bowels, the mind, the heart, and at least three or four other elements of the constituent makeup of man without setting forth an actual anthropology. Tripartitism holds that ordinary Christians have the Holy Spirit in body and soul but not yet in spirit. Average Christians are two-thirds of the way along in Christian growth, but if they want the higher, Spirit-filled life, then the Spirit of God has to affect them not only in body and soul but also in spirit. Throughout church history tripartitism has always carried some other heresy in its wake.

The Bible makes the clear distinction between the physical and non-physical aspects of our humanity; according to Scripture, we are comprised of body and soul. Only the Holy Spirit can distinguish between mind, soul, spirit, will, and the other designations we make. Fundamentally, Scripture sees us as a duality; we have a physical aspect and a nonphysical aspect. We are body and soul. Nowhere in Scripture do we find the idea that the Spirit will get to two of the three but not to the other.

That is but a brief theological preface to what Paul is setting forth here in Romans 7. In my estimation the most acute and comprehensive refutation, both theologically and biblically, of all types of perfectionism was penned by the late great Princeton theologian Benjamin Breckinridge Warfield.

He wrote a volume entitled *Perfectionism*, which will prove helpful to anyone wanting to look more deeply at the Holiness movement or the Deeper Life movements I mentioned.[1]

Perplexed

For what I am doing, I do not understand (v. 15). Paul expresses some confusion. He is perplexed but not by some abstract theological mystery. He is perplexed by his own behavior. *I don't understand myself. I just don't know why I do the things that I do.* He goes on to describe a conflict that is rooted in the will: **For what I will to do, that I do not practice; but what I hate, that I do** (v. 15). Paul is not engaging in a philosophical discussion of how the will functions; he is speaking in concrete language that we can all relate to.

Progress in Obedience

We would all like to lead a life of perfect obedience to Christ, but we do not because there is conflict in our hearts between our general desire for obedience and the specific acts of obedience that confront us. There is also the strength of the temptation toward disobedience. That is why we cry, "The spirit is willing but the flesh is weak." We are people of mixed desires, which is why life does not really become complicated until we are born again. Before we were born again we had only one principle—the flesh. We walked willingly and happily submitting to the temptations of Satan. Once the Holy Spirit has raised us from spiritual death, our lives become a battle between two jockeys, to use Augustine's analogy. Satan does not give up easily. The flesh does not die instantly. Life becomes complicated because we are involved in a war that penetrates the very deepest recesses of our souls and lasts until our glorification in heaven. This is the universal experience among Christians, and it is what the apostle Paul is talking about.

We could stop right there and say, "Why not just eat, drink, and be merry, and not be so earnest about sanctification, since we cannot reach the goal anyway?" We must remember that elsewhere Paul wrote, "Forgetting those things which are behind and reaching forward to those things which are ahead, I press toward the goal for the prize of the upward call of God in Christ Jesus" (Phil. 3:13–14). We pummel our body to subdue it. We enter into and engage in a fight, and we are admonished by the Scriptures not to yield so easily to the sin that besets us, for we have not yet resisted to the point of shedding our blood (Heb. 12:4). The very fact that we read books

1. Benjamin Breckinridge Warfield, *Perfectionism* (New York: Oxford University Press, 1931).

like this one indicates that we take our Christian life seriously. We want to dig deeper into the Scriptures because we know that through the teaching of the truth of God's Word we will be helped in the struggle. We make use of the means of God's grace to progress in our sanctification. The fact that no one makes it to the finish line in this lifetime does not mean we are supposed to stop running. We are never allowed to be at ease in Zion and say, "This far I have progressed and no farther." We are to be diligent in every way to feed the new man and kill the old man.

As we progress through our study of Romans, I hope to provide some very practical suggestions on how to increase our sanctification. I am not going to give secrets for a spiritual life, because I do not believe in those. However, I do believe that one Christian will progress farther than another, not because there are two distinct levels of Christian living—Spirit-filled and non-Spirit-filled—but because each of us is at a different place in our Christian pilgrimage. Many have never struggled to quit smoking, as I did, but they have struggled with something else. We come with different baggage, and therefore our progress in sanctification is different.

I do like that bumper sticker, "Be patient. God is not finished with me yet," because as God's people we are called to manifest love, a charity that covers a multitude of sins. This certainly does not mean we are to be soft on gross and heinous sin. The New Testament makes clear that we are not to give each other license for sin, but the average, run-of-the-mill, everyday struggles that all Christians have are to be covered by charity. We are to be forbearing and patient and encouraging toward one another.

The Danger of Victory

One of the worst sins we can commit is that of establishing our achievements as the norm by which all Christians are to be judged; however, doing so is tempting. If we have success or victory in an area of life, our tendency is to elevate it as the test of true spirituality so that we find ourselves thinking critically of those who do not measure up in that regard.

I struggled with that for many years. From the day I was born again I had a hunger and thirst for the Scriptures. Nobody had to twist my arm and say, "You have to set aside time every day to read the Bible." I cannot remember a time that I picked up the Bible from a sense of duty, but I used to wonder about my Christian friends. *I never see them reading the Scriptures. What is the matter with them?* In keeping with my vocation, God had planted a desire in my heart that made it easier to do that particular thing. Even so, I have wasted more time not studying the Scriptures than others not so called.

If we are gifted with evangelism, we want to establish evangelism as the supreme gift. If gifted in teaching, we see it as the most important gift. If gifted with generosity, then giving becomes the real touchstone of spirituality. That is why Paul had to write to the Corinthians and explain that believers have different gifts. Part of our growth as Christians is to develop an understanding that things of little difficulty to us may be very difficult for other people, and things we struggle with may never cause others to struggle. We are in this together—sharing in the Spirit and the Word, encouraging and praying for one another, and covering one another with charity.

25

THE WILL OF MAN

Romans 7:14–25, Part 2

For we know that the law is spiritual, but I am carnal, sold under sin. For what I am doing, I do not understand. For what I will to do, that I do not practice; but what I hate, that I do. If, then, I do what I will not to do, I agree with the law that it is good. But now, it is no longer I who do it, but sin that dwells in me. For I know that in me (that is, in my flesh) nothing good dwells; for to will is present with me, but how to perform what is good I do not find. For the good that I will to do, I do not do; but the evil I will not to do, that I practice. Now if I do what I will not to do, it is no longer I who do it, but sin that dwells in me. I find then a law, that evil is present with me, the one who wills to do good. For I delight in the law of God according to the inward man. But I see another law in my members, warring against the law of my mind, and bringing me into captivity to the law of sin which is in my members. O wretched man that I am! Who will deliver me from this body of death? I thank God—through Jesus Christ our Lord! So then, with the mind I myself serve the law of God, but with the flesh the law of sin.

I am going to take a break from my usual pattern of examining the text verse by verse and instead consider the passage from a theological and even somewhat philosophical perspective. We will look specifically but not exclusively at the work of Jonathan Edwards in his classic treatment of the operation of the human will.

Views of the Universe

We are always susceptible as Christians to ideas that are quite contrary to the truth of God. They tend to slip in unnoticed. We do not plan to embrace pagan notions, which are incompatible with the truth of God, but it has been said that if a lie is repeated often enough, people begin to believe it. Such information sneaks into the crevices of our brains, and we are unaware of it, particularly during childhood. We are taught that certain truths are self-evident and well attested by contemporary science and that to question them is to risk the charge of being insane.

One such idea is what we call a mechanistic view of the universe. Although somewhat passé in contemporary paradigms of natural science, it is, never-theless, still pervasive at the common level. This view holds that the universe works like a machine and functions according to fixed laws within nature. From infancy we have been told that the universe operates according to the laws of nature, and these laws are presented as if they are immutable, fixed, autonomous powers. Such thinking is on a collision course with everything the Scriptures teach us about the nature of God, which is that the world is his creation and he rules it. He governs the motion of every atom and subatomic particle in the universe, not as an absentee landlord or a cosmic spectator but through his providence. Gravity cannot function for a second apart from God's providential rule and permission. What we call "the laws of nature" are merely descriptive terms for how God ordinarily governs his creation, but in our day we are seeing a declaration of independence from the sovereign providence of God; the assumption is that the universe operates itself.

This old hymn is based on Psalm 100:

> All people that on earth do dwell,
> Sing to the Lord with cheerful voice.
> Him serve with mirth, his praise forth tell,
> Come ye before him and rejoice.

> Know that the Lord is God indeed;
> Without our aid he did us make:
> We are his flock, he doth us feed,
> And for his sheep he doth us take.

O enter then his gates with joy,
   Within his courts his praise proclaim;
   Let thankful songs your tongues employ,
   O bless and magnify his name.

Because the Lord our God is good,
   His mercy is forever sure;
   His truth at all times firmly stood,
   And shall from age to age endure.

"Know that the Lord is God indeed"—that is not the way we talk today. "Without our aid he did us make" so captures the biblical perspective of the relationship of God to his creation. We think that God cannot do anything without our assistance or consent, but he is the Lord. There is none like him, and he made us without any help or assistance. "We are his folk. He doth us feed"—there we see the sovereign providence of God. We are his sheep. He feeds us and he takes us to belong to him. This hymn, like so many of the great hymns, is rich in setting forth a Christian understanding of life and nature.

The idea of an independent, autonomous universe is the second most pervasive pagan idea that creeps into our thinking. Overwhelmingly, the most widespread pervasive pagan idea is the humanistic, secular view of the human will, which is far removed from the biblical view. So deeply entrenched is this pagan notion that when we preach the sovereignty of God in his ministry of redemption, people immediately protest, often vociferously, that it violates the free will of man. When we begin to probe what is meant by "the free will of man," usually expounded is the widespread, pagan understanding of the will.

The Will of Man

Christians agree with the pagan or humanist that humans are volitional creatures. Volitional creatures have the capacity to make choices and exercise their wills. We distinguish between voluntary actions and involuntary actions. We do not decide to start our hearts beating every morning, but deciding whether to shave is voluntary. The pagan, secular view is that the will is so free that we can respond to every voluntary matter through philosophical indifference. It means that to be truly free in the making of decisions and choices, freedom must be absolute insofar as nothing compels us to choose to the left or the right. To be free the will must have no preconceived bias or prior disposition in one direction or the other. That is the will of indifference.

When John Calvin was engaged in a dispute over free will with his opponent Pelagius in the sixteenth century, part of the debate concerned the nature of the human will. Calvin agreed with a definition of *free will* which holds that even in our sinful condition we have the power and ability to choose what we want. He did not agree with the definition of *free will* as the ability to choose from indifference, because we are all held captive by the propensity to sin. Calvin agreed that we do have free will in the sense that we have the ability to choose what we want, but that ability to choose is not only mildly influenced but is radically conditioned by the human corruption of our hearts, out of which flow the choices we make. In other words, we make evil choices not from indifference but from a prior inclination to wickedness. The Bible says that prior to regeneration, "every intent of the thoughts of his heart was only evil continually" (Gen. 6:5). This lay at the heart of the debate between Martin Luther and Desiderius Erasmus of Rotterdam. Erasmus attacked Luther's view of the sovereignty of God and election. Luther responded to the diatribe of Erasmus with his classic work *De Servo Arbitrian (The Bondage of the Will)*.

When Jonathan Edwards dealt with the question of the will in eighteenth-century New England, he did so in the context of defending his position against the rising tide of Arminian theology. Arminian theology is, in many respects, married to a view of the will as being indifferent. In his discussion Edwards began with this question: "What is the will?" Edwards answered with profound understanding, saying that the will is simply the mind choosing. The will is not an organ we find three inches to the left of the liver or the pancreas or the heart. The will describes a faculty or an ability by which human beings are able to make choices. We are not robots or inert stones. We are living, breathing people who make choices all the time. An action of the will, a voluntary action, takes place. In our thinking, in our mental approach to something, we determine what is desirable at that moment. On the basis of that activity of the mind, we exercise our choice. In fact, if the mind were not involved in our choices, our choices would have no moral basis whatsoever. A mindless choice is not a moral choice.

Edwards began to probe more deeply into the dimension of human choices, and the fundamental principle of his analysis was this: choices do not occur in a vacuum. Choices are not uncaused effects. They do not just pop up like Athena from the head of Zeus. All choices have a cause, and the antecedent cause for every choice we make is what Edwards called *inclination* or *disposition*. He set forth the principle that not only do we choose according to our desires, but we *must* choose according to our desires, and we always choose according to our strongest desire at the moment of choice. If we can get hold of this principle, it would help us avoid a multitude of serious errors about how the Christian faith works. We always choose according to the strongest inclination we have at any given moment.

Once we understand that, we will realize that never in our lives have we chosen to do something that we did not want to do. That is the ugly power of sin. We choose to sin in any particular situation because we want to. The Devil does not make us do it; we cannot make that plea on judgment day. Every sin we commit proceeds from our internal desire.

"I don't have to think about that," someone might say. "I can tell you right now that I only go to church because my wife hounds me. I decided that it is easier to sit in church for an hour and listen to the preacher than to listen to my wife rebuke me for the rest of the week. All things being equal, I do not want to go to church, but I do." However, in that example all things are not equal. The man has no desire to go to church, but he does have a desire not to be out of sorts with his wife. Each week he chooses to bear the ills of listening to the preacher rather than to disappoint his wife. His greatest inclination at the moment is to go to church. That is how it works. If we work really hard to come up with a choice we have made not according to our strongest inclination at the moment, we are not going to be able to. Every choice we have ever made, even though it might have seemed repugnant, was chosen because not choosing it was even more repugnant.

Some mistake that thinking for determinism, but Christians are not determinists. Human beings are not made of wood or manipulated by strings. They have minds. Puppets do not make choices or have desires. They have no inclinations whatsoever because they do not have minds. Without a mind there is no faculty to choose.

We live constantly with a multitude of options pressing against us, vying for our attention and submission. It would be much easier if there were only two flavors to choose from—vanilla and chocolate—but the ice cream companies outdo each other for fifty-seven flavors. If we had indifferent wills, we would be like the donkey with a bucket of oats to his left and some hay to his right. The donkey was very hungry but having an indifferent will, he had no preference of oats over hay, so he starved to death because the buckets were equal distance from him. We are not that way. When we order ice cream, we tend to order the flavor that most appeals.

The Will in Conflict

For the good that I will to do, I do not do; but the evil I will not to do, that I practice (v. 19). Paul is describing a conflict between rival goods. The most difficult decisions are not just those between good and evil but those between two goods. Such decisions can paralyze us. The desire to be perfectly obedient Christians is an inclination in our wills. The new man in our heart has the desire to please God, but there still lives in our members the vestigial remnants of the old man of the flesh, which has declared war on the leanings of the spirit. When the conflict comes, many times we would rather follow the old man than the new man. In the moment, it is more desirable to sin than to obey Christ. Part of us wants to obey Christ, but not all. We have evil inclinations and desires that bump up against our good intentions.

In the 1930s and 40s there was a baseball announcer in Pittsburgh, Rosie Rosewell, who broadcast the games by teletype. As players went to and from the bases, Rosie Rosewell would say, "Put him on, take him off." That is how my diet typically goes. I am doing fine and then someone will set a piece of cherry pie before me. I start to think, *I really want to lose weight. If I eat that cherry pie, I am not going to get very far with my diet, but oh, that cherry pie looks good. One piece will not hurt.*

We have seen the comic strips that depict the Devil talking in one ear and an angel talking in the other. That is what happens in our lives every day. We are called to be disciples or "people of discipline." Self-discipline, in the vast majority of cases, is nothing more or less than the extended habit of disciplines developed while under the authority of someone else. Someone forces us into patterned behavior and we build the pattern, and after a while it becomes part of our lives.

The Determination of Desire

In the pop psychology book *Psycho Cybernetics*, the computer was used as a metaphor to show that humans function within the GIGO principle: garbage in, garbage out.[1] The premise of the book is that people live on the basis of how they are programmed. That is not altogether false, but it is not altogether true either. If our choices are caused by the greatest inclination we have at any given moment, our choices are determined. Our choices are determined not by the stars or the fates but by what we desire. We call this self-determination, which is just another word for freedom. The essence of freedom is to be able to determine our own choices, and the essence of our

1. Maxwell Maltz, *Psycho Cybernetics* (Englewood Cliffs, NJ: Prentice-Hall, 1960).

fallen condition is that we determine our sinful choices. The concept found in the book *Psycho Cybernetics* can be translated into the spiritual realm as follows.

1) In order to grow spiritually, we need to develop a deeper prayer life. We can resolve to become prayer warriors, but we are going to fail in that discipline every time. What can we do? At the moment we desire to become more proficient in prayer, we can place ourselves in an environment, such as a prayer group, that will help us overcome our lax disposition toward prayer.

2) We have determined many times to learn the Scriptures, and we always start well. We read Genesis 1; the next day we read Genesis 2; the next day we have to go out, which means we miss our reading, so the next day we read two chapters. The next day we give up. Does that sound familiar? How much does it cost to enroll in a Bible study? We can get in a class where the discipline of the group and the commitment strengthen our resolve.

3) We can resolve that we are going to be in church on Sunday morning. We are not going to weigh the decision each week. "Should we go to church today or should we not? Let me see. What are we inclined to do this week?" We establish a principle.

That is psycho cybernetics from a spiritual perspective, and it is what the apostle Paul is talking to us about in terms of our spiritual pilgrimage and growth. He is saying that we have to put to death the old man and feed the new man. While on a spiritual high we change our routine and get into a pattern or a group where there is discipline that will help us put to death the old man and feed the new man.

That is the genius of Weight Watchers. I drove every Tuesday to those meetings. I stepped on that scale and was asked in front of the entire group, "How did you do this week?"

"I put on a pound."

"Well, that is okay, but next week we want to see less of you."

The group dynamic is a beautiful idea. If left to ourselves, personal discipline tends to lose its passion and zeal.

The Means of Grace

Once we understand how the will functions and that we are involved in the conflict the apostle sets forth in Romans 7, we can discover the way out—the means of grace. The means of grace are the instruments God gives to help us overcome the weaknesses of the flesh. Since we will always choose what we are most inclined to choose at the moment of decision, we can make use of the means of grace by programming ourselves with worship, prayer, and Scripture so that our desires become sanctified.

If we know how much God hates our sin, and if we have affection for him, we will not want to displease him by sinning. We are, however, constantly bombarded with opposing ideas. The Scriptures set before us what God delights in; we read it and say, "I want my life to be like that," but the rest of the week we hear voices from every side that lead us to lose sight of what is pleasing to God. As we take in what is pleasing to our friends and to the culture, our delight in God begins to lose its passion. We have to have the doctrine of justification by faith in our bloodstream, because there is enough continuing sin in our lives to remind us that without the righteousness of Christ, we have no hope whatsoever.

Edwards made another important distinction concerning the will. He said that fallen man has the natural ability to please God but not the moral ability. The distinction there is critical. A natural ability is one endowed by nature. A bird, for example, has the natural ability to fly unaided through the air because God gave it the equipment to fly—wings and light bone structure. The fish has the natural ability to live underwater because God gave it gills and scales. We do not have the natural ability to fly. If we want to fly, we have to ride in an airplane. We do, however, have the natural ability to obey God in the sense that we have the faculties that are necessary to be obedient creatures. God has given us a mind and a will. He has given us the equipment we need, naturally speaking, to obey him.

Arminians think that fallen humanity has the ability to incline toward God. People can choose whether to accept the offer of grace. If they do, they are saved. Yet why does one person say yes and another say no? The obvious answer is that one is inclined to say yes, and the other is not. Going even deeper, we must ask why anyone would be inclined to say yes to Christ. The only reason is that the Holy Spirit changes the disposition of the soul. In our fallen condition we have no disposition toward Christ, which is why Jesus said, "No one can come to Me unless the Father who sent Me draws him" (John 6:44a). We are in jail without bail, in bondage to sin. Augustine understood that, and so did Luther, Calvin, Edwards, and Spurgeon. Unless the Holy Spirit changes the disposition of our hearts through regeneration, we will never be inclined to come to Jesus.

If we have come to Christ, we have done so because we wanted to. We were inclined to, but not by nature. We were inclined to Christ by super-nature. God reached down and with his grace changed our desire. He changed our hearts from stone to hearts that beat with affection for him and set us free.

26

SET FREE

Romans 7:19–8:2

For the good that I will to do, I do not do; but the evil I will not to do, that I practice. Now if I do what I will not to do, it is no longer I who do it, but sin that dwells in me. I find then a law, that evil is present with me, the one who wills to do good. For I delight in the law of God according to the inward man. But I see another law in my members, warring against the law of my mind, and bringing me into captivity to the law of sin which is in my members. O wretched man that I am! Who will deliver me from this body of death? I thank God—through Jesus Christ our Lord! So then, with the mind I myself serve the law of God, but with the flesh the law of sin. There is therefore now no condemnation to those who are in Christ Jesus, who do not walk according to the flesh, but according to the Spirit. For the law of the Spirit of life in Christ Jesus has made me free from the law of sin and death.

P aul has been explaining his ongoing struggle between his spirit and his flesh. He desires to be obedient to Christ, yet that desire often gives way to failure, and he continues to struggle with the sinful inclinations of his heart. We looked at the struggle exegetically and expositionally, and then we looked at it theologically and philosophically.

Indwelling Sin

The things Paul wants to do are the things he does not do, and the things he does not want to do are the very things he does (7:19). **Now if I do what I will not to do, it is no longer I who do it, but sin that dwells in me** (v. 20). Paul is not trying to absolve himself from responsibility for his sin. His point is that he does what he does not want to do because of sin. He recognizes where that sin dwells—within him. Even though he is involved in this conflict, the new man is still what defines his personality. Despite the ongoing struggle and the failures into sin that mark his Christian life, Paul knows that he is a new creature. What God has done with him can be seen not in the remnants of his old man but in the triumph that God gives him through his Holy Spirit in the new man.

Earlier on Paul said we are to consider the old man dead; he has been crucified with Christ (6:11). Therefore, Paul says, he is not going to relate to the old man anymore. The real Paul, the Paul who has been redeemed from bondage to sin, is the Paul who is destined for glorification.

Regeneration accomplishes our rescue and release from the total bondage of sin that marks our fallen condition, the inherent corruption with which we are born that causes us to walk according to the course of the air and according to the prince of the power of the air (Eph. 2:2). When we are born of the Spirit, that bondage is broken. We are set free. We experience a liberty that man has not had since the fall, but even with the renewal by which we are dramatically changed inside, that change does not instantaneously eradicate all the impulses of sin. As we have seen repeatedly now, that struggle goes on until heaven. Paul says that although sin still dwells in him, that indwelling sin lacks the same captivating power that it had before his conversion.

Delight in God's Law

I find then a law, that evil is present with me, the one who wills to do good (v. 21). Paul is not talking about the Mosaic law or even about the moral law. He has discovered a fundamental truth that describes his current situation. His phrasing is a bit awkward but we can still see the principle. He then identifies himself not with the one who wills to do evil but with the one who wants to do right: **For I delight in the law of God according to the inward man** (v. 22). If there is any question about whether Paul is talking about his pre-conversion state or his ongoing struggle after his regeneration, this one text should put that to rest forever, because no unregenerate person delights in the law of God in the inward person. Psalm 1 makes sharp distinctions between the godly man and the ungodly man:

> Blessed is the man
>> Who walks not in the counsel of the ungodly,
>> Nor stands in the path of sinners,
>> Nor sits in the seat of the scornful;
> But his delight is in the law of the LORD,
>> And in His law he meditates day and night.
> He shall be like a tree
>> Planted by the rivers of water,
>> That brings forth its fruit in its season,
>> Whose leaf also shall not wither;
>> And whatever he does shall prosper.
>
> The ungodly are not so,
>> But are like the chaff which the wind drives away.
> Therefore the ungodly shall not stand in the judgment,
>> Nor sinners in the congregation of the righteous.
>
> For the LORD knows the way of the righteous,
>> But the way of the ungodly shall perish.

The godly man delights in the law of God and is therefore like a tree planted by the rivers of water bringing forth its fruit in season. In contrast the ungodly man is weightless, without substance, like the chaff that the wind drives away. In that portrait of the godly man we see that his godliness is defined by his delight. The godly man is the one who delights in the law of the Lord and meditates on it day and night, which is how Paul is describing his condition. Paul uses a set of words that jump right off the page. He talks about the new man, the old man, the inward man, the outer man, the sinful man, and the spiritually inclined man. This language describes the difference between pre-conversion and post-conversion humanity.

Body and Flesh

In these last few verses of chapter 7, I want to look closely at the ongoing war that the apostle describes between the mind and the flesh. **I see another law in my members, warring against the law of my mind, and bringing me into captivity to the law of sin which is in my members. O wretched man that I am! Who will deliver me from this body of death? I thank God—through Jesus Christ our Lord! So**

then, with the mind I myself serve the law of God, but with the flesh the law of sin (vv. 23–25). If we look closely at the text, we will see again two distinct Greek words. One, *sōma*, is translated by the English word *body*. We find it in the English word *psychosomatic*. The second Greek word, *sarx*, is translated *flesh*. In Latin the words are translated in the first instance by the word *corporeal*, from which we get *corporal*, and in the second instance by a word from which we get the English word *carnal*. So we have *corporal* and *carnal*, *sōma* and *sarx*, *body* and *flesh*.

This distinction between body and flesh has caused no small amount of confusion. Part of the confusion is linguistic and part is philosophical or theological. The term *sarx* is used repeatedly in the New Testament, particularly by the apostle Paul, to refer not to our physical nature but to our fallen nature. The *sarkical* nature is that which is controlled by original sin. The *sarx* describes the old man, the one that has no inclination toward the things of God and is a slave to sin, dead in sin and trespasses. That condition of radical corruption Paul describes by the term *sarx*. When Paul uses the term *sōma*, he is almost always describing the physical aspect of our humanity.

Here is the problem linguistically: not every time the word *sarx* is used in the New Testament does it refer to our fallen, corrupt nature. Sometimes it refers to our physical, earthly existence. For example, John, in writing about the incarnation of Jesus in the prologue to his Gospel, says, "The Word became flesh and dwelt among us, and we beheld His glory" (John 1:14). The word for flesh John uses is *sarx*, and certainly Jesus did not become corrupt. He was like us in every point except with respect to the condition of radical corruption. John is using the term *sarx* to refer to Jesus' incarnation, his becoming "in the flesh" in the realm of this world; yet when John records Jesus' describing the condition of man's fallen humanity to Nicodemus, he writes, "Most assuredly, I say to you, unless one is born of water and the Spirit, he cannot enter the kingdom of God. That which is born of the flesh is flesh, that which is born of the spirit is spirit" (John 3:5–6). The flesh cannot get us into the kingdom of God. Elsewhere, when John records Jesus' saying that the flesh profits nothing (John 6:63), he uses the term *sarx*.

Paul also uses the term *sarx* from time to time to refer to our physical humanity. To the Corinthians he wrote, "Therefore, from now on, we regard no one according to the flesh. Even though we have known Christ according to the flesh [*kata sarka*], yet now we know Him thus no longer" (2 Cor. 5:16). Paul meant that he never saw Jesus during Jesus' earthly ministry. He did not know him until after the resurrection and the ascension. Paul never met Jesus physically. Therein lies the linguistic problem. Not every time the word *sarx* appears in the Bible does it refer to sinful corruption, nor does the word *sōma* always refer to the physical.

There is also a theological problem, which is the influence of ancient Hellenistic philosophy and oriental dualism into early Christian thinking. Plato saw the highest dimension of human experience as being in the mind, and he saw the flesh, the body, as the prison house of the soul. Plato said that the physical aspect of our humanity blocks the mind's ability to penetrate ultimate truth, but the mind, or the soul, is eternal and free and in touch with ultimate reality. The obstruction to a vision of truth is found in the body, and therefore the body is something from which we need to be redeemed.

Plato put forth that anything physical is at best an imperfect copy of the ultimate idea. His view of the body is quite different from the biblical view, which puts forth salvation *of* the body. The Greeks believed in salvation *from* the body until that belief was influenced by oriental mysticism. The physical came to be seen as inherently imperfect or evil. Plato's view heavily penetrated the thinking of the early Christian fathers, who began to teach that the way to salvation is through denying the body all physical pleasure. Food, drink, sex—anything that involved the body—was considered inherently evil, and the method of gaining sanctification was subduing bodily appetites.

We know that physical appetites can be the occasion for human sin but not because the physical is inherently evil. It was God who made our bodies, and when he made them he pronounced his benediction upon them, calling them good. It was God who made marriage and the means of sexual procreation, which also received his benediction, but from the days of the early church down through the centuries the idea has persisted that the kingdom of God is in eating and drinking; it has to do with physical appetites. The misuse of physical appetites is an occasion for sin, but we radically oversimplify when we claim that the struggle Paul is talking about here is the struggle between the mind and the body. It is between the *sarx* and the *pneuma*, the flesh and the spirit. It is between the old man and the new man, between a fallen, corrupt nature and the renewed inner person.

There is a linguistic key that helps us over the hurdle. Almost anytime we see in the New Testament a contrast between spirit and flesh or mind and flesh, the term *sarx* is being used to describe not the physical body but the corrupt nature of the whole person. The corruption of *sarx* is not just a sinful corruption of physical appetites. *Sarx* refers to the body, the soul, the spirit, and the mind. Every part of an unregenerate person is in a state of flesh. By nature we have a mind of flesh, a soul of flesh, and a spirit of flesh, but any time we see Paul contrasting flesh with spirit or flesh with mind, he is talking about the distinction between the old man, the flesh, and the new man, the inner man, which has been made alive by the Holy Spirit.

Amazing Grace

O wretched man that I am! (v. 24). Here we have an exclamation that declares a condition of misery. Paul cries out in anguish after just relating his ongoing struggle with the weighty burden of sin pressing against the inclinations he has toward obedience. Paul uses language that is as politically incorrect as language can be in the contemporary church. In today's church we have become so narcissistic, so preoccupied with self-esteem and self-worth, that preachers must be careful never to engender feelings of guilt or worthlessness in people. That's the mentality of the church today, yet we still like to sing "Amazing Grace."

> Amazing grace, how sweet the sound,
> That saved a wretch like me.
> I once was lost but now am found,
> Was blind, but now, I see.

We don't sing, "Amazing grace, how sweet the sound, who saved a creature of self-esteem such as I." In catching one glimpse of the radiant glory and manifold holiness of God, the saints of the Old Testament would cry out in self-loathing, "I am a worm and not a man. Woe is me, I am undone" (e.g., Isa. 6:5).

There is a sense in which we can so wallow in our guilt and be so preoccupied with our failure that we almost take delight in it, like some form of masochism, but that is not the real problem we face in the church today. The problem we face is a denial of the radical character of sin. We do not hate sin the way we should. We do not abhor the disobedience that we manifest in our lives.

Because Paul was a new man, he was able to say, "I delight in the law of God in my inward man." The sin that indwelt him was not his identity, in the final analysis. "O wretched man that I am!" He is expressing an apostolic state of misery. The Latin text sheds some light on this. It speaks of being in a state of infelicity, a state without happiness or blessedness. When Paul looked at his sin, he saw his wretchedness, and he was threatened and overwhelmed by the power of this misery. He could see nothing in himself in which to put his delight.

Who will deliver me from this body of death? (v. 24). He knows in whom he has believed, and he knows who his deliverer is: **I thank**

God—through Jesus Christ our Lord! (v. 25). Who will deliver us? God. How will he deliver us? Through Jesus Christ our Lord. We have a redeemer. We have a deliverer who promises to deliver us fully and finally from the body of death, from this awful, substantive burden that plagues us all our lives.

After pouring out his heart, Paul concludes this section by saying that if we have problems walking in the Christian life, inconsistencies in our pilgrimage, we can look at him. He has the same problems. No triumphalism flows from the pen of the apostle. He was keenly in touch with who he was in his fallen condition, but he was also keenly in touch with who he was in Christ Jesus, who had rescued him from the principle that resides in the flesh.

No Condemnation

Chapter 8 is linked inseparably to what has just been articulated. We know this because it begins with the word *therefore*, which signifies a conclusion from what has come before: **There is therefore now no condemnation** (8:1). When Paul uses "therefore now," he is referring not just to the last section but to everything he has laid out up to this point. He calls attention to everything he has set forth about the redemption that is ours in Jesus Christ and concludes that there is no condemnation. He does not mean that God will never judge the world but rather that there is an end of condemnation specifically and particularly to a designated group.

If we are Christians, not only is there no condemnation for the sins we have committed, but also we have moved beyond condemnation for whatever we are going to do tomorrow or the day after tomorrow or the day after that. This is one of the most beautiful texts in Scripture for the assurance of salvation. The threat of condemnation is removed forever if we are in Christ Jesus. It is unthinkable that after what God did to his Son on the cross that he will visit more wrath upon his Son. He drank the cup of the condemnation of the Father for his sheep forever. There is no condemnation left anymore for his Son, and if we are in the Son, we are in the cleft of the rock. We are in the shelter of the Rock of Ages. We are covered and hidden, safe now and forever more.

John tells a story of a woman caught in adultery. She was dragged in her shame by the Pharisees to the feet of Jesus. In the midst of her public humiliation, the Pharisees began to test Jesus to see whether he would fully enforce the Law of Moses, which required the death penalty. Jesus knelt down in the sand and began to write. This is the only record we have of Jesus writing anything. We do not know what he wrote, but we can guess. Maybe he wrote in the sand *embezzler* while he looked at one of the men, who then dropped his stone and walked way. One by one the accusers dropped their stones and walked away, leaving Jesus alone with the woman. Then he asked her a question: "Woman, where are those accusers of yours? Has no one condemned you?" (John 8:10). The kangaroo court had disappeared, so she looked at Jesus and said, "No one, Lord" (v. 11). Jesus had addressed them all, saying, "He who is without sin among you, let him throw a stone at her first" (v. 7). Was there anybody in that group without sin? Jesus was without sin, so he had every right to pick up a stone and execute her, but he did not have a stone in his hand. He looked at her and gave her the most comforting words that the woman had ever heard in her life and was ever to hear again: "Neither do I condemn you; go and sin no more" (v. 11).

How much would it mean if Jesus looked at us and spoke those words? "From this day forward I will not condemn you; you never have to fear condemnation from me. The world may condemn you—even the church might condemn you—but if you are in me, you are safe." Only Paul's words can take us from the wretched misery of the ongoing struggle and failure with temptation and sin to the glorious conclusion that, despite the struggle, we have passed beyond the threat of death and judgment. There is no condemnation left for us. Even though we still stumble, our lives are described as those **who do not walk according to the flesh, but according to the Spirit** (v. 1). We are not enslaved by the flesh anymore. Who will rescue us from this body of death? God will, through Jesus Christ our Lord.

27

SPIRITUALLY MINDED

Romans 8:1–11

There is therefore now no condemnation to those who are in Christ Jesus, who do not walk according to the flesh, but according to the Spirit. For the law of the Spirit of life in Christ Jesus has made me free from the law of sin and death. For what the law could not do in that it was weak through the flesh, God did by sending His own Son in the likeness of sinful flesh, on account of sin: He condemned sin in the flesh, that the righteous requirement of the law might be fulfilled in us who do not walk according to the flesh but according to the Spirit. For those who live according to the flesh set their minds on the things of the flesh, but those who live according to the Spirit, the things of the Spirit. For to be carnally minded is death, but to be spiritually minded is life and peace. Because the carnal mind is enmity against God; for it is not subject to the law of God, nor indeed can be. So then, those who are in the flesh cannot please God.

But you are not in the flesh but in the Spirit, if indeed the Spirit of God dwells in you. Now if anyone does not have the Spirit of Christ, he is not His. And if Christ is in you, the body is dead because of sin, but the Spirit is life because of righteousness. But if the Spirit of Him who raised Jesus from the dead dwells in you, He who raised Christ from the dead will also give life to your mortal bodies through His Spirit who dwells in you.

T here is therefore now no condemnation to those who are in Christ Jesus (v. 1). Christians have been placed beyond the reach of the condemnation of God. The condemnation about which Paul writes refers to the last judgment, the outpouring of God's wrath in what the Scriptures describe as damnation.

Who Is Safe?

We live at a time when people look askance at any idea of a wrathful God. People believe there is no room for damnation whatsoever, but damnation is certain to come. The Greek translated in English as "condemnation" is translated in Latin as *damnationus*, from which we get the word *damnation*. Therefore, we could render the text this way: "Therefore there is now no damnation for those who are in Christ Jesus." At the end of that clause is a comma, and what follows the comma might raise in our minds a question, at least for a moment. There's no condemnation (damnation) to those who are in Christ Jesus, **who do not walk according to the flesh**, **but according to the Spirit** (v. 1). Concerning the punctuation, the terms could be restrictive. In other words, Paul could be saying that condemnation has been removed from all Christians who are not "carnal Christians," a false teaching we examined earlier. The idea, then, would be that condemnation has been removed from the Spirit-filled Christian but not from the carnal Christian. The carnal Christian, even though he is in Christ, is still exposed to the threat of condemnation. That is not what the apostle is teaching. He is saying that there is no condemnation to those who are in Christ Jesus because those who are in Christ Jesus do not walk according to the flesh but according to the Spirit.

The Failure of the Law

For the law of the Spirit of life in Christ Jesus has made me free from the law of sin and death (v. 2). Here again is a confusing use of the term *law*. Sometimes in the epistle Paul uses the term *law* to mean principle; other times he uses the term to refer to the moral standards by which God judges us. Here, the first instance of the word *law* refers to principle and the second instance refers to moral standards. The principle of life in Jesus Christ is what makes us free from the principle of sin and death. When we are not in Christ, we operate by the principle of sin. Outside of Christ, sin defines our existence, and the natural consequence of that sin is death.

Paul switches his meaning of the word *law*: **For what the law could not do in that it was weak through the flesh, God did by sending**

His own Son in the likeness of sinful flesh, on account of sin (v. 3).
Paul is speaking of the impotency of the moral law, its failure, at a certain
place and point. The law does not save because it cannot save, which is what
Paul has been laboring throughout the letter. The Holy Spirit knows how
weak we are in our grasp of the gospel, and like dogs that keep returning
to their vomit we keep falling back to the idea that somehow we can justify
ourselves by our behavior, good deeds, and morality. Paul has come at this
from every angle to get rid of that idea and to brush off the spot where that
idea once stood, reiterating that the law cannot do it.

The law is impotent. Not only does the law not save us, but it cannot. It
does not have the power. Paul is not being critical of the law. This weakness
is not the law's fault. The law cannot redeem us because it is incapable of
redeeming those in the flesh. People in the flesh are incapable of obeying
the law, so when they look to the law as a means of salvation, they exercise
futility and reach for an impossible dream. "But what the law could not do
[see the contrast here] God did." There in a nutshell is the gospel. What
our morality can never achieve, God can achieve. What our behavior and
performance are incapable of attaining, God can attain for us. That is the
gospel. We cannot; he can. It is that simple.

God did it by sending His own Son in the likeness of sinful flesh, on account of sin. What the law could not do, God could do, and he did it by
sending his Son. Later in this chapter Paul is going to talk about a different
kind of sonship, that which comes by adoption. He introduces the concept
of sonship here, but it pertains to God's only begotten Son, the *monogenace*.
What the law could not do is to give us Christ; God gives us Christ. Paul
does not say that God did it by sending his Son in the *sarx*, in the condition
of corruption, as a sinner to replace us. Notice how careful Paul is to say
that God "sent His own Son in the *likeness* of sinful flesh," not in the *identity*
of sinful flesh. Jesus Christ is like us, the author of Hebrews tells us, in all
respects except one—he is without sin. In the incarnation all that is proper
to humanity was given to the human nature of our Redeemer except for
sin. Jesus was born without original sin. Jesus was born as Adam was before
the fall. Jesus was not in bondage to a corrupt nature. Christ came in the
flesh as a human being, and he condemned the sin that binds us by taking
it upon himself.

Sin Condemned

**He condemned sin in the flesh, that the righteous requirement
of the law might be fulfilled in us who do not walk according to**

the flesh but according to the Spirit (vv. 3–4). Here Paul is describing the cross, the work of Christ in expiation. When Christ went to the cross in our place, sin was condemned. The cup that he wrestled with at Gethsemane was filled with the wrath of God—wrath that was directed against sin—and Jesus drank it. He accepted to himself the imputation of my sin and your sin. When he went to the cross, the last thing he worried about was the punitive treatment at the hands of the Romans. He went to the cross to receive the punishment for sin by the Father in order to remove our sins. That is the gospel.

In justification God pronounces us just in Jesus Christ, and with that pronouncement he removes our sin. He takes our sin away and puts it in the sea of forgetfulness. As far as the east is from the west he removes our transgressions from us. God does this; the law cannot. The law exposes and defines our sin and imposes the burden of the curse upon it. However, the law can never remove it from us. There is no earthly power to make us clean. The blot is indelible. Only God can remove our sin, which is what the gospel is. In his Son there is no condemnation for his people. There is condemnation for their sin, but it is condemned in Christ and removed. God has taken it out of the books and transferred to us the righteousness of his Son. Our only hope is the righteousness of Christ. If that righteousness is taken away from us, all we are left with is our own. If that happens not only can condemnation reach us, but it most certainly will. We must be willing to shed our blood if necessary for the sake of the gospel.

The Carnal Mind-set

Paul continues to set forth the contrast between life in the flesh and life in the Spirit, between the old man and the new man, giving us more characteristics of each state. **For those who live according to the flesh set their minds on the things of the flesh** (v. 5). The unregenerate person is described by a mind-set. If we question whether we are in the kingdom of God, the first place to look is our mind-set. What is the focus of our life? What do we think about all the time? Are we preoccupied with goals and ambitions and the desires and appetites of this world? I am not asking whether we simply think about such things but rather what our minds are set on. What is our focus?

We do not know where we are going to be a year from now or ten years from now. What really matters is where we are going to be one hundred years from now. If our minds are set on the things of the flesh, then one hundred years from now we will be in perdition, but if our minds are concerned about the things of God—the Spirit of God, the truth of God, the sweetness of God—then one hundred years from now we will be enjoying the brightness of God's glory without interruption. It is easy to fix our minds on the things of this world so that we go through our lives missing the things of eternity. Where is our mind set? Where is our heart set? Where is our treasure? Those who live according to the flesh set their minds on the things of the flesh, **but those who live according to the Spirit, the things of the Spirit** (v. 5).

Here is the second thing that marks carnality: **to be carnally minded is death** (v. 6). If we set our minds on the things of this world, there is an inescapable consequence, which is death. We would do anything in our power to escape death, but it is the only possible consequence if our mind is fixed on the things of this world. To be carnally minded, Paul said, is death, **but to be spiritually minded is life and peace. Because the carnal mind is enmity against God** (vv. 6–7).

If you repeat a lie often enough, people will begin to believe it, and they not only will believe it, but they also will defend it as a truism. Our culture is permeated with the idea that there is no war between man and God. We hear, "God hates the sin but loves the sinner." We hear that God loves everybody unconditionally, but that is the biggest lie of our day, because he does not. At the last judgment God will not send sins to hell; he will send sinners to hell. Even though sinners enjoy the blessings of God's providential love, his filial love is not their desert.

The Scriptures are graphic in describing God's attitude toward impenitent, carnally minded people. God abhors them. Nobody talks that way anymore—except for God in his Word. To set our minds on the things of this world is death. God is the supreme obstacle to people's finding happiness in their desires of the flesh. God is always standing in the way. The life of the flesh is lived not in neutrality but in opposition to God, which is Paul's point. To be carnally minded is to be at enmity with God.

People will never admit to that, **for it is not subject to the law of God** (v. 7). Why do we hate God by nature? Why, in our original state of corruption, do we have a fleshly mind-set? Why do we have what Paul earlier called debased minds (1:28)? The reason is God's law. We are at war with God because we do not want to be subject to the law of God. The media covers every ethical controversy facing mankind today, yet Christianity is held at bay in the discussion. The majority do not want the church involved in ethics because they want the right to do what they want to do. Who gave them that right? Certainly not the law of God. Every time we want to do our will, express our appetites, and live out our preferences, we run right into the wall of the law of God.

Unable to Please God

We are at enmity with God because our carnal mind is not subject to the law of God. The carnal mind is not subject to the law of God because it cannot be. Paul has made this point repeatedly, reminding us of our natural state of moral inability. Original sin has such a powerful grip on our soul and will that in our flesh we are simply not able to do the things of God. That which is born of the flesh is flesh, and the flesh profits nothing. It profits nothing because it cannot profit anything.

So then, those who are in the flesh cannot please God (v. 8). They cannot obey the law of God nor do the will of God, and the worst verdict is that they cannot do anything to please God. Those who are not Christians can do nothing to please God. So long as we are in the flesh, the only response we will have from God is a response of his displeasure, which is a euphemism for wrath. We must remember the context here: "There is therefore now no condemnation for those who are in Christ Jesus, who do not walk according to the flesh, but according to the Spirit" (v. 1). For those who do not walk according to the Spirit, those who are not in Christ Jesus, there is nothing but condemnation. That is the only possible consequence for a life defined by a mind-set of the flesh, one in which the mind is at war with God and with his law and does not want to be ruled by him.

I once made the comment that my favorite word in the Bible is *but*. It is the word that gives me relief when my life is set against the law of God, when I see myself being measured by the standard of God's righteousness, and I slip deeper and deeper into despair because I cannot begin to measure up. Relief comes with that word *but*. Paul writes to the Ephesians, "But God, who is rich in mercy . . ." (Eph. 2:4). The defining thing for the Christian is that at one point God said, "But wait a minute; there is something else."

The Necessary Condition

Paul explains that we are not in the flesh, in the painful condition he has just described: **But you are not in the flesh but in the Spirit, if indeed the Spirit of God dwells in you** (v. 9). That is the only necessary condition Paul gives. Paul does not say that we are in the Spirit if we have the victorious Christian life. We are in the Spirit if one condition is met—the Spirit of God dwells in us. This is where an understanding of the work of the Holy Spirit in our lives is so vitally necessary to a biblical understanding of what Christianity is all about. We cannot be Christians unless the Holy Spirit regenerates us and changes our hearts of stone into hearts of flesh. As Jesus said to Nicodemus, unless a man is born of the Spirit he cannot even see the kingdom of God, let alone enter it. The Spirit enters and indwells every person whom he regenerates, and everyone he indwells he gives the guarantee of future redemption. He seals the redeemed against the day of judgment. When we are born of the Spirit, we are signed, sealed, and delivered. We still fight with ongoing sin, but if the Spirit is in us, we are not in the flesh. We are in the Spirit, in Christ, and these blessed promises apply to us.

Now if anyone does not have the Spirit of Christ, he is not His (v. 9). If we are not indwelt by the Holy Spirit, if we have not been reborn, we do not belong to Christ. However, if we do belong to Christ, we have been born of the Spirit. We have been set free to live not according to the flesh but according to the Spirit.

28

ADOPTED

Romans 8:9–17

But you are not in the flesh but in the Spirit, if indeed the Spirit of God dwells in you. Now if anyone does not have the Spirit of Christ, he is not His. And if Christ is in you, the body is dead because of sin, but the Spirit is life because of righteousness. But if the Spirit of Him who raised Jesus from the dead dwells in you, He who raised Christ from the dead will also give life to your mortal bodies through His Spirit who dwells in you.

Therefore, brethren, we are debtors—not to the flesh, to live according to the flesh. For if you live according to the flesh you will die; but if by the Spirit you put to death the deeds of the body, you will live. For as many as are led by the Spirit of God, these are sons of God. For you did not receive the spirit of bondage again to fear, but you received the Spirit of adoption by whom we cry out, "Abba, Father." The Spirit Himself bears witness with our spirit that we are children of God, and if children, then heirs—heirs of God and joint heirs with Christ, if indeed we suffer with Him, that we may also be glorified together.

Several years ago a stunning novel was made into a major Hollywood motion picture starring Dustin Hoffman. *The Marathon Man* involved great intrigue and concerned a person trying to escape the clutches of a secret Nazi war criminal who was living in the United States. When the hero met with his friends in the underground he asked, "Is it safe?" Over and over again the inquiry came: "Is it safe?" The unifying theme of this entire section of Romans addresses a similar question for those who wonder if they are safe from the wrath of God. Can we be assured that indeed there is no condemnation because we are in Christ Jesus?

Indwelt by the Spirit

In our last study we looked at the distinction the apostle makes between the carnal life of the fallen flesh and the spiritual life of the Christian and came to this conclusion: "So then, those who are in the flesh cannot please God" (v. 8). Those who remain unconverted, those still defined by the corrupt nature—the *sarx* or flesh—are in such a state that nothing they do can please God. Even an unbeliever's prayers are displeasing to God because those prayers do not come from the heart. Such prayers come from some peril that the one praying is facing. The Scripture warns us that while we remain in the flesh there is nothing we can do that will please God.

But you are not in the flesh but in the Spirit, if indeed the Spirit of God dwells in you (v. 9). Previously I labored the point that what marks the life of the true believer is that he is indwelt by the Holy Spirit. Every person indwelt by the Spirit is safe. Every person indwelt by the Spirit is a new creature in Christ and enjoys all the fruits that flow from justification.

Now if anyone does not have the Spirit of Christ, he is not His (v. 9). Our safety in the kingdom of God is not determined by our church membership or whatever good deeds we have managed to perform. Rather, our safety consists of being in Christ and Christ in us. We can offer all our labors to God and belong to a church and have perfect Sunday school attendance, but if the Spirit of Christ does not dwell in us, we do not belong to him. The most terrifying warning from the lips of Jesus comes to us at the conclusion of the Sermon on the Mount: "Many will say to Me in that day, 'Lord, Lord, have we not prophesied in Your name, cast out demons in Your name, and done many wonders in Your name?' And then I will declare to them, 'I never knew you; depart from Me, you who practice lawlessness!'" (Matt. 7:22–23). That is why Paul reminds us that if we do not have the Spirit of Christ, then we do not belong to Christ.

And if Christ is in you, the body is dead because of sin, but the Spirit is life because of righteousness (v. 10). There is a bit of difficulty here in this text, a conundrum of interpretation. Translators have a close call to make. We have seen repeatedly in this section of the epistle the contrast between the spirit and the flesh. Whenever we see that contrast, the flesh refers to the fallen, corrupt nature that we inherit from Adam, and the spirit refers to the new man, the person reborn by the Holy Spirit. When the Bible speaks of the Holy Spirit, there is no doubt as to who is in view—the third person of the Trinity. However, when the word *spirit, pneuma,* occurs by itself without that adjective, *holy,* we question whether the passage in question is speaking of the Spirit of God or of Christ or whether it is simply the human spirit. The Bible teaches that we have a spirit, or soul, as it is sometimes called. In my Bible (NKJV) the word "spirit" in this verse is capitalized, which means the translators became convinced that this must be the Holy Spirit. They may be right, but if the word *holy* is not there, the only way we can distinguish between the Holy Spirit and the human spirit is by the context. I disagree with the translators in this case because the contrast is between the body and the spirit. We are talking about the human body, which is contrasted here with the human spirit. What is the result of Christ being in us? "The body is dead because of sin, but the spirit [our human spirit] is life because of righteousness." If the destiny of our human spirit is different from that of our bodies, it is only because the divine Spirit is dwelling within us.

Assurance

But if the Spirit of Him who raised Jesus from the dead dwells in you, He who raised Christ from the dead will also give life to your mortal bodies through His Spirit who dwells in you (v. 11). We are safe because we are indwelt by the Holy Spirit. All through this text the question of safety is connected to the question of the assurance of salvation. Are we really in a state of grace? How can we know for sure that we are saved and not one of those who will hear those dreadful words from the lips of Jesus on the last day: "I never knew you; depart from Me, you who practice lawlessness!"

With respect to the assurance of salvation there are four types of people. (1) Some are not saved and they know they are not saved. They are not in a state of grace. They are unregenerate. (2) Some are saved and have the full assurance of their state of redemption. They are saved, and they know they are saved. (3) Some are saved but they are not sure of their state. Their souls are restless. It is quite easy to understand those three categories. It is the fourth that muddies the water. (4) Some are not saved but think they are saved. They have assurance of salvation, which salvation they most assuredly do not possess; their assurance is a false assurance.

There are two basic reasons why people can have a false sense of assurance of salvation. The most common is a false understanding of what is necessary for salvation. If people are told that everybody goes to heaven when they die, the reasoning of the unbeliever can be very simple: "Everybody is saved; I am a body; therefore, I am saved." The false premise is that everybody who dies goes to heaven. Another false understanding is that people who live a good life will most assuredly go to heaven when they die: "I have tried to live a good life; ergo, I can be sure that I am going to heaven."

The second reason for false assurance has to do with the evaluation of ourselves. We may have a correct understanding of what is required for going to heaven. We understand that salvation requires personal trust in Christ alone for salvation, but we may deceive ourselves with respect to the profession of faith we think we have made. In other words, we may think we profess true faith when, in fact, we do not. We may think we believe in justification by faith alone because we understand the doctrine intellectually and can pass a test on it in theology class, but in our heart and soul we are not trusting in Christ alone for salvation. We deceive ourselves concerning our state of grace.

That is why Romans 7 and 8 are so important. Paul is showing us a picture of a true believer. Such a person is not controlled by the flesh. He is indwelt by the Spirit of God. If we are indwelt by the Spirit of God it has to make a difference in how we live.

After my conversion, one of the most difficult things for me was the fact that, similar to what Paul expressed in chapter 7, sin was still there. Now, these many years later, there are still sins I battle. Sometimes I ask myself, "How can I have the Spirit of Christ in my soul and still struggle this way?" It is the cry of every Christian. We know that being converted and in a state of grace does not guarantee the end of temptation or falling into momentary lapses of disobedience.

Led by the Spirit

In this section of the letter Paul is giving us pastoral counsel. He is providing information from divine revelation that should calm our spirits and increase our confidence in the state of grace to which we have been called. **Therefore, brethren, we are debtors—not to the flesh** (v. 12). We do not owe the old man anything. We are not under any obligation to fulfill the lusts of our fallen nature. We are debtors to the Spirit: **For if you live according to the flesh you will die; but if by the Spirit you put to death the deeds of the body, you will live** (v. 13).

So far, that is not very good news. If we can be sure we are saved only by putting to death all the sins of our flesh, then we have little reason to be sure of our salvation. Fortunately for us the apostle does not stop there: **For as many as are led by the Spirit of God, these are sons of God** (v. 14). If we want to know if we are in state of grace, if we want to know if we are children of God, we can look here for the answer. The first test we have as to whether we are children of God is whether we are led by the Spirit.

If any biblical concept has been thoroughly muddled in our day, it is this concept of what it means to be led by the Spirit. A danger in the Christian community is that we devise and begin to use Christian jargon, and that jargon becomes the norm that defines our theology rather than the Word of God. The way in which our jargon functions, in many instances, often has little relationship to how the same words are used in Scripture. With the enormous impact of the charismatic movement during the last century came the idea of being led by the Spirit, which is why the concept figures largely into today's Christian jargon.

When people say, "The Spirit of God led me to do this or that," what they usually mean is that they have been guided or are being directed by the Spirit to go here or there, to take this job or that job, to make this decision or that one. We use the language of "being led by the Spirit" to speak of concrete, specific guidance from God in which he opens or closes doors for us. There is nothing wrong with the idea that God leads his people where he wants them to go and into experiences that he wants them to experience, but that is not the primary biblical meaning of being led by the Spirit.

The question that I hear more than any other from Christians is, "How can I know the will of God for my life?" I explain that we have to distinguish in the Bible among various ideas of the will of God. On the one hand, there is the sovereign, efficacious will of God that we sometimes refer to as his hidden will, that which God ultimately has in view for our life and destiny. When people come to me and ask, "How can I know that will for my life?" I say, "You cannot. Quit worrying about it, because it is none of your business. If it were your business, it would not be in the hidden will of God." God has chosen not to reveal certain things.

When the Bible speaks of the will of God for our lives, it does so very differently from what we hear in Christian jargon: "For this is the will of God, your sanctification" (1 Thess. 4:3). If we would spend less time worrying about whether to marry Jane or Mabel or Ellen and more time trying to apply the biblical revelation of what God wants from his people, we would be much happier and more fruitful as Christians. The Bible is not magic. It is not a crystal ball by which we ask the Spirit to guide us into the hidden places. Where the Spirit guides his people is on the path of righteousness to holiness.

Paul has in mind those whose lives are being directed toward the righteousness of God. If our lives are being directed by the Spirit, it is a sure and certain sign that we are children of God, because that is what the indwelling Spirit does. He inclines our hearts. He gives us a hunger and thirst for obedience to Christ. He gives us an affection by which we respond to Jesus' statement, "If you love Me, keep My commandments" (John 14:15).

We must ask ourselves whether we have any inclination to follow the Spirit's leading in obedience to Jesus. If we ask whether our hearts are fully, totally, and absolutely disposed toward following the Spirit into holiness, the only answer we can give is no, but if there is a sense in which our spirits are directed to the things of Christ—any at all—it guarantees us that we are indwelt by the Spirit of God. The flesh never is inclined whatsoever to the things of God. There is where our theology is so important in terms of getting to assurance. If we know the state of someone not born of the Spirit and the state of another who is born of the Spirit, we can discern the difference in two patterns.

Sonship

Sonship is defined biblically in terms of those whose lead we follow. When Jesus talked about the Spirit of God giving liberty to those in bondage, the Pharisees were offended at that teaching. They said, "We have never been in bondage to anyone" (John 8:33). In other words, "I know that I am in the kingdom, Jesus, because I can show you my birth certificate, and my genealogy takes me all the way back to Abraham. I am a descendant of Abraham, so I am in bondage to no man. I do not need the Holy Spirit to rescue me." Jesus did not accept their claim of being Abraham's children. He said, "Most assuredly, I say to you, whoever commits sin is a slave of sin. . . . You are of your father the devil, and the desires of your father you want to do" (vv. 34, 44).

It is not a question of biology but of obedience. We are children of the one whom we obey, and if we obey the lusts of the flesh, if we obey the inclinations of Satan, then we are children of the Devil, not of Abraham or God. That is why Paul says those whose lives are directed by the Spirit of God are sons of God; they follow and obey the one leading them in the way of God.

For you did not receive the spirit of bondage again to fear, but you received the Spirit of adoption by whom we cry out, "Abba, Father" (v. 15). There is a contrast here between two kinds of spirits. One is the spirit of bondage, which is produced by the flesh. It is the spirit of the unregenerate person. Such people remain in prison. They are incarcerated by their old nature. They are slaves to the sinful impulses of their recalcitrant hearts. However, if we have the Spirit within us, we no longer have the spirit of bondage. We are no longer shaking and quaking in servile fear before the Lord God. We now have the spirit of adoption.

It is interesting that the concept of adoption is generally not found among Jewish theologians from antiquity. Adoption is a Roman idea, and Paul uses the metaphor to describe believers' relationship to God. We do not think this is such a big deal in our day and age because we have been told, as a result of nineteenth-century comparative-religion theology, that all roads go to heaven. That is as far away from the biblical view as we can get. In the Bible we see that God has one child, the *monogenēs*, the only begotten, even Jesus Christ. All the rest of his children are not naturally born children; they are adopted. We cannot get into the family of God by biological birth. The only way we can enter in is if God adopts us, and the only way we are adopted is if we are united by the Holy Spirit to the Son of God, Jesus Christ.

One of the great consequences of justification is that all who are justified are immediately adopted into the family of God and now have the unspeakable privilege of addressing God as Father. It is by the Holy Spirit shed abroad in our hearts that we have the authority to cry, "Abba, Father." We have likely heard that the word *Abba* is the common familial term of endearment translated "Daddy." There is truth in that, but it is a dangerous truth. We are invited to use that phrase, *Abba*, when we enter into the inner circle of the family of God. There is no closer relationship. We experience the use of that term in our own families. When my daughter wants something badly from me, she does not address me as *Dad*. It's *Daddy*. When she uses that term, I know she wants something. I do not want to disparage the idea that we do have the privilege of using this close term of affection with our heavenly Father, but I want to stress that the term *Daddy* can be used in a childish or frivolous way. The fact that we can address God now as "Father" and say "Abba" to him does not give us the right to enter into his presence presumptuously or arrogantly.

Toward the end of the twentieth century, German scholar Joachim Jeremias studied the use of the term *Father* for God in Jewish history. His research led him to the conclusion that though there were scores of approved forms of address the Jewish people were encouraged to use in their prayers to God, the idea of directing a prayer to God as father—immediately and directly—was unknown and, in a sense, was abhorrent to them. Jeremias said that the first occurrence of a Jewish prayer addressing God directly as

"Father" was in the tenth century in Italy, and even then it manifested a Christian influence.

One of the most radical things we find in Jesus is the claim he makes over and over again during his earthly ministry of the special intimacy that he had with the Father:

> Most assuredly, I say to you, the Son can do nothing of Himself, but what He sees the Father do. (John 5:19)

> I do nothing of Myself; but as My Father taught Me, I speak these things. (John 8:28)

> All that the Father gives Me will come to Me. (John 6:37)

Again and again Jesus referred to God as his father, which enraged the Pharisees. It is so common to us that we read over it and miss its significance. We miss how radical it was in Jesus' day that any Jewish person would pray and address God as "Father," but Jesus did it almost every time he prayed. When his disciples asked him to teach them how to pray, he said, "In this manner, therefore, pray: 'Our Father in heaven . . .'" (Matt. 6:8–9a). Jesus gave to us the unique privilege he alone held to address the God of heaven and earth as "Father." When we pray, we can call God "Father" because he is now our Father. We have been adopted into his family. It is an unbelievable privilege that we should never take for granted. Jesus never took it for granted. It is so integral to the life of Christian prayer that we would not think of addressing God without the term, but it is a privilege given only to those who have been adopted and have received that Spirit of adoption.

The Witness of the Spirit

Finally we come to the deepest and highest level of assurance of salvation that we can achieve in this world: **The Spirit Himself bears witness with our spirit** (v. 16). Here again we see that word *spirit* used to refer to both the Holy Spirit and our spirit. There is a spiritual conversation here, a spiritual communication that comes from the Holy Spirit to the human spirit, which indicates **that we are children of God** (v. 16). In the final analysis, our assurance of salvation is not a logical deduction springing from our theology. Our assurance is certainly not based on a careful analysis of our behavior. Our final assurance comes by the testimony of God the Holy Spirit, who bears witness with and through our spirits that we are children of God.

This is wonderful but also dangerous. Paul is not falling into some kind of gnostic mysticism here, a special revelation or secret pipeline through which the Holy Spirit talks to us and gives a private revelation. Paul is talking about how the Spirit of the Lord confirms a truth to our human spirit. The Spirit does not come and whisper into our ear when we are driving down the highway, "Relax, you are one of mine." We need to understand that when the Spirit communicates to God's people, he communicates to them by the Word, with the Word, through the Word, and never against the Word. There are millions who claim to be led by the Spirit into sin and disobedience. The testimony we receive from the Holy Spirit comes in and through the Word.

It is so important that we understand that. If we lack assurance and want our hearts to be at peace, we must go to the Word. The Spirit confirms his truth to us in and through the Word. If we want to be led by the Spirit of God, we must immerse ourselves in the Spirit-inspired Word. We are called to test the spirits to make sure that the spirit who is leading us is the Holy Spirit, and the only test we can apply is the test of the Word itself.

The Spirit bears witness with our spirit that we are children of God, **and if children, then heirs** (v. 17) because all God's children participate in his estate. They are all his promised beneficiaries. If we are children, we are heirs of God, **joint heirs with Christ, if indeed we suffer with Him, that we may also be glorified together** (v. 17).

29

SUBJECTED IN HOPE

Romans 8:18-27

For I consider that the sufferings of this present time are not worthy to be compared with the glory which shall be revealed in us. For the earnest expectation of the creation eagerly waits for the revealing of the sons of God. For the creation was subjected to futility, not willingly, but because of Him who subjected it in hope; because the creation itself also will be delivered from the bondage of corruption into the glorious liberty of the children of God. For we know that the whole creation groans and labors with birth pangs together until now. Not only that, but we also who have the firstfruits of the Spirit, even we ourselves groan within ourselves, eagerly waiting for the adoption, the redemption of our body. For we were saved in this hope, but hope that is seen is not hope; for why does one still hope for what he sees? But if we hope for what we do not see, we eagerly wait for it with perseverance. Likewise the Spirit also helps in our weaknesses. For we do not know what we should pray for as we ought, but the Spirit Himself makes intercession for us with groanings which cannot be uttered. Now He who searches the hearts knows what the mind of the Spirit is, because He makes intercession for the saints according to the will of God.

We have just considered the extraordinary grace and blessedness that comes with our having been adopted by the Father into the family of God as heirs of God and joint heirs with Christ. All the Father gives to the Son is shared with all those united to the Son by faith. Now Paul considers once more the afflictions, trials, tribulation, pain, and suffering that are such an integral part of the veil of tears through which we walk in this world. Through too much television exposure we have become jaded by scenes of upheaval and violence all around the world, yet the news leaves us asking, has the world gone crazy? Violence upon violence, hostility upon hostility, suffering, blood, and death all around us—when we look at the reality of all that and see the suffering that comes in its wake, we pause at times and wonder, where is God in all this?

Present Suffering, Future Glory

A philosopher, John Stuart Mill, considered the manifest presence in the world of pain, suffering, violence, and wickedness, and he concluded that what we encounter on a daily basis belies any hope of a good and loving God. In skepticism he said that if God is a God of love yet he allows such pain and suffering, then he is powerless to prevent it and is nothing more than a divine weakling incapable of administering peace and justice. If, on the other hand, he has the power to prevent evil but chooses not to, standing by and allowing it, then he may be powerful but he is not good or loving. The complaint Mill raised against historical Christianity is that either God is good but not all powerful, or he is all powerful but not good.

What is missing from Mill's oversimplified equation concerning the economy of grief and pain in the world is the reality of sin. God not only tolerates violence and suffering, but he also—even more so—actually ordains it, yet we cannot leave sin out of the equation. It is not that God lacks in goodness; it is that we lack in goodness. The entrance of human sin into the world plunged the whole creation into ruin, a ruin that includes not just people but animals and the land itself; the earth mourns because of us. When the transgression came in paradise, the curse of God extended beyond Adam and Eve and even beyond the serpent; the land itself was cursed.

Throughout the prophetic oracles of the Old Testament, we see God chastening his people Israel for their hard-necked disobedience, and he tells them through the prophets that because they do not listen to his word, violence follows upon violence. The land mourns; the ground suffers. When the Bible rehearses the repercussions of the fall, it does so in cosmic terms. The effects of the fall on the human species and the ruination of the whole creation are laid at our doorstep. This reflects God's judgment upon us, which spills over into the domain in which we were created to be God's vice-regents in exercising dominion over the earth, the animals, and the ground. When we were ruined, everything under our dominion was affected by it.

That is what Paul is concerned to reflect in the passage before us, but first he sets a contrast between the present and the future, between the present sufferings and the future glory that God has prepared for his people. Paul is quick to point out that this is not a simple formula of ratio and proportionality. There is no analogy between the present climate of pain and the future climate of blessedness. The comparative here is in terms of *how much more*. The usually articulate Paul cannot seem to find words, even under the inspiration of the Holy Spirit, to describe the radical difference between the now and the then: **For I consider that the sufferings of this present time are not worthy to be compared with the glory which shall be revealed in us** (v. 18). The difference between the present degree of pain we experience and the blessedness to which God has appointed his people is so immensely different that there is no way to compare them. Any comparison we come up with falls short.

Notice that Paul considers the sufferings of this *present* time; in other words, suffering is real, not just an illusion. Paul was not a practitioner of Christian Science. He understood in a visceral way, in a way few of us have experienced, the stark reality of human suffering. One of the most persecuted, afflicted men ever to grace this fallen planet was the apostle Paul. Indeed, his Savior was even more acquainted with grief and sorrow; nevertheless, there are few who have approached Paul's personal experience of suffering. He shook off that suffering in light of the hope God has given in Jesus Christ. He said that it is not even worthy to talk about the suffering in comparison to what God has laid up for us in the future.

Christians have been ridiculed for their hope of heaven and future redemption. We are told that this is pie in the sky. Karl Marx believed that religion was invented for economic reasons. He said that in a society dominated by class, the owners are always in the minority to the workers, and if ever the majority—the laborers—understood the strength inherent in their number they would rise up in revolt against the owners. Therefore, the owners gave the workers religion and the promise of a future benefit. In the meantime, workers lived in chains and in sweat and toil while the owners, according to Marx, laughed all the way to the bank.

Consider that in the American experiment with slavery. If we look carefully at some of the songs that enrich our hymnody, we hear the motif of the slave who sings:

Swing low, sweet chariot,
Comin' for to carry me home;
Swing low, sweet chariot,
Comin' for to carry me home.

I looked over Jordan,
And what did I see,
Comin' for to carry me home,
A band of angels comin' after me,
Comin' for to carry me home.

A slave's only hope lay in another world, in heaven. Marx said that religion is "the opiate of the people." Opium is a narcotic given to dull the senses, to minister to pain, to give people hope when there is no hope.

I do not believe what Marx said. I believe that God's promises are eternal, immutable, and unbreakable. Again and again God says to his people, "Yes, the pain now is real, but wait. We are not finished yet. I have a plan for my people, and that plan is glorious. I have established my Son upon his throne, and I have called a people to myself that I have given as a gift to my Son, and together with him they will reign forever." That redemption will extend far beyond the realm of the human; the whole world, which has been plunged into ruin, will be redeemed. There will be a renovation—a new heaven and a new earth. This is our Father's world. It is his property, and he may dispose of it however he sees fit, and he has seen fit to appoint it for glory for those who love his coming. Paul is eloquent here, rhapsodic, in considering this future promise.

Expectation

For the earnest expectation of the creation eagerly waits for the revealing of the sons of God (v. 19). We find here a personification. Even the impersonal forces of nature are brought into the arena of celebrating God's redemption:

Let the rivers clap their hands;
Let the hills be joyful together
before the LORD,
For He is coming to judge the earth.
With righteousness He shall judge the world,
And the peoples with equity. (Ps. 98:8b–9)

> The mountains and the hills
> Shall break forth into singing before you,
> And all the trees of the field shall clap their hands. (Isa. 55:12)

All creation rejoices in the expectation of what lies in the future.

There is something I always notice when I walk into the woods to go hunting: the absolute silence. I hear no birds singing. I hear only my footsteps as I make my way to the tree stand from which I wait and watch. Once I have been up in the tree stand for fifteen or twenty minutes, however, I begin to hear the chatter of squirrels, the songs of birds, and the gobbling of turkeys. The woods come alive. I have sat in tree stands and looked down from my perch and seen wild boar, turkeys, and deer feeding—a variety of beasts coexisting in the wild in a spirit of peace—but as soon as they realize that man is present, a pall of fear falls over the bird, the squirrel, the deer, and the turkey. It was not supposed to be like that. God intended that the animals rejoice in the presence of those who have been given dominion over them, but now the animals suffer because of us, and they are no longer comfortable when we intrude into their domain. Nevertheless, these dumb brutes, as they are called, have an earnest expectation, a conviction of hope, for the day when that will all change, when the glory of God will be revealed in us, **for the creation was subjected to futility, not willingly, but because of Him who subjected it in hope** (v. 20).

The word *futility* is one of the ugliest words in the English language. Nothing can drive the human being to despair more quickly or deeply than the idea that our pain and labor are mere exercises in futility and utterly meaningless. What could be worse than the sentence given to Sisyphus in the Greek myth? Sisyphus uses all his energy to push a gigantic rock to the top of a mountain, but as soon as he gets it to the top, the rock falls back to the bottom, and he has to push it back to the top again and again, forever. He was sentenced to vain labor. Paul's words to the Corinthians stand in contrast to what happens in the myth: "Therefore, my beloved brethren, be steadfast, immovable, always abounding in the work of the Lord, knowing that your labor is not in vain in the Lord" (1 Cor. 15:58). That is the hope of the gospel, that our pain is not meaningless. Our toil is not futile. Every ounce of effort we expend in this world, every tear that falls across our cheek, is not meaningless.

For the present time the whole creation has been subjected to the appearance of futility, something which did not occur by vote. It was set by divine decree. This world is filled with pain and suffering, not because God is not good but because he is good and will not tolerate evil. God has subjected the entire creation to pain and affliction because of our sin. The next time we hurt and become angry with God and shake our fist in his face and ask, "Why me?" we must listen for the reply: "Why not you?" The real question is why God in his grace should store up for us in heaven a glory and blessedness so great that the suffering we endure now is not worthy to be compared with it.

Creation Delivered

The creation itself also will be delivered from the bondage of corruption into the glorious liberty of the children of God (v. 21). We have seen what the gospel has done to deliver us. By nature we are people in bondage, but Paul has just explained that through the power of the Holy Spirit, we have been set free. We are no longer under those bonds of sin. We have been released from that incarceration. We have been set free, and that release from bondage does not end with us. The goal of the finished work of Christ is to rescue the entire creation so that even the land will stop mourning and the animals will no longer be afraid. Though nature may be red in tooth and fang, the bloody crimson violence will be done away with in the new heaven and the new earth, where the lion will lie down with the lamb. Paul says that the creation itself will be delivered from the bondage of corruption into glorious liberty.

Just as the created world has suffered because of our sin, the whole creation will participate in the liberation from the consequences of sin at the time of the manifestation of the children of God. **We know that the whole creation groans and labors with birth pangs together until now** (v. 22). Here we see the metaphor of a woman in labor, at that threshold of pain prior to the delivery. It is excruciating. She cries; she groans. Paul says the whole creation is like that, crying and groaning in birth pangs, but the pain of that labor is not worthy to be compared with the joy that follows when the child is born.

Not only that, but we also who have the firstfruits of the Spirit, even we ourselves groan within ourselves, eagerly waiting for the adoption, the redemption of our body (v. 23). We have already been adopted, so there is a present sense in which we experience the adoption into the family of God, but there is still a "not yet" dimension of what it means to be adopted, which will be revealed when we receive the inheritance stored up for us in heaven. How wonderful it is to hear the promise of what God will say: "Come, my beloved. Inherit the kingdom that I have prepared for you from the foundation of the world." That is our expectation and hope.

For we were saved in this hope, but hope that is seen is not hope; for why does one still hope for what he sees? (v. 24). Paul talks constantly about hope. As I noted earlier, he does not use the term *hope* the way we commonly use it. We use the term *hope* to express our desire for some future result that is at present uncertain, but the concept of hope in the New Testament indicates a situation in which the future is absolutely certain. It is faith looking forward. It is faith being certain and receiving the assurance of what God promises for tomorrow. Our hope is the anchor for our souls. It is what gives stability to our faith. When we stumble and trip today, when we become uncertain in our faith because of afflictions, hope kicks in. We are reminded of God's promise for tomorrow. That is the great explanation for the behavior of the saints of the ages who were willing to go up against the lions in the arena and to be human torches in the garden of Nero. They knew where they were going. They had a hope that would never embarrass them or leave them ashamed. Paul says that hope in what is seen is not hope, **but if we hope for what we do not see, we eagerly wait for it with perseverance** (v. 25). Paul has linked perseverance and character many times in this epistle. It is hope that keeps us going.

The Help of the Spirit

One of the most important passages in the Bible that instructs us about the nature of godly prayer is this one: **Likewise the Spirit also helps in our weaknesses. For we do not know what we should pray for as we ought, but the Spirit Himself makes intercession for us with groanings which cannot be uttered. Now He who searches the hearts knows what the mind of the Spirit is, because He makes intercession for the saints according to the will of God** (vv. 26–27). We understand that our communion with God the Father is not a simple one-on-one communication. We pray in the name of Jesus because one of the most important roles that Jesus exercises even now is that of our high priest in heaven. He makes intercession for us every day. We do not dare appear in our own garments to make our requests, but we come before the throne of grace garbed in Christ's righteousness, and we plead for his intercession. We should always keep in mind when we pray that Jesus is praying for us. Prayer is a Trinitarian activity; it is more than simply praying to the Father through the Son. In this text we see that our great Helper, the Holy Spirit, assists in the articulation of our prayers addressed to Christ and the Father.

When we pray, we must remember to ask the Holy Spirit to assist us because so often we do not pray rightly. If we really want to see answers to prayer that will put strength in our souls, we pray according to the leading of the Holy Spirit. The Spirit helps us pray according to the will of God rather than according to the will of our flesh. We will see prayers answered when they correspond to the will of the Father. If we ask God to do something against his will, we are going to be frustrated. He will answer those prayers—he will say no. When the Spirit, who searches the deep things of God and knows our souls and the mind of the Father, helps us to pray as we ought, we begin to pray according to the will of God.

30

ALL THINGS FOR GOOD

Romans 8:28–30

And we know that all things work together for good to those who love God, to those who are the called according to His purpose. For whom He foreknew, He also predestined to be conformed to the image of His Son, that He might be the firstborn among many brethren. Moreover whom He predestined, these He also called; whom He called, these He also justified; and whom He justified, these He also glorified.

We know from the teaching of Scripture that our ultimate destiny as Christians is to enter into heaven, a place, we are told in the book of Revelation, where there will be no night, no death, and no tears. In heaven we will live forever without affliction and pain. The environment of heaven will never be marred by the presence of evil or sin. Heaven is a place where nothing goes wrong and no evil takes place. Heaven is a place to which we look forward with joyous anticipation, as the apostle did in the verses just preceding our current text. In those verses, Romans 8:18–27, Paul shows that there is no comparison between the afflictions we endure in this life and the glory that has been stored up for us in heaven.

A Sure Promise

What about now? We are not in heaven. We are still in a vale of tears. How would we feel if Jesus walked in the door and spoke directly to us, saying, "I have good news for you: I promise that nothing bad will ever happen to you again"? In a very real sense he has already said that, although he does so in a sideways manner. It is basically the affirmation we are given here in Romans 8:28. Paul says with assurance, **And we know . . .** (v. 28). He is not speaking with the editorial *we* or the magisterial *we*; he is speaking inclusively of all who are in the faith. The one thing that all true believers know for sure is **that all things work together for good to those who love God, to those who are the called according to His purpose** (v. 28). Paul gives us an astonishing affirmation when he says with certainty that all things are working together for good for those of us who love the Lord and who are the called according to his purpose.

Good versus Evil

One of the most fundamental principles of biblical Christianity is that we are never to call good evil or evil good. That is essentially the lie of Satan, which has been spread abroad through every generation. The great seduction of the enemy is to convince us that sin is really not so bad. In fact, it is actually good. If we are to experience the best that life has to offer, the Devil says, we must indulge ourselves in things that God prohibits. Because Satan lies, he calls evil good and good evil. Someone who mentored me during my theological training was fond of making a distinction between four types of actions:

1) Actions that are good-good.
2) Actions that are bad-good.
3) Actions that are bad-bad.
4) Actions that are good-bad.

1) *Actions that are good-good.* Good-good actions display the sort done by Christ, by God, and by the saints in heaven, where there is no alloy of evil mixed in. Whatever good we are able to do as we are being sanctified never reaches the level of good-good, because there is a pound of flesh in all the virtue we accomplish in this life. Augustine well said that our best works, because of the way in which they remain tainted by our human pride, are, at best, splendid vices.

2) *Actions that are bad-good.* These actions are accompanied by the intention for virtue and obedience to God but nevertheless contain shortcomings

and failures. Such actions are in keeping with what Calvin called *civic virtue*, in which righteousness is achieved even by the unregenerate pagan. Even an unbeliever can, through enlightened self-interest, stumble at times upon the good and do good, though not of a heavenly sort. Someone who drives his car according to the speed limit and is obedient to the civil magistrate is doing a good thing, even though not by God's standard. God weighs actions in terms of both outward conformity to his law and inward motive. The pagan may have external righteousness. He may drive his car according to the speed limit, but the reason he drives his car at 55 mph is not that he has a desire in his heart to please the Lord; rather, he is trying to escape a speeding ticket or another negative impact. We find people driving at 55 mph on the interstate simply because they like to drive at 55 mph. We find these same people driving 55 mph in a 35-mph speed zone or even in a 25-mph speed zone. From time to time their outward behavior corresponds to the law but not from any virtuous intent. That is *bad-good*. The good is not motivated from a pure heart.

3) *Actions that are bad-bad*. Bad-bad actions are so bad that no virtue is mixed in. Such actions are pure transgression outwardly, motivated by a hostile heart to God inwardly. Such are the sort of actions undertaken every moment by Satan and his fallen angels.

4) *Actions that are good-bad*. It is easy to understand the first three categories. The more difficult one to understand is the one we call *good-bad*. When certain actions take place, they are simply evil; nevertheless, under the providence of God, under his sovereignty over human events, he has the power to bring good out of them, which is a glorious thing we can experience as Christians. Everything we are called upon to suffer, even things that are truly bad, are, nevertheless, being used by God for our ultimate good. Viewed from a proximate perspective, such actions are indeed bad, and there is no redemptive virtue in them, but from the ultimate perspective it is good that they are happening because God is using them for his ultimate purpose. That is a critical point to grasp if we are to understand anything of the providence of God.

The fact that evil is redeemed for good is based on what theologians call, under the heading of providence, "the doctrine of concurrence" or confluence. The doctrine of concurrence holds that certain actions in which humans exercise their will to do what they wish, even to making diabolical choices, are, nevertheless, under the providence of God, who is at work in them. He has the power to trump our evil inclinations and desires and bring good to pass.

The Sovereignty of God

The best illustration in the Bible of the doctrine of concurrence occurs at the end of the book of Genesis. Joseph suffered greatly at the hands of his treacherous and jealous brothers. He was separated from his family and countrymen, sold into slavery, falsely accused, and thrown into prison. Finally, through the providence of God Joseph was rescued and elevated to the right hand of Pharaoh, becoming the prime minister of Egypt. Then famine came to Joseph's homeland of Canaan, and Jacob, Joseph's father, sent his other sons as emissaries down to Egypt to seek relief. In the process they met Joseph. They did not recognize him, but Joseph recognized them. What follows is one of the most poignant narratives in the entire Old Testament. The moment of truth came when Joseph revealed his identity to his brothers. They were terrified of his wrath and begged for his forgiveness. Joseph said, "As for you, you meant evil against me; but God meant it for good" (Gen. 50:20). What an incredible, incomprehensible biblical revelation that is.

God orders his providences so as not to cancel out secondary causes. He does not annihilate the actions of the human will, which are undertaken freely. In the Genesis text we see that Joseph is aware that his brothers not only sinned against him and committed something that was really evil, but they also sinned with intent, with malice aforethought. They had conspired and schemed to get rid of their brother of whom they were so jealous. We have in this text the appearance of what we call *intentionality*. As rational beings, the brothers of Joseph fully intended to bring harm to him, so their sin was intentional. But Joseph said that despite their intentions and their efforts to bring them about, God was involved in the whole thing. God was acting, and his intention was purely righteous; there was no mixture of evil in it. His sovereign providence in it was altogether good.

We see the same thing operating in the story of Job. Satan worked through the Sabeans and Chaldeans to exercise intentional actions of harm against Job. All the while they were fulfilling the plan of God, whose purposes in these things is never evil but altogether good and glorious.

People choke when I tell them that God ordains whatsoever comes to pass, at least, in some sense. The Westminster Confession says that God ordains whatsoever comes to pass, but it is quick to add that this does not occur in such a way as to eliminate secondary causes or to make of no significance the will of the creature. God does not do violence to the will of the creature. Nevertheless, God's sovereignty prevails in every instance.

Some have said, "God's sovereignty ends where human freedom begins," but it is blasphemy, and a moment's thought will reveal it to be so. The sovereignty of God is not in any way limited, conditioned, or dependent on man's authority. Our freedom is a gift from God. It is real. We exercise and enjoy freedom, but it is everywhere limited by God's sovereignty. That is what we mean by *sovereignty*. God is sovereign; we are not. Even the fall of the human race was in some sense ordained by God.

Some time ago I was misunderstood as having said that God needed the fall in order to bring about his plan of election. I would cut my tongue out before I would make a statement like that. God does not need anything. He did not need the fall. He can bring to pass his sacred will however he desires, and not because he needs it. Karl Barth, in his qualified supralapsarianism, speaks as if God needed the fall to bring about his plan of redemption, but I do not hold to that. I have said that God ordained the fall in some sense, but I say it simply because the fall happened, and God is sovereign and omniscient.

God knew before the fall that Adam and Eve were going to fall. God also had the power and authority to intervene to crush the head of the serpent before the serpent opened his mouth. God could have prevented the fall from occurring, but he did not. However, he did not force Adam and Eve to sin. If he chose not to stop them from sinning, then in some sense he ordained that they not be stopped. If he ordained that they not be stopped, then that means he ordained that they would, in fact, sin. If the Lord God omnipotent permitted the fall for his purposes, he must have had a good reason for it. Even though evil is in the world, the fact that it is here has to be good, or it could not possibly be here. Whatever God ordains should come to pass according to his inscrutable and eternal purpose must be ultimately for good.

Evil is evil, but it is within the broader, eternal purpose of God and ultimately for his glory. What if the Creator would permit the creature to be engaged in evil only to manifest in the final judgment his perfect justice in punishing wickedness? I do not know if that is the reason, but I know that whatever God does, he does well.

We have that affirmation here in Romans 8:28. Not all things are good. Paul is not an illusionist who says there is no such thing as evil, but he does say that all things are working together for good; that is, the ultimate purpose is a good purpose. In the meantime, even though evil befalls and afflicts us such evil is working for our good. The Greek word Paul uses here is *sunergeō*, from which we get the word *synergy*. A work of synergy, or synergism, is a cooperative venture. When two or more parties work together on a task, we say that there is synergy involved in the activity, a working together. That is the word Paul uses to describe the way in which God's providence works with our afflictions for good.

Good for Whom?

Notice the limitation that Paul gives here: God's working all things together for good is not for the benefit of everybody. Rather, all things are working together for good "to those who love God, to those who are the called according to His purpose." The drama of concurrence of synergy, whereby God is making all things work together for good, is simply for those who love him. Obviously that does not include everybody because the vast majority of mankind lives and dies at enmity with God. However, if we are Christians and the love of God has been shed abroad in our hearts, we have nothing to fear.

Paul's statement is part of Romans 8, where we are still dealing with the question, is it safe? Are we in a place where we now have no condemnation to fear? If so, we have nothing to fear for eternity. We have nothing to fear from the afflictions we have to endure in this present life, because all these things are every moment working together under the sovereignty of God for good. If we love him, good is working for the believer.

Those who love God are **those who are the called according to His purpose** (v. 28). Debates ensue constantly about election and predestination. Every generation of Christians has to fight this battle, as if election were some esoteric doctrine that only elite intellectuals and professional theologians can grasp though the doctrine is on every page in the Bible. Even if the doctrine were backed up only by the verse before us in Romans, it would be enough to establish the doctrine of election forever. In this verse, Romans 8:28, assurance is given to those who love God, and those who love God are identified as the ones who are the called according to his purpose. Some say that "those who are called" is referring to those who respond positively to the preaching of the gospel. It is a nice theory, but it is not what the apostle is saying. Paul is defining those who love God as the ones "who are the called according to God's purpose."

Effectual Calling

In almost every instance where the Bible speaks of the call of God, it is speaking of what we call the "effectual call." *Effectual calling* is a term that describes the fact that what God calls forth occurs; what he purposes to effect by his call is effected. It started with creation. When God called the world into existence *ex nihilo*, it was not an invitation. God did not plead with the darkness to produce light. He did not woo the universe to come into being. When God in his omnipotent power said, "Let there be light," that call was always and everywhere effectual. What God purposes in whatever call he gives, that purpose can never be frustrated because God is God. He is not a president elected by majority vote. He rules sovereignly from all eternity because he is the Lord God omnipotent who reigns. Nothing—no darkness, emptiness, threat of chaos, or sinful disposition—can ultimately resist the power of his call because his grace in the call is irresistible.

It is not that we lack the capacity to resist. Our whole lives demonstrate that we can and do resist grace. *Irresistible grace* means that even though we resist with all our might, God's grace trumps our resistance and brings to pass what his eternal plan has been and is. When God and Christ called Paul to be an apostle, it was no mere summons. Paul explained that he was called to be an apostle not by men but by the will of God (Gal. 1:1). He was referring to that divine purpose, which is effected by the call itself.

When we talk about "the called" or "the elect," we mean those who have been summoned not only outwardly but also inwardly by the Spirit, who changes the disposition of their hearts and effects the transformation of their souls—the resurrection from spiritual death to spiritual life. If we are believers today, it is not because we made God's call effectual in our lives; it is because God did. We were called according to his purpose.

God's Purpose

What is a purpose? A purpose is a desired end, a planned consequence. When we set forth our goals and articulate our purposes, our plans are fallible at best. We know the best-laid plans of mice and men can go astray. Fortunately, the poet Robert Burns was talking only about the plans of mice and men; he did not include God in that category, because the best-laid plans of God never come to naught. A pervasive doctrine in the Christian world today strips God of his sovereignty and, in effect, of his very deity. According to this doctrine, a poor, impoverished deity rings his hands in heaven, hoping, at times against hope, that somebody will take seriously the sacrifice that his Son made and bring his plan of salvation to fruition. That is not God nor is a deity like that worthy to be given the title *God*.

God is the Lord God, the God who says to Pharaoh, "Let My people go" (Ex. 10:3). Pharaoh's heart was hardened, which is attributed in Scripture to both God and to Pharaoh himself. Paul will explore that in Romans 9. For now, we need only keep in mind that even Pharaoh, the most powerful man in the universe at that time, was clay in the hands of our Creator and our Redeemer, who had a purpose for his people, and through those people he had a purpose for the whole world: exodus, liberation, redemption, and salvation.

It is not as if God considered the exodus only after hearing the cries of the Israelites as they groaned about the burdens laid on them by Pharaoh. It is not as if God noticed the calamitous situation and said, "I had better do something about it." God spoke to the children of Israel through Joseph, whom the enslaving Pharaoh did not know, saying, "You meant evil against me; but God meant it for good, in order to bring it about as it is this day, to save many people alive" (Gen. 50:20). God planned the bondage of Israel. He planned the exodus from Egypt just as much as he planned the betrayal of Joseph and his imprisonment to demonstrate that all the afflictions and suffering that Joseph endured were working together not only for Joseph's good but for Israel's good and the good of all saints of every age.

No Tragedies

Immediately following Paul's dramatic affirmation that all things work together for good to those who love the Lord, Paul launches into the Golden Chain: **For whom He foreknew, He also predestined to be conformed to the image of His Son, that He might be the firstborn among many brethren. Moreover whom He predestined, these He also called; whom He called, these He also justified; and whom He justified, these He also glorified** (vv. 29–30).

What we get from Romans 8:28 is this: in the short run each of us is visited at some point by tragedy. We are actors in the theater of the tragic. Tragedies are on our minds every day, but what Romans 8:28 teaches is that ultimately—not proximately but ultimately—there are no tragedies for the Christian. Tragedy now is blessing later. In every tragedy we experience, God is working with it, molding it and shaping it, for our eternal blessedness. The tragic is ephemeral and temporary. It is in the world but never permanent.

The other side of the coin is this: for the unbeliever who persists in his unbelief, every blessing he receives from the hand of God in this life is ultimately working for his damnation. Every blessing the impenitent person ungratefully receives from the hands of God adds more sin to that depository of sin that Paul mentioned earlier: "In accordance with your hardness and your impenitent heart you are treasuring up for yourself wrath in the day of wrath and revelation of the righteous judgment of God, who will render to each one according to his deeds" (Rom. 2:5–6). Every blessing that goes unthanked, unacknowledged, and unappreciated by the pagan will end up as a tragedy for the ungrateful one.

We live in a topsy-turvy world in which the tragedy for the Christian is a blessing for eternity, but the blessing for the pagan is a tragedy for eternity. God works all things together for good for those who love him.

31

THE GOLDEN CHAIN

Romans 8:29–31

For whom He foreknew, He also predestined to be conformed to the image of His Son, that He might be the firstborn among many brethren. Moreover whom He predestined, these He also called; whom He called, these He also justified; and whom He justified, these He also glorified. What then shall we say to these things? If God is for us, who can be against us?

A ll through Romans 8 Paul is dealing with the position of safety we have in our state of salvation in Jesus Christ. After we are justified, there is no more condemnation. The entire chapter is filled with encouragement to those who are in Jesus Christ. The acme of that encouragement comes in verse 28: "We know all things work together for good to those who love God, to those who are the called according to His purpose." The idea that God effectually calls certain people according to his good pleasure and purpose introduces the so-called Golden Chain in the verses before us now.

TULIP

In terms of the theological significance of the Golden Chain, let me introduce it by reviewing some background that we covered earlier in our study of Romans. In seventeenth-century Holland, a group of theologians rose

up from the Dutch Reformed Church to protest against historic Reformation theology, and with Arminius and his friends they entered into what was
called Remonstration, that is, a protest against some of the sixteenth-century
Calvinist doctrines. Five doctrines in particular were given the weight of
their theological criticism: (1) the doctrine of man's total moral inability as
the result of the fall; (2) the idea of a predestination that is rooted in God's
sovereign decrees from all eternity in which the number of the elect is fixed;
(3) the idea that the atonement of Christ was designed by the Father as the
sole means by which he would bring his elect to salvation; (4) the doctrine of
effectual calling; that is, when the Holy Spirit calls people and effects their
regeneration, that work of divine grace is so powerful that no human resistance can overcome it; and (5) the idea of eternal security, which holds that
once a person is in a state of grace, he will remain in that state forever.

These five points of remonstration provoked the judgment of the senate
of Dordrecht, and the protestors were labeled as heretics and disciplined for
their errors. As a result of the controversy, these five issues became known
as the five points of Calvinism and fell under the rubric of the acrostic
T-U-L-I-P: T for total depravity; U for unconditional election; L for limited
atonement; I for irresistible grace; and P for perseverance of the saints.

Unconditional Election

What we are concerned about here is the U in TULIP, the doctrine of unconditional election. The phrase *unconditional election* simply means that from
all eternity God chose, or elected, a fixed number of fallen human beings
to be redeemed and to be conformed to the image of his Son. This election
was unconditional in the sense that it was not based upon some foreseen
conditions of the creature.

At the time of the Reformation and the recovery of biblical soteriology,
the magisterial reformers were of one mind on the issue of election. The
Reformed doctrine of predestination is so often identified with the Swiss theologian John Calvin, but that is a little bit of a distortion historically, because
there is nothing in Calvin's doctrine of predestination that was not first in
Martin Luther's doctrine. Luther defended this doctrine vigorously against the
diatribe of Erasmus of Rotterdam. There was nothing in Luther's doctrine
of predestination that was not first articulated by the great Augustine, and
nothing in Augustine's doctrine of predestination that was not first in the
mind and teaching of the apostle Paul. Additionally, there was nothing in
Paul's doctrine of predestination that was not first articulated by our Lord

himself, and there was nothing in Jesus' doctrine of predestination that was not first articulated by Moses in the Old Testament.

As convinced as Luther was of the supreme doctrine of God's electing grace, his chief lieutenant, Philip Melancthon, a brilliant theologian in his own right, modified Luther's view when Luther died. Melancthon's modification became the view that was embraced by later Lutheranism, a doctrine of predestination called the *prescient* view of predestination.

The word *prescience* comes from a prefix and a root. The prefix *pre-* means "beforehand" and the root word *science* means "knowledge," so *prescience* is a kind of prior knowledge. We often use the term *foreknowledge* to describe the same idea. Melancthon's view, which has become the majority report in modern evangelical Christianity, is this: God knows in advance which people will render a positive response to the gospel and choose by their free will to come to Jesus Christ. On the basis of that prior knowledge, God chooses them to be saved. I mention it because the text before us now is the standard proof-text for the prescient view of predestination, and it is important that we understand the parameters of the controversy as we look at Romans 8:29–30.

Foreknowledge

Immediately after Paul says that "all things work together for good to those who love God, to those who are the called according to his purpose," he introduces the idea of foreknowledge: **For whom He foreknew, He also predestined to be conformed to the image of His Son** (v. 29). The first link in the Golden Chain is the link of foreknowledge. It is important to understand that *predestination* is not a concept or a word invented by Calvin or Luther or Augustine. It is a biblical word, one we find here in Romans and in Ephesians also. The idea of election is found throughout the whole of Scripture. The question is not whether we are going to have a doctrine of predestination; as we have seen, predestination is a biblical concept. If we want to be submissive to the Word of God, we have to wrestle with this and come to understand some kind of doctrine of predestination. The question is, what is the correct understanding of the doctrine of predestination?

I am convinced that the prescient view of predestination that relegates it simply to an act of God's omniscient foreknowledge is not an explanation of the biblical doctrine but is precisely a denial of the biblical doctrine. Because Paul starts with foreknowledge, those who hold to the prescient view say, "That is what predestination is about—foreknowledge." They claim that since foreknowledge comes before predestination in the Golden

Chain, obviously what the apostle is teaching here is that predestination is based upon foreknowledge. Nowhere does Scripture say that; it is an inference read into the text by virtue of the order of the words. The fact that foreknowledge comes before predestination leads people to the conclusion that predestination is based upon God's prior knowledge of a condition that people will meet, but those who come to that conclusion about Romans 8 have not read Romans 9.

The mere fact that the word *foreknowledge* comes before the word *predestination* does not necessitate that predestination is based upon a foreknowledge of human actions. If we are debating predestination and someone says that the basis of it is God's prior knowledge of our human behavior, we respond that God cannot predestine anyone from all eternity that he does not first know from all eternity. God does not predestine a nameless, faceless group of elect people. Obviously, if he predestines a people from the foundation of the world he has to know what people he is predestinating. In that sense, before he acts in the decree of election with respect to certain people, he has to know what he is doing.

We also have to look at the word *foreknowledge* in the Greek language. It is even harder to find it in the Greek text than in the English. The word used here by the apostle Paul, which is translated "foreknowledge," is the word *prŏginō*. It comes from a form of the noun *gnosis*, which is the Greek word for knowledge. When we are sick and go to the doctor, he offers a diagnosis. When we ask, "Am I going to get better?" he may offer a prognosis. Both have to do with *gnosis*, or knowledge.

The word for *knowledge* in New Testament Greek is used in two distinct ways. We have seen that by God's self-revelation in and through nature, people know that he exists (Rom. 1:18–20). Knowing God, we refuse to acknowledge him as God; neither are we grateful. We don't honor God as God. Paul declares in Romans 1 that by general revelation everybody in the world has some *gnosis*, some knowledge of God, yet when Paul writes his first epistle to the Corinthians, he says that the unregenerate person, the pagan, does not know God. We could get away from this seeming contradiction if Paul had used different words for *knowledge* in each of those instances, but that escape hatch will not work, because he uses the same word in both letters.

Paul is not speaking with a forked tongue, slipping into contradiction. He is talking about two aspects, two nuances, of the Greek idea of knowledge. The first has to do with cognition, or intellectual awareness. That is the fundamental reference point for the Greek word *gnosis*—a cognitive awareness of some reality. In addition to that cognitive aspect there is a deeper dimension that we might consider in terms of personal, spiritual, or redemptive knowledge. In the Old Testament we find statements such as "Adam knew Eve his wife, and she conceived." In the Septuagint, the word translated "knew" is the same word used for the knowledge that we are talking about here. It takes more than cognitive knowledge for a baby to be conceived in the mother's womb. It takes a more intimate, personal form of knowledge. When the Bible speaks about a man knowing his wife, it is not an attempt to avoid a description of a sexual relationship; rather, it is making use of the full measure of the word *knowledge* or of the verb form *to know*.

To clear up the apparent discrepancy between Paul's teaching in Romans and his teaching in 1 Corinthians, we can say that general revelation gives to all men an inescapable cognitive knowledge of God, and though we seek to destroy it and do not want to have it in our minds, we cannot eliminate it altogether. Therefore, we are left without excuse. On the judgment day we can never say with impunity that we did not know that God was there. We do have that *gnosis* as a result of revelation. At the same time, such *gnosis* never rises to a redemptive level of spiritual apprehension and personal knowledge of God. Personal, redemptive, spiritual knowledge of God comes only as a result of the work of the Holy Spirit within our hearts and minds.

Now, why labor this when we are talking about a particular text in Romans 8? We do so because it is the root of the term that starts the Golden Chain: "For whom He foreknew [*prŏginō*], He also predestined." The full import of the word includes not mere cognition on God's part but a redemptive knowledge that is spiritual and affective—not *e*ffective in this case, but *af*fective. Therefore, we could reasonably translate this text, "Those whom he foreloved [those whom he knew in a personal, intimate, redemptive sense from all eternity] he predestined."

Predestined

The word *predestinate* in the Greek text also contains the prefix *pro-*. The word is *prŏŏrizō*, which means, according to the Greek lexicons, "a sovereign determination in which a fixed or definite limit is sovereignly decreed." So, as the English word suggests, there is a destiny for certain people that God, from the foundation of the world, has established. He has fixed it. He has determined it according to the sovereign good pleasure of his will. Nowhere in Scripture is a foreseen, conditional, human response ever given as the rationale for the eternal decree by which God fixes for all eternity those whom he ordains and chooses for redemption.

The language Paul uses here with respect to the goal of predestination is not immediately linked to redemption or salvation. Paul does not say, "Those whom he foreknew, he also predestined unto salvation." The concept is certainly there, but it is not the language Paul uses. "Whom He foreknew, He also predestined," but predestined to what? What are people predestined to? They are predestined **to be conformed to the image of His Son** (v. 29). The purpose of predestination is that the elect may be brought, by God's grace, into a relationship with the Son of God. When Paul—and all the New Testament—writes about predestination, the focus is always and everywhere related to Christ. Predestination is never discussed in the abstract; it is always related to our relationship with Christ.

Christ the Firstborn

Why does God, from all eternity, predestinate certain people to be in conformity to Jesus? We come next to a subjunctive clause, which indicates purpose. The apostle is setting forth very clearly the purpose of predestination: **that He might be the firstborn among many brethren** (v. 29). Predestination is for Christ's sake. It is that Christ may see the travail of his soul and be satisfied.

It is not, as so many today say, that Christ provided a potential atonement and offered a potential redemption for a potential number of people. The God of Scripture is one who, from all eternity, had a sovereign purpose of salvation in mind, and he sovereignly sent his Son into the world to effect the atonement for his people, that they may be adopted into the family of God. We are heirs of God, joint heirs with Jesus, because God sovereignly decreed that people would come to Christ. The only reason we find anywhere in Scripture as to why anyone is saved is for Christ's sake.

In Jesus' prayer in the upper room, he thanked the Father for giving people to him, and he said, "As You have given Him authority over all flesh, that He should give eternal life to as many as You have given Him" (John 17:2). Arminians reverse that to read, "All who come to me, the Father will give to me." No, those whom the Father gives to the Son come to the Son. We who have come to Christ have done so because we are gifts of love that the Father had given to his Son. That is the *why* of predestination.

The Good Pleasure of God's Will

Elsewhere the apostle says that God chooses people according to the good pleasure of his will (Eph. 1:5). That "according to" tells us the basis upon which God chooses or determines the elect. As we will see in Romans 9, "it is not of him who wills, nor of him who runs, but of God who shows mercy" (v. 16). In Romans 9 Paul uses Jacob and Esau to show that before they were born, before they had done anything good or bad, God decreed that the elder would serve the younger. "Jacob I have loved, but Esau I have hated" (v. 13). We will wait until we get to Romans 9 to look more deeply at it, but in Ephesians and elsewhere Paul speaks about God's choosing or predestinating according to the good pleasure of his will.

If God's choosing us is not based on some foreseen thing we have done or will do, if his election is unconditional, then on what basis does God make his choice? At first glance it might seem completely arbitrary, as if God just closed his eyes and said, "I will take some of these and some of those." God does not do anything by chance. The fact that our election is not in us does not mean that there is not a reason for it, and the reason we are given is that God's electing is according to the good pleasure of his will. Paul describes the pleasure of God's will as the *good pleasure* of his will. The only pleasure God takes in his will is good pleasure, not bad pleasure. Whatever he pleases and wills to do always flows from his character, which is altogether righteous.

When people hear the doctrine of election, they think, *God must be unfair.* People are willing to accept what the Bible says about God until they get to the doctrine of election: *I cannot love a God who does that. There must be something wrong with God if from all eternity he chooses a fixed number of people to be conformed to the image of Christ.*

Moreover whom He predestined, these He also called; whom He called, these He also justified; and whom He justified, these He also glorified (v. 30). This is called the Golden Chain because several links are bound together. First is foreknowledge, which is followed by predestination. We find calling next, then justification, and finally glorification.

The Ordo Salutis

In theology we talk about something called the *ordo salutis*, which is Latin for "the order of salvation." There are several aspects to the *ordo salutis*, but Paul does not mention all of them here. He does not mention sanctification, which follows justification. Justification, sanctification, and glorification occur in a certain logical order in the plan of salvation. The order Paul gives us here in Romans 8 begins with foreknowledge and then moves to predestination. The ones God has predestined are also called, and these same ones are also justified and glorified. Tacit here in the text is the concept *all*. All whom God foreknows, in the way Paul is speaking of here, are predestined, and all those in the category of the predestined are also in the category of the called.

From a prescient perspective, an Arminian or Langtonian viewpoint, the predestinated are those whom God foreknew would respond to the gospel. Those who give the right answer to the call are saved; those who give the wrong answer to the call are lost. The fact that God calls all whom he predestines stands the Arminian distortion on its ear. The Golden Chain makes clear that all whom God knows, he predestines. He does not call only some of the predestined; he calls all.

Is the calling that Paul describes in verse 28 an external call, a general call, or the internal, effectual call of the Holy Spirit? God called the world into existence; he did not invite it but commanded it, and it came. When Christ called Paul to be an apostle, Paul became an apostle. When Jesus called Lazarus out of the tomb, it was no mere external call that he hoped Lazarus would respond to; it was a sovereign call, an effectual call, one that brought to pass what God had designed. So which kind of call is Paul writing about here in the Golden Chain? Paul writes that those whom God calls, he justifies. Not all who are called outwardly are justified, because many who receive an outward call say no. All who are called inwardly, effectually, come to faith by the power of the Holy Spirit, and they are justified. We see in the Golden Chain a doctrine of predestination that is completely removed from the Arminian view. Paul says that those whom God foreknew, he predestined, and all whom he predestined, he called, and all whom he called, he justified, and all the justified he glorified.

Remember the context: are we safe in our salvation? Once we are justified, can we lose our salvation? We cannot if the Golden Chain is true. It tells us that all the justified will be glorified, so if we are saved now, we are saved forever. That is the Golden Chain. It is not a rusty chain, but one made of the precious truth of the gospel.

Our Response

After declaring the Golden Chain in all its links, Paul asks a question of his readers: **What then shall we say to these things?** (v. 31). In other words, what should the response be? I read a book in which the author described a woman whose husband became convinced of the doctrines of grace and the Reformed faith, a conviction that nearly broke up the marriage. The man's wife said that she could not believe in a God who elects some people to salvation but passes over the rest so they will perish forever. Her answer to the apostle's question, "What then shall we say to these things?" is that she does not want anything to do with a God who elects people in that manner.

That is not how Paul answers his own question. His answer is this: **If God is for us, who can be against us?** (v. 31).

One of the greatest Latin phrases in church history is *Deus pro nobis*, "God for us." Karl Barth said the most important word in the Greek language is *huper*, which means "in behalf of." What should our response be to the Golden Chain? What should our response be to the fact that we have been rooted and grounded in the eternal purposes of God? The response is this: "If God is for us, who can be against us?" I will tell you who can be against us: everybody in the world. Paul is not suggesting that if God is for us, nobody will ever stand to oppose us. The import of his declaration is simple: all the human opposition that rises against us is meaningless in the final analysis, because all the opposition in the world cannot overthrow the glory that God has laid up for his saints from the foundation of the world.

If God is with us from all eternity, and if God is for us in his decree of election, in effectual calling, and in justifying us by his grace, and if God is for us by glorifying every one of his people, then whose opposition can mean anything? It is amazing that people kick and scream against the doctrine of sovereign grace and election. It is one of the most comforting doctrines we will ever learn from sacred Scripture.

32

GOD FOR US

Romans 8:31–39

What then shall we say to these things? If God is for us, who can be against us? He who did not spare His own Son, but delivered Him up for us all, how shall He not with Him also freely give us all things? Who shall bring a charge against God's elect? It is God who justifies. Who is he who condemns? It is Christ who died, and furthermore is also risen, who is even at the right hand of God, who also makes intercession for us. Who shall separate us from the love of Christ? Shall tribulation, or distress, or persecution, or famine, or nakedness, or peril, or sword? As it is written:

> "For Your sake we are killed all day long;
> We are accounted as sheep for the slaughter."

Yet in all these things we are more than conquerors through Him who loved us. For I am persuaded that neither death nor life, nor angels nor principalities nor powers, nor things present nor things to come, nor height nor depth, nor any other created thing, shall be able to separate us from the love of God which is in Christ Jesus our Lord.

D*eus pro nobis*, "God for us." **If God is for us, who can be against us?** (v. 31). Paul sets forth that phrase in a conditional sense; in other words, the language suggests a kind of uncertainty. The apostle says "*If* God is for us," as if it were a matter open to some doubt or further speculation, but Paul is not indicating uncertainty about God's being for us. He has labored thus far through the epistle to demonstrate how deeply God is for his elect. Paul is speaking in the language of logic, even of a syllogism, which gives a first premise and then a second premise and then rushes toward a conclusion. The conclusion of a syllogism is one that follows inexorably from the premises, if the premises are sound. If A and B are true, then C must of necessity follow. So when Paul asks, "If God is for us," he is writing syllogistically, not with respect to uncertainty. We could just as easily translate it with the word *since*: "Since God is for us, who can be against us?"

Obviously, if God is for us, the whole world can be against us, because man in his revolt against God not only protests against his Creator but against all the redeemed. Implicit in the apostle's statement is not just who *can* be against us, but who *could possibly* stand against us. This is, of course, a rhetorical question; the answer is obvious. No one can stand against us if God is standing with us. An aphorism that has since become something of a cliché goes like this: one person with God on his side is in a majority against all the rest of the human race.

Spared

He who did not spare His own Son, but delivered Him up for us all, how shall He not with Him also freely give us all things? (v. 32). We notice first the idea of sparing. When people are rescued from an almost certain doom at the last second, we say that they have been spared a disaster that was about to befall them. When we read such language in Romans 8, how can we not think back to Genesis 22, where God commanded Abraham to offer his son Isaac, the son whom he loved, on the altar at Mount Moriah? In obedience Abraham took his son on an arduous journey and placed him on the altar, bound in ropes, and he lifted up the knife to slay him, but at the last second God stopped him: "Do not lay your hand on the lad, or do anything to him" (Gen. 22:12). God commanded Abraham to spare his son.

It was on Mount Moriah, later named Mount Calvary, just outside the city of Jerusalem, where, one thousand years after Abraham's experience, our Savior on the night before his death went into the garden of Gethsemane and sweat drops of blood pleading with the Father to allow the cup to pass from him. "Nevertheless," Jesus said, "not what I will, but what You will" (Mark 14:36). In that moment of the grand passion of Christ, the Father said no. The Father would not spare his Son.

How can we not understand the posture of God toward his people after he has gone to such lengths to effect our redemption? God spared nothing, not even his Son, so that we might be saved. Therefore, Paul says, "He delivered Him up for us all." I don't believe for a moment that God did this for all mankind. God gave his Son to redeem his elect, those who are a part of the Golden Chain.

Because of Christ's perfect obedience for us, the Father bestows every conceivable blessing upon him. His inheritance is the world and everything in it. Paul says that because the Son died for us and the Father did not spare him, he will also give us everything that he gives his Son. Here Paul adds to the idea of our adoption, which he developed earlier in Romans 8. We are heirs of God and joint heirs with Christ; the Father is pleased to give all things to his Son, whom he did not spare, and not only to his Son but to all those whom he had given to his Son for his Son's glory.

No Charge

Paul continues with his list of questions. **Who shall bring a charge against God's elect?** (v. 33). Satan works to bring every conceivable slanderous charge against God's elect. Satan never ceases accusing the brethren. He never stops harassing us and getting at our consciences, telling us how wicked we are and that we do not deserve to be in fellowship with Christ. The principal work of Satan in the life of the believer is not temptation, though he is engaged in that; his chief work is accusation. He accuses us in order to take away our assurance and joy and the consolation that is ours in Christ. He keeps reminding us of our sin. He keeps telling us of our shortcomings. He lays against God's elect every conceivable charge that he can bring; yet, there is no work more futile, which is why Paul mocks Satan with this question. What can be sillier than to bring accusations against those who have been redeemed through the blood of the Lamb? The one who justifies is the judge of all, and he has declared us just by the imputation of the perfect righteousness of Christ.

Who can rightly bring any charge against Jesus? He said to his contemporaries, "Which of you convicts Me of sin?" (John 8:46). He is sinless, so any attempt to charge Jesus with sin is an exercise in futility. It is a waste of time and breath because the Father knows that Christ is without sin. Christ's perfect obedience is transferred to the account of all who put their faith in him. It is just as futile for anyone to lay a charge against us as it is to lay a charge against Christ, because we are clothed in his righteousness. We are justified by his merit. God has not pardoned or exonerated us, but having clothed us with the righteousness of Christ he has pronounced his verdict of righteous. Once the supreme, sovereign judge declares us righteous in his sight, all the slander in the world can make no impact on God's assured, final judgment. There is now no condemnation for those who are in Christ Jesus because the judge has declared us just.

Justification is not just an abstract doctrine, and we must never negotiate it. It is the very heart and soul of the gospel. Because of our justification in Jesus Christ, we need fear no slander from Satan or from the world.

No Condemnation

Athanasius was driven into exile countless times. His tombstone reads, *Athanasius contra mundum*, that is, "Athanasius against the world." *Deus pro nobis*, Athanasius; God was for you though the whole world was against you. My mother taught me to say, "Sticks and stones can break my bones but words will never hurt me." The first time I tried it I discovered that words can hurt. Slanderous accusations can be more painful than sticks and stones, but they bounce off the skin of the Christian in the presence of God, because God has declared us righteous in his sight. The verdict is in. There is no higher court of appeal than the verdict rendered by the sovereign Judge of all the earth.

It is God who justifies. Who is he who condemns? (vv. 33–34). Once God has justified us, who can condemn us? Condemnation is gone. **It is Christ who died, and furthermore is also risen, who is even at the right hand of God, who also makes intercession for us** (v. 34). It is Christ who died; it is Christ who was raised for our justification; it is Christ who ascended to the right hand of God, where he is seated in the position of cosmic authority. He is the King of kings and Lord of lords. The highest tribunal in the cosmos is the one who died for us. When Stephen's enemies stoned him, they acted with great fury, gnashing their teeth in hatred. They threw rocks that opened gashes on that saint, yet while his blood poured from his veins and life drained from him, he looked up, and God gave him a vision into heaven. He saw the Son of Man standing at the right hand of God (Acts 7:54–60). The earthly court condemned him to death, but at that very moment in the heavenly court the Judge of all the earth was Stephen's defense council. What matters is where the court sits, and it sits at the right hand of God.

Our Intercessor

Not only is our Savior our judge and defense attorney, but he is also our intercessor. He is our great high priest, pleading our case before God every minute. It is foolish, therefore, to worry about the slander of men. Who shall lay any charge against God's elect? God is the one who justifies. Christ is the one who died and was raised for our justification. Christ is the one sitting at the right hand of the Father, and Christ is the one who intercedes for us every day. **Who shall separate us from the love of Christ?** (v. 35). Those who live a life of uncertainty thinking they can lose their salvation if they fail to persevere to the end need only remember the finest flower in God's garden, the tulip.

Paul explores things that have the potential to drive a wedge between us and our Savior: **Shall tribulation, or distress, or persecution, or famine, or nakedness, or peril, or sword?** (v. 35). In these very things we have assurance of Jesus' presence with us. If anything seals his love for us, it is his promise to be with us in the midst of persecution and peril and sword and famine and everything that the world, the flesh, and the Devil can throw against us. The things Paul anticipates here are not exhaustive; this list is representative. Paul could go on forever naming things that try to separate us from the love of Christ.

As it is written: "For Your sake we are killed all day long; we are accounted as sheep for the slaughter" (v. 36). The image of sheep is used often in the Bible to refer to the flock of God and to Christ, who is our good shepherd. During Jesus' trial before Pilate, Jesus was "as a sheep before its shearers is silent, so He opened not His mouth" (Isa. 53:7; Acts 8:32). Our Lord, the great shepherd, became the sheep, the docile one who went willingly to the slaughter. We participate in that vocation by participating in his humiliation, his tribulation, and his death.

Conquerors

In the nineteenth century some of the most cynical attacks ever written against Christianity came from the pen of Friedrich Nietzsche. He declared the death of God. According to Nietzsche, God died of pity. Nietzsche was convinced that Western civilization, particularly Western Europe, had become completely decadent by his day, primarily due to the baleful influence of Christianity. He could not stand that Christianity exalted virtues like mercy, love, and pity. He believed that such virtues strip human beings of their natural humanity. Nietzsche argued that what most defines humanness is the will to power. Every human being has a drive to dominate, conquer, and rise to the top. Nietzsche said that Christianity with its false piety takes away the strength of humanity, leaving a race of impotent men. Nietzsche called for a new humanity, the dawn of a new superman, the Übermensch. This superman would serve as an example of authentic human existence, the father of biological heroism. Is it any wonder that Hitler sent copies of Nietzsche's *Spake Zarathustra* to his henchmen as Christmas presents when he was trying to develop the super race of Aryans in the twentieth century?

The chief characteristic of superman, according to Nietzsche, is that of conqueror. He is the man, Nietzsche said, who sails his ship into uncharted waters. He is the Hemingway of his day who grabs the bull by the horns. He will bow to no opposition and show fear before no power of nature, such as a volcano. He is defiant to the end. He is Übermensch, the superman, in counter-distinction to the weak, pitiable Christian who turns the other cheek.

I always think of Nietzsche when I read Paul's words about our being more than conquerors in pestilence, tribulation, peril, and sword and in being led as sheep to the slaughter. The Greek word Paul uses for "conquerors" comes from the term *hupernikaō*. We are hyper-conquerors. The Latin is even better—*super vincēmus*: in all these things we are supermen through him who loved us.

We have a superman, an Übermensch, in Christ. He has conquered the world. Nietzsche believed that dialectical courage would mark the superman; dialectical courage is irrational courage. Nietzsche also declared that life is meaningless and that there are no real values. Since life is meaningless, he said, people can be of good cheer. There is no reason for rational courage because it only leaves people at the bottom of the sea. How different that is from Jesus' charge to his people: "Be of good cheer, I have overcome the world" (John 16:33). There is reason for our cheer and joy—the Lord Jesus Christ has conquered powers, principalities, and every wickedness in the cosmos.

No Separation

For I am persuaded that neither death nor life, nor angels nor principalities nor powers, nor things present nor things to come, nor height nor depth, nor any other created thing, shall be able to separate us from the love of God which is in Christ Jesus our Lord (vv. 38–39). We may feel at times that God has departed from us, but that is when we have to believe his Word rather than our feelings. The Word of God promises and guarantees that death cannot separate us from

Christ's love, nor can life or earthly governments. Men could throw Joseph in prison for years, but they could not separate Joseph from the love of his God. Principalities in the demonic world or Satan and his angels cannot separate us from the love of Christ, nor can anything that happens today or tomorrow. What about height? What about depth? Paul is giving us selective examples of what might separate us from the love of Christ. His point is that nothing—height, depth, life, death, powers, principalities, or any creature—can separate us from the love of God that is in Christ Jesus.

Is it safe? That has been the theme of our study of Romans 8. If we have been saved, we are safe from anything this world can put against us because God from all eternity has loved and redeemed us. We are his elect. We have been chosen by God to be conformed to the image of Christ and to be Christ's possession—not for a day or a week but for eternity. If we do not like the idea of God's sovereign grace, if we are still kicking against it, why? It is our guarantee that nothing can separate us from the great love wherewith he loves us.

33

THE DOCTRINE OF ELECTION

Romans 9:1–5

I tell the truth in Christ, I am not lying, my conscience also bearing me witness in the Holy Spirit, that I have great sorrow and continual grief in my heart. For I could wish that I myself were accursed from Christ for my brethren, my countrymen according to the flesh, who are Israelites, to whom pertain the adoption, the glory, the covenants, the giving of the law, the service of God, and the promises; of whom are the fathers and from whom, according to the flesh, Christ came, who is over all, the eternally blessed God. Amen.

T he doctrine of God's sovereign election is not an arcane item found rarely in obscure passages of Scripture, nor does it require the pursuit of a diligent scholar to uncover it. The doctrine of election appears on virtually every page of the Bible, from Genesis to Revelation. No section of Scripture sets it forth, however, more definitively and persuasively than Romans 9.

Contending for the Doctrine

The great Swiss theologian Roger Nicole made tremendous contributions to the church in the twentieth century and continues to do so today. He once made the observation that we are, by nature, Pelagian. We assume that we have the power to incline our hearts to Christ while we are yet in the flesh.

Our natural hostility to the sovereignty of grace is not instantly cured by conversion, which is why a majority of Christians still ride the horse of semi-Pelagianism and seek to escape the full implications of the doctrine of election.

I struggled with the doctrine for at least five years after my conversion, despite my godly and able professors who tried to explain the Scriptures. The built-in resistance to the sovereignty of God's grace found a root in my soul. Not until I was exposed to a careful treatment of Romans 9 was I brought, kicking and screaming against my will, to an initial acquiescence of pure Augustinianism. I was assisted in my understanding by John Gerstner, that great defender of Reformed theology. He forced me to read carefully Luther's *Bondage of the Will* and Edwards's *Freedom of the Will*. Those Christian classics deal at length with the content of Romans 9. Finally, as I studied the biblical text, I could only throw up my hands and say, "I can fight this battle no more, and now I have to embrace this doctrine even though I don't have to like it."

When I was a seminary student, I had a card on my desk on which I had written these words: *It is your duty to believe and to teach what the Bible teaches, not what you would like it to teach.* That bothered my conscience because I did not like Romans 9, but the sheer force of the text overwhelmed me, and afterward it became my lot in life to teach and defend the doctrine of election against those who hold the position I formerly held. Although the doctrine set forth in Romans 9 is absolutely clear, people use three basic ways to get around it.

1) The easiest and most common way of getting around the doctrine of election is to ignore or avoid it. People direct the discussion to other portions of Scripture, staying studiously away from Romans 9. This tends to happen with those who know enough to realize the force of it.

2) Others say that Paul in Romans 9 is not writing about God's sovereign election of individuals but about God's sovereign election of nations to a particular historic destiny, specifically Israel as distinguished from Syria, Babylonia, Greece, Rome, or other nations of antiquity. The grace that the apostle is expounding here, they argue, is not saving grace but the promise of earthly benefits, such as the inheritance of a piece of real estate, which is still very much contested, even with violence.

3) The doctrine of election is also gotten around by a method we have considered repeatedly during our study of Romans—God's foreknowledge. Supposedly, God looks down the corridor of time and knows in advance how people will respond when they hear the gospel. He chooses for salvation

those whom he knows will say yes to Christ, but he rejects those whom he knows will reject him.

A Sober Beginning

For decades I understood the opening of Romans 9 to be Paul declaring a formal oath, the taking of a vow. **I tell the truth in Christ, I am not lying, my conscience also bearing me witness in the Holy Spirit** (v. 1). In times past I pointed to this passage as an example of the sort of lawful vow or oath that Scripture permits. I reasoned that if Paul takes an oath in his writing, then such oaths are indeed permissible. I learned, however, that I was mistaken in my understanding of this text. Paul uses the preposition *en* instead of *pros*: "I tell the truth in Christ [*en Christos*]." Historically, when people swore in the name of Christ, they used the preposition *pros* rather than *en*. So, in all likelihood, Paul was not swearing an oath here or giving a sacred vow.

Although Paul's opening statement falls short of a vow or oath, Paul is giving a declaration with the deepest solemnity he can muster. He is about to deal with issues that are problematic for the Jews. Before Paul looks at how God has taken the gospel from the Jews to the Gentile community, grafting Gentiles in the place of Israel (Romans 9–11), he wants to make sure that the Jewish community in Rome might read his epistle through his tears. He is not angry or hostile toward his kinsmen—quite the contrary. He speaks as a Christian who embraces and loves truth, *alētheia*, which is embodied in Christ.

Paul is speaking in Christ, in the Holy Spirit, from the depths of his conscience. In other words, Paul's conscience witnesses to him that he speaks the truth. There is no deceit or malice. He is speaking the sober, unvarnished truth to those in Christ, and he is doing so by the Holy Spirit.

Acquainted with Grief

Paul is declaring a solemn truth: **I have great sorrow and continual grief in my heart** (v. 2). He is going through what the text calls *dolor*, a Latin term we find in the name of an ancient street in Jerusalem, *Via Dolorosa*, which means "the way of grief or pain." Paul's grief is not passing. It attends his life and perturbs his heart continually.

When Jesus approached Jerusalem, he considered how the people of the city had hardened themselves against the Word of God. He cried out in a lament, "O Jerusalem, Jerusalem, the one who kills the prophets and stones those who are sent to her! How often I wanted to gather your children together, as a hen gathers her chicks under her wings, but you were not willing!" (Matt. 23:37). That is why Jesus is known as a man of sorrows, acquainted with grief.

Some time ago I was given the assignment of writing an article about grief for *Table Talk* magazine. The editors asked me to write from personal experience. As I contemplated the assignment, I thought of the loss of my father when I was seventeen years old. I was stricken with grief, which has never completely left my soul. I think also of the loss of my friend Jim Boice. Upon his death I lost a friend and a comrade. Yet, as I searched my heart, I discovered that most of my grief experiences have involved departures from biblical truth. In that sense I relate to the apostle Paul. He loved his fellow Jews and cared about their well-being. When they did not respond to Christ as the Messiah, Paul was grieved in his heart.

I dearly love many non-Christian friends in my hometown and all over the country. I hurt that they do not know the Savior. The same feeling is revealed about Paul as he begins this important chapter. He has a great sorrow, a continual grief, in his heart.

Accursed

Paul escalates the description of his pain to a degree unprecedented in his writings: **For I could wish that I myself were accursed from Christ for my brethren, my countrymen according to the flesh, who are Israelites** (vv. 3–4a). Paul loves his people so much that he would be willing to give up his salvation for his brothers and sisters, his fellow Jews. I cannot imagine too many things that I would be unwilling to do to see my friends come to Christ, but I have never said I would be willing to trade my salvation for theirs. I do not think I have that much love for anybody, but the apostle did.

The word Paul uses is *anathema*, which means he would willingly place himself under the very curse of God and be delivered to total destruction if by doing so his people would know Christ. *Anathema* is the word Paul uses when he writes to the Galatians as they were being seduced away from the true gospel: "But even if we, or an angel from heaven, preach any other gospel to you than what we have preached to you, let him be *anathema*" (Gal. 1:8). Let him be damned. Any threat to the gospel provoked the wrath of the apostle. To the false teachers Paul would say, "Damn you for destroying the gospel," the worst kind of curse against a human being. It goes back deeply into the Old Testament. At the time of the conquest of Canaan, God put the Canaanites under the ban, which meant that he forbade the people of

Israel to spare Canaanite lives or to take their goods. God delivered them to absolute destruction. That is the meaning of *anathema*, and Paul was willing to know it personally if that would save his kinsmen.

Privileges Missed

Paul's natural kinsmen are those **to whom pertain the adoption, the glory, the covenants, the giving of the law, the service of God, and the promises** (v. 4b). First, the adoption pertains to the Israelites. We think of adoption almost exclusively in New Testament categories; it is the great benefit received by all who are justified and welcomed into God's family. The idea of God's adopted children, however, goes back into the pages of the Old Testament. Israel was the adopted son of God.

In his Gospel Matthew makes application from Old Testament prophecy. After Jesus was born and Herod issued the threat of infant slaughter, an angel warned Joseph in a dream to flee from Bethlehem and not return to Nazareth but to go into Egypt until the threat had passed. Matthew tells us that Joseph took Mary and the babe and fled to Egypt. When the Herodian persecution was over Joseph returned to Israel, thereby fulfilling the Old Testament prophecy, "Out of Egypt I called My son" (Matt. 2:15). The original reference to adoption is found at the exodus, when God redeemed his people from the yoke of slavery under Pharaoh, calling the nation his son (Hos. 11:1). The Israelites were those who had been called to enjoy adoption, and it pains Paul that they had missed their privilege.

Glory is also on Paul's list of Israelite privileges. In high school I had a friend who was a tremendous athlete. He excelled in several sports, but his best was ice hockey, and we played together on the team. After scoring a goal, he would raise his stick high and yell to the fans, "My people, my people." I asked him why he did that, and he replied, "I'm basking in the glory." After hockey we played golf together, but eventually we lost touch. Several years later, when I was living in Pittsburgh, I got a call from him. "R. C., I'm coming to Pittsburgh. Let's get together and play golf. I want to recover the glory." We have such a superficial understanding of glory.

I've mentioned before that the Greek word for *glory* is *doxa*. From it we get *doxology*. When we sing the Doxology on Sunday mornings, we are giving glory to God. The Latin equivalent is the word *gloria*, from which we get the Gloria Patri:

> Glory be to the Father, and to the Son, and to the Holy Ghost.
> As it was in the beginning, is now, and ever shall be. Amen.

Glory attributes supernatural majesty to God. His glory is so brilliant that human eyes are not permitted to behold it, yet God allowed his glory to dwell in the midst of his people Israel. The Old Testament glory hovered over the mercy seat and the ark of the covenant in the Holy of Holies. When the ark of the covenant fell into the hands of the conquering Philistines, the cry of God's people went up:

> Phinehas' wife, was with child, due to be delivered; and when she heard the news that the ark of God was captured, and that her father-in-law and her husband were dead, she bowed herself and gave birth, for her labor pains came upon her. And about the time of her death the women who stood by her said to her, "Do not fear, for you have borne a son." But she did not answer, nor did she regard it. Then she named the child Ichabod, saying, "The glory has departed from Israel!" because the ark of God had been captured. (1 Sam 4:19–21)

Glory in Israel was connected to the *shekinah*, a blazing light that manifested God's glory and made him a consuming fire. Ezekiel saw the glory of God rising from the city of Jerusalem and departing (Ezekiel 10). At the birth of Jesus, the glory of God flooded the landscape (Luke 2:8–9). That *doxa* or *gloria* pertained to Israel. God first manifested his glory in the community he formed from the slaves in Egypt.

Israel had been given the covenants—with Adam, with Noah, with Abraham, Isaac, and Jacob, with Moses, and with David. The covenants we inherit come from the Jews, not the Gentiles. They come from Paul's kinsmen. The covenants belonged to them.

The Israelites also had been given the law. The law did not come through Hammurabi; it came through Moses. The law did not come from Babylon, Phoenicia, or Egypt; it came from the people of Israel through the mediatorial work of Moses. We owe our law to the Israelites.

The Jews had been given the service of God. Paul uses the word *latreia*, which actually refers to the worship of God. Our instructions about how to bring praise sacrifices to God in corporate worship did not come to us from the Greeks or the Romans. The principles of worship that shape our devotion were born in Israel. God delivered to Israel the principles by which he is to be worshiped, adored, and sanctified.

The promises we have also began with the Jews. I once heard J. Vernon McGee say on the radio that the problem with people in the church today is that they sing the old gospel song "Standing on the Promises" while they are sitting on the premises. Those promises we stand on did not come *de novo* from the mind of Paul or John or Peter in the New Testament era. The promises of God came through centuries of prophetic utterances going all the way back to the *protoevangel* in Genesis 3, where God promised that the Seed of the woman would crush the head of the serpent (v. 15). The thousands of promises of the one to come out of Israel from the root of Jesse pertained to the Israelites.

All these things—the adoption, the glory, the covenants, the giving of the law, the worship of God, and God's promises—came through Paul's kinsmen, Israel. Do we wonder, then, at the weight of Paul's tears?

Christ over All

Paul adds more about his kinsmen: **of whom are the fathers and from whom, according to the flesh, Christ came, who is over all, the eternally blessed God. Amen** (v. 5). What primarily pertains to the Israelites is Jesus, a Jew, from the seed of David.

Some time ago I received a letter in which I was asked a question, one that I am asked frequently:

> Dr. Sproul,
> You frequently quote Martin Luther, and obviously you are a fan of his, and you hold him in high esteem. We hear that in his later years he became viciously antagonistic to the Jews in Germany and became exhibit *A* for the worst kinds of anti-Semitism. Some people even say that he sowed the seeds for the holocaust and that Hitler was just following in the train of Luther with his hatred of the Jews.

At the end of his life, in the sixteenth century, Luther did lash out against Jews for various reasons, and he did so in a manner not that unusual in the polemics of his day. Earlier in his ministry, however, Martin Luther had written a magnificent essay on the debt the church of Christ owes to the Jews. In this great essay Luther pointed out the biblical principle that *salvation is of the Jews*. In that essay, which is often overlooked in the debate, Luther said we have nothing apart from the legacy of Israel.

Paul notes that Christ came from the seed of David "according to the flesh," *kata sarka*; Paul affirms Jesus' Jewish ancestry, but he does not stop there. He gives one of the clearest and most decisive affirmations of the deity of Christ that we find anywhere in Scripture. Christ is over all things, the entire universe. The Jews used this expression to refer to God's dominion over the entire creation; he is the Most High God. Here Paul says that Christ is over all. Some attack the biblical concept of Christ's deity by trying to change the syntax of the verse, translating it "Christ who is blessed eternally by God." In other words, Jesus' lordship was God's gift to him, a manifestation of divine blessing rather than a mark of divinity. That is a torturous approach to the syntax of this particular passage because the same could be said of any Christian—that he or she is blessed of God. The apostle is referring to Jesus as *the* eternally blessed God.

After Paul makes this profound affirmation of the full deity of Christ, he interjects "Amen," which is the word the Jews used to affirm the truth of a statement. In some churches people respond to the preaching of the Word with a shout of "Amen," but it is rarely heard in our more staid assemblies. The shout, "Amen," is an affirmation of the truth they are hearing. "Amen" is the term Jesus used when prefacing his teaching to the disciples: "Amen, amen, I say to you." We translate "Truly, truly I say to you" or "Verily, verily I say to you." The word *amen* comes from *emut*, which means "truth." Paul punctuates his profound affirmation of the divine nature of Christ with this word, which every Jew understood to be a clear affirmation of truth. Here Paul says "amen" about his own words: "Christ came, who is over all, the eternally blessed God. Amen."

34

JACOB AND ESAU

Romans 9:6–13

But it is not that the word of God has taken no effect. For they are not all Israel who are of Israel, nor are they all children because they are the seed of Abraham; but, "In Isaac your seed shall be called." That is, those who are the children of the flesh, these are not the children of God; but the children of the promise are counted as the seed. For this is the word of promise: "At this time I will come and Sarah shall have a son." And not only this, but when Rebecca also had conceived by one man, even by our father Isaac (for the children not yet being born, nor having done any good or evil, that the purpose of God according to election might stand, not of works but of Him who calls), it was said to her, "The older shall serve the younger." As it is written, "Jacob I have loved, but Esau I have hated."

I want you to follow closely the reasoning of the apostle Paul. He has lamented the fate of his fellow Jews. Although his kinsmen had been given the covenants and promises, they had missed out on the redemption brought to them by the Messiah; therefore, it seemed that the promises and covenants that God had made with his people in antiquity were to no avail. Jesus "came to His own, and His own did not receive Him" (John 1:11). His very people had turned against him.

Does this mean that all the promises of salvation that God made through the centuries have come to naught? Does this mean that because the Jews have failed to understand those promises and have missed their Messiah that God's plan of redemption has ended? Paul says no: **But it is not that the word of God has taken no effect** (v. 6a).

I once jokingly asked my congregation, "What am I doing here? Why do I bother to expound the Word of God to people who can't remember the sermon three weeks later?" In a real sense, that doesn't bother me, because my job is to open the Scriptures and expound them as carefully, accurately, and persuasively as I know how. The efficacy of that preaching, the power of the exposition, never lies with me. I am not responsible for the effect that the Word of God has upon the hearer. God takes his Word and applies it to people.

The Spirit of God works with the Word of God to pierce our souls. It is impossible for the Word of God to be without effect. If my congregation forgets something I say or even the whole sermon, I know the Holy Spirit is going to take that word where he wants to take it, and he will hide it in our hearts. We may not know it's hidden there; we may not be able to remember, but we have been affected. That is the power of the Word. That is why Paul says that although the Jews of his generation along with those who heard the prophets earlier have rejected God's Word, that rejection has not nullified the Word of God. God will not permit his Word to return to him void (Isa. 55:11).

True Israel

Paul reminds his readers, **they are not all Israel who are of Israel, nor are they all children because they are the seed of Abraham** (vv. 6b–7a). He has to work against the idea that salvation is passed on biologically or through the visible nation of Israel. Following Augustine, we distinguish between the visible church and the invisible church. The point of the distinction is that not all members of a visible church are redeemed. Not everybody in the visible church is numbered among the elect but only those in the invisible church. It's called "invisible" because we cannot read the hearts of the congregation. I don't know who has made a true profession of faith. Some might have made a profession with their lips but their hearts remain far from God. I cannot read people's hearts, but I can hear their words. People cannot read my heart, but God can. The invisible church is absolutely manifest to the scrutiny of Almighty God. He knows his own, and though we may seek to fool our fellow citizens about our state of grace, nobody has ever fooled God about the state of his or her heart.

Paul makes that same distinction. Just because somebody is an ethnic Jew, a member of the commonwealth of Israel, does not mean that he is saved. The Pharisees fell into that trap. They said, "Abraham is our father" (John 8:39), as if that automatically guaranteed them entrance into the kingdom of God. Not every Jew is a child of promise. Looking to the Old Testament, Paul says that belonging to the seed of Abraham is no guarantee of entry into the kingdom of God. Ishmael was a child of Abraham, but Ishmael was not the child of promise. Paul reminds his readers that in Isaac the seed was called; that is, the children of the flesh are not the children of God. The children of promise are counted as the seed. **For this is the word of promise: "At this time I will come and Sarah shall have a son"** (v. 9).

Denial of the Doctrine

There is much at stake in the reading of Romans 8 and 9, so something I said earlier bears repeating. In my opinion and in the opinion of church history, there is no portion of Scripture that teaches the unconditional election of God in his sovereign grace more persuasively than Romans 9. It is so clear that I wonder how any Christian can closely read this chapter and not come away utterly convinced of the unconditional character of our election, that our salvation rests ultimately on the grace of God alone, not on anything we have ever done or will do.

Despite the perspicuity of the text, the majority of professing evangelicals in our day deny the doctrine of unconditional election. Earlier I noted three ways that people try to get around the doctrine. I repeat them here and add a fourth.

The first and most common way is a systematic avoidance of the text. I did a radio interview not too long ago in which the radio host was against anything regarding the sovereignty of God in election. Every time I tried to take him to Romans 9, he steadfastly refused to go there. Instead, he recited text after text from other portions of the Bible that tell us people have to choose Christ and believe in him. The one I hear most often is John 3:16: "God so loved the world that He gave His only begotten Son, that whoever believes in Him should not perish but have everlasting life." The radio host recited that text to me at least ten times. I said, "I not only am aware of John 3:16, but I see it every time someone at a golf tournament holds up a placard. Let's reduce it to logical propositions: whoever does *A* will not have *B* and will have *C*. If you put your faith in Jesus Christ, you will not perish but have everlasting life. I believe that. Now, tell me what this text says about who will believe or even who can believe?"

He replied, "Obviously, if all who believe will be saved, it must mean that everybody has the ability to believe."

I told him, no, it does not necessarily mean that, particularly when in that same chapter (John 3) our Lord had just told Nicodemus that unless a man is born again he cannot see the kingdom of God, let alone enter it. In John 6 Jesus labors the point that nobody in the flesh can come to him. If left to ourselves, we are in a state of spiritual death because our hearts are corrupt. Unless the Holy Spirit opens our eyes and ears, we will never believe in or choose Jesus. John 3:16 and related texts do nothing to undercut the clear teaching that Paul gives in Romans 9.

The second way in which people get around the doctrine of election is by arguing that Paul in Romans 9 is writing about nations, not individuals. The Arabs came from Ishmael, and the Jewish people came from Isaac. Furthermore, Arabs came from Esau whereas the purity of Israel came through Jacob. So, they say, Paul is referring to God's sovereign, merciful selection of nations set apart to receive a particular blessing. However, when Paul makes his point about election, he mentions individuals. He writes about Jacob and Esau. Paul specifically discusses the selection of one individual over another, Jacob over Esau. The reference to individuals cannot be ignored, so the argument falls by its own weight. I do not know any serious New Testament scholar that advocates it.

Closely related to that argument is a third one: in Romans 9 Paul is writing about God's election of individuals for temporal blessings. Some are elected to inherit land, possessions, herds, and goats, but not salvation. I cannot imagine a more astonishing interpretation of the text. In order to interpret Romans 9 in this manner, it has to be pulled away from its connection to Romans 1–8. Paul introduced the doctrine of predestination in chapter 8:

> Whom He foreknew, He also predestined to be conformed to the image of His Son, that He might be the firstborn among many brethren. Moreover whom He predestined, these He also called; whom He called, these He also justified; and whom He justified, these He also glorified. (vv. 29–30)

There Paul clearly puts the idea of predestination in the context of personal salvation, a theme he has been developing since chapter 1. To see the apostle as describing in chapter 9 anything other than real salvation is to clutch at straws.

The fourth attempt to escape the teaching of Romans 9 is the most popular view, the doctrine of prescience, which I explained earlier. If you recall, this doctrine holds that God does elect individuals to ultimate salvation, but the ground of that election is rooted in his prescience, his prior awareness of what people will do when they are given the gospel. Paul writes: **Not only this, but when Rebecca also had conceived by one man, even by our father Isaac (for the children not yet being born, nor having done any good or evil, that the purpose of God according to election might stand, not of works but of Him who calls), it was said to her, "The older shall serve the younger"** (vv. 10–12). The doctrine of prescience is not only denied, dear friends, but it is demolished. The apostle dusts off the spot where it stood, because he addresses unambiguously the very concept that lies at the heart of the prescient view of predestination. The apostle guides us to look at the two unborn children Jacob and Esau. They were not only brothers; they were also twins. They had the same environmental background, the same mother, father, and birthday. Paul reminds the reader of God's decree that the elder should serve the younger and that this decree was made before either boy was born. It is manifestly obvious that if these two boys were the subjects of divine election, then their election had been settled before they were born.

The Ground of Election

Notice Paul's use of the words "purpose" and "calls"—"that the purpose of God according to election might stand, not to him who works but of Him who calls." In both instances he is referring to the one who elects. The decree came before the boys were born, before they had done any good or evil, to make certain that the purpose of God according to election might stand. Their election was based not on what the boys would do but on what God does. The decree was issued according to the purpose of God so that his purpose would be exalted and established. His purpose is the ground of election.

Our election is never found in us. "So then it is not of him who wills, nor of him who runs, but of God who shows mercy" (v. 16). The prescient advocates say that in the final analysis our election is rooted in some work we do, but election would be conditional if we had to meet a condition in order for God to elect us. A conditional election flies in the face of the very point the apostle is laboring to make.

Inevitably discussions of predestination come down to the free will of the creature, but bringing the notion of free will to this text is humanistic. The idea of a human will not enslaved by sin is an unbiblical understanding. At the heart of this text is indeed a profound affirmation of free will. It teaches that our salvation rests ultimately and eternally on free will, but it is not our free will; it is God's. It is the free will of the Creator, the Redeemer, who, in his sovereign grace, pours his mercy out upon those he chooses. In this case, God distinguishes between Jacob and Esau, the younger and the elder.

The Nature of God's Love

Jewish custom held that the elder received the inheritance and the blessing, but in the case of Jacob and Esau, God turned it upside down and declared that the elder would serve the younger. **"Jacob I have loved"**—Jacob, the supplanter, the liar, the one with very little to commend himself—**"but Esau I have hated"** (v. 13). Some say, "You are teaching that God hates people, and my minister told me that God loves everybody unconditionally."

How do we deal with Paul's words? I've written an entire book on just this verse, "Jacob I have loved, but Esau I have hated." We have to be careful to distinguish between the various ways the Bible refers to the love of God. The Bible speaks of God's universal love, that is, the love he has for all people. The first has to do with God's *love of benevolence*. The word *benevolence* comes from the prefix *bene-*, which means "good" or "well," and the word *volēns*, *will*, so *benevolence* means "good will." God has a basic attitude of goodwill to all his creatures, and that posture or attitude of good is shown by his love of beneficence. God's love of benevolence underlies God's giving good gifts to people indiscriminately.

There is, however, a special dimension of God's love, his *love of complacency*. It is a love that takes delight in the object of one's affection. This is the love the Father has for the Son. Christ is the beloved, but the Father, in pouring out his love of complacency upon his only begotten Son, extends that love to all who are in Christ Jesus. Our adoption includes us in that special, redemptive love of God in a way that those outside the fellowship of Christ do not share.

The fact that God loved Jacob and hated Esau does not indicate that God had a malicious sense of odium within his being against Esau. God was not filled with loathing toward him, although there are times in the Old Testament where that kind of loathing is attributed to God against evildoers and impenitent people. Here we are seeing a love-hate contrast, which is intended to communicate the truth that those who receive only God's benevolent love might consider it hatred when compared to God's complacent love, because his benevolent love is such a lower degree of love.

Jesus spoke similarly when he said, "If anyone comes to Me and does not hate his father and mother, wife and children, brothers and sisters, yes, and his own life also, he cannot be My disciple." (Luke 14:26). Jesus was not advising his disciples to have an attitude of hostility toward their earthly parents. Jesus knew that people are called to honor their father and mother, something they certainly are not doing if they despise them. Jesus was making a comparison. Those who want to love him must love him before all others. Jesus requires that the love we have for our friends, spouse, mother, father, or children be so much less than the love we have for him that it could be seen as hatred.

Early on in the Old Testament Leah complained about Jacob's lack of love for her; Jacob's deepest affection was for Rachel. Rachel was the apple of his eye, yet he was married first to Leah through the chicanery of Leah's father. Jacob was not cruel to Leah, but Leah said that she was hated by her husband (see Genesis 29–30 KJV). If you look at the context, she is saying that she knew herself to be second in terms of Jacob's preference.

If there remains any doubt that Paul is talking about sovereign election, just wait until our next study, because Paul is just now getting warmed up.

35

THE RIGHTEOUSNESS OF GOD

Romans 9:14–16

What shall we say then? Is there unrighteousness with God? Certainly not! For He says to Moses, "I will have mercy on whomever I will have mercy, and I will have compassion on whomever I will have compassion." So then it is not of him who wills, nor of him who runs, but of God who shows mercy.

My first assignment as a college professor was to teach the history of philosophy. Many students know that the study of philosophy can be exceedingly difficult. The ideas that are analyzed tend to be abstract and heavy. Otherwise excellent students stumble when they come into the arena of philosophy. It takes a certain kind of mind to track with philosophical inquiry. As I recounted earlier, I tried to give my students some helpful hints on how to wade through the writings of Hume or Descartes or Kant. I told them, "When you read these men, see if you can discover what problem they are trying to solve and what question they are trying to answer. If you can isolate the problem and clarify in your mind the question they are addressing, it will help you understand how they came to various conclusions."

In my early days of teaching I disagreed with most of the content I taught on the history of philosophy, but integrity demanded that I try to be scrupulous in setting forth the ideas espoused by various philosophers. If I dared to offer a critique, I had to avoid setting up straw men. I stated my opponent's position with as much force as I knew how.

I discussed with my students how to argue over various ideas and for different positions when controversy arises. I advised that they try to think the way the opponent thinks and track with the opponent's process. I instructed them that when debating, they ought to state the opponent's position more cogently than even the opponent can so he will know that his position is at least understood. I wanted my students to know that approaching debate that way provides opportunity to address the issues head-on.

I provide that background to aid our understanding Paul, the master teacher. Paul was the greatest theologian ever to walk the face of the earth. He had the equivalent of two PhDs by the time he was twenty-one years old. It has been argued that he was the most learned man in Palestine. Had Paul not become a Christian, we would likely know of him anyway due to his superior intellect. When we deal with a genius of the scope of the apostle Paul and find ourselves struggling with what he is saying, we need to ask, what problem is he trying to solve and what question is he trying to answer?

In our last study we came to a rigorously difficult portion of Romans 9. Although Jacob and Esau had the same mother, and before either had been born or had done any good or evil, the purposes of God according to his election prevailed. God decreed that the elder would serve the younger. We ended up with Paul's very troublesome declaration: "Jacob I have loved, but Esau I have hated."

God Unrighteous?

Afterward the apostle does what any good teacher does, particularly one steeped in the rigors of debate: he anticipates the reaction of his students or opponents. Paul anticipates the point of tension, the argument, in what he is teaching about the sovereignty of God in election, and he raises a rhetorical question: **What shall we say then? Is there unrighteousness with God?** (v. 14a). The word translated "unrighteousness" comes from the Greek word *adikia*. When a word is prefaced with that simple letter, *a*, it is a negation of the root. (*Agnosticism* comes from the word *agnosis*, which means "without knowledge" or "non-knowledge.") The root of *adikia* is *dikaios*, which means "righteous" or "just." When you put that prefix, *a-*, in front of *dikaios*, it negates the root. Paul is using the term that defines injustice or unrighteousness. If we go to the Latin text we find, "What do we say then?

Is there iniquity, *iniquitos*, in God?" There is force behind Paul's rhetorical question.

Why would Paul raise a question like this one? Is there anything more fundamental than the clear manifestation that God is altogether righteous? It is unthinkable. It is blasphemous to attribute to God any smear of iniquity, any tinge of unrighteousness, or any hint of injustice. Words like *injustice, unrighteousness,* and *iniquity* simply do not belong as predicates of God's character. Paul raises a rhetorical question with an unthinkable answer, but why does he raise it? He is anticipating a response to his teaching on the sovereignty of God in election, which he has been setting forth since chapter 8. As soon as Paul makes the radical statement about Jacob and Esau, he can hear the hisses and boos in the gallery: "That's not fair!" It certainly does seem unfair if, for nothing found in Jacob or Esau, God chooses one over the other. The fact that it seems unfair is a chief reason why Christians kick against this doctrine.

There are two principle objections in the Christian community—never mind the pagan community—to the doctrine of election. It seems to dispense with any significance to the free will of man, and, even more importantly, it seems to cast a shadow on the integrity of God. The doctrine seems to make God arbitrary, whimsical, and capricious and, even worse, it seems to show a shadowy side of God's character, one that indicates that even he is infected by sin in the sense of being unjust or unrighteous.

Paul's rhetorical question convinces me that the Reformed understanding of predestination is the biblical one and the one that Paul is teaching. I have been defending the doctrine of election for more than forty years in many contexts, and I have heard the objection against predestination and election—that it represents God's unfairness—countless times. Every time I teach the doctrine, somebody objects and says, "That's not fair."

My Arminian friends and some of my Lutheran friends who borrow this prescient view of predestination have had to defend their position against various objections, but I trust that no one has accused them of calling God unrighteous. Why would anybody think of God as unjust, unrighteous, or iniquitous for choosing people on the basis of the decisions they make—either good or bad? What could be fairer than that? Here in Romans 9 Paul anticipates accusations because the doctrine provokes that kind of response from his audience.

Sovereignty and Grace

Paul answers his rhetorical question: **Certainly not!** (v. 14b). Those strong words are translated in different ways such as "By no means!" or "God forbid!"

I think the most accurate translation is "May it never be!" In other words, no one can dispute the fact that in God is no unrighteousness, injustice, or iniquity, though indeed it may seem that way initially.

After answering his question with that demonstrative reply, Paul inserts a revelation from the Pentateuch: **For He says to Moses, "I will have mercy on whomever I will have mercy, and I will have compassion on whomever I will have compassion"** (v. 16). Paul reminds us of the absolute sovereignty of grace. Obviously, if God is not sovereign, then he is not God. To be God is to be sovereign. When we consider divine sovereignty, we generally look at it in three specific domains. The first domain of God's sovereignty is the universe, which he governs. God, who made the universe, called it into being from nothing by the sheer power of his command. He exercises his sovereign authority over the stars, the floods, and the rivers; he exercises it over history and all things.

The second domain in which God's sovereignty reigns is law. God has the sovereign right to legislate the manner of behavior and response that his creatures should render to him. Do you believe that God has the right to impose obligations upon his creatures and to bind your conscience with his laws that command "you shall" and "you shall not?" Contrary to the moral relativism so pervasive in our culture, you certainly know, if you have the slightest understanding of the Christian faith, that God has the authority to command you to do what he says is right.

Most Christians hold to God's sovereignty over nature and law, but when it comes to the third domain—the sovereignty of God's disposition of grace—90 percent get off the train. To them, God is not sovereign in his disposition of grace because if he were, he would show the same mercy to everyone. Scripture paints a different picture of God's exercise of grace: "I will have mercy on whomever I will have mercy, and I will have compassion on whomever I will have compassion."

How can God say that and still be just? He can, because he is exercising mercy upon sinners. No one can shake his fist at God justly, yet plenty do, saying, "That's not fair. You have given me a bad deal." No sinner has the right to say with impunity, "God, you owe me grace." If grace is owed, it is not grace. The very essence of grace is its voluntary character. God reserves to himself the sovereign, absolute right to give grace to some and withhold that grace from others.

The study of logic includes making distinctions of categories, an example being theism. Theism incorporates within a broad circle of thought any type of religion that affirms the existence of any kind of god or gods. Theism is a broad concept, and any affirmation of a *theos* or *theoi*, a god or several gods, makes it inside that circle. The term *atheism*, which means non-theism, incorporates everything outside that circle. If you believe in any kind of god, you are in the circle of theism. If you do not believe, you are in the realm of atheism.

When we come to the concept of justice, there is a circle of righteousness, or justice, and everything just or righteous fits in that circle. However, when we consider the concept of non-justice, it gets confusing. Non-justice points to and includes everything outside our circle of justice. We have justice inside the circle and non-justice outside the circle, but what about injustice? Injustice is outside the category of justice; it falls into the realm of non-justice. Injustice is a bad thing. It is evil to commit an injustice. Mercy is not bad, so is mercy inside the circle of justice? The answer is no; mercy is non-justice. There are two things outside the circle of justice: one is injustice, which is evil, and the other is mercy, which is not evil. So is there injustice in God? No. Is there unrighteousness in God? No. Is there iniquity in God? No. Is there non-justice in God? Yes, there is. There is mercy and grace, but grace is never inside the circle of justice. Over the years I have told my students, "Don't ever ask God for justice—you might get it."

Through the entire epistle Paul has been laboring to show that all are sinful; none is just. We have no hope of standing before the judgment of a holy and righteous God, but the wonderful grace of the gospel is that God has provided for us a justice not our own. This justice is the righteousness of Christ, which is imputed to us. This is how Paul has explained the gospel all along. The fact that we are adopted into the family of God and receive the gift of the transfer of the righteousness of Christ to our account is, from beginning to end, the result of God's grace. "For by grace you have been saved through faith, and that not of yourselves; it is the gift of God" (Eph. 2:8).

Justice and Mercy

God in his sovereign disposition of grace interrupts our life while we are alienated from him, dead in sin and trespasses, and the Holy Spirit comes and quickens us from death to life and changes the disposition of our heart. Where formerly Christ seemed repugnant, now he is the sweetest thing in the world. We rush to him, we choose him, we embrace him, and we trust him, because God in his grace has given us the pearl of great price. If God does that for us, is he obligated to do it for everybody? If the president of the United States exercises executive clemency and pardons somebody in prison, is he then obligated to pardon everybody? No. What Jacob got was grace;

what Esau got was not injustice. God withheld his mercy from Esau—mercy to which Esau had no claim—but the withholding was not an act of injustice on God's part. Jacob got mercy; Esau got justice. The elect get grace; the non-elect get justice. Nobody gets injustice.

We have to hold on to that point with all our might, and Paul is laboring for that. "I will have mercy on whom I will have mercy." God does not have to have mercy on everybody. God called Abraham out of paganism, out of Ur of the Chaldeans, and made him a covenant promise, not because Abraham had done any good thing but so that the purposes of God, according to his grace, might stand. God did not do that for Hammurabi or Nebuchadnezzar.

Jesus faced his enemies. There was Caiaphas the high priest; there were the members of the Sanhedrin. Jesus was condemned by Pontius Pilate, who spoke on behalf of the Roman magisterium. However, the most vicious and hateful opponent of Jesus on the pages of the New Testament was the man who wrote the very words we are studying. The apostle Paul had hated Jesus more than Pilate or Caiaphas or the scribes and Pharisees. There was never a day when Paul walked along the street and said, "Maybe I had better think this over a bit more clearly," and after giving it further scrutiny changed his mind and decided to exercise his free will and become a disciple of Jesus. No, Paul became a disciple while breathing out animosity and hostility. Jesus knocked him off his horse, blinded him with the brilliance of his glory, and called him to be his apostle. Jesus intervened in the life of Paul in a way he did not do for Pontius Pilate or Caiaphas or for the scribes and Pharisees.

If we read the Bible from Genesis to Revelation, we see that God does not treat everybody the same way. If he did, we would all have the same place in hell, but he exercises mercy to some so that the glory of his purposes may be known.

So then it is not of him who wills, nor of him who runs, but of God who shows mercy (v. 16). Paul sets forth the doctrine of election with such clarity in Romans 8 and 9 that he leaves us without excuse. How can we look at this text closely and still say, "It really is of him who wills and him who runs. My free will is the basis of my salvation." No, it is God's free will. Perhaps you have heard it said that God's sovereignty ends where human free will begins. Maybe you have even said it. It is blasphemy, of course, because if God's sovereignty is limited by our free will, then we are sovereign. We do have free will. We have the ability to choose what we want to be. That is true freedom, but it is always and everywhere limited by God's sovereignty. Any time man's free will bumps up against God's free will, who wins? It is no contest. It is God's good pleasure to save his elect that he may show forth his grace in salvation.

Let me end with a rebuke. I do not want to be harsh—I understand how difficult this doctrine can be and how much baggage we carry into the discussion of it. If you are hanging on to your semi-Pelagian views of election, get rid of them. Your theology is undermining the sovereignty of God, his grace, and the sweetness of his mercy. We do that when we want to exalt our decisions above his, and it is the very essence of sin. We have to bow before him and acquiesce not only to the sovereignty of his grace but to the *goodness* of the sovereignty of his grace.

So far we have nothing by which to protest against the goodness and the sweetness of God's grace. If you have struggled with it thus far, you will really squirm and struggle when we consider in our next study God's hardening of Pharaoh's heart and creating vessels fit for destruction.

36

PREDESTINATION

Romans 9:17–20

For the Scripture says to the Pharaoh, "For this very purpose I have raised you up, that I may show My power in you, and that My name may be declared in all the earth." Therefore He has mercy on whom He wills, and whom He wills He hardens. You will say to me then, "Why does He still find fault? For who has resisted His will?" But indeed, O man, who are you to reply against God? Will the thing formed say to him who formed it, "Why have you made me like this?"

John Calvin said that the doctrine of election is one of the most difficult doctrines of sacred Scripture and must be handled with care, caution, tenderness, and patience among those who struggle with it, but it should not be neglected. The doctrine comes from the Word of God, and even though we struggle with it, we must not sweep it under the rug; we must deal with it, albeit carefully.

I have participated in numerous call-in radio programs, and I know before the phones start ringing what is going to be at the top of the list—predestination and election. Every time somebody asks me about that in a radio call-in context, I would prefer not to answer. I would rather say nothing than say too little. I just cannot deal with this subject in a two-minute radio response because a short response generates more questions than it answers.

Double Predestination

I am asked frequently whether I believe in double predestination. Here is where we face what I have to call "double or nothing." If some of humanity is elect, then others are non-elect. The non-elect are those whom we call the reprobate. So as far as I'm concerned, unless we are universalists there is no way to avoid the idea of a double aspect to divine predestination. Of course predestination is double. There is election and reprobation. We cannot avoid that fact with mental gymnastics. However, once we affirm double predestination, we have to ask what kind of double predestination we affirm. Even within the communion of Reformed theology there is ongoing debate about that very question. Most agree that predestination is double; the debate is over how to understand the double aspect.

One view, sometimes called hyper-Calvinism, teaches a symmetrical view of predestination, or equal ultimacy. A symmetrical view of double predestination holds that in the case of the elect, God decreed their election from eternity and in the fullness of time intervenes in their lives and creates saving faith in their hearts by his grace. God invades the soul of the elect and quickens them from spiritual death to spiritual life and brings them to faith in Christ. In a symmetrical manner, the reprobate are doomed from eternity, and God in the fullness of time intrudes into their lives and creates fresh evil in their souls, ensuring their ultimate reprobation and damnation. This symmetrical view believes that God works grace by direct intrusion, and he works hardening by creating evil in the reprobate in an equal manner. However, that is not the orthodox Reformed doctrine of double predestination, and I do not hold to that symmetrical view, or equal ultimacy. I hold to a positive-negative view of double predestination.

A positive-negative distinction in predestination is this: in the case of the elect, God positively intervenes in their lives to rescue them from their corrupt condition. The Holy Spirit changes their hearts of stone to hearts alive to the things of God. That is his positive intervention. In the case of the reprobate, God works negatively insofar as he passes over them. He leaves them to their own devices, but he does not intrude in their lives to create fresh evil. In the mass of fallen humanity, some receive the saving grace of God; God intervenes to rescue them from their sinful condition. He passes over the remainder. Those whom he passes over are not elect; they are reprobate. They are judged because of the evil already present in them, which is in view in this portion of Romans 9.

God and Pharaoh

Paul quotes what God says to Pharaoh, **"For this very purpose I have raised you up"** (v. 17a). In this case, it is not enough to say that God permits Pharaoh to sin. It is not enough to say that God's will is involved only so far as God stayed out of the picture altogether and left Pharaoh to his own devices. That is an attractive way to handle the text, but I do not think it is sufficient to deal with Paul's teaching. God not only has allowed Pharaoh to continue in willful disobedience, but he also has raised him up. A better way to translate that text is this way: "I have appointed you to this task."

The eternal God Almighty raised up Pharaoh, sat him in the seat of power over the Egyptians, and gave him power to rule over his own people and the Israelite slaves. God put Pharaoh in a position of power for the purpose of showing his own power: **". . . that I may show My power in you, and that My name may be declared in all the earth"** (v. 17b). Luther said that the people of Israel were *machtlos*, "without any might." All the power was invested in Pharaoh, and it was invested there by the Lord God omnipotent. In the face of God's power, Pharaoh's power was impotent. It is as if God said to Pharaoh, "I appointed you to this position not to show the world how much power you have, Pharaoh, but to show the world my power. That's why I appointed you to this task, so that my people, in their powerlessness, their *machtlos*, might know where the power of their salvation lies."

Removal of Divine Restraint

Therefore He has mercy on whom He wills, and whom He wills He hardens (v. 18). On the surface it sounds once again as though there is a balance, a symmetry, in which God melts the hearts of the elect and calcifies the hearts of the reprobate. The Bible does say, not only here but throughout the exodus account, that God repeatedly hardens the heart of Pharaoh. How are we to understand that? First, both Pharaoh and God were involved, so in a very real sense God was actively involved in the hardening of the heart of a human being, but how exactly did God harden the heart of Pharaoh? How does he harden anybody's heart? He does so not by mere permission but by a divine decision that we see again and again, particularly in the book of the prophet Jeremiah, where God deals with impenitent sinners by giving them over to their sin.

In the book of Revelation we find that the final disposition of the wicked is through this very means: "He who is unjust, let him be unjust still; he who is filthy, let him be filthy still" (22:11). God does not have to create any new evil in the human heart. To make someone more wicked than he already is,

God need only remove his restraints. One of the great mercies God gives us is keeping us from being as sinful as we possibly could be.

Earlier in our study I mentioned that Reformed theology uses the acronym TULIP to describe our situation of original sin. The T in the acronym stands for *total depravity*. I do not like the term *total depravity*; it is misleading. I prefer *radical corruption*. The term *total depravity* suggests that we are as bad as we possibly could be; that is, we are utterly depraved. Think, however, of all of the sins you have committed in your lifetime. As bad as they have been, they could have been worse. You could have committed more sins, and the sins you have committed could have been more vicious. The same could be said of Ted Bundy, Charles Manson, and Adolf Hitler. No one has been as sinful as he theoretically could be—not because some island of righteousness holds him back from utter depravity, but because the restraining power of God is a bridle that keeps all in check. When we abuse God's patience and longsuffering, our hearts become harder and harder, and at any moment God can remove the restraints and give us over to our sin.

From Genesis to Revelation we see that God's abandoning a sinner to wickedness is not an act of unrighteousness on his part; it is a manifestation of his perfect justice. It is as if he is saying, "You want to sin? Be my guest. I am not going to strive with you anymore. I am going to take the wraps off. I am going to loosen the leash and let you do what you want, because I know that the desires of your hearts are only wicked continually."

Being given over to sin is itself a judgment on sin—that is a biblical principle. It presupposes an existing sinful condition. God did not look around Egypt for somebody to appoint to resist Moses and in the process stumble upon the poor, innocent, righteous young man Pharaoh and say, "I will take this benevolent young fellow because he is an able administrator, and I will put him on the seat of power over the Egyptians and make him as evil as I can so that I can get my will done and show my power to the whole world." That would be sheer cosmic tyranny, and it is not what God did. He hardened a man who was already hard. Pharaoh could not say before God, "God, what's going on here? You are punishing me for the hardness of my heart while you have been making sure that my heart gets hardened. That is not fair." Yes, it is fair. It is perfect justice for God to give an evil one over to evil.

Potter and Clay

At this point in the text Paul is expecting another objection. He has already heard this one: "Is there unrighteousness with God?" (v. 14). Now, as soon as

Paul mentions Pharaoh's hardening, he heads off the objection he knows will follow: **You will say to me then, "Why does He still find fault? For who has resisted His will?"** (v. 19). Paul does not answer that question. He does not slip into Arminianism and say, "The reason he still finds fault is that all sin is found in man, so it is dependent on what people do with their choices." We find none of that here.

Paul's response to this anticipated objection is simply a moral rebuke: **But indeed, O man, who are you to reply against God?** (v. 20a). Before Paul begins to answer the question, he calls the objector to remember who he is and who God is. He is basically saying to those who constantly carp against God's sovereignty, "Who do you think you are?"

Remember Job. He was the victim of much injustice at the hands of men and Satan; he suffered affliction without relief. Finally he raised his fist against heaven and shook it in the face of God. God answered Job by means of a lengthy, relentless interrogation:

> Who is this who darkens counsel
>   By words without knowledge?
> Now prepare yourself like a man;
>   I will question you, and you shall answer Me. (Job 38:2–3)

God's interrogation of Job continues: "Can you bind the cluster of the Pleiades, or loose the belt of Orion?" (v. 31). Job answered no. "Can you draw out Leviathan with a hook, or snare his tongue with a line which you lower?" (41:1). The answer was no, chapter after chapter, and finally Job said, "I abhor myself, and repent in dust and ashes" (42:6). Even when we struggle, even when we do not fully comprehend the mystery of God's sovereign will, let that not lead us to blasphemy.

The absolute integrity and righteousness of Almighty God is not to be questioned. **Will the thing formed say to him who formed it, "Why have you made me like this?"** (v. 20b). Pharaoh could not shake his fist at God and ask, "Why have you hardened my heart?" God owed Pharaoh no explanation. Pharaoh's heart had no inherent righteousness. God used Pharaoh for his glorious, holy, merciful, and gracious plan of salvation.

37

VESSELS OF WRATH AND MERCY

Romans 9:20–24

But indeed, O man, who are you to reply against God? Will the thing formed say to him who formed it, "Why have you made me like this?" Does not the potter have power over the clay, from the same lump to make one vessel for honor and another for dishonor? What if God, wanting to show His wrath and to make His power known, endured with much longsuffering the vessels of wrath prepared for destruction, and that He might make known the riches of His glory on the vessels of mercy, which He had prepared beforehand for glory, even us whom He called, not of the Jews only, but also of the Gentiles?

But indeed, O man, who are you to reply against God? Will the thing formed say to him who formed it, "Why have you made me like this?" Does not the potter have power over the clay, from the same lump to make one vessel for honor and another for dishonor?** (vv. 20–21). I want to look at this passage more closely in light of a classic controversy within the Reformed tradition, that between *supralapsarianism* and *infralapsarianism*. This controversy has been labeled as an arcane principle of theology, but as difficult and controversial as the issue has been historically, it is not without significance. It makes a big difference which side we come down on, and I address it here because the controversy is provoked by the text before us.

Supralapsarianism and Infralapsarianism

The debate between supralapsarianism and infralapsarianism has to do with the relationship of God's decrees to election and the fall, particularly to the fall—the lapse of the human race into sin—hence, the root of both terms, *lapsarianism*. Both *supra* and *infra* deal with God's involvement with the fall and the order of God's decrees with respect to it and to election.

Some think that those who hold to the doctrine of infralapsarianism claim that God's decree of election came after the fall, and those who hold to supralapsarianism claim that God's decree of election came before the fall. That is a false distinction. Both sides understand that God's decrees regarding election and reprobation are rooted in eternity. God did not issue a decree to save people as a plan B, as if his original purpose in creation had been ruined by Adam and Eve's sin. In other words, God did not have to remedy the mess of the fall by coming up with a plan of salvation. Both sides agree that God's sovereign plan of salvation was determined before the foundation of the world—before Adam and Eve existed. The question is not *when* the decrees were executed by God in his eternal plan but rather the *order* of the decrees.

The infralapsarian position, held by the vast majority of historic Calvinists and Reformed theologians, claims that God's decree of election was made in view of the fall. When God makes from one batch of clay vessels fit for destruction and from another vessels fit for honor, it does not mean that he planned from eternity to make some people bad and other people redeemable. God applies his redeeming grace to a mass of humanity completely dead in sin and trespasses. The decree of electing grace is made in light of the fall. In fact, if it were not made in light of the fall, it would not be a decree of grace.

On the other side of the coin is the supralapsarian position, which teaches that God decreed the fall in light of his doctrine of election. God first elected certain people to salvation and others to reprobation, and in order to accomplish that eternal purpose, he decreed the fall of humanity. The purpose of the fall was to provide the necessary clay for God to choose some to salvation and others to reprobation. Supralapsarians say that God planned to save some and condemn others, and in order to make that possible, he consigned the whole world to ruin. Therefore, the purpose of the fall was to provide the necessary condition through which God shows his grace and wrath. That is problematic because it violates what we call the biblical *apriori*—God is not the author or creator of sin. God does not choose to create people in a fallen condition so that he can condemn them to eternal damnation. It is not God's purpose to force people to sin and then punish them for that sin.

I do not believe that God creates people wicked and then punishes them for their wickedness, nor is Paul teaching that here in Romans 9. At the same time, as Augustine said, in some sense God did ordain the fall. There are two reasons why I believe that God, in some sense, did ordain the fall. God's sovereignty is one reason. God is sovereign over nature and human history. He rules all things by his power and authority. He is sovereign over the disposition of his grace. Nothing can happen apart from God's sovereign action. If I plan to steal a car tonight, my evil intentions might be a secret from the car's owner, but they are not hidden from God. He knows what I am going to do before I do it, and he knows what I am going to say before I say it. Before a word is even formed on my lips, he knows it all together (Ps. 139:4). God knows my intentions, even though others do not unless I tell them.

God has the power to stop me from stealing a car, but does he have the *authority* to stop me? He does. God has the authority and power to prevent anything from happening that does, in fact, happen. God can exercise his authority and power and sovereignty by stopping something from happening or by not stopping it. Those are God's options always in every way. Since the fall happened, God knew it was going to happen, and he could have prevented it, but he chose not to. His purpose in not stopping it, however, was not to provide himself with a wicked batch of clay on which to exercise his sovereign decree of reprobation. Why God allowed it is something we cannot fully know. The answer Scripture gives is that somehow the lapse into sin, which produced a batch of fallen humanity and fragile, corrupt clay, was for his glory.

Wrath Made Known

Paul addresses this question to the Roman Christians, but by extension he addresses it to us: **What if God, wanting to show His wrath and to make His power known, endured with much longsuffering the vessels of wrath prepared for destruction?** (v. 22). Would there be anything wrong with a just and holy God displaying his power and wrath? We might struggle with that because we live in a culture that has rejected any idea of a wrathful God, but Paul refuted that back in Romans 1: "For the wrath of God is revealed from heaven against all ungodliness and un-righteousness of men" (v. 18).

When God was going to visit his wrath on Sodom and Gomorrah, Abraham asked him, "Would You also destroy the righteous with the wicked? Suppose there were fifty righteous within the city; would You also destroy the place and not spare it for the fifty righteous that were in it?" (Gen. 18:23b–24). Abraham, the father of the faithful, fell into an abysmal heresy even suggesting the possibility that God would punish innocent people. Abraham came to his senses and said to God, "Far be it from You to do such a thing as this, to slay the righteous with the wicked, so that the righteous should be as the wicked; far be it from You! Shall not the Judge of all the earth do right?" (v. 25). Abraham had no idea how far it is from God to do such a thing. The distance between the likelihood of God's punishing the innocent with the guilty, the righteous with the wicked, is infinite. It is absolutely unthinkable.

When we see Paul talk about God's showing his power—his wrath for vessels fit for destruction and dishonor—we must not think that God punishes innocent people or that he finds fault with the faultless. "Will not the Judge of all of the earth do what is right?" It is right for the Judge of the earth to show his wrath. We may not like his wrath; we may choke on the very idea of it. It should take us no more than five minutes to think about the justness of a holy God displaying anger against sin. When Jesus made a rope from cords, went into the temple in Jerusalem, kicked over the tables, and drove out the moneychangers in a fit of rage, it was a demonstration of justifiable anger. Every time the New Testament mentions the last judgment, it shows everyone standing before the judgment seat of God with their mouths shut. The whole world is found guilty before him.

My late friend James Boice and I frequently flew together to various conferences and events. I am a white-knuckle flyer whereas he loved the bumps and the feeling of exhilaration that comes from flying through the air. While I looked anxiously out the window, he said, "What is the matter, R. C.? Don't you believe in the sovereignty of God?" I replied, "Jim, that is my problem. I do believe in the sovereignty of God, and I know that he would be perfectly just to crash me into the ocean right now. That is why I am nervous."

Even though I delight in my adoption into the family of God, I still fear God. I am not thinking solely of an adoring fear of awe and reverence; sometimes I experience the stone-cold fear of provoking him. I know that my justification is not on the line; I know that I will never experience condemnation at his hands. I will and do, however, experience his chastisement, his corrective wrath. When I receive it, I am not to think of it as unjust. Paul wants us to consider that. We do not enjoy his chastisement, but we cannot fault God for "wanting to show his wrath and to make his power known."

The writer of Psalm 2 paints a picture of a summit meeting. Attending are the most powerful rulers of the world. They come together and join in a conspiracy, plotting against the Lord and his anointed, declaring their independence and autonomy from God. They say, "Let us break Their bonds in pieces and cast away Their cords from us" (v. 3). How does God respond? He laughs. The Lord holds them in derision (v. 4). If we were to amass all the power on the planet and aim it at heaven, it would be to no avail. No one can withstand God's power, yet in the folly of our sin and the hardness of our heart, we sin daily, and when we get away with it, we assume that God is powerless to do anything about it. That is a foolish assumption for any creature to make. Throughout history God has interrupted his forbearing. He does at times temporarily suspend his patience with us and remind us that he is sovereign.

Riches of Glory Made Known

God's sovereignty in election is revealed so **that He might make known the riches of His glory on the vessels of mercy, which He had prepared beforehand for glory** (v. 23). The treasure of God's glory is likened to riches untold, riches that can never be counted. That is what the doctrine of election is about. We must never study the doctrine of predestination in the abstract. In the final analysis, although predestination certainly involves God's sovereignty—his omnipotence and omniscience—the doctrine is about the riches of God's glory. Paul cannot rehearse these things without soon breaking into doxology: "Oh, the depth of the riches both of the wisdom and knowledge of God!" (11:33a). I initially struggled to embrace the doctrine of election, but contemplating the riches of God's glory enabled me to see the sweetness of this doctrine. It screams not so much sovereignty as unfathomable grace and mercy.

This doctrine more than any other reveals that grace really is amazing. "Amazing grace, how sweet the sound that saved a wretch like me. I once was lost, but now I am found"—we sing the hymn not because we were searching but because the hound of heaven found us with the sweetness of his mercy and grace. That is why we talk about doctrines such as justification and election as the doctrines of grace. Grace is the idea here in the text we are considering. From a corrupt mass of clay God chose to make vessels of glory. If you are in Christ Jesus, that is what God has done for you in his mercy and grace. He has made you a vessel of mercy that he prepared before the foundation of the world for glory. We are bound from God's eternal plan for eternal glory in his family, **even us whom He called, not of the Jews only, but also of the Gentiles** (v. 24).

To underscore the riches of this mercy and the central accent on grace Paul goes back to the prophet Hosea. We will consider this portion of the text in our next study, but I will introduce it here. The lesson of mercy and grace that God taught Israel through the prophet Hosea came at great personal expense to Hosea. In order to show the riches of his glory and the sweetness of his mercy, God commanded Hosea to marry a prostitute who was flagrant in her promiscuity and infidelity. The children that came from their union received the judgment of God: "When she had weaned Lo-Ruhamah, she conceived and bore a son. Then God said: 'Call his name Lo-Ammi, for you are not My people, and I will not be your God'" (Hos. 1:8–9). That is an object lesson of divine rejection. God told the nation of Israel that because of their sinfulness, they had become Lo-Ammi, "not my people."

Paul then introduces a motif that he will develop through the remainder of chapter 9 and into chapters 10 and 11. He is going to show that God will have mercy on whom he will have mercy and call a people who were not his people. Paul is talking about us. We who were no people now are his people by grace. We are the wild olive branch grafted into the root of the tree. We bring nothing to the table. Nothing in us could move God to include us in his kingdom. Our only hope is the riches of his glory and mercy. That is what election is all about.

38

GOD'S PEOPLE

Romans 9:25–10:4

As He says also in Hosea:

"I will call them My people, who were not My people,
And her beloved, who was not beloved."
"And it shall come to pass in the place where it was said to them,
'You are not My people,'
There they shall be called sons of the living God."

Isaiah also cries out concerning Israel:

"Though the number of the children of Israel be as the sand of the sea,
The remnant will be saved.
For He will finish the work and cut it short in righteousness,
Because the LORD will make a short work upon the earth."

And as Isaiah said before:

"Unless the LORD of Sabaoth had left us a seed,
We would have become like Sodom,
And we would have been made like Gomorrah."

What shall we say then? That Gentiles, who did not pursue righteousness, have attained to righteousness, even the righteousness of faith; but Israel, pursuing the law of righteousness, has not attained to the law of righteousness. Why? Because they did not seek it by faith, but as it were, by the works of the law. For they stumbled at that stumbling stone. As it is written:

> "Behold, I lay in Zion a stumbling stone and rock of offense,
> And whoever believes on Him will not be put to shame."

Brethren, my heart's desire and prayer to God for Israel is that they may be saved. For I bear them witness that they have a zeal for God, but not according to knowledge. For they being ignorant of God's righteousness, and seeking to establish their own righteousness, have not submitted to the righteousness of God. For Christ is the end of the law for righteousness to everyone who believes.

Paul introduced the grand theme of justification in Romans 1. Immediately after, Paul interrupted the good news to declare that the wrath of God has been revealed from heaven against the ungodliness and unrighteousness of men. God has made the knowledge of himself so clear through the works of nature and to our consciences that we are without excuse. Despite our clear knowledge of the righteousness of God, we have fled from God's presence. Then Paul shows that both Jew and Gentile are equally guilty under the law before God. He spells out in chapter 3 the degree of our corruption, pointing to the fact that no one can be justified in the sight of God through the works of the law. Then Paul sets forth the grand doctrine, that of justification by faith alone. After that he lays out the benefits of justification, sanctification, and adoption.

In chapter 8 Paul sets forth the order of salvation. It began in eternity in God's decree to elect some. Paul defends that most pointedly in chapter 9 using the example of Jacob and Esau. Before either boy was born, God decreed that the elder would serve the younger, and through the mercy of God's sovereign election Jacob was loved in a way that Esau was not. Paul anticipated objections. In fact, since Romans was received in the Christian church in the first century, people have been objecting to Paul's teaching on election, primarily because it seems to indicate unrighteousness in God. Paul answers that objection emphatically in the negative. The righteousness of God is evident throughout the epistle. The Greek word for *righteousness* is *dikaiosunē*. The word is sometimes translated "justification" because the concept of being justified in the sight of God is inseparably related to the idea of God's righteousness, which is made available to us by faith.

As we come to the end of chapter 9, Paul looks to the past, to the pilgrimage of Old Testament Israel, and he reminds us that Hosea was required to marry an adulterous woman and that their children's names had symbolic significance. One child was called Lo-Ammi, which means in Hebrew "not my people." In that name God expressed his judgment against the ten tribes of Israel that had become apostate, but afterward: **"I will call them My people, who were not My people, and her beloved, who was not beloved"** (v. 25). The failure of one group became the occasion for God's expanding his mercy to those outside the community.

God's People

Mercy has been extended to the Gentiles. The Jewish people, who had been the stewards of the oracles of God, had missed the coming of the Messiah. When we are adopted into the family of God, we experience an affection from God that we have no claim upon. There is nothing lovely in us in the sight of God, but he has been pleased in his mercy to call us his people, to adopt us into his family where we have no birthright or entitlement. In Christ he calls us his beloved.

The culture in which we live endlessly repeats the myth that God loves everybody equally, so it is no big thing to be loved by God. "Of course God loves us. He is a loving God. God loves everybody." To the contrary, to be loved by God is a privilege, not a birthright. We have no claim on the love of God. Nothing in us would make him desire us, yet he has, by his mercy, turned his affection to all who put their trust in Christ.

We must understand the mystery of the doctrine of election in terms of election being *in Christ*. We are not Christians while others are not because of any righteousness in us. We are Christians by the sheer grace of God alone. We might wonder why God redeems anyone. The only answer I can provide is the great love the Father has for his Son. The Father will not allow the Son to see the travail of his soul and not be satisfied. Throughout John's Gospel we see this taught from a different perspective. There, believers are a gift the Father gives to the Son. Because the Father loves Christ, he gives Christ a people as his legacy, and by God's mercy we are included in that.

Warning to the Visible Church

Paul continues citing the Old Testament prophet: **"It shall come to pass in the place where it was said to them, 'You are not My people,'**

there they shall be called the sons of the living God" (v. 26). We participate in the family of God, but God has only one Son. Because God has placed us in Christ, we participate in that sonship. We have become sons of God who are not by nature children of God.

Isaiah also cries out concerning Israel: "Though the number of the children of Israel be as the sand of the sea, the remnant will be saved" (v. 27). Paul is looking back to the promise God made to Abraham: "I will multiply your descendants as the stars of the heaven and as the sand which is on the seashore" (Gen. 22:17). There were countless descendants, yet out of that vast multitude only a remnant would actually be saved.

Theologians in the eighteenth century debated whether, in the final analysis, the majority of human beings will be redeemed. The consensus, based on Scripture, was that the vast majority of people will not enter the kingdom of heaven. We hope for a remnant, even from among the household of God, who will actually make it into the kingdom. Of all those whom God redeemed from the oppression of Pharaoh in Egypt, only a couple were permitted to enter the Promised Land; the vast majority did not make it. Jesus warned about this:

> Enter by the narrow gate; for wide is the gate and broad is the way that leads to destruction, and there are many who go in by it. Because narrow is the gate and difficult is the way which leads to life, and there are few who find it. (Matt. 7:13–14)

What about the Christian church? Are we safe by virtue of our membership in the visible church? We have learned that people outside the commonwealth of Israel were saved while people inside were not. Paul has already taught that one is not a Jew outwardly but inwardly. Receiving circumcision in an ecclesiastical ritual was not enough to get someone into the kingdom of God; circumcision of the heart was necessary. The same applies to the Christian community. Church membership or receiving baptism is no guarantee of redemption. A true Christian is a Christian internally, not just externally.

Therefore, what good is it to be in the visible church? There is much advantage in every way, because to the church has been given the oracles of God (see Rom. 3:2). Augustine was the one who fathered the distinction between the visible church and the invisible church. He made the distinction because not everyone in the visible church is in the kingdom of God. Jesus warned that tares would grow along with the wheat (Matt. 13:24–30) and that people can honor him with their lips while their hearts are far from him (Matt. 15:8).

The most dreadful warning he gave concerns what will happen on the last day: "Many will say to Me in that day, 'Lord, Lord, have we not prophesied in Your name, cast out demons in Your name, and done many wonders in Your name?'" (7:22). Jesus will say to them, "I never knew you; depart from Me, you who practice lawlessness!" (v. 23). Some will claim, "I was baptized," or, "I was a deacon," or, "I taught Sunday school," and the Lord will say, "I never knew you."

Jesus' warning was given to people in the visible church. That is why it is dangerous to seek assurance of our status before God by looking to church membership as proof of our inclusion in the kingdom. Augustine said it is easy to count the people in the visible church, but their souls cannot be seen. I do not know who is trusting in Christ alone for redemption, but I do know this—those who have affection for Christ and trust him for salvation are certainly in the invisible church. The state of our soul is invisible to man, but it is manifestly visible to God. The Bible tells us that "man looks at the outward appearance, but the LORD looks at the heart" (1 Sam. 16:7). God knows everyone within his adopted family in ways we cannot possibly know. The invisible church is the true church; it is the full number of the redeemed.

When Augustine was asked where the invisible church is to be found, he replied the invisible church is found almost totally within the visible church. It is remotely possible to be a true believer in Christ but not be involved in the visible church. Such a circumstance is one I do not think can last for long. If we are truly in Christ, and if we are in the Word of God, we know it is our duty to be part of the visible fellowship of God's people. If our hearts are really in tune with God, we will, sooner or later—in most cases sooner—unite ourselves with a visible church.

When some think of the thief on the cross who became a member of the invisible church before his death but had no opportunity to join the visible church, they are tempted to think church membership does not matter. It does matter because the church is where the means of grace are concentrated. Where else can we go to hear an exposition of the Word of God? We are not going to hear it in the halls of Congress. We are going to find it only in the church. I realize there are churches all over the world that have absolute hostility to the Word of God; we can go to such churches week after week and never experience the means of grace. It is, however, in the visible church that the means of grace are most heavily concentrated.

Augustine said, "He who does not have the church for his mother does not have God for his father." That is an overstatement, because you can be led to Christ outside the church. I was led to Christ outside the church, but I was nurtured by the church, in the church, through the ministry of the church. We must never despair of the church, because it is where the remnant is found.

And as Isaiah said before: "Unless the LORD of Sabaoth had left us a seed, we would have become like Sodom, and we would have been made like Gomorrah" (v. 29). If no remnant existed, if no seeds spilled out from the core of the flower or grain, then the harvest would end forever. Even as God brings his judgment upon Israel, there remains a seed that will bring forth its fruit in season. The prophet said that if God had not left a seed, they would have become like Sodom and Gomorrah, cities God made short work of when he visited them in judgment.

Whose Righteousness Matters?

Paul gives us another rhetorical question: **What shall we say then?** (v. 30a). In other words, what is our response to that grim history of Old Testament Israel? **The Gentiles, who did not pursue righteousness, have attained to righteousness, even the righteousness of faith** (v. 30b). We receive the benefits of the gospel even though we never sought them. It is not in our nature to pursue the things of God. The Gentiles, to whom Paul is writing here in Romans, had no clue about the history of redemption. They were not concerned with studying the Old Testament Scriptures. They did not care about the Law of Moses; they were not pursuing the righteousness of God. In God's mercy they found what they had not pursued.

Several years ago a national evangelism campaign was launched with the title "I Found It." The title appeared on bumper stickers all over America. The truth is, however, that they had found nothing; God found them. God found you and me. We were not looking; we were not pursuing. By his grace he pursued us, and we were found. That is the Christian message. "I once was lost but now am found."

But Israel, pursuing the law of righteousness, has not attained to the law of righteousness (v. 31). How can it be, Paul asks, that those outside the redemptive historical covenant community found the pearl of great price while those on the inside missed it? "He came to His own, and His own did not receive Him" (John 1:11). **Why? Because they did not**

seek it by faith, but as it were, by the works of the law. For they stumbled at that stumbling stone (v. 32). The one whom God appointed as the cornerstone of his kingdom became a stumbling block, a stone of offense. Israel tripped over grace. They fell over their Messiah because they could not fathom receiving God's favor apart from their righteousness. The multitudes in Israel sought the righteousness of God through their endeavors and missed the kingdom of God, and that same error is deeply ingrained in churches all over the world. I venture to say that at least 80 percent of Christian church members in our country believe that they can get to heaven through their good works.

I was involved in Evangelism Explosion years ago in Cincinnati. I trained over two hundred people, and we went out twice a week to evangelize. We asked, "Have you come to the place in your spiritual life where you know for sure that when you die you will go to heaven?" We asked thousands that question, and the overwhelming majority answered that they were not sure. They did not think anyone could be sure, and they were suspicious of those who were sure. That first diagnostic question opened discussion for the second question: "If you were to die tonight and stand before God, and God were to say to you, 'Why should I allow you into my heaven?' what would you say?" Ninety percent of people gave what we called a "works righteousness" answer: "I tried to live a good life," or "I went to church," or "I gave my money to a good cause." Only one in ten said, "There is no reason why God should let me into heaven, except that he promised if I put my trust in his Son that he would bring me into his family. That is my only hope in life and death—not my own righteousness but his."

This has been the issue all the way through Romans. Whose righteousness matters? Whose righteousness justifies? Not ours. The tragedy for the Jewish nation is that they sought the kingdom of God on their righteousness so they missed their Messiah. They did not seek it by faith but by the work of the law. They stumbled at that stumbling stone. Paul again quotes Isaiah: **As it is written: "Behold, I lay in Zion a stumbling stone and rock of offense, and whoever believes on Him will not be put to shame"** (v. 33). Israel was offended by the rock. They were ashamed of a suffering servant. Those who put their trust in that stumbling block and don't trip over it will not be put to shame.

Zeal according to Knowledge

At the beginning of Romans 10 Paul reaffirms something he stated earlier: **Brethren, my heart's desire and prayer to God for Israel is that**

they may be saved. For I bear them witness that they have a zeal for God, but not according to knowledge (10:1–2). His heart was heavy because he loved his kinsmen, and his deepest desire was that they would all be saved. He recognized that they were zealous for religion; they never missed the meetings in the synagogue. They had a zeal for God, but their zeal was based on ignorance. A fanatic is somebody who loses sight of where he is going but redoubles his effort to get there. He is full of zeal, but he has no knowledge or understanding of that for which he is zealous.

Paul wrote in Romans 1 that God has revealed himself clearly to everyone in creation, but people suppress that knowledge and exchange it for a lie. They serve and worship the creature rather than the Creator. Paul announced judgment on the human race, not because it is given to atheism but because of false religion. The judgment of God is provoked by religion in which the object of devotion is an idol, where the truth of God is swapped for the creature. God alone is worthy of our adoration, devotion, and service. It is not enough to be religious or to be a zealot.

When Jesus appeared on the scene the most zealous people in Jerusalem were the Pharisees and scribes. They spent their lives pursuing righteousness. A Pharisee was "a separated one." Pharisees were consecrated to the pursuit of righteousness, but when true righteousness came into their midst to redeem them, they killed him. They were looking for justification by works, so they stumbled over Jesus. They did not realize they were required to give up any claim to merit and all boasting and say, "Nothing in my hand I bring, simply to the cross I cling." They were zealous but not according to knowledge. **For they being ignorant of God's righteousness, and seeking to establish their own righteousness, have not submitted to the righteousness of God** (v. 3). Paul's kinsmen had sought to build their house upon the foundation of their merit and goodness. That is how they wanted to do it, and that is how we want to do it by nature. Grace is for the weak.

A friend of mine went to Germany recently and asked if he could bring something back for me. I asked him to bring me some paperback copies of Perry Mason and Earl Stanley Gardner published in German. When he returned from Germany he brought me a bag full of Perry Mason books. I asked him what I owed him for the purchase.

"You can't pay me; it's a gift," he replied.

He wanted to be gracious, but I wanted to pay my own way. It's hard to rely on grace alone, because it is the end of boasting. We have no bragging rights. The only thing we can boast in is the perfection of the Redeemer.

They have not submitted to the righteousness of God, Paul says, **for Christ is the end of the law for righteousness to everyone who believes** (v. 4). Almost every Sunday we read one of the Ten Commandments in the liturgy of our worship service. We do so because if we do not listen to the law, we will never see our need for the gospel. The goal and purpose of the law is Christ. God did not give the law as a way for us to attain status in his family. The law was given to show us the righteousness of God. It was given so that we can see the perfect righteousness of God and by comparison see ourselves, warts and all, and despair of our own righteousness. The law sends us rushing to the cross and running for grace. The law exposes our sin, and anything that exposes our sin screams to our need for the Savior, whose righteousness alone can justify.

Paul said that this is the tragedy of the people he loved. They had missed it. They had sought the righteousness of God through their obedience to the law and had failed to see that the goal of the law is Christ and his righteousness, which can never be earned, bought, or deserved.

I hope that each of us has a heart on fire with zeal. Jesus warned those who were neither hot nor cold but lukewarm he would vomit them out of his mouth (Rev. 3:16). He wanted his people to be filled with zeal, but a zeal according to knowledge, zeal that is informed by his Word. The fire in our hearts is not simply heat but also light, which comes from God's Word.

39

TRUE CONFESSION

Romans 10:5–15

For Moses writes about the righteousness which is of the law, "The man who does those things shall live by them." But the righteousness of faith speaks in this way, "Do not say in your heart, 'Who will ascend into heaven?'" (that is, to bring Christ down from above) or, "'Who will descend into the abyss?'" (that is, to bring Christ up from the dead). But what does it say? "The word is near you, in your mouth and in your heart" (that is, the word of faith which we preach): that if you confess with your mouth the Lord Jesus and believe in your heart that God has raised Him from the dead, you will be saved. For with the heart one believes unto righteousness, and with the mouth confession is made unto salvation. For the Scripture says, "Whoever believes on Him will not be put to shame." For there is no distinction between Jew and Greek, for the same Lord over all is rich to all who call upon Him. For "whoever calls on the name of the LORD shall be saved." How then shall they call on Him in whom they have not believed? And how shall they believe in Him of whom they have not heard? And how shall they hear without a preacher? And how shall they preach unless they are sent? As it is written:

> "How beautiful are the feet of those who preach the gospel of peace,
> Who bring glad tidings of good things!"

P aul began Romans 10 with a lament that his kinsmen, Israel, had a
zeal for the things of God but not according to knowledge. They had
failed to understand that the doctrine of justification was no novelty;
it had been set forth early on in the Old Testament, particularly in the life of
the patriarch Abraham. Justification before a holy God is by faith alone.

The Righteousness of Faith

Paul follows up his lament: **For Moses writes about the righteousness
which is of the law, "The man who does those things shall live
by them." But the righteousness of faith speaks in this way, "Do
not say in your heart, 'Who will ascend into heaven?'"** (that is,
to bring Christ down from above) or, **"'Who will descend into
the abyss?'"** (that is, to bring Christ up from the dead) (vv. 5–7).
Paul's thoughts seem somewhat oblique at first glance. He is setting forth
two ideas that represent manifest impossibilities. It is just as impossible for
a person to be justified by the law or by their works as for a human being to
ascend into the highest heaven and drag the Messiah from heaven to earth.
The only way the Messiah can descend from heaven is if God Omnipotent
sends him, which is exactly what God the Father did in sending the Son into
the world to be our mediator.

It is also equally impossible for any human being by strength of his virtue
or righteousness to descend into the pit of hell and bring Christ back from
the dead. When Christ was executed, the disciples fled as sheep without a
shepherd. They were in despair because they knew it was totally beyond their
power to bring Jesus back from the grave. Paul is saying that it is impossible
for someone to be saved through the works of the law just as it is impossible
to bring Jesus back from the dead or to bring him down from heaven.

In stark contrast to that manifest impossibility Paul quotes Moses concerning God's Word: **But what does it say? "The word is near you, in
your mouth and in your heart"** (that is, the word of faith which
we preach) (v. 8). In other words, the central truth about justification is not
so high or abstract or deep or profound as to be beyond our understanding.
Understanding the gospel does not require a PhD in theology. We are not
Gnostics, who believe that the gospel can be understood only by an elite
group of scholars. The gospel is "near you," a Hebrew idiom meaning that
it is within our grasp. It is right in front of us. The word of faith is simple.
I have said to you throughout our study of Romans that to understand
the doctrine of justification by faith alone—the very heart and soul of the
gospel—is not a difficult thing. A child can understand it. To get it in the

bloodstream, however, is something that requires a life of concentrated study of God's Word. Embracing what God has put in front of us requires hearing the Word of God day in and day out.

Paul reminds us of the ease with which we can understand the message, and he boils it down to this: **if you confess with your mouth the Lord Jesus and believe in your heart that God has raised Him from the dead, you will be saved** (v. 9). Paul conjoins two elements here. He does not just say that you must confess with your lips and profess with your mouth in order to be saved. Every Christian is called to profess their faith. We are to profess the faith, but the profession without authentic faith attending it will justify no one. I do not tire in repeating that, because one of the great perils of the church in our day is the way in which we do evangelism. We are so zealous to win people to Christ and to persuade them of the truth of the gospel that we are not satisfied with simply proclaiming the gospel and then allowing the Holy Spirit to take that truth and pierce human hearts with it. We want to give our assistance to make sure our evangelistic statistics are good.

We have come up with various techniques for doing so. The technique employed at a general crusade is the altar call. People are asked to respond to the gospel by coming to the front of the church or coliseum, or to raise their hand, pray a prayer, or sign a card. All these techniques are designed to urge people to take a step to finalize their commitment to Christ. Nothing is actually wrong with those things unless we think that walking down an aisle, raising our hand, signing a card, or saying the sinner's prayer will get us into the kingdom of God. If we think so, we are in trouble. We have to understand that a profession of faith alone will never justify us. The possession of faith, not the profession of it, is the necessary condition for our justification.

That is why Paul does not say that we will be saved if we confess with our mouth. He adds a condition: you must "believe with your heart." I used to get cantankerous with my seminary students when I would ask for their opinion about a particular issue and they would answer, "Well, professor, I *feel* that such and such is the truth." I would reply, "I did not ask you how you feel about it; I am asking what you think." Conviction of truth is not a sensual matter; it is primarily the assent of the mind. We live in such a sensuous culture that people intertwine feeling and thinking. Paul understood that it is impossible to possess a mental persuasion that never gets to the heart.

The Ingredients of Faith

When the Reformers were proclaiming the doctrine of justification by faith alone, the great objection raised against it was its seeming implication of cheap grace or easy believism. Anyone can say they believe in Jesus, but saying so is no manifestation of true godliness. What are the necessary ingredients of saving faith?

Luther, following James's teaching that faith without works is dead (James 2:20), asked, "Can a dead faith justify anybody?" Luther answered emphatically in the negative. Luther said the only kind of faith that justifies is a *fides viva*, a living faith, one that is manifested in a life of obedience to God. The first ingredient of faith is *notae*, which means there is *content* to the faith we embrace. We have heard the cultural adage, "It does not matter what you believe as long as you are sincere," but let me suggest that it matters eternally and profoundly what we believe. People can put their trust and faith in the Devil and be sincere about it. There is no comfort to be found from faith in a false object. Saving faith requires content, information, and knowledge.

The second ingredient of saving faith is *assensus*, intellectual assent to the truth of the data. We might understand and believe the facts of the resurrection of Jesus and the atonement, but that does no more than qualify us to be demons, because every demon from hell knows that information is true. That is why Lutheran Reformers said that data and intellectual assent to the data are not enough. Intellectual affirmation of the truth claims of the gospel must be embraced with personal trust and affection for the truth, something no demon will do. That is why Paul says it is not enough to believe it in our heads; we have to believe in our hearts. The Old Testament teaches that as a man thinks in his heart, so is he (Prov. 23:7). The Old Testament writer has not confused organs of thinking with organs of feeling. The point is that we can say we agree with something intellectually without its ever getting to the core of our being.

I study the text of Scripture in order to take the text from the Bible and communicate it to others, but every time I prepare a sermon, I have to prepare it for myself. At the end of the day I have to look in the mirror and say, "R. C., do you believe what you proclaimed today?" Sometimes I find myself answering, "I believe it in my head." When that happens, I must ask myself, "Do you believe it with your life, or is this just an exercise in theology?" Ministers and teachers are in danger if the truth does not get down into the bloodstream of their hearts.

The third ingredient of saving faith follows by resistless logic, as any syllogism yields its conclusion: we shall be saved. Someone once asked me, "How can I know I'm saved if I have been elected?" I replied, "That is what you are elected to—salvation." Instead of worrying about the intricacies that attend the doctrine of election, we must get down to the simplest principle: if we confess with our mouths and believe with our hearts, we shall be saved. We will not do that unless we are elect. Do you believe in your heart and trust in Christ alone? If so, then I can give you full assurance of your salvation. **For with the heart one believes unto righteousness, and with the mouth confession is made unto salvation. For the Scripture says, "Whoever believes on Him will not be put to shame"** (vv. 10–11). If you put your trust in Christ from the heart, you have no need of future embarrassment. You will not be put to shame for having held to a false hope or having devoted your life to a myth.

For there is no distinction between Jew and Greek, for the same Lord over all is rich to all who call upon Him. For "whoever calls on the name of the Lord shall be saved" (vv. 12–13). Paul makes that statement within a broader context. Even within the immediate context he is not saying that anybody who calls for Jesus in a moment of trial will be saved. The Lord warns us that when he appears and God's wrath is manifest against the unrepentant, they will be screaming for the mountains to fall and the hills to cover them. People will say in that moment, "Jesus, help me! Save me!" It will be too late. Paul's statement applies to those who call upon the name of the Lord in the terms he has just used. A true call issues from the heart. It is an authentic reaching for the Savior. Anyone who calls truly will not be denied.

We may be elect or we may not, but we cannot know for sure until we die. We may be like the thief on the cross and be brought to the Lord through the mysterious work of God through the Holy Spirit in our fleeting breath. We do not have to work through all the intricacies of doctrine so long as we understand that if we sincerely call upon the name of the Lord, we will be saved.

Election and Missions

Paul gives a series of related questions, which are very important. The text bears heavily on the missions outreach of the church. **How then shall they call on Him in whom they have not believed? And how shall they believe in Him of whom they have not heard? And how shall they hear without a preacher? And how shall they preach unless they are sent? As it is written: "How beautiful are the feet of those who preach the gospel of peace, who bring glad tidings of good**

things!" (vv. 14–15). This series of *how* questions follows all Paul said about divine election in Romans 9. It is appropriate that chapter 10 follows chapter 9, because chapter 10 addresses one of the most common objections raised by people about the doctrine of election.

When I was taught the doctrine of predestination years ago in one of my seminary classes, the professor seated the students in a semicircle. There were eighteen in the room. He asked us, "Gentlemen, if the doctrine of election is true, why should we be engaged in evangelism?" Nobody raised a hand, so he went around the semicircle interrogating each student for a response. I breathed a sigh of relief because he started on the left side of the semicircle; I was sitting on the extreme right end, so I had seventeen points of buffer between me and the relentless interrogation of the professor. He asked the first student, "If predestination is true, why should we be involved in evangelism?" The student did not know. The professor moved along to the second student, who also did not know. The third student answered, "Evangelism would be a Herculean waste of time if salvation has been settled by divine decree."

Those answers did not satisfy the professor, so he continued around the semicircle. My buffer disintegrated, and he finally got to me. "Well, Mr. Sproul, what do you think?"

Sheepishly I said, "I know the answer has to be far more profound than this, but one of the reasons that we should be engaged in evangelism is that Jesus commanded us to do it."

The professor said, "Mr. Sproul, can you possibly think of a more significant reason to do evangelism than that Jesus Christ commands you to do it?"

The professor went on to say that engaging in evangelism must not be done from a sense of duty. Evangelism is one of the greatest privileges that God gives to the church. He explained that God could have preached his Word from the clouds without any human participation, but he chose the means to accomplish it, chiefly, the foolishness of preaching. God gave us the unspeakable privilege of participating in his majestic program of redemption, which he planned from the foundation of the world.

No preacher is indispensible. Cemeteries are filled with indispensible people. God does not need preachers to accomplish his purposes of redemption. He did not need Isaiah, he did not need Jeremiah, and he did not need the apostle Paul. God has given men the most sacred vocation possible—carrying this treasure in earthly vessels.

Nobody is going to put their trust in a Savior whom they do not believe is capable of saving them. When I have a plumbing problem I do not call the grocer, because I have no reason to believe the grocer can fix my problem. Likewise, when I face the deepest problem of human existence—escaping from the wrath to come—why would I put any trust in or call upon somebody unless I first believed he was able to redeem me? Belief is a precondition, a necessary condition, to calling upon him.

"How then shall they call on Him in whom they have not believed? And how shall they believe on him of whom they have not heard?" (v. 14a). Millions have never heard the name of Jesus, and they are not going to put their trust in someone they know nothing about. They cannot possibly believe in Jesus because they know nothing about him. I said earlier that saving faith requires information. That is why the church is commanded to go to every corner of the world and make that message plain to all people.

"How shall they hear without a preacher?" (v. 14b). The answer to Paul's question is that they will not. No one is going to hear about Jesus unless somebody tells them. Nobody is going to believe a gospel they have never heard, and without a preacher they will never hear it.

"And how shall they preach unless they are sent?" (v. 15a). The Latin word for *send* is *missia*, from which we get the word *mission*. Missionaries are sent. We see throughout the pages of the Old Testament that God anointed prophets and sent them to people. Just so, missionaries cannot go unless somebody supports and sends them. Not everyone in the church is called to be a missionary, but every member of the church is responsible to make sure that the missionary activity gets done. We all have a part to play in that endeavor.

Paul quotes from Isaiah: "How beautiful are the feet of those who preach the gospel of peace, who bring glad tidings of good things!" (v. 15b). The full quote from the Old Testament reads, "How beautiful upon the mountains are the feet of him who brings good news, who proclaims peace, who brings glad tidings of good things, who proclaims salvation, who says to Zion, 'Your God reigns!'" (Isa. 52:7). In the fifth century BC when the Greeks were at war with the Persians, three great historic battles occurred. In the Battle of the Plain, so called because it occurred on the Marathon plain, a man named Pheidippides was commissioned as a runner. He took messages from the battlefield back to the city of Athens. He ran the entire distance, twenty-six miles, which is why we call races of that duration *marathons*. Pheidippides ran all the way from the plain into the city of Athens to bring the gospel, the good news of the Greek victory at Marathon.

The person who led me to Christ was the third person of the Trinity, the Holy Spirit. No mortal has the ability to bring anyone to faith, yet God worked through a human instrument, a man who told me about Jesus, on September 13, 1957. I am eternally grateful to that person, not because he had the power to change my heart but because God enlisted him for that sacred task, and he was faithful to it. So as long as I live, his feet will be beautiful in my eyes.

Paul gives the reason why, if election is true, we should preach. We preach not simply as a matter of duty but because God gives us the blessed privilege of having beautiful feet in the eyes of those who hear and respond to the gospel.

40

THE OBEDIENCE OF FAITH

Romans 10:16–21

But they have not all obeyed the gospel. For Isaiah says, "Lord, who has believed our report?" So then faith comes by hearing, and hearing by the word of God.

But I say, have they not heard? Yes indeed:

> "Their sound has gone out to all the earth,
> And their words to the ends of the world."

But I say, did Israel not know? First Moses says:

> "I will provoke you to jealousy by those who are not a nation,
> I will move you to anger by a foolish nation."

But Isaiah is very bold and says:

> "I was found by those who did not seek Me;
> I was made manifest to those who did not ask for Me."

But to Israel he says:

> "All day long I have stretched out My hands
> To a disobedient and contrary people."

I n our last study we examined Paul's series of rhetorical questions: "How then shall they call on Him in whom they have not believed? And how shall they believe in Him of whom they have not heard? And how shall they hear without a preacher? And how shall they preach unless they are sent? Paul concluded with a reference to the Old Testament prophet Isaiah: "How beautiful are the feet of those who preach the gospel of peace, who bring glad tidings of good things!"

But they have not all obeyed the gospel (v. 16a). The gospel is being proclaimed widely, not only to Israel but also to the Gentile nations. Paul's point is that not everybody who hears the gospel obeys, or embraces, the gospel. At the beginning of the epistle Paul established that the gospel is "the power of God to salvation" (1:16). Elsewhere, Paul writes that God has chosen the foolishness of preaching as his method to save the world (1 Cor. 1:21). When we considered the doctrine of election, or predestination, we saw that God ordains from all eternity not only the ends of people and nations but also the means to those ends. We saw that the primary means God uses to awaken faith in the hearts of the elect is the preaching of the gospel. Faith comes through the Word, specifically, the preaching of the Word.

Earlier I distinguished between a necessary condition and a sufficient condition. A necessary condition for igniting a fire is the presence of oxygen. If all the oxygen is removed, the flame goes out. Thankfully, oxygen is not a sufficient condition for a fire; otherwise, every time we draw in a breath of air we would set our lungs on fire. A sufficient condition is one in which something need only be present for the effect to take place. If we apply that to what Paul is saying, the preaching of the Word is a necessary condition for faith but it's not a sufficient condition. You can't have faith without it, but you can have unbelief even with it.

Faith Comes by Hearing

For Isaiah says, "LORD, who has believed our report?" (v. 16b). The prophet was uttering a lament. There was a remnant who believed the report of the suffering servant of Israel, but Isaiah knew, as every prophet did, that the Word of God must be proclaimed over and over again. The gospel has been announced, but has anybody believed it?

So then faith comes by hearing, and hearing by the word of God. But I say, have they not heard? (vv. 17–18a). Of course they have heard: **"Their sound has gone out to all the earth, and their words to the ends of the world"** (v. 18b). God had published his gospel throughout the borders of Israel and into the Gentile community. **But I**

say, did Israel not know? First Moses says, "I will provoke you to jealousy by those who are not a nation, I will move you to anger by a foolish nation" (v. 19). In other words, why should anyone be surprised that the gospel is being proclaimed to the Gentiles? This was not a last-minute switch in God's plans. God had told the people of Israel that he would make them jealous by taking their proffered benefits across the border to all nations. Paul has in view here the universal proclamation of the gospel so that, as Paul said earlier, "whoever calls on the name of the Lord shall be saved" (v. 13).

When we talk about the doctrine of election, we are bound to be asked, "Isn't there something dishonest about offering salvation to all when, in fact, God never intended to save all people?" The question touches heavily on the controversy surrounding the doctrine of limited atonement—definite or particular redemption. The doctrine teaches that the atonement of Jesus was not designed by God to make salvation possible to all men. Looking at Paul's words—"Whoever calls on the name of the Lord will be saved"—it certainly seems that Paul is making a universal offer, and if so, how can we talk about the atonement being limited to certain people?

Unlike universalists we understand that the benefits of the atonement are limited to those who believe. The New Testament does not claim that Jesus automatically saves everybody in the world. The condition for salvation is clear. To receive the benefits of the cross people must put their trust in Christ. At very least we must say the atonement is limited to believers. Jesus did not die for all indiscriminately; he died for believers.

So, who are the believers? Paul answers that question: believers are the elect. Believers who are numbered among the elect will surely be brought to faith. The issue of limited atonement ultimately goes back to God's purpose in the covenant of redemption, where the Father covenanted with the Son and the Holy Spirit to bring about God's plan of salvation. Did God propose to send his Son into the world to die on the cross because he hoped that people would take advantage of that? Did he not know from all eternity the names of everyone who would embrace Jesus and those who would not? Did he send his Son to die to make salvation possible, or did he send his Son to die to make salvation certain? The doctrine of limited atonement holds that God knew what he was doing from all eternity. He constructed a plan of salvation, and in perfect agreement the Son came into the world to die for those whom the Father had given him, knowing that those whom the Father had given him would come and that his atonement would not be an exercise in futility or a hypothetical possibility. The Son knew that there would be a people saved as a result of his sacrifice, and the Holy Spirit knew all those to whom he would apply that work of the Son for salvation.

No Universalism

Why all the talk about a universal offer? The language of evangelism in our day is: "God loves you and has a wonderful plan for your life." What if that promise had been made to Judas? "God loves you, Judas, and has a wonderful plan for your life—your destination is eternity in hell." That plan was not wonderful.

The Bible tells us that God loves everybody indiscriminately in terms of his love of beneficence, but the love that he gives to the redeemed is his love of complacency, which is limited only to believers. The Bible says that God abhors the wicked, but we tell everybody indiscriminately that God loves them unconditionally. That is considered the universal offer of the gospel, but the universal offer of the gospel is really to proclaim to every living creature the gospel of Jesus Christ.

You cannot know you are not elect until you die, but you can know right now that you are not a believer. You may conclude that since you are not a believer you are not among the elect, but you might yet believe. So we are called, as the apostle tells us here, to go to the four corners of the world to preach the gospel. In that sense, there is to be a universal proclamation of the gospel. The Apostles' Creed declares, "I believe . . . in the holy catholic church." Earlier in church history, the creed declared belief in "one, holy, catholic, and apostolic church." Historically, the four marks of the church are unity, sanctity, catholicity, and apostolicity. If we take away apostolicity, sanctity, unity, or catholicity we do not have the church. The church is in every nation. The voice of the gospel has gone to every corner of the planet, and there are people from every tongue and tribe and nation right now incorporated into the church of Jesus Christ. That is what we mean when we say the church is "catholic." It is not limited to one denomination or nation, be it Israel or America. The church is everywhere, because God has reserved for his Son people from every corner of the world.

To whom is the gospel offered? Is it offered to everyone indiscriminately, with no strings attached? No, the good news is offered only to those who believe. If you are not willing to put your faith in Christ, then the gospel is not offered to you. The gospel is proclaimed universally, but its benefits are offered only to believers, those who hear the Word and are brought to faith in and through the Word.

But Isaiah is very bold and says: "I was found by those who did not seek Me; I was made manifest to those who did not ask for Me" (v. 20). The overwhelming majority of churches in the United States, particularly evangelical churches, have embraced a seeker strategy for church growth, but the Bible says that apart from regeneration, no person seeks after God. Those who seek the kingdom of God—the main business of the Christian life—do not start seeking until they have been converted. Many unbelievers are desperately trying to find the benefits that only Christ can give them, but all the while they are actually fleeing from Jesus.

Paul, quoting Isaiah again, says, "I was found by those who did not seek Me." Was Paul looking for Jesus on the road to Damascus when the bright light knocked him from his horse? No, he was looking for Christians to throw into prison and kill.

The last thing I was seeking was Jesus—until he found me. Once he found me, I wanted to know everything I could about him. I wanted to go to church to learn more.

Preach the Word

I got a request some time ago from a sister church that was without a pastor. The church was suffering from serious financial shortfalls and had to lay off staff. The session of that church asked me if I would come preach and offer encouragement to the downcast congregation. I accepted the invitation and began to plan what I would say. I decided not to address their particular struggles because their most important need was that of every Christian church—the need for biblical preaching. A church might have good programs for youth or singles, but if it lacks biblical preaching, it has nothing. Other things are desirable, but biblical preaching is the only thing a church actually needs.

Paul wrote his final admonition to Timothy from the Maritine prison, which was no more than a piece of rock hewn from the ground. The prison had been used as a cistern to hold water. To enter, one had to go down stairs. The prison space, carved from solid rock, spanned about fifteen feet across and stood about seven feet high. There in the cold, wet darkness Paul awaited execution, and while he was waiting he wrote his last epistle to his beloved Timothy. He wrote, "I charge you therefore before God and the Lord Jesus Christ, who will judge the living and the dead at His appearing and His kingdom: Preach the word!" (2 Tim. 4:1–2a). Timothy's preaching was not to be political commentary, pop psychology, or entertainment; Paul told his disciple to preach the Word, which means doing expository preaching. Such preaching exposes the Word and makes it clear to people.

At the end of his life Princeton theologian Charles Hodge said, "I never had a novel idea." He was determined to know nothing except what he had learned. A preacher's opinions are not what matters. The power of God is the Word of God, which is why Paul wrote, "Preach the Word!" and to that he added, "Be ready in season and out of season" (v. 2). In other words, "preach the Word all the time." Part of what it means to preach the Word is to be ready any moment to open the Scriptures for the people of God.

That was the mandate Jesus gave to Peter before Jesus ascended. "Simon, son of Jonah, do you love me?" . . .

"Lord, You know all things; You know that I love You."

Jesus said to him, "Feed My sheep" (John 21:17).

Peter was not to poison Jesus' sheep or give pabulum to adult sheep. Peter's call was to take care of Jesus' sheep. Those sheep belonged to Jesus, not to Peter, and he was to feed them God's Word.

Manna

God was found because his word went out to all the earth, and he "was made manifest" because his character and plan were revealed through that word. **But to Israel he says: "All day long I have stretched out My hands to a disobedient and contrary people"** (v. 21). Earlier Paul said there is no difference between Jew and Gentile because both are under sin. Paul brought both before the tribunal of God, saying, "All have sinned and fall short of the glory of God" (see Rom. 3:9–23). A true Jew is one inwardly; nobody is saved by circumcision.

In Romans 2 Paul took his readers through all the failures of Israel and then he asked, "What advantage then has the Jew, or what is the profit of circumcision? (3:1). If circumcision does not save, what good is it being a Jew? "Much in every way," Paul replied, "chiefly because to them were committed the oracles of God" (3:2). The Jews had the Scripture.

In the wilderness God provided food for his people through manna. He nurtured and fed his sheep by providing bread from heaven. He instructed the Israelites to take some manna out of the wilderness and preserve it so that future generations would know that the Lord God omnipotent had fed his people with bread from heaven (Ex. 16:33) until later when one would stand up and say, "I am the bread of life" (John 6:35). The Old Testament Scripture pointed beyond the manna that was gathered from the dew of the earth to the manna that comes down from heaven.

There is a divine agreement within the Godhead—Father, Son, and Holy Spirit. They are working together in and through the Word. The Spirit does not divorce himself from the Word. Many want to be led by the Spirit without the Word, but they cannot distinguish between the leading of God and indigestion, because they have nothing concrete against which to check their inclinations and hunches. The Holy Spirit leads and teaches in the Word and through the Word, but never against the Word. "So then faith comes by hearing, and hearing by the Word of God" (Rom. 10:17).

Have you heard God through his Word? When the Bible is expounded, does it tickle your ears or inflame your soul? Does the Spirit of God take this Word and bother you with it? Does he pierce, comfort, strengthen, and encourage you with it? There is nothing else.

Revival would come to our country if every church member in America would say, "I am never again going to ask the minister to administrate the church or be responsible for its finances. I want somebody to feed me the Word of God." If every church member in America would ask that the Word of God be preached in an expository manner every Sunday, it would blow the lid off this country, because that is where the power is. It is not in our programs, buildings, or parking lots. It is in the Word.

41

A REMNANT

Romans 11:1–10

I say then, has God cast away His people? Certainly not! For I also am an Israelite, of the seed of Abraham, of the tribe of Benjamin. God has not cast away His people whom He foreknew. Or do you not know what the Scripture says of Elijah, how he pleads with God against Israel, saying, "LORD, they have killed Your prophets and torn down Your altars, and I alone am left, and they seek my life"? But what does the divine response say to him? "I have reserved for Myself seven thousand men who have not bowed the knee to Baal." Even so then, at this present time there is a remnant according to the election of grace. And if by grace, then it is no longer of works; otherwise grace is no longer grace. But if it is of works, it is no longer grace; otherwise work is no longer work. What then? Israel has not obtained what it seeks; but the elect have obtained it, and the rest were blinded. Just as it is written:

> "God has given them a spirit of stupor,
> Eyes that they should not see
> And ears that they should not hear,
> To this very day."

And David says:

> "Let their table become a snare and a trap,
> A stumbling block and a recompense to them.

Let their eyes be darkened, so that they do not see,
And bow down their back always."

One of the most controversial subdivisions of systematic theology is
eschatology. Eschatology is the science or study of the last things.
It has to do with future prophecies found in the Bible in both the
Old and New Testaments. A biblical scholar once pointed out that two-
thirds of the doctrinal material in the New Testament focuses in one way or
another on eschatology. The church in our day is divided among competing
eschatological camps. There is post-millennialism, pre-millennialism, amil-
lennialism, preterism, partial preterism, dispensationalism, and others. Books
pertaining to eschatology, such as *The Late Great Planet Earth* by Hal Lindsey,
have made the best-seller lists, and the *Left Behind* series swept through the
fiction market of America.[1]

How we understand eschatology is, to a large degree, connected to how
we understand Romans 11. This chapter is Paul's most complete teaching
on the future of the nation of Israel. Much of the dispute about eschatology
in our time focuses on what, if anything, is still to happen with ethnic Israel,
the Jews that exist today.

When the Six-Day War occurred in the 1960s and Jerusalem was recap-
tured by the Israelis, theologians were reading the Bible in one hand and the
newspaper in the other. In fact, since the reconstitution of the Jewish state of
Israel in 1948, there has been a strong concentration of interest as to whether
we are living in that last generation. Are we living in the end times? Many
answers to that question may be found locked within Romans 11. For that
reason, I approach chapter 11 with a spirit of trepidation. There are some
knotty problems in the text.

The History of the Jews

Paul begins, as he has done so often throughout this epistle, with a rhetorical
question: **I say then, has God cast away His people?** (v. 1a). In Old
Testament times Israel was called out of paganism and set apart as a theo-
cratic nation with God as its ultimate king. Israel was given a mandate and a
destiny. It has been said by some historians, "How odd of God to choose the
Jews." I believe it was George Bernard Shaw who once asked a theologian

---

1. Hal Lindsey, *The Late Great Planet Earth* (Grand Rapids, MI: Zondervan, 1970); Tim LaHaye
and Jerry B. Jenkins, *Left Behind: A Novel of the Earth's Last Days* (Wheaton, IL: Tyndale, 1996) began
the series.

for certain proof of the existence of God, and the theologian replied to Shaw, "I can prove the existence of God with one or two words—the Jews." The history of Israel all the way back to Abraham up to the present day is a striking testimony of God's providential government of human history, especially redemptive history.

The history of ancient Israel is quite remarkable. After the Romans conquered Jerusalem in AD 70, the Jews were dispersed and sent out of their homeland. Despite two thousand years of exile they have never lost their ethnic and national identity. Jews say to one another, "Next year in Jerusalem." For two thousand years this people has dreamed of returning to Mount Zion.

When I was a little boy there were two days during the year on which my mother allowed me to skip school. One was opening day for the Pittsburgh Pirates baseball season at Forbes Field. The other was St. Patrick's Day on which the annual Orangeman's Parade was held in Pittsburgh. My grandfather marched in that parade. When I was a baby my mother sang Irish lullabies to get me to sleep. I also heard stories of my great-grandfather migrating from Ireland to America during the potato famine and settling in Pittsburgh in the middle of the nineteenth century. While I am aware of my family's roots in the old sod, I do not sit and dream about next year in Dublin. I have been assimilated into the American culture; I do not think of myself as an Irishman. I am an American.

We all assimilate—except for the Jews. They still have an unquenchable awareness of their ethnic and national identity. Paul lamented earlier the fact that Israel has missed the gospel by seeking salvation through the law, and now he poses a question about the consequences. Has God exercised a full and final rejection of the Jewish people? **Certainly not!** (v. 1b). God has not categorically rejected Old Testament Israel. Paul argues from the lesser to the greater. If God had rejected all the Jews, he would have rejected Paul, too, because Paul is one of them: **For I also am an Israelite, of the seed of Abraham, of the tribe of Benjamin** (v. 1c). Paul cites his pedigree, including a brief recounting of his genealogical background. He traces his roots to the tribe of Benjamin and all the way to Abraham.

God has not cast away His people whom He foreknew (v. 2a). God is incapable of rejecting a people he foreknew from the foundation of the world, the elect, of whom Paul has been writing since chapter 8. Here he brings the concept of election to the Jewish people. He wrote earlier, "For they are not all Israel who are of Israel" (9:6). He argued that the circumcised were not automatically saved but only those circumcised in heart. Not all from the seed of Abraham were chosen from the foundation of the world. Ishmael was the seed of Abraham, but he remained a foreigner to God's redemptive purposes. "In Isaac your seed shall be called" (9:7). Paul does not want his readers to conclude from all the weighty things he has said about the Jews—their rejection of the Messiah and despising the gospel—that God has rejected them totally. Paul's readers cannot come to that conclusion because Paul himself is numbered among the Jews.

Apostasy

Or do you not know what the Scripture says of Elijah, how he pleads with God against Israel, saying, "LORD, they have killed Your prophets and torn down Your altars, and I alone am left, and they seek my life"? (vv. 2b–3). This cry from the prophet Elijah was uttered during a terrible time—perhaps the worst time—of apostasy in the history of Old Testament Israel. Elijah made this plea while Ahab was king. Ahab ruled with his consort Jezebel, a priestess of the cult of Baal. Using her influence with the king, Jezebel invited pagan idolaters into the royal house and persuaded Ahab to sanction the idolatrous religion in the high places of Israel. Under Ahab and Jezebel, a massive persecution was instituted against the classical religion of the Jews. In this iconoclastic movement of pagan-ism, the sacred altars of the Jewish people were physically dismantled and burned while shrines were established to the pagan god Baal (see 1 Kings 16:29–34; 18:1–19:10).

Elijah challenged the prophets of the priests of Baal to use their power to bring down fire from heaven. An altar was placed on Mount Carmel, and Elijah told the prophets of Baal to ignite the fire of sacrifice on the altar. Those prophets prayed, wept, and called, but heaven was silent. Elijah mocked them, saying, "Cry aloud, for he is a god; either he is meditating, or he is busy, or he is on a journey, or perhaps he is sleeping and must be awakened" (18:27). Although the prophets called and performed their sacred rituals, cutting themselves, there was no response. Elijah ordered that the altar be doused with water. After it was saturated he prayed, and the Lord God Omnipotent sent fire from heaven that consumed the altar (18:30–39).

In the midst of Israel's hellish reversion to paganism, the soul of Elijah was tried to the uttermost. He experienced persecution daily and became a fugitive from the power of the throne. He was exhausted with living. In the midst of it he cried out to God, "It is enough! Now, LORD, take my life, for I am no better than my fathers! . . . I have been very zealous for the LORD God of hosts; for the children of Israel have forsaken Your covenant, torn down Your altars, and killed Your prophets with the sword. I alone am left; and they seek to take my life" (19:4, 10). I call that the Elijah Syndrome; it is what true believers experience when surrounded by apostasy.

Apostasy is not the same as paganism. An apostate is one who, at some point, professed the true God. Apostasy can take place only in the house of God. People become apostate by repudiating the faith they once professed. Whole churches can become apostate. When churches denounce essential truths of the Christian faith, they are apostate churches. Denominations— Protestant denominations—can become apostate. The church in which I grew up and was ordained is, I believe, part of an apostate denomination. It celebrates the imaging of pagan goddesses. It sanctions abortion on demand. Its official church councils have argued that to affirm the deity of Christ or his atonement is not a necessary qualification for pastors of the denomination. When a church does that, it is apostate.

True Christians might be in such churches, but they should not be. When a group becomes apostate, we have a moral obligation to leave and distance ourselves from it. We do not have to break fellowship over every difference of doctrine, but when real apostasy is manifested, it is time to shake the dust from our feet and get out. Not every Christian does that, however. Multitudes of Christians are still working, striving, laboring, and preaching within apostate bodies all over the world. Those who do might experience the Elijah Syndrome.

Paul tells his readers the response Elijah received: **"I have reserved for Myself seven thousand men who have not bowed the knee to Baal"** (v. 4b). Not just one or five or even one hundred—God has kept for himself seven thousand from within that godless nation. They had not kept themselves for God, but God had kept them. Some might have been found within the courts of Ahab and Jezebel; others were perhaps in areas that Elijah would not have guessed. Wherever they were, there were seven thousand preserved from apostasy by God himself.

I believe I am not apostate, but the only reason I can give is that the Lord God in his sweet grace and mercy has preserved me. I believe in the perseverance of the saints only because I believe in the preservation of the saints. The Lord God in his grace preserves his people.

A Remnant by Grace

Even so then, at this present time there is a remnant according to the election of grace (v. 5). Throughout the Old Testament God speaks of preserving a remnant. If you go to a carpet store because they happen to be having a remnant sale, you are not going there to purchase whole rugs. You are buying what is left over after the rugs have been trimmed. Seed left after the field has been plowed, dregs found in the bottom of a cup, loose ends fit only for the trash barrel, and the stump left from a felled tree are all metaphors for the people of God. That is what we are—the dregs reserved by God in election. He has preserved his remnant, which he determined to redeem from the foundation of the world. That is why I know the church of Jesus Christ will never be erased from the face of the earth. Parishes may fall and denominations may crumble, but God will preserve his elect in every generation. You will never be asked to stand alone in a dying world, because God has a people who cannot fail.

The church belongs to Christ. It is his bride, and the bride has been given to the Son by the Father. Before going to the cross Jesus prayed in the upper room: "I do not pray for the world but for those whom You have given Me, for they are Yours. . . . Those whom You gave Me I have kept; and none of them is lost except the son of perdition [Judas], that the Scripture might be fulfilled" (John 17:9, 12).

The remnant is according to the election of grace. **And if by grace, then it is no longer of works** (v. 6a). Those two concepts—grace and works—are mutually exclusive, as we have seen throughout this epistle. Grace by definition is unmerited, unearned, and undeserved. Paul makes this simple—it is one or the other, grace or works. Our only hope is grace. Paul is writing about the Jewish people as a whole, ethnic Israel, his kinsmen. **What then? Israel has not obtained what it seeks; but the elect have obtained it, and the rest were blinded** (v. 7).

Spiritual Blindness

Paul quotes the Old Testament again: **Just as it is written: "God has given them a spirit of stupor, eyes that they should not see and ears that they should not hear, to this very day"** (v. 8). The people of Israel were blind because God had made them blind. Their blindness was punishment for their sin. They did not want to see the things of God, so, as he has done throughout redemptive history, he abandoned them to their sinful desire. This is God's poetic justice. If you do not want to hear the Word of God, be careful, because God will make you deaf, and then you will never hear it. If you do not want to see the kingdom of God, whatever you see even vaguely now will be taken away. If you are not alive and energetic to the things of the Spirit, be careful that God does not visit you with the spirit of lethargy, taking from you whatever weak zeal you have. When God works that way, it is always a punishment for evil inclinations.

Paul cites David, who was speaking about the enemies of God's kingdom: **"Let their table become a snare and a trap, a stumbling block and a recompense to them. Let their eyes be darkened, so that they do not see, and bow down their back always"** (vv. 9–10). Elsewhere, in Psalm 23, David writes: "You prepare a table before me in the presence of my enemies" (v. 5a). This is the table of the banquet feast, a table of blessing prepared by God made visible to the enemies of the kingdom. "You anoint my head with oil; my cup runs over" (v. 5b). Concerning this imagery Luther said that ultimately this table, bestowed by the Lord God in his grace upon the nation of Israel, is the table of his Word. He has spread the banquet feast with the oracles of God.

The supreme advantage that God gave to Israel was his Word. He did not give it to the Assyrians, the Babylonians, or the Acadians; he gave his Word to Israel. They had the oracles of God. David saw how his enemies hated the Word of God and the church in its Old Testament manifestation. Elsewhere David wrote, "Let their table become a snare before them, and their well-being a trap" (Ps. 69:22). When God's enemies come to that table and see the sumptuous food placed upon it, like a trap baited with meat that will spring when the animal pounces, the table will be a snare, a hammer on the heads of those who hate it.

Luther, looking at Psalm 69:22, said it is like a flower in the field whose nectar is used to make honey for the bee, but the nectar is poison to the spider. To those who are being saved, the Word of God is sweetness and honey, but for those who are perishing, it is poison. May it be for you nothing but sweetness and honey so that you may feast on the table God has prepared for you from the foundation of the world.

42

GRAFTED IN

Romans 11:11–24

I say then, have they stumbled that they should fall? Certainly not! But through their fall, to provoke them to jealousy, salvation has come to the Gentiles. Now if their fall is riches for the world, and their failure riches for the Gentiles, how much more their fullness! For I speak to you Gentiles; inasmuch as I am an apostle to the Gentiles, I magnify my ministry, if by any means I may provoke to jealousy those who are my flesh and save some of them. For if their being cast away is the reconciling of the world, what will their acceptance be but life from the dead? For if the firstfruit is holy, the lump is also holy; and if the root is holy, so are the branches. And if some of the branches were broken off, and you, being a wild olive tree, were grafted in among them, and with them became a partaker of the root and fatness of the olive tree, do not boast against the branches. But if you do boast, remember that you do not support the root, but the root supports you. You will say then, "Branches were broken off that I might be grafted in." Well said. Because of unbelief they were broken off, and you stand by faith. Do not be haughty, but fear. For if God did not spare the natural branches, He may not spare you either. Therefore consider the goodness and severity of God: on those who fell, severity; but toward you, goodness, if you continue in His goodness. Otherwise you also will be cut off. And they also, if they do not continue in unbelief, will be grafted in, for God is able to graft them in again. For if you were cut out of the olive tree which is wild by nature, and were grafted contrary to nature into a cultivated olive tree, how much more will these, who are natural branches, be grafted into their own olive tree?

In the Greek language, unlike English, rhetorical questions have a specific structure that tells us conclusively whether the answer is yes or no. Once again Paul begins a section of the epistle with this literary device: **I say then, have they stumbled that they should fall?** (v. 11a). Paul has already told us that Israel had missed their calling. Holding to works righteousness, they had become blind to the truth of redemption. They had tripped over the Messiah. He was a rock of offense and a stumbling block to his own people. Now Paul explores the purpose of their stumbling; in other words, what was God's design in it?

The result of stumbling is usually falling. When we trip, we fall, and when we fall, we often get hurt. Sometimes we fall and cannot get up. Did God want his people to fall, not just temporarily but fully and finally? Paul gives the same emphatic response that he has so often in the epistle: **Certainly not!** (v. 11b). Other translations have "by no means" or "God forbid!" We should not conclude that God's purpose in the stumbling of Israel was their permanent fall into destruction.

Salvation for the Gentiles

But through their fall, to provoke them to jealousy, salvation has come to the Gentiles (v. 11c). This passage reeks with irony. Later (v. 25) Paul will elaborate on this principle, calling it a "mystery." Paul refers to *mystery* frequently in his New Testament writings, particularly in his epistle to the Colossians in which he writes of the *mustērion*. The Latin translation of the Greek *mustērion* is *sacramentum*, which is why some churches refer to the sacraments as the "sacred mysteries." There is a linguistic connection between the Greek and the Latin words.

Although the word *mustērion* is translated as *mystery*, there is a great chasm between our understanding of the word and the Greek concept in Paul's day. When we do not understand something in God's Word or in the realm of science, we refer to it as a "mystery." Mystery is a term we also apply to whodunit novels and crime dramas on television. The New Testament understanding of the term *mystery* or *mustērion* refers to something that was at one time hidden but has now been revealed and made plain. The most important mystery with which the apostle grapples time and again in his writing is this: "To them [the saints] God willed to make known what are the riches of the glory of this mystery among the Gentiles: which is Christ in you, the hope of glory" (Col. 1:27).

The grand mystery so heavily veiled in the Old Testament is now made clear: the Gentiles are included in the people of God. Even though it was veiled in Old Testament history, it was not totally hidden. God made a covenant with Abraham in which Abraham would be blessed in order to be a blessing to all the nations of the world. Implicit in that promise to Abraham was that, at some point, the non-Jews (the Gentiles) would participate in the blessedness of the covenant. Later on the prophet Jonah was sent as a missionary to a Gentile land (Jonah 1:1–2). As we see, God's intention to include the Gentiles in the covenant promise was not completely unknown in Old Testament Israel, but it was certainly vague and in shadows. The grand design of God, the mystery of the stumbling of Israel, is "to provoke them to jealousy."

The vast majority of us are of Gentile descent. We are the Gentiles who are now a part of the mystery that has been revealed. Salvation has come to us, and the means through which that salvation has come is the fall of the Jews. God has done it. He has worked through the disobedience of one group to bring a larger group into his household of faith.

Paul uses another literary device common not only in his writings but also in the teaching technique of Jesus—the comparison. Jesus' comparisons were not simply between good and bad or good and better; his comparisons were in the nature of "how much more," a phrase he used frequently. In the parable of the unjust judge (Luke 18:1–8), Jesus describes an unfortunate, disenfranchised widow. She sought her justice from a judge who had no regard for man or God. The judge would not hear the widow's case, but she persisted in her request. Finally the judge agreed to hear the case. He had no concern for the woman; he just wanted some peace. The judge heard her case and gave her a favorable verdict. Jesus said, "Hear what the unjust judge said. And shall God not avenge His own elect who cry out day and night to Him, though He bears long with them? I tell you that He will avenge them speedily" (vv. 6–8a). Jesus' point is that if an ungodly judge will render a just verdict, *how much more* will God, who is just, vindicate his people who cry unto him day and night? Paul uses the same device here when he says, **Now if their fall is riches for the world, and their failures riches for the Gentiles, how much more their fullness!** (v. 12). If God brings a good thing out of the failure of Israel, how much more blessedness will he bring through their restoration?

Paul began this section of the epistle with the promise of his passionate concern for his kinsmen, ethnic Israel (9:1–5). **For I speak to you
Gentiles; inasmuch as I am an apostle to the Gentiles . . .** (v. 13a).
Even though Paul was a Jew, he was called by Christ as a missionary and
apostle to the Gentiles. Paul magnifies his ministry, not to magnify himself
but to remind his Roman readers that Christ had chosen him for the work,
of which they were a part. **I magnify my ministry, if by any means I
may provoke to jealousy those who are my flesh and save some
of them** (vv. 13b–14). He articulates passion for brothers and sisters of his
own nation. He uses the term *jealousy*. The Jews were hostile, bitter in their
opposition to the Christian church, but Paul hopes that as the glory of the
church is continually made manifest, his kinsmen will see the greatness of
the gospel. If that happens, his kinsmen will be jealous rather than angry
and will try to pursue what believers enjoy.

Years ago I ministered with the founder of Jews for Jesus, Moshe Rosen.
I do not know of any organization that has been more effective in leading
people of Jewish ancestry to Christ. At the same time, I do not know of any
missionary organization that has provoked more controversy or hostility
than this one. It has particularly provoked the religious establishment of
American Judaism, which is deeply resentful of Christian evangelism to its
people. American Jews are profoundly opposed to any type of proselytism. I
tell my Jewish friends that I am puzzled by that. I ask them, "Do you believe
that Judaism is true and Christianity is false?"

"Yes," they reply.

"Do you believe that Jesus is the Messiah?"

"No," they reply.

They believe our religion is false, that we are the ones stumbling in darkness. They think we are guilty of idolatry because we worship a man and
deny the monotheistic foundation of their Jewish faith, yet they have an
antipathy toward evangelism. They do not evangelize Christians. If they
believe that Judaism is the truth of God, why don't they crawl over glass to
bring us into the true religion of Abraham? When I ask, they have nothing
to say. They mumble, "It is not for you; it is just for us."

Paul wants to break through those barriers. He wants to cut through the
hostility and resistance by making the Jews jealous of what God has given
to us. **For if their being cast away is the reconciling of the world,
what will their acceptance be but life from the dead?** (v. 15). If their
being rejected is God's plan for the reconciliation of the world, how much
more would their acceptance bring blessedness to humanity? What would

it be but life from the dead? Some commentators believe that Paul is giving us an eschatological hint, saying with *The Late Great Planet Earth* that the final sign of Christ's coming and the consummation of his kingdom will be the conversion of Israel. I certainly believe that the conversion of Israel is in view later in this chapter, but I do not think that is in this part of the text.

Bones and Branches

"What will their acceptance be but life from the dead?"—This image has its roots in the Old Testament where we find Ezekiel's vision of the valley of the dry bones:

> The hand of the LORD came upon me and brought me out in the Spirit of the LORD, and set me down in the midst of the valley; and it was full of bones. Then He caused me to pass by them all around, and behold, there were very many in the open valley; and indeed they were very dry. (Ezek. 37:1–2)

The bones had dried up in that arid environment into a state of hopeless death. God asked Ezekiel, "Son of man, can these bones live?" (v. 3). When God's word came over the valley of dry bones, suddenly there was a stirring and the bones began to rattle. They began to move together and were knit one to another, and then flesh came upon the bones, and then life began to course through the veins of those skeletons. From death in the valley came life, and that is the image Paul has in view here when he declares that if rejection brings salvation, the acceptance will bring so much more.

Paul changes metaphors: **For if the firstfruit is holy, the lump is also holy; and if the root is holy, so are the branches** (v. 16). Paul mentions firstfruits, lumps, and roots. Firstfruit refers to the offerings that were brought into the temple in the Old Testament. The firstfruits were the initial blossomings, the best of the fruit, but the whole crop was consecrated as sacred unto the Lord. The lump is an analogy for bread leaven. A small amount of leaven introduced into a small piece of bread makes the whole loaf rise. When the leavening agent was made sacred to God, holy and set apart, so too was the whole loaf. Paul also uses a tree metaphor: "If the root is holy, so are the branches." The branches are not made holy; only by their connection to the root are the branches considered sacred.

Paul presses the tree analogy further: **If some of the branches were broken off, and you, being a wild olive tree, were grafted in among them, and with them became a partaker of the root and fatness of the olive tree, do not boast against the branches** (vv. 17–18a). The broken-off branches are the disobedient, apostate Jews, the ones who stumbled and were cut off from the promises of God and thrown into the fire, just as Jesus said. The metaphor focuses on the olive tree, which was very important to the economy of Old Testament Israel. Olive oil was one of the most important, if not *the* most important, agrarian products in the land. The precious olive oil came from olives that grew on olive trees, which were very valuable in the land of Palestine. The olive tree is the most durable of all trees. The roots go deep, and the trees can live for three or four hundred years.

The Mount of Olives separates the village of Bethany from the city of Jerusalem. When Jesus went to Gethsemane, when he agonized in prayer the night before he was executed, the slope of the mountain between Bethany and Jerusalem was covered with olive trees. One of the tragedies of Jewish history is the felling of those trees. During the Roman siege of Jerusalem in AD 70 the Romans encamped on the Mount of Olives and waited for the resources of food and water to dry up within the city. They kept warm by cutting down those olive trees, using the tree branches to build fires. The Mount of Olives was completely denuded of olive trees by the Roman soldiers. Nevertheless, the symbol of strength and durability to the Jew was the olive tree.

Other olive trees grew wild; they were not cultivated so they bore no fruit. They were worthless, giant weeds, which is how Paul describes us: "Some of the branches were broken off, and you, being a wild olive tree, were grafted in among them." God cut off the branches of the precious, durable, valuable olive tree and made a graft. The graft he put on the tree was taken from wild, worthless olive trees that could not be commended to God. "You . . . became a partaker of the root and fatness of the olive tree." These spindly, worthless, wild olive branches were plugged into the root from which they get the sap, the nutrients. The grafted branches draw everything valuable from the root of the cultivated olive tree. Salvation is of the Jews, and we must never forget that.

It should be the deathblow of anti-Semitism among Christian people. **But if you do boast, remember that you do not support the root, but the root supports you** (v. 18b). How could Paul be any more graphic? Remember where you came from, and remember the grace of God in bringing you where you are.

You will say then, "Branches were broken off that I might be grafted in." Well said. Because of unbelief they were broken off, and you stand by faith. Do not be haughty, but fear (vv. 19–20). Sometimes Christians read this text and say, "Shame on the Jews. They rejected the promises of God, but we have accepted them, so now we are God's chosen people." Paul warns us against that. We are not to get haughty.

Cutting

Just as apostasy polluted Israel, it can pollute us. We have seen the unbelievable corruption of mainline churches that have become monuments of unbelief and apostasy. Just as God cuts off the branches of Israel, he will cut off the unproductive Gentile branches. **For if God did not spare the natural branches, He may not spare you either. Therefore consider the goodness and severity of God: on those who fell, severity; but toward you, goodness, if you continue in His goodness. Otherwise you also will be cut off** (vv. 21–22). We are to think about the goodness of God—it is an incredible and awesome goodness—yet while we are doing that, we are to consider the severity of God. Our God is an all-consuming fire, and when his judgment comes, when it falls upon wicked people, the judgment is severe.

The principle of cutting is deeply rooted in Old Testament faith. When covenants were made in the Old Testament, they were cut. Cutting rites were associated with the most important covenants of the Old Testament. The sign of the Old Testament covenant was circumcision. It may seem crude when you think about it, but cutting the foreskin of Jewish male children had a twofold symbolic significance. First, the Jewish males were cut to symbolize being cut out of the world, separated from the rest of lost humanity and consecrated to God through this covenant. Second, circumcision signified that failure to keep the terms of the covenant meant being cut off from God's blessing. That negative sanction was contained in the symbol that every Jewish boy carried on his body. The worst thing ever to befall a human being is being cut off from God.

When you join a church, you agree to submit to its discipline. If you become involved in gross sin or public scandal, the church is responsible to call you to account and plead with you to repent. If you refuse to repent, you are first suspended from the sacraments in hope that it will make you jealous to get back into the safety of the fold. If you persist in your impenitence, the final act of punishment is excommunication, which means that the church of Jesus Christ turns you over to Satan by cutting you out of its fellowship. We practice excommunication because Jesus commanded us to do so.

Many do not take church discipline seriously, but Jesus was speaking about the church when he said, "Assuredly, I say to you, whatever you bind on earth will be bound in heaven, and whatever you loose on earth will be loosed in heaven" (Matt. 18:18). We take that seriously.

43

THE FULLNESS OF TIME

Romans 11:25–26

For I do not desire, brethren, that you should be ignorant of this mystery, lest you should be wise in your own opinion, that blindness in part has happened to Israel until the fullness of the Gentiles has come in. And so all Israel will be saved, as it is written: "The Deliverer will come out of Zion, and He will turn away ungodliness from Jacob."

A war took place in 1967 that lasted only a few days, but it culminated in the Jewish, or Israeli, troops coming into the old city of Jerusalem. Television gave us images of soldiers arriving at the Wailing Wall, the portion of the temple still standing. Even though firefights were going on, the soldiers threw down their weapons and rushed to the Wailing Wall and began to pray. It was an astonishing moment in the history of civilization. Many serious scholars then and now believe the return of the Jews to the Holy Land has absolutely no redemptive-historical significance, nor do they believe it of the 1948 Balfour Declaration. Others believe that what happened in 1948 and again in 1967 has everything to do with redemptive history, so much so that they keep a constant eye out for the rebuilding of the temple and the reinstitution of the sacrificial system in Jerusalem as harbingers of the imminent return of Jesus. I don't think there has ever been a period in church history in which more frenzied attention has been focused on the expected return of Jesus. This intense focus, which we have witnessed over the past few decades, is due largely to those events in Israel and Jerusalem.

I remember that day in 1967. I watched the proceedings on television from my home in Massachusetts, and then I got in my car and drove to the house of a friend, now one of the most distinguished Old Testament scholars in the world. He had never believed that such events have redemptive-historical significance, but when I went to see him that day, he was not so sure. Even someone steeped in biblical knowledge was struck by the sensational events unfolding at that time.

The Mystery Revealed

The question before us is whether there is a future for ethnic Israel. Is God going to work again in history with the people who are Jewish *kata sarka*, according to the flesh? Thus far in Romans 11 Paul has addressed his concern for his kinsmen, Israel. In the course of redemptive history the fall of ethnic Jews has led to our being incorporated into the family of God as wild olive branches grafted into the root. If the fall of the Jewish people redounded to the blessedness of the nations, how much more will their restoration. That is why we have to pay close attention to what he says here.

As Paul introduces the subject of Israel's blindness, he talks about a mystery, which, as we noted earlier, in Paul's vocabulary is something once hidden but now made manifest by God. He knows how destructive ignorance is to godliness. God has given us the Bible so that we might become mature in our understanding of the things in it and not seek comfort in ignorance. **For I do not desire, brethren, that you should be ignorant of this mystery, lest you should be wise in your own opinion** (v. 25a). Paul desires that his readers rest upon the revelation of God rather than their personal opinions, explaining **that blindness in part has happened to Israel until the fullness of the Gentiles has come in** (v. 25b).

The word *until* is a timeframe reference. It means "up to a certain point in time," and such a point in time has a terminal dimension to it. Beyond it something changes. When Paul says blindness has happened to ethnic Israel, to the Jews, it has not happened forever. At the beginning of chapter 11 we saw that the state of apostasy into which the Jews had fallen was neither full nor final. Paul reminded us of his own Jewish ancestry as a way to show that not all the ethnic Jews had fallen away from the covenant. Here he points out that the fall of Israel is not only not full but also not final. It is not the end of the story. The blindness that has come upon them has a historical limit to it, which is "until the fullness of the Gentiles has come in."

The Greek word translated "fullness" is *plērōma*; the Latin word is *plentitude*, the plentitude of the Gentiles. Both words refer to something that reaches its saturation point. Presumably there is a point in history where God's extension of his salvific call to the Gentiles will reach its saturation point, after which God's relationship to ethnic Israel will change.

The Bible contains a parallel expression to the one Paul uses. It is not verbatim, but virtually every New Testament scholar notices it and sees significance between Paul's language and that of his co-missionary Luke in his Gospel. Luke 21 contains one of the most important prophetic discourses given by Jesus during his earthly ministry. It took place very close to the end of Jesus' life, after he had come to Jerusalem. There he made the prediction that the temple would be destroyed and not one stone would be left upon another, and he talked about the destruction of Jerusalem. Jesus' forecast of the destruction of the temple and Jerusalem by Roman invaders was given about forty years before the actual events took place in AD 70. This event is of the utmost significance in understanding the Christian faith, but there is a difficulty with the biblical record of the event.

Signs of the Times

Jesus' discourse is called the Olivet Discourse because it took place on the Mount of Olives. It is recorded in all three synoptic Gospels. In addition to Luke's version, we find it in Matthew 24 and a brief version of it in Mark 13. My Bible contains a subhead over this section of Luke 21 titled, "Jesus Predicts the Destruction of the Temple." Such subheads have been added to help us locate sections of Scripture; they were not in the original text. This subhead in my Bible does no harm to the text. It is exactly what happened. The next subhead in my Bible is titled, "The Signs of the Times and the End of the Age," but there is no language in what follows about the end of the age. In Matthew's version of the Olivet Discourse, however, Jesus said a great deal about the destruction of the temple and the signs of the times and the end of the age.

Almost every time we see such language about the end of the age, we must ask which age is under consideration. Was Jesus referring to the age of the Enlightenment, the age of reason, the age of empiricism, the Cenozoic era, the Ice Age, the Iron Age, or the Bronze Age? The assumption most bring to that phrase, "the end of the age," is that it must be referring to the end of time as we know it, the consummation of the kingdom of God. Maybe it does, but I do not think so.

Jesus said, "They will fall by the edge of the sword, and be led away captive into all nations. And Jerusalem will be trampled by Gentiles until the times of the Gentiles are fulfilled" (Luke 21:24). Jesus goes on to predict the destruction of the temple, and he gives the signs of the times—wars, rumors of wars, and signs in the sky (vv. 25–27). Our Lord predicted Jerusalem would be trampled underfoot by Gentiles, which is exactly what happened in AD 70. We see, however, the Greek word that means "until" or "up to a certain point but not beyond," which renders, "Jerusalem will be trampled underfoot by the Gentiles *until* the times of the Gentiles are fulfilled." What does Luke mean by the "times of the Gentiles," and what does Paul mean by "the fullness of the Gentiles"? Those two ideas are close. The difficulty is this terminal point for the destruction of Jerusalem and its being in captivity and trodden underfoot by the Gentiles is a detail found in Luke but not in Matthew or Mark. What are "the times of the Gentiles," and does that phrase suggest anything about other times? Jews and Gentiles are always in contrast in the Bible. We find in redemptive history times of the Jews and times of the Gentiles. The thrust of Paul's argument is this: there is a time in redemptive history when the focus of God's redeeming grace is on the Jews and a time when it is on the Gentiles.

In AD 70 the temple was destroyed and sacrifices ceased, and for all intents and purposes the Jewish nation was scattered throughout the world. The Jews' identity with Jerusalem was broken except for their wistful hope and oath that sometime they may be restored to it. Before AD 70 most people saw the Christian church as a subdivision of Judaism, but that stopped in AD 70 when the judgment of God came with a vengeance on Israel. Her temple was removed block by block, and her holy city was devastated and given over to the control of the Gentiles, but not forever, according to Luke 21 and Romans 11. There is a future for ethnic Israel and the city of Jerusalem.

Jesus the Prophet

Jesus' prediction of the future destruction of the temple and Jerusalem is the clearest proof anywhere in recorded literature of Jesus' being a prophet sent from God. He predicted things about the future that nobody could possibly predict with such uncanny accuracy. The irony is, however, that this prophecy, which so compellingly proves the truth claims of Jesus, is the very text that the higher critics use more than any other New Testament text to argue against the inspiration of the Bible and the infallibility of the prophetic utterances of Jesus. I made mention earlier of Bertrand Russell's book *Why I'm Not a Christian*. In that book, along with other objections to Christ and Christianity, he mentions that these words from the Olivet Discourse are the clearest proof that Jesus was a false prophet.

The temple and city were destroyed as Jesus said they would be, but this text is used as the compelling proof against Christianity because of the time references Jesus used. When Jesus told his disciples that not one stone would be left upon another and the temple would be destroyed, the burning question in the minds of the disciples was this: "When will these things be? And what sign will there be when these things are about to take place?" (Luke 21:7). I believe they are asking about the end of the Jewish age. They ask a straightforward question, and Jesus is not the least bit oblique in his response: "Assuredly, I say to you, this generation will by no means pass away till all things take place" (v. 32). This includes his coming, presumably, in judgment on Israel.

Jesus referred to wars and the rumors of wars, the signs of the times, and the signs of his coming, and people presume he was talking about his final return at the end of time. I do not think so, because the "all these things" of which Jesus spoke specifically, refer to the temple and to Jerusalem and to some kind of Jesus' coming, which the New Testament broadly speaks of as a visitation of God's wrath, which, of course, fell with fury in AD 70.

To the Jew, a *generation* referred to a particular age group of approximately forty years. Elsewhere Jesus said, "Assuredly, I say to you, there are some standing here who shall not taste death till they see the Son of Man coming in His kingdom" (Matt. 16:28). If you had been among those listening to Jesus say, "This generation is not going to pass away until all of these things take place," would you understand him to mean that two thousand years would go by before his prediction would come to pass? I do not think so. As every liberal critic understands, Jesus was predicting that those events would occur within the next forty years, before some of the disciples had died. The plain meaning of the text is that Jesus put forth a timeframe for the fulfillment of the prophecies.

I was in seminary in the midst of a stronghold of higher critical theory, and I had this text referred to every day in attacks against the inspiration of the Bible. I would say, "What if Jesus was not wrong? What if everything he said would take place within forty years did take place within forty years?" When he spoke about the signs of the times, he warned the people, "When you see Jerusalem surrounded by armies, then know that its desolation is near. Then let those who are in Judea flee to the mountains, let those who are in the midst of her depart, and let not those who are in the country enter her" (Luke 21:20–21). His instructions were the exact opposite of what typically took place in the ancient world when an army approached a walled city. When the Roman soldiers marched through Israel, the people left their homes and flocked to the city with the greatest walls. Josephus tells us that at the time of Jerusalem's destruction 1.1 million Jews were slaughtered because they went to the city. Jesus told his disciples not to go there; he told them to go to the hills instead. Christians were spared the destruction that did take place within forty years.

Books such as *The Late Great Planet Earth* and the *Left Behind* series point to earthquakes and wars and conclude we are on the brink of Jesus' return, but I do not think such events have anything to do with the consummate return of Jesus. I think these events already took place. I hold that view because it is what the text says.

The moon has not turned to dripping blood and the heavens have not rolled up like a scroll, some argue, and they are right. There are two types of terminology in the Olivet Discourse. There is simple, didactic language and apocalyptic language, which uses catastrophic images to describe God's visitation of wrath and destruction. By using the basic hermeneutic of interpreting Scripture by Scripture when considering the language of destruction in the prophets of the Old Testament, we see that such language was used to describe the actual destruction of cities such as Tyre and Sidon. When we encounter highly imaginative language, it is appropriate to allow for an imaginative interpretation. When we encounter simple, declarative, indicative statements, we must treat them as such. When Jesus gave the timeframes in the Olivet Discourse he did not use imaginative language; he used straightforward, direct, indicative passages. He said that some listening to him were going to live to see it. Was he wrong? At stake here is the trustworthiness of Jesus and the Bible.

Evangelicals apply Jesus' words about the generation that will not pass away (Luke 21:32) to unbelievers; in other words, unbelievers will not pass away until all Jesus has described is fulfilled. If that were the case, Jesus would not have answered the disciples' question; his answer would have amounted to nothing more than an evasion. The disciples asked him a straightforward question, and he gave them a straightforward answer. We see the same thing in the book of Revelation. The language of the timeframe references in the first nineteen chapters indicates things that are about to happen, not something that is going to take place three or four thousand years later.

Israel Saved

I do not hold to the view of preterists. They say all the prophecies about the return of Jesus and the fulfillment of the kingdom of God took place in AD 70. I do not believe that for a minute. I think something of dramatic significance took place in AD 70—the end of the Jewish age as they knew it. It was the end of the temple and of Jerusalem but not the end of God's economy of redemption for his people. I believe Paul is saying here and throughout Romans 11 that God is not finished with the Jews.

I have been concerned since 1967. It may be in the economy of redemption that God is going to bring Gentiles into his house for another five thousand years, but when I see what is happening in Jerusalem, I do not think so. We may be on the very cusp of the last roundup of Gentiles. We may be very close to the next step of redemptive history—God's work with ethnic Israel. No time since AD 70 has seen such a concentration of evangelism to ethnic Jews as that taking place in our day, nor has any time in church history mirrored the vast number of converts to Christianity from Judaism. I do not believe that God has two agendas, one for the Jew and one for the Gentile. He has one agenda that incorporates both the Jew and the Gentile in his kingdom.

So all Israel will be saved (v. 26a). If Paul is referring to spiritual Israel, he is departing from the way he uses the term *Israel* here and in the preceding three chapters. Since chapter 8 Paul has been talking about ethnic Israel. Does he mean each and every Jew? The word *all* in Scripture does not function the way we characteristically use it to indicate each and every. I believe Paul to be saying that the full complement of God's elect from Israel will be saved and that this will come in a new redemptive-historical visitation by the Holy Spirit when the time of the Gentiles is fulfilled.

I am much interested in Luke's use of the phrase "the times of the Gentiles being fulfilled" and its parallel here in Romans 11 concerning "the fullness of the Gentiles." The apostle tells us he does not want us to grope in the darkness; he wants to take away the mystery. He is telling us about the future of the kingdom of God, which we must take with great earnestness, joy, and consolation. I don't mean to suggest that God's work was finished in AD 70, but when he said, "This generation will not pass away," he meant exactly what he said. That generation did not pass away until the temple and Jerusalem were destroyed and our Lord visited his people in the time of their wrath.

44

OUT OF ZION

Romans 11:26–35

And so all Israel will be saved, as it is written:

> "The Deliverer will come out of Zion,
> And He will turn away ungodliness from Jacob;
> For this is My covenant with them,
> When I take away their sins."

Concerning the gospel they are enemies for your sake, but concerning the election they are beloved for the sake of the fathers. For the gifts and the calling of God are irrevocable. For as you were once disobedient to God, yet have now obtained mercy through their disobedience, even so these also have now been disobedient, that through the mercy shown you they also may obtain mercy. For God has committed them all to disobedience, that He might have mercy on all.

Oh, the depth of the riches both of the wisdom and knowledge of God! How unsearchable are His judgments and His ways past finding out!

> "For who has known the mind of the LORD?
> Or who has become His counselor?"
> "Or who has first given to Him
> And it shall be repaid to him?"

A s it is written: "**The Deliverer will come out of Zion, and he will turn away ungodliness from Jacob; for this is My covenant with them, when I take away their sins**" (v. 26b). This is a compilation of more than one Old Testament text, but the apostle Paul provides a summary that gets to the heart of all he has been teaching to the people at Rome. Paul has labored to show his Roman readers—and us—that we, the Gentiles, are the wild branch grafted onto the root of the tree. We have no intrinsic claim to the promises God gave his people in the Old Testament because the Deliverer—the one who will redeem—came not from the Gentiles' lands; he came out of Zion.

One thing the Messiah will accomplish is found in this Old Testament prophecy. The prophecy is referring to Israel. Israel had fallen into apostasy, into unspeakable sin against the Messiah himself, and yet the redemptive work of the Messiah will provide the framework for the final redemption of Israel.

The Future of Israel

Paul gives a reason why the Deliverer will turn away ungodliness from Jacob. Jacob has rejected the covenant by saying no to God's yes in his promises of redemption. Jacob has turned away into consistent disobedience, but God is going to turn them back. Why will God do this? Does he owe them a second chance? He will turn them back because of his covenant promise and electing grace. When Paul began his treatment of the plight of the Jews in chapters 8 and 9, he examined it in light of the broader question of divine election. When he talked about the final restoration of Israel after the age of the Gentiles, he put it in the context not only of the covenant promises but also of the doctrine of election.

The reason we can be absolutely certain God is not finished with the Jews is that God predicted it. Whatever God says will happen in the future must necessarily come to pass, but how does God know what will happen eventually with the Jews? For that matter, how does God know what is going to happen tomorrow to us? The open-theism movement, which is penetrating the Christian world with ungodliness, says that God does not and cannot know the future choices of human beings. Open theists claim that God's future knowledge is limited by human free will and that even God's knowledge is finite. He is not really omniscient, they say, and he certainly lacks the foreknowledge of human choices in the future. They deny the biblical doctrine of God. From our perspective, how does God know what is going to happen? How does he know what people will choose tomorrow?

It is not as though God has a mysterious psychic sense about the future through which he peers down through the corridor of time and sees what we cannot see from our vantage point. God knows what is going to happen tomorrow before it happens because he has ordained it. His knowledge of future things is based upon his ordination of future things. God knows that the people of Israel will be restored in the last hour because it is his sovereign will that it should happen.

That is why the doctrine of election is so vitally important to Paul in the midst of his struggle about the future of his people. He knows that their future is in the hands of God, not in the hands of the Pharisees. God has the power, authority, and will to turn people away from their disobedience. Had God waited in heaven for us to turn from our sins and come to the cross, he would still be waiting. In his sovereign mercy and grace God does not wait for us to turn or incline ourselves; God brings us away from our disobedience to respond to him.

An Irrevocable Call

Concerning the gospel they are enemies for your sake, **but concerning the election they are beloved for the sake of the fathers** (v. 28). One of my favorite stories in the Old Testament is that of the lame son of Jonathan, Mephibosheth. When Saul and Jonathan were killed, a messenger came to David with that news, and David tore his garments because of his great love for Jonathan. Then he asked, "Is there still anyone who is left of the house of Saul, that I may show him kindness for Jonathan's sake?" (2 Sam. 9:1). All Saul's kin had fled for their lives. They assumed David wanted to get rid of them to prevent another uprising against his monarchy. Among Saul's relatives was a boy named Mephibosheth. He had been dropped by his nursemaid when he was a baby, and he became lame in both feet. He was whisked away into hiding. David sent his soldiers into the countryside to search for Saul's survivors, and they discovered Mephibosheth and brought him back to David. Mephibosheth was terrified, sure that he would be executed, but David brought him into his house and treated him as a son. David honored Mephibosheth, not because he had affection for the boy but for the sake of his love for Jonathan.

That story illustrates the history of redemption. The only reason we are included in the kingdom of God is God's love for his Son. Our election, our adoption, is always in Christ Jesus. God will visit his mercy upon the seed of Abraham through the line of Isaac because of his promises to the fathers

Abraham, Isaac, and Jacob. We have seen this theme woven throughout this epistle.

For the gifts and the calling of God are irrevocable (v. 29). That is one of the most comforting verses in Scripture as we struggle with our sins. It is politically incorrect today to use terminology that might reflect negatively on Native Americans, but I am going to risk that here. In my youth we used to label some as Indian givers. An Indian giver was one who gave a gift and then took it back. I have no idea where the expression originated, but we certainly knew while growing up that being labeled an Indian giver was negative. Paul is making the point here that God is not an Indian giver. When the Lord God gives a gift, it is irrevocable. When the Lord God exercises his redeeming call on someone, it is final; he never takes it back. The supreme gift we have been given is grace, the gift of the mercy by which we have been called and brought into the kingdom and the fellowship of Christ and adopted into his household. God will never under any circumstances revoke it. Even our disobedience, which may displease him and provoke him to corrective wrath, will not cause him to take that gift away. In like manner, God made promises to his people, to Abraham, Isaac, and Jacob. He called them and gave gifts to them, and that, too, was without revocation. The sovereign election of God is always and ever final.

For as you were once disobedient to God, yet have now obtained mercy through their disobedience, even so these also have now been disobedient, that through the mercy shown you they also may obtain mercy (vv. 30–31). God gave gifts to the nation of Israel, but they became disobedient, and through their disobedience, our mercy was received. Through the mercy we receive, God is going to work to bring his mercy on those who were once disobedient. "He will turn away ungodliness from Jacob" (v. 26). He will say no to their sin and overcome it for the sake of his redemptive plan.

In Romans 3 Paul brought the Jew and the Gentile together before the judgment seat of God and said that both are guilty of sin: "All have sinned and fall short of the glory of God" (v. 23). Here Paul says, **God has committed them all to disobedience, that He might have mercy on all** (v. 32).

The Unfathomable Depths of God

Paul follows his extraordinary affirmation with a sigh, a holy groan, the first word of which is simply "Oh": **Oh, the depth of the riches both of the wisdom and knowledge of God!** (v. 33a). When we read this

carefully, the text is almost palpable. Reading between the lines we can see
Paul's bare emotions as he pens these words, emotions that spring from his
profound concern for his kinsmen, Israel. As Paul sets forth the promise of
God for a final restoration of his people, his soul groans in passion, and what
follows is a doxology.

I noted earlier that my professor in Holland once said, "Gentlemen, all
sound theology begins and ends with doxology." He was speaking of the
fear of the Lord, reverence for God, a heartfelt sense of worship, which is
the beginning of wisdom. The first lesson in systematic theology deals with
the incomprehensibility of God. The fullness of the essence of God's glory
so far transcends human ability to sound its depths that we are left in a state
of awe before him. I am not saying that we are involved in some sort of
mystery religion where the things of God are unintelligible; what God reveals
we can grasp, to a certain degree. Central to the teaching of John Calvin
was the axiom *finitum non capax infinitum*: "the finite cannot contain or grasp
the fullness of the infinite." Even after we are in heaven—when we are no
longer looking through the glass darkly but basking in the refulgent glory of
God—we will not have an exhaustive knowledge of the Creator.

Eternity is not long enough for the creature to come to a comprehensive
knowledge of God, because even in eternity we will be creatures, and as
creatures we are finite and will remain subject to Calvin's axiom. Never
in this world or the next will the finite be able fully to contain or grasp the
infinite, so as we stand in wonder and awe before what God has revealed of
himself in his Word we are moved to doxology. The depth is so deep that
we cannot plumb it.

In the deeper parts of the ocean, the water becomes murky. Some fish
survive at the bottom of the ocean where the sunlight never penetrates, but
we cannot see them. Our vision into the ocean is limited to the shallows.
Just so, Paul is contemplating not the shallow water of God but the infinite
depths of his being. That is why he groans, "Oh, the depth of the riches . . ."
We can speak at the human level of the depths of degradation, corruption,
and poverty that no one can grasp, but here the apostle is speaking of the
riches of the glory of God.

Some time ago I read a small devotion by Charles Spurgeon in which
he made mention of fine jewels, silver, and gold—imagery used often in
the Bible to describe our faith. In order for gold to reach a certain level of
purity, it has to be refined by fire. Just so, God puts us through the crucible,
through the flames and the fire of persecution, so that the gold of our faith
may be purified. Spurgeon talked about the fire that purifies gold, and then

he contrasted that to garbage. You can throw garbage into the fire, but it will never be refined. In our souls there is garbage but in God only riches.

Who can reach the depth of the riches of God's wisdom and knowledge? We are impressed by people who have advanced degrees and yet the most brilliant human mind is filled with enormous gaps in knowledge. The mind of the brightest human being has more ignorance than knowledge, but in the mind of God there is no ignorance or folly. There is nothing but wisdom and knowledge.

God Unchangeable

I am often asked, "Does prayer change God's mind?" To ask the question is to answer it. Nothing could be more absurd than to think our prayers would change the mind of God. Our prayers do change things—they change us. If God has determined to do something, what would possibly move him to change his mind as a result of communion with us? Am I giving him knowledge when I pray? "God, I know you intend to do this thing, but I don't think you have considered fully the consequences. Let me try to show you what will happen if you do it." No prayer has ever added a subatomic particle of knowledge to the mind of an infinite God.

Consider something even worse: when we think we can change God's mind, we are demonstrating that we think God's intentions are somehow foolish or, even worse, evil, apart from the benefit of our counsel. There is no folly in the mind of God. God does not need our prayers to gain more knowledge or wisdom. Through our prayers God gains our affection and reverence as we bow before him. The first law of prayer is this: remember to whom we are speaking, and the second law of prayer is this: remember who we are. When we come with our prayers to God, we say, "Oh, the depth of the riches both of the wisdom and knowledge of God! **How unsearchable are His judgments and His ways past finding out!**" (v. 33b).

His judgments are unsearchable. In Paul's teaching to the Corinthians he tells us of the Spirit, who searches all things of God. The apostle's teaching there is easily misunderstood. Some think that even the Spirit is searching, groping in the darkness of the Father, trying to figure out what the Father is up to. No, when Paul speaks of the Spirit searching the things of God, he is not implying that the Spirit is searching for information. Rather, the Spirit is putting the searchlight on the things of God to illumine them for our understanding. To us, the things of God are unsearchable, but thanks be to God that the Spirit searches them for us. That is why, when we come to the biblical text, we pray that God will condescend to our weakness and give us the assistance of the Holy Spirit to make his ways intelligible to us.

The Mind of the Lord

Now we come to another quotation from the Old Testament, this time from Isaiah, Jeremiah, and Joel. It begins this way: **"For who has known the mind of the LORD?"** (v. 34a). Has anybody ever questioned your motives? When people question my motives I tell them they could not possibly know why I do what I do unless I tell them, and even then I might not be telling the truth. Additionally, I might not be telling myself the truth, because I do not always know why I do what I do. Are you always in touch with your motives? I can never get inside the secret chambers of others' hearts, so how can I know their motives?

Because we are sinful, we attribute the worst possible motives to people who injure us, and when we hurt others, we impute to ourselves the best motives. We tend to save the judgments of charity for ourselves. We need to be instructed. We cannot plumb the depths of someone else's mind, but that inability cannot be compared to our inability to know the mind of the Lord. "The secret things belong to the LORD our God, but those things which are revealed belong to us and to our children forever" (Deut. 29:29). The only way we can know the mind of the Lord is if the Lord is pleased to reveal it. When he does, we can know for sure that what he reveals about his mind is not deceitful or inaccurate. That is why I love the Bible—it reveals the mind of God to us.

Nothing in My Hand I Bring

Paul continues the Old Testament quote: **"Who has become His counselor?"** (v. 34b). God does not have any counselors because he does not need any counselors. What would we counsel him about? We do not go to God to give him our advice; we go to God to hear his advice. During my formal education there was an emphasis on learning the tools of critical analysis. We were taught not to jump to conclusions but to learn the difference between legitimate and illegitimate inferences. In our classes we were forced to critique statements made by various philosophers such as Kant, Plato, Aristotle, and Mill and to point out errors. We were taught how to read literature with a critical comb rather than just accept what we find in print. Approaching texts in that way has been a habit for me ever since. When I read a newspaper, a book, or a manuscript, that critical apparatus is always there. This is not a negative spirit but a spirit of analysis, and, as I said, it is always with me, except when I come to the text of Scripture. When I come to the Scripture I realize it is criticizing me. My only analysis in that case is to examine what it says and then examine my heart for my nonconformity to it. We cannot improve on God. We are not qualified to be his counselor.

"Or who has first given to Him and it shall be repaid to him?" (v. 35). James writes, "Every good gift and every perfect gift is from above" (1:17). When God gives us a gift, he is not paying us back for something we have given to him. What can we give him that he does not already have? That is the marvel of his grace in election. In electing us he is not repaying a debt. The gift of his grace is given freely from the abundance of his mercy and love.

45

ALL THINGS

Romans 11:36

For of Him and through Him and to Him are all things, to whom be glory forever. Amen.

We have come to the end of Paul's treatment of the doctrines of grace that began in Romans 1 with the announcement of the gospel of God and justification by faith alone. The apostle described the universal exposure of the human race to the wrath of God for repressing God's revelation. Man's repression led to manifold sins in the radical corruption of the race, sins both of the Jew and of the Greek. In Romans 3 Paul brought the whole of mankind before the tribunal of God saying, "All have sinned and fall short of the glory of God" (v. 23).

What followed from that was the exposition of the doctrine of justification by faith alone, which, in turn, was followed by a treatment of sanctification—our growth in Christ after we are justified. Then came a magnificent statement of the providence of God over all things: "All things work together for good to those who love God" (8:28). This introduced the Golden Chain of the doctrine of election, which Paul expounded in great detail in chapter 9. In chapter 10 Paul covered the great missionary enterprise of the church—we should be sending people throughout the world so that the gospel may be preached to all people.

Thus far in our study of chapter 11 we have seen Paul's profound treatment of the place of ethnic Israel in the future of God's redemption. That was brought to a close in a doxology: "Oh, the depth of the riches both of the wisdom and knowledge of God! How unsearchable are His judgments and His ways past finding out!" (v. 33).

Now we come to the last verse of chapter 11, which is also the last verse of Paul's unfolding of the gospel of God: **For of Him and through Him and to Him are all things, to whom be glory forever. Amen** (v. 36). In this single verse we find the sum and substance of the whole biblical revelation of the being and character of God. Paul sets it forth with a succinct use of three prepositions, each of which is virtually loaded with significance: "For *of* Him and *through* Him and *to* Him are all things." These three prepositions teach us about the nature of God. Through these three prepositions the apostle is saying that God is the source and owner of everything that is. He is also the ultimate cause of everything that comes to pass, and everything that comes to pass occurs through the exercise of his sovereign will. God is not only the means of all things but also the end or the purpose of all things.

All of Him

We begin with the preposition *of*—"All things are *of* him." In Greek the word *of* is a simple preposition that can be translated as either *of* or *from*. A distinction can be made between these two renditions. Both call attention to a profound truth about God. Everything is *of* God in the sense that it is his possession. God is not simply the owner of the gospel or the world. He owns everything in the world. The cattle on a thousand hills are his, and to that we add sheep, donkeys, camels, automobiles, homes, and the whole of creation. This is our Father's world.

Beyond this obvious element of God's ownership of all things, we also see that he is the *source* of everything. The first affirmation about God in Scripture is that he is the source of the universe: "In the beginning God created the heavens and the earth" (Gen. 1:1). In the New Testament John's Gospel begins this way: "In the beginning was the Word, and the Word was with God, and the Word was God. He was in the beginning with God. All things were made through Him, and without Him nothing was made that was made. In Him was life, and the life was the light of men" (1:1–4). In the same chapter John introduces the *Logos*, the second person of the Trinity, as the creative agent of the universe: "He was in the world, and the world was made through Him, and the world did not know Him" (v. 10).

Paul expands the cosmic work of Jesus in his letter to the Colossians, an epistle rich in affirmations of the dignity and glory of Christ:

He is the image of the invisible God, the firstborn over all creation. For *by* Him all things were created that are in heaven and that are on earth, visible and invisible, whether thrones or dominions or principalities or powers. All things were created through Him and for Him. And He is before all things, and in Him all things consist. (1:15–17)

The passages in John and in Colossians, which amplify what the apostle says so briefly in Romans 11, are staggering in their assertions about the function of Christ as the cosmic substance, creator, and author of all things, for whom all things are made, and in whom all things consist. The New Testament speaks of at least three dimensions of human experience of which God is the source.

The Source of Truth

First, God is the source of all truth. We live in a time when theories of relativism have become widely accepted. Francis Schaeffer, in the latter days of his life, spoke about the death of true truth. He meant that objective truth has been undermined. It began with the influence of existential philosophy and continued later with pluralism and relativism. When Schaeffer spoke about true truth, he meant truth that goes beyond the preferences of individuals. Søren Kierkegaard used to teach that truth is subjectivity, which, in the twentieth century, came to mean that truth is, like beauty, in the eye of the beholder. Something can be true for you but not true for me.

"Do you believe in God?" a young lady once asked me.

"Yes, I do," I replied.

"Do you find it meaningful to believe in God?"

I said, "Yes, I do."

"Do you pray to God?"

"Yes."

"Do you sing hymns of praise to God?"

"Yes, I do."

"Is that meaningful to your existence?"

"Yes."

She said, "God is true for you, but I do not believe in God. I do not pray to God. I do not sing praises to God. So, for me, there is no God."

I said, "We are not talking about the same thing. If God does not exist, then my faith and prayers and devotion and singing do not have the power to conjure him up. Conversely, if this God of whom I am speaking does exist, then your unbelief, disinterest, and perhaps even hostility toward him do not have the power to destroy him. I am talking about objective truth, the nature of reality."

If we were to do a word study of the biblical concept of truth, *alētheia*, we would find in the theological dictionary of the New Testament, for example, a lengthy entry about it. We would see that the biblical concept of truth is defined as that which describes real states of affair. In the eighteenth century when philosophers were very much concerned about the science of epistemology, of how we know anything, they wrestled at great length with the question that Pontius Pilate asked of Jesus. During Jesus' trial Pilate asked him, "What is truth?" (John 18:38). In reading the printed Word we do not get to see facial expressions or hear inflections of tones of voice. Was Pilate being cynical, or was he caught in a pensive moment of meditation after being confronted by Jesus? I do not know, but it is a question that philosophers through the ages have tried to answer. The quest came to a heightened intensity in the eighteenth century.

During the eighteenth century, John Locke became famous for introducing the correspondence theory of truth, which states, quite simply, that truth is what corresponds to reality. Locke was very close to the New Testament definition of truth as that which describes real states of affair as distinguished from fantasy, mirage, or imagination. However, no sooner had Locke laid the groundwork for the definition of the correspondence of truth than the next generation of philosophers began to talk about the way in which our individual perceptions determine our understanding of truth. So this question was raised: if truth is that which corresponds to reality, what if my perception of reality is different from yours?

The Christian response is this: truth is that which corresponds to reality as perceived by God. Only God has a comprehensive knowledge of all reality. God knows reality in its absolute fullness. There is no nuance or microscopic, subatomic particle of the universe unknown to the mind of God. What he knows, he knows perfectly, eternally, and exhaustively. The one who knows all things without error is the source of all truth.

That is why the battle for the Bible is so vital and why Christianity was founded upon the conviction that the Bible gives to us not the individual existential subjective insights of mortals, but the self-disclosure of truth that comes to us from the very fountainhead and source of all truth. God is the standard of all truth, which is what makes truth so sacred. When we are willing to play with the truth, to allow truth to be slain in the streets in order to maintain relationships, we are striking a blow against the very nature and character of God. No possession we have is more precious, more valuable, and more powerful than truth.

In his diatribe against Martin Luther, Desiderius Erasmus said, "On matters of this kind of ultimate theological truth, I prefer to suspend judgment. I prefer not to make assertions." When Luther was confronted by Satan, he threw an inkwell at him, and he reached for the same inkwell to throw against Erasmus, essentially saying, "You prefer not to make assertions? You call yourself a Christian? Do you not know that making assertions is at the very heart of the Christian faith? *Spiritus sanctus non et skepitus*—the Holy Spirit is not a skeptic. The things he has revealed in his Word are more certain than life itself." Luther knew the source of truth and how precious it is.

The Source of Goodness

Not only is God the source of truth, but he is also the source of goodness. The ultimate norm for ethics and righteousness is the character of God himself. Frequently we make distinctions between positive law and natural law or even biblical law. The primary meaning of the term *natural law* is laws that can be extrapolated from a study of nature or science. Theology also speaks of natural law as that which proceeds ultimately from the nature of God. How can we discern between good and evil? We look to the law of God to reveal to us the source of good and evil.

God's law is not some arbitrary legislation that God decided to impose on his creatures; rather, God's law flows from his very being. Theologians make a distinction between the internal and the external righteousness of God. External righteousness refers to what God does in his management of the universe. It refers to God's behavior in which there is no shadow of turning (James 1:17). His works are altogether righteous. God's external righteousness flows from his eternal being. God does what is right because he is the source of all righteousness, and when God behaves in a righteous way, he is simply working out his own being, which is altogether righteous. He is the source and standard of all that is good.

The Source of Beauty

God is also the source of beauty. Our church once produced a brochure that expressed our hopes for a building campaign, and the theme for the project was "for beauty and for holiness." St. Andrew's did not invent that theme; it is the theme God gave to the people of Israel when he commanded that they build a house for him. Anything we undertake must be driven by those twin concerns—God's glory and God's holiness.

We are told in the Old Testament to worship the Lord in the beauty of holiness (1 Chron. 16:29). If you look up every Old Testament passage that refers to beauty, you will see that God is not only the wellspring of the true and the good but also of the beautiful. Everything beautiful comes from him and points back to him. Pagans compose magnificent music or art, and their work points to the author of everything beautiful even though they have no affection for God in their hearts. There is nothing virtuous in the ugly.

All Things through Him

The next preposition is *through*: "For of Him and *through* Him are all things." If everyone believed that one phrase, the Arminian-Calvinistic debate would end forever because this text refers to the means by which God governs and orders his universe. The word *through* has to do with means, the instrument, by which things come to pass. Paul is simply reiterating here what he taught in Romans 8, that God in his providence exercises his sovereignty over, in, and through all things. All things that come to pass in this world ultimately come about through the sovereign agency of God himself. We need to embrace this because the great joy of the Christian is to know that all things are in God's hand and are being used by him for his purposes, regardless of the causal means he uses to bring about whatsoever he pleases. There are no accidents in a universe governed by God, in an ultimate sense. If God exists, sovereignty is an essential attribute of his very deity. If there were one maverick molecule in this universe running loose outside the scope of God's sovereign control, God would not be sovereign, and if he were not sovereign, he would not be God.

All Things to Him

The third preposition is *to*: "For of Him and through Him and *to* Him are all things." The word *to* indicates the purpose toward which everything is moving. Where is everything going? What is the goal of the universe? What is the ultimate purpose of all history? In a word, the answer is God. He is the alpha and the omega, the beginning and the end. He is the source. All things are moving in history and in the universe to fulfill the purpose of God.

We observe many things that cause us to ask, "How can that possibly fit in with the purposes of God?" We see much evil and corruption, and we say that God cannot possibly have anything to do with it, but over against all that is wicked stands a mighty God who orders all things together for his glory. One theologian said this last verse of Romans 11 is Paul's version of the *non nobis Domine*— "Not unto us, O LORD, not unto us, but to Your name give glory" (Ps. 115:1). Your destiny has been appointed by God from the foundation of the world for his glory. The destiny of nations, history, and planets and the orbiting of the heavenly bodies have been created, designed, and ordained by God to display his glory. That is why the psalmist looked at the stars and was overcome with awe: "The heavens declare the glory of God; and the firmament shows His handiwork" (Ps. 19:1).

To Whom Be Glory

There is also a pronoun, *whom*, in Paul's summary verse: "to *whom* be glory forever. Amen." The Hebrew word for glory, *kavod*, literally means "weightiness." It refers to God's significance or value. God's glory is his singular transcendent dignity, which no creature can possess in similar magnitude. God's glory is in a class by itself. In the Bible we see God manifesting his glory through the Shekinah cloud. The Shekinah cloud is so excellent in its brilliance that human beings must shield their eyes from it lest they go blind. That is the outward manifestation of the eternal inward dignity of God.

Revelation 21 and 22 describe the holy city coming down out of heaven. Strangely, it is described as a place where the sun does not shine. There are no candles nor moon nor artificial source of light. You would think that such a place would be bathed in perpetual darkness, but the author of Revelation tells us there is no need of sun or artificial light in heaven because the glory of God and the radiance of his Son bathe the holy city in light perpetually. The glow from the face of God—the manifestation of his glory—illuminates every inch of the kingdom of heaven. The light of the glory of God is never extinguished, which is why the apostle says ". . . to whom be glory forever." The glory of God began in eternity and will continue for eternity.

When we come into God's presence to worship him, the only appropriate response is reverence, awe, humility, and submission. The contemporary church all too often displays a cavalier approach to worship. Many have no idea about the one they are dealing with, the one for whom the angels themselves have to cover their eyes when they sing of his glory. Our glory comes and goes but the glory of God endures forever.

46

HOLY SACRIFICES

Romans 12:1–2

I beseech you therefore, brethren, by the mercies of God, that you present your bodies a living sacrifice, holy, acceptable to God, which is your reasonable service. And do not be conformed to this world, but be transformed by the renewing of your mind, that you may prove what is that good and acceptable and perfect will of God.

In the English language there is a variety of word forms—nouns, verbs, adverbs, adjectives, and prepositions—but there is also an abundance of symbols such as the plus sign and the minus sign. One symbol with which you may not be familiar contains three dots in the form of a triangle. There is a dot at the top and another on either side. The triangle is the symbol for the word *ergō* or *therefore*. The symbol usually indicates the conclusion to an argument that has just been set forth; it indicates the *therefore*. As I have said before, any time we see the word *therefore* in Scripture our attention ought to perk up because we are coming to the sum of the matter.

As we come now to the beginning of Romans 12 we are faced immediately with a question. Concerning Paul's words, **I beseech you therefore, brethren** (v. 1a), does the *therefore* refer to the conclusion of Paul's doxology in chapter 11? That might be the case, but the majority of Pauline scholars would argue that the *therefore* is intended to follow the entire unfolding of

Paul's argument for the gospel that began in chapter 1. At the beginning of Romans 12, Paul makes a clear transition from the doctrinal portion of the epistle to the application portion. In light of all he has unfolded about the things of God, there is a practical conclusion that Paul wants his readers to reach. He is not simply making a logical argument, although he is certainly doing that; he is making an apostolic plea. Now that his readers have been shown the true gospel—justification, sanctification, the doctrines of grace in election, perseverance, and the sweetness of God's providential care—Paul wants his readers to consider its implications and applications.

Paul pleads with the brethren **by the mercies of God** (v. 1b). Paul makes his plea in light of God's tender mercies, which he has just finished expounding in chapter 11, and those mercies are these: (1) we are justified by faith; (2) our sins are forgiven through the atonement of Christ; (3) God works all things together for our good; and (4) God calls people to himself. Everything Paul has expounded throughout the doctrinal section of the epistle, chapters 1–11, points back to God's mercy. The mercies of God lead us to the "therefore."

A Thank Offering

The first thing Paul asks his readers, by way of practical application, is to bring a thank offering to God: **present your bodies a living sacrifice, holy, acceptable to God, which is your reasonable service** (v. 1c). His request hearkens back to the Old Testament system of worship, which was established on the basis of sacrifice. The first sacrifice propagated by God in the Old Testament was the worship that he enjoined upon Adam and Eve and their sons. The sons came with their produce or livestock and offered a sacrifice on the altar. Such sacrifices were the very definition of early worship. The liturgical structure of the tabernacle and the temple in the Old Testament expanded on that mode of worship. Bulls, goats, lambs, turtledoves, and cereal offerings were brought into the sanctuary and sacrificed.

We think of *sacrifice* as the giving away of something of extreme value. There is an element of that in biblical sacrifice, but the primary point is not that we should lose something but that we should express something. The whole principle of giving to God is an expression of worship.

During Sunday morning worship services we hear, "Let us now worship God with the giving of our tithes and offerings." When that request comes, we are not asked to give something back to God from a sense of duty. We are asked to make an offering as an act of worship. Such giving is one way we show our submission to the transcendent majesty of God. He is worthy of our praise, devotion, substance, and time—everything we have.

In the Old Testament, the animal sacrifices had to be killed before they could be offered. The lamb or goat or bull was slain, and its blood was poured on the altar. In stark contrast to that, in light of the gospel, we are to offer ourselves as living sacrifices—not our animals, vegetables, or cereal, but our bodies. We tend to think of worship as spiritual rather than physical, so we might wonder why Paul asks us to present our bodies rather than our souls. Actually, Paul is writing about the entire person. God wants us to give ourselves. Christ, in the ultimate sense, gave *himself*, not his *self*. He gave himself for us, and we are to respond by giving ourselves to him. Of course, we cannot give ourselves to Christ the way that he gave himself for us. He gave himself to redeem us; we give ourselves to thank and serve him.

When are we to give ourselves to God as living sacrifices? We are to do so the minute we come to Christ. The sacrifice is not something offered on the Day of Atonement or on Sunday morning; it is an offering of our whole self for our whole life. It is easy to see but hard to do. Our spiritual growth is weak, so we hold back. We want to keep for ourselves a part of ourselves. I used to tell my seminary students: "You may think you are studying for a glamorous enterprise in which you are going to make a difference in people's lives. I want you to know before you go into a church and get ordained that it is a throw-away life. When you enter into the service of Jesus Christ, you are throwing your life away. By the world's standards, you are wasting your life."

My father died shortly before I made the decision to go to seminary and become a minister. He had been the president of a large corporate bankruptcy firm in the city of Pittsburgh, and working with him were a number of attorneys. The name of that company was R. C. Sproul & Sons. It was begun by my grandfather, whose name was R. C. Sproul, and it was continued by my father, R. C. Sproul Jr. I was the heir to that prosperous company. I had only to get my CPA license in order to step into the presidency. When I expressed my plans to go into the ministry, I was descended upon by a battery of attorneys with one message: "Are you out of your mind? You are being handed a company that guarantees you prosperity, and you want to go into the ministry?" They spoke to me with great passion, but I was not tempted. They did not understand that I was a sinner who had experienced the mercies of God, and that same God had called me to serve him.

It is a throwaway life, and not only for pastors but for every Christian. Our lives are to be given over, body and soul, to the service of God. To be a Christian is to present ourselves as living sacrifices.

A Holy Sacrifice

Our sacrifice is to be living, and it is to be holy. The animals offered to God in the Old Testament economy were required to be the firstfruits of the flock, the animals without blemish, but Christ has already taken our sin. Therefore, when we give ourselves as living sacrifices to God, he wants that sacrifice sanctified or consecrated. In the words of the old hymn, "Give of your best to the Master." We are to give the most sanctified portion of our lives as an act of praise to God.

Paul is giving us a tough job. Remember that he starts out begging: "I beseech you . . ." We can sense the way in which the Old Testament economy is informing Paul's understanding of the metaphor of sacrifice. Not all the offerings that God received from his people in the Old Testament delighted him. Offerings were brought to the Lord while the people were living in hypocrisy, offering him false worship. Through the voice of the prophets God would say to his people, "I hate, I despise your feast days, and I do not savor your sacred assemblies" (Amos 5:21).

We often overlook the type of sacrifice God requires of us. We think any act of religion or spiritual sacrifice will necessarily be delightful to God. It will not. God requires that we offer ourselves in a way that is acceptable to him. We are to offer ourselves in humility and repentance so that the sacrifice of our praise will provide a sweet aroma.

Reasonable Service

Paul grounds his appeal for living, holy sacrifices: it is our "reasonable service." Other translations read, ". . . which is your spiritual worship." The apostle actually says, "logical worship." What could be more logical or reasonable than offering our whole selves to God in thanksgiving, praise, worship, and adoration with the saints behind the altar? We sing, "Worthy is the Lamb who was slain"; that is our logical response. If we understand the gospel, then indifference and apathy are irrational responses. The worship we are to offer God is not a mindless worship.

Many Christians today do not want to think. They do not want to grapple with the content of the Word of God. They want their religion to be one of feeling. "God calls us to have a childlike faith," they say. They are right about that, but it is not to be a childish faith. We are to be childlike in our morality and in our trust; we are not to be hardened professionals in sin. We are to be children in one sense, but we are called to be adults in our understanding. The Word of God repeatedly rebukes those who are satisfied with a diet of milk and pabulum in their Christian life. We are called to go for the meat of the gospel. We are called to grow up to the fullness of maturity in Jesus Christ. Our reasonable worship is one that, as we will see very soon in the text, involves the mind in an engaging way.

I host a daily radio program called "Renewing Your Mind." The title is based on Paul's words in verse 2: **Do not be conformed to this world, but be transformed by the renewing of your mind** (v. 2a). A contrast is presented in Romans 12:1–2 between what we are not to do and what we are to do. Both have to do with morphology, the study of forms. In English the root words for *form* can either describe shape or indicate style. Paul is contrasting conformity with transformation; we are to flee from one to the other. To present our bodies as living sacrifices entails not being conformed to the world.

Christian Nonconformity

The single greatest social pressure a teenager faces is conformity. Those who march to the beat of a different drummer are considered dorks or nerds or fools. Similarly, what saps the strength of Christian witness in our day is the Christian community's conformity to the world. We do not want to be seen as foolish any more than a teenager does. Yet that is exactly what we are called to be—fools for Christ. The things we cherish and follow are the things the world considers foolish and rubbish. Paul says a Christian is to be a nonconformist.

I find myself scared by polls about the behavior of so-called Christians. Today it seems there is no discernable difference between the professing, born-again Christian and the secularist when it comes to divorce, abortion, or sexual immorality. We are still adolescents. We watch what the world is doing, and we want to win its approval. We do not want to be social pariahs, so we allow the standards and customs of our culture to dictate our behavior instead of the Word of God. The apostle is reduced to pleading because he understands our frames. He knows the tremendous pull upon our psyches to conform to the world.

Throughout history there have been movements of Christian nonconformity. I went to college in a town where the largest indigenous population was Amish, and we had to be careful while driving at night because the Amish were hard to see in their poorly lit, horse-pulled buggies. It seemed that every month there was a terrible collision between an Amish buggy and a car. The Amish use white sheets for curtains. They have hooks and eyes on their denim clothing. They do not believe in the use of buttons or electricity. They have none of the modern amenities. They live that way because they are trying to obey this text. If the world does some particular thing, the Amish do not, which shows what happens when nonconformity degenerates into nonconformity for nonconformity's sake.

Various Christian groups say that the essence of Christian piety is refraining from movies, lipstick, and dancing. They reduce the spiritual matter of eternity to trivial things. The kingdom of God, however, is not about avoiding lipstick, card games, movies, or dancing. It is about obeying the law of God and living lives of godly spiritual obedience.

Paul's exhortation not to be conformed to the world is not solely negative. The Latin translation of "world" here is, ironically, the word *seculum*, not the word *mundus*, another Latin word for *world*. *Mundus* refers to the spatial world, its geographical location. The word *seculum* refers to this age, the present time. Contemporary secularism asserts that the time, or *seculum*, on this planet is the only time there is; there is the *hic et nunc*, the here and now, and nothing more. There is no eternity. There is no life beyond the grave. This explains why our young people are bombarded with advertisements like "You only go around once," "Grab all you can get," and "Go for the gusto now." The Scriptures refute that emphatically. We are not secularists. We live in the sphere of the world, but we do not live according to the precepts and principles of this passing age. We are to live our lives in the light of eternity and the truth that comes to us from above.

Transformed

The Greek word Paul uses in verse 2 for "transformed" is *metamorphosis*. We use that word to describe the transition a caterpillar undergoes in order to become a butterfly. The word indicates a radical change of form. Therefore, the goal of the Christian life is not merely nonconformity, which is the easy part, but transformation. The prefix *trans-* added to the word *formed* means "above and beyond the forms of this world." Living as Christians means we do not live by the drumbeat of this world but by a higher calling—the calling of God—and when we do that, the form of our life changes. We are not conformed to this dying age, but our lives are transformed by the power of God.

This transformation happens through mind renewal. If we want a transformed life, the most important thing is to get a new mind. The beginning of the Christian life is rooted in repentance. The Greek word for repentance is *metanoia*, which means "a change of mind." Prior to our initial repentance, we thought according to the precepts of this world. We thought just like our secular neighbors, who do everything in their power to bury their sin in their subconscious, but when the Holy Spirit awakened us to our absolute need for a Savior and we rushed to the cross, our minds and the direction of our lives were changed. The mind is central, because transformation comes from a renewed mind.

While a changed mind is a *necessary* condition for transformation, however, it is not a *sufficient* condition. People can study the Word of God and get a perfect score on every theological examination without that knowledge ever getting into the heart. No one is transformed apart from heart change. God has designed us in such a way that the avenue to the heart is through the mind. The book of Romans was given for our understanding, so that we would begin to think as Jesus thinks and begin to approve what he approves and despise what he despises. That is how our lives are changed. When we begin to think as Christians, we get a new mind. From that new mind our heart is changed, and when the heart is changed, our life is changed. That is how we become transformed people.

God's Will for Your Life

Transformation happens for this purpose: **that you may prove what is that good and acceptable and perfect will of God** (v. 2b). Many years before "Renewing Your Mind" was on the radio, Ligonier produced a five-minute radio program called "Ask R. C." People contacted the program with questions and asked for theological comments and biblical references. The primary question we were asked was this: "How can I know the will of God for my life?" The answer is found not from a Ouija board or from signs or from fleeces—it is found by the renewing of the mind through feeding on the Word of God. A renewed mind begins to think God's thoughts after him. When our minds are informed by the Word of God, we are able to certify, prove, and recognize what is that good, acceptable, and complete will of God.

When people ask me, "What's the will of God for my life?" I reply, "Are you asking me if you should be a lawyer or a baker, or whether you should marry Jane or Virginia?" We will address this subject more in our next study; here I tell you simply what the Bible says about it: "This is the will of God, your sanctification" (1 Thess. 4:3). It doesn't matter what our job is or whom we marry or what city we live in. If we are not growing in sanctification, seeking God's will about such things is worthless. God's will for each of us is that we grow into spiritual maturity, that our lives become more fully set apart and consecrated by the Holy Spirit, and that our minds are changed. After that we will be able to tell what is pleasing to God. Then we will be able to know what he wants us to do—that good and acceptable and perfect will of God.

47

COMMUNION OF THE SAINTS

Romans 12:3–8

For I say, through the grace given to me, to everyone who is among you, not to think of himself more highly than he ought to think, but to think soberly, as God has dealt to each one a measure of faith. For as we have many members in one body, but all the members do not have the same function, so we, being many, are one body in Christ, and individually members of one another. Having then gifts differing according to the grace that is given to us, let us use them: if prophecy, let us prophesy in proportion to our faith; or ministry, let us use it in our ministering; he who teaches, in teaching; he who exhorts, in exhortation; he who gives, with liberality; he who leads, with diligence; he who shows mercy, with cheerfulness.

While I was in grade school my English class was asked to write a one-page descriptive essay. I wrote mine and turned it in. The next day, the teacher stood before the class and said, "Before I return this assignment to you I want to take a moment to read one of them to the class." To my utter astonishment, she read my essay. Afterward she walked to the bulletin board and affixed it there with a thumbtack, saying, "This deserves to be here because it is a work of art." After class I walked up to the bulletin board to admire my tremendous achievement. She had written on the top of the page "*A+*," and on the bottom she had written, "R. C., don't ever let anybody tell you that you can't write." I took that woman's compliment to heart. A compliment is different from flattery. A compliment is something we can believe because it comes to us from somebody we regard with a certain authority. My English teacher's generous compliment became a part of my life's story.

Sober Esteem

We live in a culture obsessed with self-esteem. Developing a good self-image has become almost cultic. Some years ago an international test in mathematics was administered to children from ten nations, including the United States. The test had two parts. The first pertained to mathematical competency, and the second pertained to feelings of self-esteem with respect to the students' performance. Two ironies stood out. First, the Korean students were last in their estimation of their performance but first in actual competency. The reason is that along with the rigorous pursuit of academic excellence Korean students are taught principles of humility. Conversely, and to our national shame, the American children scored last in mathematical competency but first in self-esteem. The American students had a high view of their competency in spite of their miserable performance. Self-esteem, as important as it is (we are not to brutalize people by tearing them apart with unnecessary criticisms and insults) can be damaging if we provide people with a higher opinion of themselves than they should have.

What does all that have to do with Romans? Paul writes, **For I say, through the grace given to me** (v. 3a). Paul is writing to them as one gifted and called by God, through no merit of his own, to the position of apostle. Despite his calling, he considered himself the chief of sinners (1 Tim. 1:15). It is through the grace given to him that Paul writes an admonition **to everyone who is among you, not to think of himself more highly than he ought to think, but to think soberly** (v. 3b). Unfortunately, the English juxtaposes Paul's words "to think . . . more highly" with "to think soberly." The play on words present in the Greek cannot be translated into English. The Greek term for "to think soberly" is the same term used for "to think" but with a different prefix added to it. Therefore, Paul is not talking about an intellectual enterprise or analysis of our skills or ability or status; he is connecting the cognitive aspect, thinking, to the aspect of affection. He is not writing about estimation so much as about esteem. Simply, Paul is saying that we should not esteem ourselves too highly but rather to think soberly and carefully about ourselves.

When the apostle calls us to a sober self-evaluation, particularly with respect to our abilities, he puts on us a tremendous responsibility. People come to me asking, "How do I know if I am called to the ministry?" "How do I know if I should accept the office of deacon in the church?" "How do I know if I am qualified to be an elder?" We must remember that the church is the context in which Paul is giving this practical instruction. To those who are considering a vocation in the ministry I say, "Before you think about the glory and drama of the ministry, you need to sit down and make a sober analysis of your gifts." I ask them to consider whether they really have what it takes to be a minister or a deacon or an elder or any other calling they might consider pursuing.

One good thing we get from the secular world is psychological testing. There are profiles designed to help us see if we have the necessary equipment to enter into a certain vocation. I have seen in the course of seminary teaching many students with stars in their eyes about going into the ministry, but they lack the necessary gifts for the service of God in this particular vocation. Someone perhaps has flattered them or they have flattered themselves; along the way the evaluation was not a sober one. When that happens, people are doomed to failure, frustration, disappointment, discouragement, and sometimes lifelong depression. Each year in the United States sixteen thousand clergy demit the ministry, some for moral reasons but most because they deem their job to be a bad fit for their abilities. That is a dreadful experience for people, and it starts because they were intoxicated rather than sober in their self-esteem.

The closest follow-up to the instruction Paul gives here is found in his first letter to the Corinthians. The Corinthian community was torn apart with strife because everybody was elevating their gifts and offices above everyone else's. There was an ongoing battle for power and status in that church. If that can happen in a first-century church, it can certainly happen in our churches today. To both the Corinthians and the Romans Paul uses one of his favorite metaphors for the church—a body. A body is made up of many parts, and each part needs the help of the other. To the Corinthians Paul writes, "If the ear should say, 'Because I am not an eye, I am not of the body,' is it therefore not of the body?" (1 Cor. 12:16). Through unity in diversity, grace is given to everybody in the church, and everybody in the church has a role to play. We are not to despise the roles that other people play, nor are we to elevate our roles as the most important for the life of the church.

One Body

Here is how Paul spells it out to the Romans: they are not to think of them-selves more highly than they ought but to think soberly, **as God has dealt to each one a measure of faith** (v. 3c). Paul wrote, "For by one Spirit we were all baptized into one body" (1 Cor. 12:13).

Persistent in the church today is the troubling idea that some believers are gifted by the Holy Spirit while others are not. In addition to the Spirit's work of regeneration in the life of the Christian, the Spirit also distributes gifts or abilities to every Christian. The church is to help believers find their particular gifts so that all work together for the good of the church.

For as we have many members in one body, but all the mem-bers do not have the same function, so we, being many, are one body in Christ, and individually members of one another (vv. 4–5). Some ten years ago I was approached about starting a church and becoming the pastor of it. I already had a full-time job so I could not take on a full-time pastorate, but the request was persistent, so I gave it more thought. I was aware that something had been missing in my ministry, and that was a pulpit. After much discussion, prayer, consideration, and, I hope, a sober analysis of my limitations, I agreed. That is how St. Andrew's was born. Since then I have spent much time at conferences with pastors from all over the country, and now that I am a pastor I have an ability to hear their cries in a way I could not before. Pastors are expected to be jacks of all trades and masters of none. They are expected to be administrators, statesmen, and psychological counselors. They are expected to be biblical experts, theologians, preachers, and teachers.

We need a reformation in the church in terms of what is expected from ministers. The primary task of the minister is the preaching of the Word of God, the feeding of the flock. I tell young pastors that 90 percent of their time should be taken up with preaching and teaching. God has not called them to be psychological counselors or brilliant administrators. He has called them to preach the Word and feed the sheep. The pastor should be free to spend his time preaching and teaching, because what Christians need above all is to be nurtured in the Word of God.

Gifted for Service

Everyone has a task: **Having then gifts differing according to the grace that is given to us, let us use them** (v. 6a). God has given us gifts, and he has not given them to be wasted or set on a shelf or buried in the ground. God expects us to use them. Those with the gift of teaching should teach. Those gifted to preach must preach. Anyone with the gift of evangelism is called to evangelize.

Prophecy

Paul adds to the gifts list: **if prophecy, let us prophesy in proportion to our faith** (v. 6b). Some believe the gift of prophecy refers to the immediate, supernatural, Spirit-given ability to interpret tongues and to make predictions for the future, just as prophets in the Old Testament did, and this is a struggle for those who believe that the supernatural gifts of the apostolic age ceased with the death of the last apostle. I believe that the gift of apostleship was intended for the first century only and did not pass on to the next generation. In one sense the gift of prophecy Paul is describing here applies only to the immediate time of the apostolic age, but there are other problems involved.

In the Old Testament the supreme agents of revelation were the prophets. The New Testament counterpart to the Old Testament prophet is not the New Testament prophet; it is the New Testament apostle. There is parity between the Old Testament prophet and the New Testament apostle—both are authoritative agents of revelation—but here Paul distinguishes between the gift of prophecy and the gift of apostleship. One way that scholars deal with this is to make a distinction between the terms *Prophet* and *prophet* and *Apostle* and *apostle*. The term *Apostle*, with a capital *A*, refers to those selected by Christ and endowed with his authority, specific individuals such as Peter, Paul, and John. At the same time all the church was involved in the apostolic mission of spreading the Word of God to all nations. In that sense, every church member was an *apostle* (lowercase *a*). The same thing can be said about the office of prophet.

In New Testament terms the prophet functioned as an interpreter of the Word of God. We like to think of the Old Testament prophets as those who predicted the future, what we call foretelling, yet their primary task was not predicting the future; it was forthtelling, communicating the word of God to the people. Old Testament prophets were God's prosecuting attorneys against a covenant community that had broken its vows. The Old Testament prophets were called upon to interpret God's word to the people. In like manner, the New Testament prophet was one gifted in interpreting or exposing the word of God. In contemporary terms, such a prophet is a preacher. Today it is the preacher who fulfills the task of interpreting and exposing the Word of God. What continues to this day from the role of the first-century prophet is interpreting the Word of God and expounding it to the people. Those are the primary tasks of the preacher.

Therefore, anyone whose vocation is that of preacher must start preaching. Preachers are not to enter the pulpit on Sunday morning with the latest analysis of the culture or with an agenda for entertainment, trying to turn the church into an ecclesiastical Starbucks. Preachers are to interpret the Word of God and expound it to the people. Paul's last injunction to Timothy was this: "Preach the word! Be ready in season and out of season" (2 Tim. 4:2). Preachers have the awesome responsibility of preaching the Word of God.

Ministry

If our gift is **ministry, let us use it in our ministering** (v. 7a). In view here principally is the ministry of the deacons, those who serve by taking care of the orphans, the widows, and the poor. Certain people with a servant's heart have been gifted by God to be deacons. It is a marvelous gift for the church. No church can be a healthy one without a heavy commitment to service—taking care of the oppressed, the poor, and the lonely. Ministry is not just preaching the Word of God. Deacons were appointed to serve the needs of the people so that the apostles could preach without being encumbered with other tasks, but not all the deacons were content with being deacons. They sought to establish policy and rule the community; they wanted a higher status than that of servant.

King Uzziah came to the throne in Jerusalem when he was sixteen years old, and he reigned for fifty-two years (see 2 Kings 15:1–7; 2 Chronicles 26). His monarchy, for the most part, was marvelous because he did what was right in the sight of the Lord, but in his later years his status went to his head. He became dissatisfied with being the king. He wanted to be the priest too, so he went into the temple and tried to offer the sacrifices. The priests were horrified, and when they tried to stop him Uzziah went into a wild rage. At that moment God struck Uzziah with leprosy. He died alone, cut off from the temple and the royal house in shame and disgrace. Uzziah was discontented with the office that God had given him.

The same thing happens in every church in every age in every part of the world, but we are not to let it happen. We are to identify our gifts and exercise them. We are not to be jealous of others' gifts, and we are not to elevate our gifts over the gifts of others. During my forty-plus years of ministry, I have seen that happen repeatedly. People get passionate about the gift they have received and begin to think that others' gifts do not matter.

I have heard some gifted with evangelism say they do not understand how anyone not doing evangelism can actually be a Christian. They question the resources invested in church education. What matters is winning souls, they say, not learning doctrine. In like manner I have seen those whom God has gifted with a heart of compassion for the poor move to the inner city and invest their lives there. If God gives somebody the gift of teaching and the zeal for learning and communicating truth and doctrine, they must fight the tendency to question why others do not seem to care as much about it. What good is evangelism if we do not teach those who come to the faith? We fear they will remain spiritual infants. Teachers think that way from time to time; it is human nature. The eye wants to say to the ear, "I do not need you," but ears do not help us see anything more clearly than we already see. The ear does not want to see; it wants to hear, so it says, "Who needs the eye?" How foolish.

Generosity

Everybody has an obligation to give, but some really have the gift for it, and if so, this is how they must use it: **he who gives, with liberality** (v. 8). There are people who not only give but do so generously. They give beyond what is required. Paul said elsewhere that God loves a cheerful giver (2 Cor. 9:7). Nobody wants to get a gift from a sourpuss who cannot stand to be separated from his money. God does not want such gifts.

My father was the most generous person I have ever known. He was relatively affluent before the years of debilitating illness took it away. Before his illness, when he saw somebody in need he would reach into his pocket and hand over not just a quarter or a dollar; he would give lavishly. I watched that as a boy; I never saw in him a selfish spirit. I saw a man who loved to use what God had given him for the sake of the kingdom and for the sake of his neighbor. I realize now that he had a gift, one that not everybody has. But it is a wonderful gift, and it is why churches are able to accomplish what they do.

Leadership

Leadership is another gift to exercise: **he who leads, with diligence** (v. 8). I once traveled to Germany with a group to tour the sites of the Reformation. One day we went to examine the spot where the Diet of Worms had been assembled. We were given a lunch break and told to return afterward to where the buses were parked. We split up in different directions, and the group I joined had lunch near one of the town squares there. After lunch

I could not remember how to get back to the bus, but a girl in our group said she knew the way back. We all got in line behind her, and she started marching with great confidence toward the bus. I did not recognize anything that looked familiar, so I asked her, "Are you sure this is the right way to the bus?" She said, "Yes, R. C., I am sure." Finally, she stopped and said, "I am always sure but seldom right." She had not done due diligence; she should have spent some time with a map. If a gifted leader is going to be followed, he or she had better know the way to go.

Mercy

The gift of mercy is to be shown this way: **he who shows mercy, with cheerfulness** (v. 8). We receive God's mercy from a heart glad to give it. To be gifted in mercy is a wonderful thing, and it is as much needed among the people of God as the preaching of the Word. Scripture tells us that love covers a multitude of sins (1 Pet. 4:8). There are disagreeable people in every congregation who make big issues of minor matters. They have no sense of charity or mercy—no sense of grace. We exist by grace. We cannot do anything apart from the tender mercy of God. Mercy is to be dispensed with cheerfulness.

Paul is mapping out for us the communion of saints. The word *communion* comes from the prefix *com-*, which means "union" or "with oneness." In order for a communion of saints, there first has to be a plurality. If we are Christians, we are supernaturally in Christ, and if we are in Christ, Christ is in us; however, the relationship we enjoy with Jesus is not simply a unilateral relationship. We have a supernatural bond, a union among ourselves, that flows from Christ. We are to like one another for Christ's sake, because we are in him and we are with each other forever. That is the communion of saints, warts and all.

48

BROTHERLY LOVE

Romans 12:9–15

Let love be without hypocrisy. Abhor what is evil. Cling to what is good. Be kindly affectionate to one another with brotherly love, in honor giving preference to one another; not lagging in diligence, fervent in spirit, serving the Lord; rejoicing in hope, patient in tribulation, continuing steadfastly in prayer; distributing to the needs of the saints, given to hospitality. Bless those who persecute you; bless and do not curse. Rejoice with those who rejoice, and weep with those who weep.

We find in the passage before us now another shift in the literary style of Paul's writing. Throughout the epistle he has given us lengthy, weighty concepts, and he has done so with long sentences and paragraphs. Here, however, Paul writes in staccato shots, giving us something almost like bullets in a PowerPoint presentation. In a terse manner Paul sets out ethical injunctions, one after another, which we are to manifest in the Christian life. Paul was not present when Jesus gave his Sermon on the Mount, but much of the information communicated by our Lord there is recapitulated in brief form here. This section of the epistle is also reminiscent of the apostle James's writings. He gave ethical injunctions in a similar manner to Paul's style here.

Love and Hate

The first injunction is not just part of a loose list of virtues; rather, it is the thematic statement for all the responsibilities that follow. Paul begins with love: **Let love be without hypocrisy** (v. 9a). We are to manifest love that is genuine, sincere, and authentic. When Paul wrote to the Corinthians, he devoted an entire chapter to the meaning of love (1 Corinthians 13). We might consider this Romans passage as a similar exposition. God expects from us authentic love, that which is not mixed with hypocrisy or false sentiment.

Paul makes immediate application with two strong statements: **Abhor what is evil. Cling to what is good** (v. 9b). We are to hate one thing and to love something else. The hatred about which Paul writes is hatred of the highest dimension. He uses one of the strongest words for hatred found anywhere in the Bible. The word implies not mild displeasure or mere dislike; Paul is commanding in the name of the Lord that we loathe evil. We are to see evil as an unveiled assault on the character of God and on his sovereignty. As we seek to grow in grace, we seek to gain the mind of Christ, which is to think like Jesus, to love what Jesus loves, and to hate what Jesus hates. Hatred is one of the strongest emotions that can inhabit the heart of a human being. Hatred is destructive and demeaning, but not when it is directed against evil.

I believe that the greatest ethical issue today is that of abortion. In recent years many have come to see terrorism as more concerning than abortion. I am baffled by that, because more people were killed on September 10 in the womb of U.S. women than were killed on 9/11 in New York City. More babies were slaughtered on September 12 than adults were killed on 9/11. If we had a camera on the womb so that CNN could show us graphic videos of what actually happens in the slaughter of unborn children, abortion would be quickly abolished, but the reality of it is covered up. If there is one thing I know about God, it is that he hates abortion. The German ethicist Helmut Thielicke indicated something unusual in his massive mid-twentieth-century work on Christian ethics. The work appeared before *Roe v. Wade*; that is, before Western civilization had embraced abortion on demand. In his book Thielicke wrote that abortion has always been considered a monolithic evil in Christian thought among both liberals and conservatives. That is clear from the very first century, in the Didache, which called abortion "murder." Abortion is an unspeakable evil that God abhors, one that the American church tolerates and winks at. That troubles me deeply, and I do not understand it.

As we are to despise what is evil, we are to cling to what is good. Paul uses intense language here. This term translated "cling" is the root of the Greek word *glue*. We are to hang on tightly to that which is good, allowing it to be cemented to our souls so that we do not drop or lose it with the next wind of cultural fantasy that comes our way.

Affection, Honor, and Diligence

Paul's next comments are addressed specifically to the fellowship of believers, the household of faith: **Be kindly affectionate to one another with brotherly love** (v. 10a). We find here the idea of *philadelphia*, brotherly love. It is love among those who share a common family. The love we have for one another in the church is to be the same kind of love we experience in our families between parents and children and between siblings. We are to imitate that kind of love—brotherly affection—in a spirit of kindness toward one another. Kindness is one of the most important virtues in the Bible. It is a fruit of the Holy Spirit. The tombstone of an honorable person might read, "He was a kind person." The deceased might have been unsuccessful by worldly standards, but a kind person is successful in the eyes of God.

In addition to affection and love, we are to live **in honor giving preference to one another** (v. 10b). There is some ambiguity in this statement, so it has been translated in various ways. The text is generally thought to be saying that we ought to prefer each other for honor. We are not to seek honor for ourselves but rather to reflect or deflect honor to others. In other words, it is a call to humility. Paul's basic thrust, however, is that believers are to be leaders in establishing the principle of honor among one another. Even if no one in the congregation is manifesting respect and honor, then we must demonstrate a spirit of humility. That is the heart of a servant, and it is to be the heart of the Christian.

My translation for the next phrase reads **not lagging in diligence** (v. 11a). An older translation reads "not slothful in business" (KJV). We are not to be lazy in business; however, Paul is not talking about commercial enterprise. The word *business* comes from the term *busy-ness*, which means we should be busy people, busy with the things of God. Jonathan Edwards gave a sermon about pressing into the kingdom of God. "From the days of John the Baptist until now the kingdom of heaven suffers violence, and the violent take it by force" (Matt. 11:12). Edwards said that those who have come to Christ have been born again and given a spirit of zeal to pursue the things of God with a sense of urgency and with hunger and passion. Therefore, it is the duty of every Christian to press into the kingdom of God, making that the main business of life. The kingdom of God cannot be a secondary interest for a true Christian. We are to be diligent and active in the things of God.

Hope, Patience, and Prayer

Paul's bullets continue: **rejoicing in hope, patient in tribulation, continuing steadfastly in prayer** (v. 12). A custom has developed in our day in which ministers or teachers are asked to sign people's Bibles. Another contemporary custom is the idea that everybody should have a life verse. The first time I tried to come up with a life verse, I chose Romans 12:12: "Rejoicing in hope, patient in tribulation, continuing steadfastly in prayer." Another translation has "be constant in prayer" (AMP).

Christianity can be reduced to three dimensions. First is the dimension of joy, which we should manifest at all times. We are called to rejoice in hope. I mentioned earlier in our studies that tribulation is inseparably related to hope, because when we are forced to suffer, the Holy Spirit uses those tribulations to work character in us and to provoke in our souls the virtue of hope. In his first epistle to the Corinthians Paul mentions the triad of virtues that are to mark the life of the Christian: "Now abide faith, hope, love, these three; but the greatest of these is love" (13:13). To make it into the top three is pretty significant, and it is interesting that the apostle elevates hope to that top drawer of virtues.

As I have said before, the biblical concept of hope differs from the common meaning of the term in our language today. We hope that certain things will come to pass, even if we doubt they will, but the biblical concept of hope has nothing to do with such uncertainty. The New Testament concept of hope has to do with absolute certainty that the promises of God for the future will come to pass. Faith looks backward, trusting in and relying on what God has done in the past, but faith also looks forward and finds its anchor for the soul in the future promises of God. That is the foundation for our joy. No matter how painful the present moment may be, we can still have joy because we know that the pain and suffering and tribulation we endure now is but for a moment. God has laid up for us such treasures in heaven that the brief moments of pain and suffering we have to endure now are not worthy to be compared to them. No matter how bad things are in this life, we can still be happy. We can still have joy because we have this hope of which we will never be ashamed.

The second dimension of the Christian life is patience. Although I had initially chosen Romans 12:12 as my life verse, I later abandoned it for a different verse because of my ongoing struggle with patience. I am impatient.

I want to get past the finish line in order to get on to something else. I have never had the quiet spirit of patience that we are supposed to have, particularly in the midst of tribulation.

Paul is writing about patience here, the virtue of forbearance, of hanging in when things are tough. We are to remember the patience of Job, who cried out in the midst of his agony, "Though he slay me, yet will I trust him" (Job 13:15). That is the kind of patience that gives perseverance and the ability to endure in the midst of difficulty.

The glue that brings those dimensions together is the third one: continuing steadfastly in prayer. The Christian life is one of prayer, but not simply prayer offered at certain hours or appointed times. There is to be an ongoing dialogue between our hearts and God all the time. We are to be always conscious of God's presence, relying on him and communicating with the Father in our thoughts.

A friend I had in seminary had to endure great suffering. In fact, his suffering led to his death while we were still in school. At that time he sought a deeper level of spiritual growth. I remember him saying to me, "R. C., I won't know that I'm really progressing in my sanctification until my dreams change. I want to dream about loving God. In my dreams I want to see myself praying rather than doing something like winning a baseball game." I have never before or since heard anyone talk about sanctification in those terms; my friend was a living, walking prayer. He wanted his communication with the Lord to be so much a part of his life that he would even dream about it.

Blessing Others

Rejoicing in hope, patient in tribulation, continuing steadfastly in prayer, **distributing to the needs of the saints, given to hospitality** (v. 13)—Paul is still explaining what it means to love without hypocrisy. We are to be those who meet the needs of our Christian brothers and sisters, and we are to be known for our hospitality. Hospitality has always been and continues to be an important virtue in the Middle East. It goes back to the Old Testament when the Jews were slaves in Egypt. They had no place to call their home. After God liberated them, they wandered for decades in the wilderness, and they longed for a place to call home. When God gave it to them, he admonished them not to forget where they had come from. They were to show hospitality to the stranger in their gates. They were to open their homes and hearts to those around them (e.g., see Ex. 22:21; 23:9; Lev. 19:34; Deut. 10:18–19; Ps. 146:9; Jer. 7:6).

Verse 14 is also reminiscent of the Sermon on the Mount: **Bless those who persecute you; bless and do not curse** (v. 14). This is not simply a call to bless those who insult us occasionally. Paul was constantly attacked by people. His entire ministry was conducted under persecution, just as his Lord's ministry had been. Paul's response to persecution was to bless his enemies, not curse them. Refraining from cursing our enemies is not too difficult, but to bless them, to pray that God would bestow upon them his favor and grace, is much harder. Doing so is tough, but it is what love means.

A tremendous text follows: **Rejoice with those who rejoice, and weep with those who weep** (v. 15). Perhaps our brother or sister gets an award that we were hoping to get. Maybe our friends' team beats our team in the Super Bowl; can we rejoice with them? Can we participate in others' joy and forget about our sense of loss? That is how the body of Christ is knit together. If one rejoices, everybody rejoices. There are no politics of envy in the kingdom of God—none. If a brother prospers beyond how we prosper, we should delight in his prosperity and blessing rather than say, "He doesn't deserve that; why should he get this wonderful advantage?"

When one of us weeps, we all should weep. That is what the body of Christ is about. When Paul came to sorrowful people, he sorrowed with them. He stood beside them in their tribulation; he wept with those who wept. When Jesus came to the home of Lazarus, Mary, and Martha, the Bible tells us that he wept (John 11:35). He knew he was going to raise Lazarus from the dead, but he wept because people around him were weeping. Jesus wept with those who weep, and we are supposed to do that too.

One of the most difficult things I have had to endure was the protracted illness of my father. It took him three years to die, and he was incapacitated the entire time. He liked to sit outside in the summertime, and I had to help him out into the lawn chair where he sat all day long. One time I vented my anger about the situation to my mother. "Mom, where are Dad's friends? When he was healthy and wealthy, we had no end of visitors in the house. I do not understand it. Where are they now?" I was angry—at God. Why did God allow that? I never once heard my dad complain that no one came to see him. My mother, always a patient woman, said to me, "Son, you have to understand something. Your dad's friends cannot stand to see him the way he is. They feel inadequate. They do not know what to say."

Young ministers tell me, "I have to learn how to do hospital calling," or "I have to go to a funeral. What should I say?" I reply, "There is no speech. It does not matter what you say. Just be there, and if they cry, then you weep with them. You do not have to have a magic word to dissolve their tears."

My mother's words failed to provide me much comfort at the time, but later I understood.

We like to distance ourselves from pain. We feel that we have enough of our own pain without having to weep with everybody else who is weeping, but doing so is love without hypocrisy. Sharing in others' joy is the same. When a young woman is about to be married, that is all she can talk about. We should share in her joy. We should share in the joy of marriages, just as we share in the sorrow of the bereaved. That is what love looks like.

49

REGARD FOR GOOD THINGS

Romans 12:16–21

Be of the same mind toward one another. Do not set your mind on high things, but associate with the humble. Do not be wise in your own opinion.

Repay no one evil for evil. Have regard for good things in the sight of all men. If it is possible, as much as depends on you, live peaceably with all men. Beloved, do not avenge yourselves, but rather give place to wrath; for it is written, "Vengeance is Mine, I will repay," says the Lord. Therefore

"If your enemy is hungry, feed him;
If he is thirsty, give him a drink;
For in so doing you will heap coals of fire on his head."

Do not be overcome by evil, but overcome evil with good.

I n our last study we began to look at a list of virtues that Paul sets forth in a series of staccato shots, and we concluded our look with his injunction in verse 15: "Rejoice with those who rejoice, and weep with those who weep."

Affection and Ambition

Paul adds something to that injunction, telling his readers to **be of the same mind toward one another** (v. 16a). He is referring here to more than doctrinal unity. Certainly it is important for the people of God to believe the same things. After all, we have one Lord, one faith, and one baptism. We agree about the content of our faith, which is why churches produce confessions of faith, but intellectual agreement, such as we find in our creeds and doctrinal statements, is only a portion of what Paul is speaking about. In this context, "being of the same mind" has to do with affection. We are to have a certain kind of affection for one another as believers. We are not to reserve our love for a small group or clique within the church; we are to distribute our affections to the whole body of Christ.

Do not set your mind on high things, but associate with the humble (v. 16b). The second phrase amplifies—indeed, explains—the first. If we looked just at the first phrase, "Do not set your mind on high things," it would seem to contradict what the apostle enjoins on many other occasions, telling us to set our mind on high things and to focus our attention on the lofty principles of the kingdom of God. Considering the first phrase together with the second phrase enables us to see that Paul is not talking about spiritually high things but about high positions in the world. Some people are driven by status; they desire to be exalted over others. In Mark's Gospel we find Jesus' rebuke of the scribes, who were guilty of that very thing: "Beware of the scribes, who desire to go around in long robes, love greetings in the marketplaces, the best seats in the synagogues, and the best places at feasts" (12:38–39).

Paul is warning against a life driven by fleshy ambition. Such ambition can drive us to ruthlessness in our relationships so that we do not hesitate to step on others in our desire to reach the top of the ladder. Therefore, we are not to set our minds and hearts on the positions of esteem and exaltation in this world; rather, we are to associate with the humble. This is another example of how we are to imitate the life of Jesus. He associated with those of low esteem. When Mary rejoiced in the news that she would be giving birth to the Son of God, she sang what we call the Magnificat:

My soul magnifies the Lord,

And my spirit has rejoiced in God my Savior.
For He has regarded the lowly state of His maidservant. (Luke
1:46–48)

Mary was overcome that God would notice her. She had no earthly claim to riches, status, or significance. She was a humble peasant girl whom God noticed and chose to be the mother of his incarnate Son. No woman in history has been visited with greater blessedness than Mary the mother of Jesus.

Not many of the great and powerful have been called into the kingdom; God gives himself to those of no reputation, to the lowly and meek. Jesus, as the Son of God, practiced this same process. We, in turn, are called to follow his example of associating with the humble.

Wisdom and Personal Opinion

I struggle with Paul's next point: **Do not be wise in your own opinion** (v. 16c). I have spent so much of my life working to understand matters of faith and theology that I often have more confidence in my judgment than I have in the judgment of others. Paul writes that I am not to rely solely on my opinion. I am not alone in this struggle. In the final analysis everyone comes to his own conclusions. We give intellectual assent to whatever conclusion we come to after sifting through evidence. No one else can think for us; we have to think for ourselves. Although we are not to rely on our opinions, Paul is not denying the reality of human thought and conviction. We have to think for ourselves.

Sometimes as we listen to others we find ourselves disagreeing with most of what we hear. Why do we come to such radically different conclusions about so many important things even though we believe in the same God, the same Lord, and the same Bible? When I find myself in disagreement with somebody, I try to find something that we can agree on, even if it is only the weather. At least that gives us something to work from. If we can start at a point of agreement and trace it to where we come to a fork in the road, we can better see why and where we went in different directions.

Along her journey Alice in *Alice in Wonderland* came to a fork in the road. She did not know which way to go. In her confusion she looked up and saw the Cheshire cat smiling at her, and she asked him which way she should go. The Cheshire cat said, "That depends. Where are you headed?" Alice said, "I don't know." The Cheshire cat said, "Then it doesn't matter." Again, however, we have to ask the question, why are we inclined to take one road over another? Answering that question involves an analysis of not only other people's thinking but also our own. In attempting to deal with differences of opinion, disagreements, and the frequent controversies that arise among Christians, we must take the guns we have aimed at our adversaries and turn them on ourselves. Why do we believe what we believe? Are we just opinionated? Are we fighting for an idea we inherited from the denomination or home or school in which we were raised? The next question to ask is, are our opinions consistent with the teaching of the Word of God? In the final analysis, our opinions do not mean anything; what matters is truth as God defines it. We are prone to error and given to delusion, so we ought never to trust merely in our own views.

The preacher who stands in the pulpit should study the text of Scripture diligently and examine as much as possible the original languages in an effort to get an accurate understanding of the text. If he relies solely on his intellect, he is doomed. He must also allow the wind of the ages to blow through his mind. When he comes to a text, he will want to know what the greatest minds in the history of the church have understood about it. If he relies only on his own understanding, he will miss the insights and counsel of those who might be far more knowledgeable and wiser than he. We all must examine our opinions and see if they are just that—opinions—or whether they have some solid foundation in truth.

During the golden age of Greece the civilization was threatened with collapse because people abandoned the pursuit of ultimate and objective truth. In those days skepticism and cynicism brought to the fore the sort of political relativism that reigns in our culture today. Everybody was doing what was right in his own mind, until the gadfly of Athens, Socrates, began to ask penetrating questions. Socrates forced people to question why they thought and acted in particular ways. Of course, no one more brilliantly incorporated Socrates' pursuit than his star pupil, Plato.

Plato tells an imaginary story of men held captive in a cave since childhood. They were chained so that their field of vision was restricted to a wall directly before them. Above them people walked around, and the glow from some dimly burning candles cast shadows of those people on the wall before the prisoners. The prisoners' only perception of reality came from the shadows they saw; the actual reality was beyond their field of vision. Eventually the prisoners were freed, and only when they came out of the cave into the sunlight could they see how different reality was from what their perceptions had been. Plato told his story to make a distinction between knowledge and opinion. In his view, opinion is the dancing shadow on the wall that cannot stand up to the light of day. Can our opinions stand the scrutiny of the Word of God? Can they stand the light of divine revelation or must they be discarded?

Evil for Evil

Repay no one evil for evil (v. 17a). The words *evil* and *sin* are not synonymous. All sin is evil, but not all evil is sin. Sin is one particular, although poignant, manifestation of evil. When the Scripture speaks of evil, it includes many things besides moral failure in human behavior. In the Old Testament, for example, the Hebrew word for *evil* has at least eight nuances. It can refer to any experience we do not welcome as pleasant or good, an example of which we see in the prophet Isaiah: "I form the light and create darkness, I make peace and create calamity; I, the LORD, do all these things" (Isa. 45:7).

Another Old Testament nuance for *evil* is natural disasters such as famines and earthquakes. Such catastrophes can bring upon us all kinds of bad consequences, but we do not go to the field that fails to yield its fruit or to the earthquake that destroys a town and accuse them of sin. Such occurrences are bad things, evil happenings, but they are natural evil as distinguished from moral evil.

Moral evil has to do with the behavior of moral agents, those whom God has created with the faculty of choosing and are therefore capable of obeying or disobeying the commandments of the Creator. The Westminster Confession gives this definition of sin: "Sin is any want of conformity to or transgression of the law of God." In other words, sin is defined as a failure to obey one of God's commands or prohibitions. Historically, the concept of evil has been defined by great minds of the church, such as Aquinas and Augustine, as a negation or a privation of good. Evil is *provadio*, a lack of the good. When a bumper crop is harvested, we call it a good crop, but when famine strikes and ruins the harvest, we call it evil. It is not, however, a moral evil. Moral evil has in common with other kinds of evil the idea of a lack, a negation, because sin lacks righteous obedience. Sin is defined in negative terms. It is unrighteousness, godlessness, and disobedience. The negative use of these terms indicates a lack of virtue.

When Paul writes, "Repay no one evil for evil," he is indicating the moral realm. Today when we are hurt or offended, we are prone to say, "It is payback time. What goes around comes around." We look for an opportunity to wound the one who has wounded us. We want to get even. In fact, we are very seldom satisfied with getting even. Getting even is simply tying the score. We do not want to get even; we want to get one up. We want to win in the battle of human relationships. Paul says that such a disposition, which reigns in the human heart, is a manifestation of corruption and an example of moral evil. If we are victims of someone's sin, the flesh wants to get even, and the payback involves us in sin. That is not the way the Christian life is to be. We are not to return evil for evil.

Goodness and Peace

People are watching us; they know who we are. Can unbelievers see something different about us that they cannot deny, even when they slander us? Do they see that we have tender hearts? Do they see that our word can be trusted? Do they see that we are not out to destroy them? **Have regard for good things in the sight of all men** (v. 17b). As hostile as unbelievers may be to Christians, they are not blind, and they can see certain virtues that they do not perhaps acknowledge but know are there.

If it is possible, as much as depends upon you, live peaceably with all men (v. 18). Do we have any enemies? Do we have broken relationships? If we say yes to those questions, I suggest that we need to reevaluate our opinions. We all experience broken relationships and significant conflicts with others. Nevertheless, Paul says, we are to live peaceably with all men. Our Lord said, "Blessed are the peacemakers, for they shall be called sons of God" (Matt. 5:9). The making of peace should be part of our Christian character. We ought to endeavor to live peaceably with everybody.

We are warned in the Bible, however, to beware of the peacemakers of the flesh. There are the Neville Chamberlains of this world who think they have achieved peace for our time when they have not. There were the false prophets of Israel about whom Jeremiah complained, "They have also healed the hurt of My people slightly, saying, 'Peace, peace!' when there is no peace" (Jer. 6:14). Martin Luther described a fleshly peace, one based on falsehood rather than truth, a peace born of cowardice rather than courage. There is a wrong kind of peace, and because of that it is impossible to live at peace with all men.

Notice how Paul qualifies his admonition: "If it is possible, *as much as depends on you*, live peaceably with all men." Paul is addressing a problem that strains possibility to its limit. Our burden is to live peaceably with all men as much as doing so depends on us. When somebody offends us, we can have a spirit of retaliation, revenge, or vengeance, but that only exacerbates the tension and deepens the chasm that separates us from the offender. According to Paul, if somebody offends us, we are not to strike back. Instead, we are to seek peace. Doing so is hard, but it is what our Lord did throughout his earthly ministry. He did not have the word *doormat* printed on his forehead. No one could accuse Jesus of being a doormat. The same is true of Paul. Paul is not advocating that we emulate Caspar Milquetoast; rather, he wants us to be people who do not love a fight.

As we consider the word *offense*, we must make a distinction between an offense given and an offense taken. If with malice aforethought we crush someone's toes under our heel, intentionally seeking to hurt him, then we have offended him. He has every right to take offense because we have given offense. However, we live in a world where people take offense even when none has been given. People are offended when we say or do something that they do not like. They have no just grounds for taking offense in such cases. When people take offense when none has been given, they are giving an offense by taking one. We must be careful, however, because we might have given offense, which is why we must guard ourselves in the exchanging of offenses. As much as it depends on us, we are to be sensitive to people.

No Revenge

Paul then escalates his warning, but he does so with a term of affection: **Beloved**. When in my preaching I come to something that may be hard for people to hear, I try to remind them that I love them, and I do so by prefacing the teaching with the term *beloved*. It is a signal to my congregation that a punch is coming. Paul was not flattering his readers; he loved them and understood their temptations, weaknesses, and struggles for Christian maturity and obedience. When he prefaces his admonition with a term of endearment, he is preparing them for something difficult: **do not avenge yourselves** (v. 19a).

When we are injured, we are not to seek revenge. Once wounded, our deepest natural desire is for revenge. One of the most important concepts we find in the New Testament is vindication. Vindication takes place when someone accused of a crime or an evil is found to be innocent of the charge, or when someone's labor is shown to be of great value after it was ridiculed or scorned. Vindication has to do with justice. Justice is served when innocent people are shown to be innocent and are exonerated of charges brought against them.

Our Lord gave a majestic parable about vindication. A widow brought her case to the court and sought justice, but the judge would not hear her; he had no regard for man or God. The widow persisted and eventually wore down the judge with her ceaseless entreaties. Finally, just to get rid of her, he heard her case (Luke 18:1–7). The point of Jesus' parable is if an unjust judge will from time to time execute justice, how much more will the heavenly Father be quick to bring justice? Jesus asks the question rhetorically: "Shall God not avenge His own elect who cry out day and night to Him, though He bears long with them?" (v. 7).

When Jonathan Edwards was unjustly accused of sin by a malicious man in his congregation, he was kicked out of his parish in Massachusetts, exiled into ministry to the Indians. When Edwards's friends heard the scandalous charges against him, they begged him to speak in his own defense, but he refused to do it. Although he wanted to be vindicated, he feared that if he sought to vindicate himself, his efforts, however successful, would still be less than the vindication the Lord would eventually work on his behalf. His response may seem foolish because in many cases the Lord's vindications will not take place until we stand before the bar of justice in heaven. In Edwards's case, his accuser was so overcome by conscience that after ten years he confessed to the congregation that he had lied about Professor Edwards, and Edwards lived to see his vindication. We see the same thing with Job, who received vindication during his lifetime.

There is a difference between vindication and vengeance. Vindication reveals innocence whereas vengeance is payback for harm. Vengeance is a desire for revenge. Actually, revenge is not a bad thing. It is a good thing, because God takes revenge. Therefore, revenge in and of itself is not evil. What makes it evil is who undertakes it. Revenge belongs to God, who tells us that we ought not to avenge ourselves: **but rather give place to wrath; for it is written, "Vengeance is Mine, I will repay," says the Lord** (v. 19b). Revenge is God's prerogative to dispense, although he delegates to the civil magistrate the responsibility of vengeance, as we will see in Romans 13. In the final analysis vengeance belongs to God. There will be payback. Our offenses will be avenged, but the one who is to do it is God. When God brings vengeance, he brings it perfectly. His justice never punishes more severely than the sin. If vengeance were left to us, our fallen condition is such that we would not be satisfied unless we could inflict more pain than the crime deserves. God never does that.

Good for Evil

Paul again hearkens back to the Sermon on the Mount: **If your enemy is hungry, feed him; if he is thirsty, give him a drink** (v. 20a). We are not to ask our enemy why he is hungry or thirsty. If somebody is high on drugs and falls into a ditch, we are not to ask him how he got into the ditch. Our job is to bind up his wounds, and if he is hungry and thirsty, we are to feed him and give him a drink, which is the ministry of mercy. If somebody suffers from a sexually transmitted disease, we minister to him in the midst of his suffering. Jesus did that, and we are to do likewise, **for in so doing you will heap coals of fire on his head** (v. 20b). We are to repay our enemy with good rather than evil. We are to repay him with kindness. When we respond to evil with good, we expose our enemy to God's wrath. If someone persists in treating us evilly while we persist in repaying him with good, we increase our enemy's guilt before God, although we certainly are not to repay evil with good in order to get evildoers into trouble. The point is that the burden is no longer on us. If we return good for evil, our hands are clean.

When I was a senior in seminary, I served as a student pastor in a Hungarian refugee church in a steel town in western Pennsylvania. The church had less than one hundred members. One lady in our congregation was somewhat vexing, and I once made a remark that she found offensive. Afterward she came to church on Sunday mornings and looked out the window during my sermon so that everybody could see her ignoring me. This created a real problem for me. I went to see her and apologized for my offensive remark. I apologized in tears and asked her forgiveness, but she would not forgive me. I went a second time and asked her forgiveness, but again she refused.

During that seminary assignment I was required to meet monthly with my appointed mentor, an eighty-five-year-old retired missionary who had spent fifty years in China. During his time in China, he and his wife had been incarcerated in concentration camps for five years. I went with hat in hand and gave him the report about my trouble with the unforgiving woman. He told me, "It was a mistake to say what you said, but your biggest mistake was apologizing for it twice. Once you apologized sincerely and asked her forgiveness, the ball was placed in her court. Her refusal to forgive is far worse than the offense you caused in the first place. Do not keep pursuing it. The coals of fire are on her head."

Do not be overcome by evil, but overcome evil with good (v. 21)—that is the grand strategy of Jesus, the apostolic church, and the Christian life.

50

CHURCH AND STATE

Romans 13:1–3

Let every soul be subject to the governing authorities. For there is no authority except from God, and the authorities that exist are appointed by God.
Therefore whoever resists the authority resists the ordinance of God, and
those who resist will bring judgment on themselves. For rulers are not a terror
to good works, but to evil. Do you want to be unafraid of the authority? Do
what is good, and you will have praise from the same.

P aul begins the theme of civil government here. In our study of Romans 12 I distinguished between three important concepts. First is
justification, the central theme of the epistle. Second is vindication,
which occurs when someone accused of wrong is found innocent. Every
Christian is slandered from time to time, yet we are called to patiently await
our vindication from the court of heaven. Third is vengeance, or payback.
When we are injured, we are never to become vigilantes for revenge. Revenge
does not belong to us. "'Vengeance is Mine, I will repay,'" says the Lord"
(12:19). Vengeance is not inherently evil; it is a legitimate enterprise when
carried out justly, which only God can do.

That is a precursor for Paul's treatment of civil government. God keeps
for himself the prerogative of vengeance, and he establishes an order on
earth—the civil magistrate—for justice to be carried out in his name and

under his authority. The civil magistrate did not come into being through the machinations of man; rather, civil government is an institution established by God. God has established the church with its redemptive mission and the government for the well-being of everyone. Government might well be called a common-grace ministry. The church dispenses the elements of special grace, that which has to do with our salvation, whereas civil government attends to the common good of the human race, not only for Christians but for all people.

Both church and state are established and governed by God, which we need to understand in light of the contemporary outcry for separation of church and state. Such separation originally meant a division of labor between the institution of the church and that of human government. Today it has come to mean the separation of the state *from* God. The state declares its independence from God and seeks autonomous rule apart from him. When the government does that—whether the United States, Russia, or any other nation—it becomes demonized and exists as an agent of opposition to God himself. Such nations become truly godless. We face that clear and present danger every moment in our nation, and we must be aware of it.

Models of Civil Obedience

It is the duty of every Christian, indeed of every person, to be subject to the authorities: **Let every soul be subject to the governing authorities** (v. 1a). We struggle with this. In our sinful corruption we kick against the authorities placed over us. We are called to submit to authorities at every stage of life. During our youth we are under the authority of our parents. While in school we are under the authority of our teachers and principal. After obtaining a driver's license we are under the authority of the police department as they patrol the highways. All our lives we are under the authority of state and federal government.

The universal call to submit to authority touches the root of our corruption. Everyone is a sinner, and every sin is an act of revolt against authority. If we respected the authority of God perfectly, we would never sin. Sin is a refusal to submit to the governing authority of God himself, and God knows that about us. If we are not willing to submit to God, it is more difficult to submit to the police department, the government, and other authorities that rule over us. It is the duty of every Christian to be in subjection to the authorities.

From a theological perspective, the principle is that of civil obedience. Christians are called to be extraordinary models of civil obedience. We are called to bend over backwards to be submissive to authorities. Throughout redemptive history there have been great models of civil obedience, both men and women.

Jesus was born in Bethlehem, just as Micah had prophesied (Mic. 5:2). Certain events occurred which led Mary and Joseph to be in that prophesied location at the time of the birth: "It came to pass in those days that a decree went out from Caesar Augustus that all the world should be registered. This census first took place while Quirinius was governing Syria. So all went to be registered, everyone to his own city" (Luke 2:1–3). All people were required to be registered so that they could be taxed by a conquering emperor, one who had no regard for the cost to the people of doing so. The census required people to make an arduous journey to their birthplace to enroll for taxation, so Mary and Joseph made the journey. They risked their lives and that of the unborn child in obedience to the civil magistrate. That is an example of godliness.

The second-century apologist Justin Martyr, who gave a defense of the faith to the emperor Antoninus Pius, argued that the emperor should examine the lives of Christians to see that they, above all other citizens in the empire, were the most scrupulous in paying their taxes and in their obedience to the civil magistrate. Throughout the New Testament we find this strong motif of civil obedience.

When to Disobey

Must we always obey the civil magistrate? When the Sanhedrin told the apostles to preach no more in the name of Jesus, Peter said, "We ought to obey God rather than men" (Acts 5:29). Conflict arises when the civil magistrate commands or forbids something that conflicts with the commandments of God. In such cases, not only may you disobey the civil magistrate, but you must disobey. We are always and everywhere to obey the authorities over us—boss, police, governor, whatever that authority may be—unless that authority commands us to do something that God forbids, or forbids us from doing something that God commands. Sometimes we must disobey. If the civil magistrate calls us to sin, we must say no. History is replete with examples of governments that have commanded the citizens to do evil. It can happen in any country, even our own.

Women have asked me about submission to their husband: "I am trying to be submissive to my husband, but my husband will not allow me to go to church. What should I do?" I tell them to disobey their husband in that instance because God commands us not to forsake the assembling together of the saints.

The principle is easy; the application is difficult. We are not free, however, to disobey the civil magistrate when we disagree with it or when authorities make us suffer or experience inconvenience. It is ironic that this master text on civil obedience was written to the Roman Christians who were under the heavy hand of imperial Rome.

All Authority Belongs to God

Paul then gives the theological grounds for the ethic: **For there is no authority except from God** (v. 1b). Ultimately, the only one who possesses inherent authority is God himself, and the authority that God possesses is the eternal right to impose obligations upon his creatures. God has the inherent authority to command our obedience and submission to him. "It is He who has made us, and not we ourselves" (Ps. 100:3). God's authority rests in his authorship and ownership of the entire world. All other authority we experience is not intrinsic but extrinsic. It has been delegated by God.

The apostle Peter sounds the same message as Paul's: "Submit yourselves to every ordinance of man for the Lord's sake, whether to the king as supreme, or to governors, as to those who are sent by him for the punishment of evildoers and for the praise of those who do good" (1 Pet. 2:13–14). How is our submission to the police department, the state government, and the housing development association honoring God? I find myself frustrated in seeking to comply with the zoning restrictions for building a church, but at St. Andrew's we painstakingly jump through the necessary hoops so that Christ may be honored.

Is Jesus honored by our submission even to corrupt authorities? The universe is not structured as a democracy. It is a theocracy. The government of the universe is God, and he has appointed his only-begotten Son as the King of kings and the Lord of lords. The Father has given to the Son all authority on heaven and earth. At the end of his life, the president of the United States will have to stand before Jesus Christ and be held accountable for how he held his office. The Senate, the House of Representatives, and all such authorities will be answerable to the King of kings as to how they executed justice in their labors. The king of England and the chairman of China will be held accountable to the King of kings. We often overlook the fact that at the heart of the biblical message is a political message. We live in a kingdom where the supreme political authority is vested in Jesus Christ.

When we disobey lesser authorities, we are disobeying those whose authority rests on Christ and has come from him and through him. The president of the United States could not exercise his office for five minutes apart from the will of the King of kings. It is the God of providence who raises kingdoms and brings them down. Every king in the history of the world rules and has ruled only by the providential will of God. God casts the final ballot in every election.

The authorities that exist are appointed by God (v. 1c). Every authority is established, in the final analysis, not by referendum or democratic vote but by the single appointment of the supreme ruler of heaven and earth; every authority is appointed by God. Paul is making clear that God appointed the Roman authorities. I wonder whether Paul, when his life was about to end by the sword, rued the day he wrote these words. He faced a vicious and unjust execution by the decree of Nero. More than likely, when Paul put his head on the block, his last thought was that Nero's authority to execute him came ultimately from God, and he died willingly.

Can we look past such authorities and see the authority that stands behind them? "Shall God not avenge His own elect who cry out day and night to Him?" (Luke 18:7). Will not God set the scales of justice right? When we are victimized by unjust, demonic governments that do everything but work for the glory and honor of Christ, God notices. Our Lord will vindicate his people who seek to be faithful to him despite the injustice that comes their way from earthly authorities.

Living under Authority

Therefore whoever resists the authority resists the ordinance of God (v. 2a). In the eighteenth century, Christians struggled over whether to pick up arms against the British government and declare their independence. One of the most heated discussions in Christian history occurred over how to understand Romans 13 in light of the War of Independence. The colonists were fighting for the maintenance of their governmental system, which the parliament of England wanted to change. The colonists decided that British common law gave them the right to resist. That was a very complicated situation, which Christian scholars debate to this day, and the reason for the debate is this text in Romans 13. Whoever resists the authority resists the ordinance of God, **and those who resist will bring judgment on themselves** (v. 2b). That is a sober warning. If we resist the authorities that God has appointed, we might be regarded as heroes by some, but we can expect only the visitation of God's judgment.

For rulers are not a terror to good works, but to evil. Do you want to be unafraid of the authority? Do what is good, and you will have praise from the same (v. 3). This is a proverbial point of wisdom. It is true in the main, but it is not true absolutely. Nobody did more good in the Roman Empire than the apostle Paul, yet he did not, in the final analysis, receive praise from the civil magistrate. Instead, it gave him his death sentence. In general, even under corrupt governments, those who receive the harshest treatment are criminals, people involved in the worst forms of corruption. The whole point of civil government is to restrain evil, by force if necessary.

Several years ago I shared a meal with a United States senator. In the course of our discussion we covered certain ethical issues facing our nation at that time, and the senator said to me, "R. C., I don't believe that the federal government has the right to force its people to do anything." I replied, "Senator, do you realize that you have just told me you do not believe the federal government has the right to govern, because government is legalized force? Government has the right to enact legislation and to enforce the legislation that is enacted. A government that has no right to exercise force is a government that can make only suggestions, not laws."

The essence of government is its power and authority to force conformity. We do not get a letter from the IRS every year requesting that we pay our taxes. If we do not pay taxes, we face penalty under the law, and every weapon in the United States arsenal can be used to bring us into conformity.

We hear that morality cannot be legislated. Every time an ethical issue comes up for political discussion, such as abortion or euthanasia, we hear that cry from every corner. It is true that we cannot change behavior just by changing the law, but that is not typically what people mean when they use that phrase. The phrase is used by those who claim that the government has no right to pass laws that have to do with moral matters. If we cannot legislate morality, however, what can we legislate—the state bird? Even that has ecological and ethical ramifications. Many laws of the land are moral, such as those pertaining to bank robbery and first-degree murder. That is exactly what legislation is about—restraining evil. In simple terms, Paul is saying that although the government we have to live under may be corrupt, the worst government is still better than anarchy, when evil goes forth without any restraint whatsoever.

Several years ago I was invited to give a message at the inaugural prayer breakfast for the Florida governor. Within hours of the breakfast, the governor-elect was set to be installed. He would take his oath and become the governor of the state. In my address I explained that when we are consecrated to the ministry, set apart for the church, we are ordained. Ordination is a sacred occasion because we take vows to be faithful to God in the execution of our ministerial office. I told the governor, "Sir, today is your ordination day, because you are being ordained as God's minister of civil righteousness," and I talked about Romans 13. People told me afterward that they had never thought about government authority in such terms. Indeed, it was the governor's ordination day because civil magistrates are ordained by God. They are God's ministers, and they are called to serve God's good pleasure.

We will consider more about civil government in our next study, focusing especially on its God-given power of the sword.

51

THE POWER OF THE SWORD

Romans 13:4–7

For he is God's minister to you for good. But if you do evil, be afraid; for he does not bear the sword in vain; for he is God's minister, an avenger to execute wrath on him who practices evil. Therefore you must be subject, not only because of wrath but also for conscience' sake. For because of this you also pay taxes, for they are God's ministers attending continually to this very thing. Render therefore to all their due: taxes to whom taxes are due, customs to whom customs, fear to whom fear, honor to whom honor.

For he is God's minister to you for good. But if you do evil, be afraid; for he does not bear the sword in vain; for he is God's minister, an avenger to execute wrath on him who practices evil (v. 4). Romans 13:4b is one of the most important verses in Scripture in terms of the development of historic, classic Christian ethics, especially with respect to two monumentally important issues. The first is capital punishment and the second is warfare and whether Christians can, in good conscience, engage in war. We see here that God himself has given to the civil magistrate the power of the sword. "The power of the sword" is an idiomatic expression referring to capital punishment. God has given

447

the civil magistrate the power to use a weapon to bring death in order to enforce the law.

The Sword as Restraint

The idea of the sword's being used to enforce the law of God was established exceedingly early in the biblical record. The third chapter of Genesis records the circumstances of the fall of the human race into sin, the seduction of Adam and Eve by the serpent in the garden:

> Then the LORD God said, "Behold, the man has become like one of Us, to know good and evil. And now, lest he put out his hand and take also of the tree of life, and eat, and live forever"—therefore the LORD God sent him out of the garden of Eden to till the ground from which he was taken. So He drove out the man; and He placed cherubim at the east of the garden of Eden, and a flaming sword which turned every way, to guard the way to the tree of life. (Gen. 3:22–24)

When Adam and Eve sinned, the curse for sin came upon them, the earth, and all things in it. Then God drove Adam and Eve out of the garden of Eden, and they were forced to live east of Eden, outside the presence of the paradise in which they had been placed by their Creator. Human beings were forbidden to enter again into the garden, and God established a sentinel to block the way back in. He put angels at the gateway to the garden armed with a flaming sword.

We see here the first establishment of physical force as a governing restraint upon sinful people. The image of that sword is used throughout Scripture to indicate the authority given to those responsible for enforcing the law of God. In the Old Testament several offenses were considered so heinous that for the commission of them, God, in the civil code of Israel, required the death penalty.

The Bible and Capital Punishment

In Genesis 9, we find another important text for understanding the power of the sword:

> So God blessed Noah and his sons, and said to them: "Be fruitful and multiply, and fill the earth. And the fear of you and the dread of you shall be on every beast of the earth, on every bird of the air, on all that move on the earth, and on all the fish of the sea. They are given into your hand. Every moving thing that lives shall be food for you. I have given you all things, even as the green herbs. But you shall not eat flesh with its life, that is, its blood. Surely

for your lifeblood I will demand a reckoning; from the hand of every beast I will require it, and from the hand of man. From the hand of every man's brother I will require the life of man.

> "Whoever sheds man's blood,
> By man his blood shall be shed;
> For in the image of God
> He made man." (vv. 1–6)

We find there the biblical institution of capital punishment for murder. The way in which the text is expressed can be easily misunderstood. "Whoever sheds man's blood, by man his blood shall be shed." We could misinterpret that to mean "he who lives by the sword dies by the sword," a sort of cryptic prophecy of the consequences of living a violent life, but the original text indicates not a prophetic prediction but an imperative: God is requiring the death penalty for murder. In the law code of the Old Testament, the offense of murder is carefully explained. Distinctions are made in Old Testament law that correspond to our distinctions between first- and second-degree murder, or murder and manslaughter. In the case of manslaughter the penalty was not death but banishment to cities of refuge. When first-degree murder was committed, the civil magistrates of Israel were commanded to execute the guilty one.

Several years ago the question of capital punishment came before the state legislature in Pennsylvania. Originally, of course, Pennsylvania had the death penalty for murder, but it was repealed for a season. When it came back before the legislature, the motion to restore capital punishment was vetoed by the Pennsylvania governor, who was Jewish. He believed capital punishment is unbiblical because the Bible says, "You shall not murder" (Ex. 20:13). Since God prohibits killing human beings, the governor said, the execution of murderers through capital punishment must not be tolerated. Eventually, however, the law was restored in Pennsylvania in cases of first-degree murder. If the governor had read just a few pages further in the Old Testament he would have seen that God requires the death penalty for murder.

Many Christians have been strongly misinformed about this biblical position. When capital punishment was instituted by God, it was part of a renewal of the covenant of creation. There are many biblical covenants. God made a covenant with Abraham and with Isaac and Jacob. God mediated a covenant through Moses. God made a covenant with David, and, of course, we have the new covenant, which was instituted by Jesus. We call the original covenant the "covenant of creation." The laws established at creation were not intended just for Jews or for Christians; the laws built into creation were given to every human being. Every person alive today is under the authority of the terms of the creation covenant.

Many do not believe in creation, so they do not think they have any covenant responsibility toward God, but unbelief and denial of the covenant do not eliminate the covenant. Every human being remains inescapably in a covenant relationship with God. Everyone is either a covenant keeper or a covenant breaker. The vast majority of the human race exists in a state of covenant rebellion.

After the creation covenant was established, sin spread throughout the world so rapidly that God decided to virtually wipe out the human race, saying that he would no longer strive with wicked people. Noah and his family were the exceptions. On one hand the flood account is God's judgment on the mass of fallen humanity, and on the other hand it is an account of God's grace toward Noah and his family and Noah's being the instrument of rescue of the world's wildlife. After the flood receded, the ark came to rest, and God reestablished a covenant with Noah, setting his bow in the sky and saying he would never again destroy the world by flood. In that covenant, the Noahic covenant, we see the restitution and repetition of the ordinances and laws of the creation covenant (see Genesis 7–8).

The point is this: the law of capital punishment for murder is not restricted to the law code and civil penalties of Israel in the Old Testament, nor is it a portion of the jurisprudence of the New Testament; it is a law rooted and grounded in creation. So as long as creation lasts, the principle of capital punishment is in effect in cases of first-degree murder.

A few years ago I read an article by Larry King in which he criticized the Christian community for its gross inconsistency. He complained that the Christian community protests against abortion on demand while arguing in favor of capital punishment. Larry King said he would not support the Christian opposition to abortion until the church stops its support of capital punishment. I have never had the opportunity to tell Mr. King that there is no inconsistency here at all. There is a strong point of consistency behind both the church's opposition to abortion and its support of capital punishment—the sanctity of human life. The principle that resounds on virtually every page of Scripture and reiterated emphatically by Jesus in the Sermon on the Mount is that human life is so sacred that we must never take it with malice aforethought or for personal convenience.

Human life is sacred not because of some inherent value in humans that is lacking in whales, eagles, and turtles. Human life is so significant because of this: "Whoever sheds man's blood, by man his blood shall be shed; for in the image of God He made man" (Gen. 9:6). That is what makes us different from chickens and kangaroos; we have been stamped with the image of God. That is why, if somebody rises up as Cain did and kills his brother with malice aforethought, God sees it as an attack on himself.

Human life is so sacred that if you rise up without just cause and kill your neighbor, you forfeit all rights and privileges to your own life. God gives the forfeited life not to the victim's relative for vengeance but to the civil authorities. God has given the government the sword, and government is to see to it that punishment is carried out. We hold to this in order to communicate to the world that we will not tolerate the murder of human beings.

That is the biblical rationale. We see it in the Old Testament and again in Romans 13. When God gives the power of the sword, he does not give it merely to see it rattled. The power of the sword is given to be used to enforce law and justice.

The Just-war Theory

This same verse, Romans 13:4, also serves the *locus classicus* in historical Christian ethics concerning the just-war theory. The fundamental principle of the just-war theory is this: if a nation or a people aggressively invades or attacks another nation, the attacked nation is the victim of external aggression, so it has the right and the responsibility to protect itself from the invading aggressor. When Hitler invaded Poland, Czechoslovakia, and other nations, the local governments of those nations had the moral duty to try to stop the Blitzkrieg from coming and enslaving their people.

The just-war theory has a long history. Augustine said that all wars are evil with the exception of the divinely ordained conquest of Canaan. Apart from that, he said, we do not have direct instructions from God to wage war, and we are left to make such decisions on the basis of human understanding and the application of principles drawn from sacred Scripture alone. He said, however, that not all involvement in war is evil. Thomas Aquinas seconded the motion, and in his moral theology he worked out the details of what is involved in a just war.

The sanctity of life principle lies behind the just-war theory. Human life is so sacred that the civil magistrate has been given the sword to protect the innocent from the evildoer, just as the policeman has been given arms and the right to use arms to stop rape, robbery, and murder. When the civil magistrate uses reasonable force to restrain the evildoer, he serves not only the community but also God. In terms of just war, those principles are simply elevated to the larger domain of national security.

In our day and age we have the opportunity to invade without sending soldiers across borders. We send missiles across oceans. With the sophistication in modern weaponry, issues of just war become increasingly complex. The New Testament and the Christian church do not encourage a bellicose national posture or a militaristic style that exists by the threat of intimidation. The church historically has encouraged nations to be good neighbors to other nations and to use the sword as the last resort—when the defense of the people becomes a clear and present necessity.

Conscientious Objectors

When I was a college professor in the mid-1960s, many of my students were vehemently opposed to the war in Vietnam, and many of them applied for conscientious-objector status. Those opposed were required to file affidavits with the government and with draft boards in which others gave testimony under penalty of perjury that they believed the conscientious objection was sincere. I filled out countless such affidavits for students. My responsibility in those cases was not to give my view on the war; that was beside the point. The only responsibility I had was to give my honest view as to whether a particular student was sincere in his objection to the conflict in Vietnam.

So many students filed objections to the war that the Supreme Court of the United States made a decision that was, in my judgment, one of the worst miscarriages of justice I have ever seen, and it was made without a peep from the Christian community. The Supreme Court ruled that no one could be given conscientious-objector status unless he could demonstrate that he was opposed to all wars. To this day that remains the rule of the land. Someone cannot be a conscientious objector unless he can demonstrate that he is opposed to all wars.

At the Nuremburg trials, when war crimes committed during World War II were tried, officer after officer pled the same excuse for the atrocities they had committed in the death camps. They said they were merely carrying out orders, which meant that their superiors were responsible. As good German soldiers, they simply did what their commanding officers commanded them to do. The United States government argued that each soldier had a responsibility to disobey a command given to him by a superior officer if that superior officer commanded him to do something evil. As we considered in our last study, our responsibility is to be obedient to the civil magistrate unless that magistrate commands us to do something God forbids or forbids us from doing something God commands. In other words, after World War II the United States held that those German soldiers should have been conscientious objectors even if they did not believe that any involvement in war is evil.

Today the Christian is discriminated against if he believes that involvement in war is legitimate only if the cause is just. If I see my nation getting involved in an unjust war (even though I hold the position that there are just wars), I do not have legal recourse to say that I refuse to submit to that order. That is a very serious matter. As Christians, we must make sure that the cause is just before we pick up a gun or a sword and kill anybody. It is silly to assume that a government can be trusted to engage in only just military activity. I do not know of any nation in history that has not, at one point or another, used its power and authority in an unjust manner. That is why we have to be vigilant. When the nation is involved in the just defense of its borders, and the civil magistrate calls us to pick up the sword, it is our duty to use the sword. However, if the nation conscripts us to engage in an unjust aggression or invasion of an innocent nation, I am equally obligated to say no.

No one ever said that living the Christian life is simple or that making ethical decisions is an easy matter. The principle is easy: we are always to obey the authorities over us unless those authorities command us to do something God forbids, or forbids us from doing something that God commands. We cannot disobey the civil magistrate because it inconveniences us or burdens us with heavy taxation or because we disagree with its wisdom. Those are not just excuses for civil disobedience. At the same time, we are not to render slavish obedience to any authority, because authorities can work against the Word of God. We have to be careful to ensure that our decisions are motivated by an earnest desire to obey God in all he commands.

Responsibilities of Sword Carriers

According to Paul, the civil magistrate has been appointed by God to execute God's wrath on those who practice evil. Paul's words provide the biblical basis for the establishment of force given to civil magistrates. If the civil magistrate uses the sword to promote evil, then the civil magistrate will be judged by God. It is the Lord who raises up nations, and it is the Lord who brings them down. The Christians who received this letter from the apostle Paul knew all about the corruption of the Roman system, and yet they listened to their apostle defending the authority that God had given to the Roman Empire.

When we object to capital punishment or warfare in principle, we object to what God himself has instituted and established. The sword is necessary because there is sin in the world, and the sword is given to work against and to restrain evildoers in order to protect the lives of the innocent. The primary responsibility of any civil government, whether in China, Russia, the United States, or Iran, is to protect, defend, and maintain human life. When any government turns its back on that primary responsibility, it is acting in utter defiance of the law of God and is exposing itself and the nation it governs to the judgment of God.

52

FOR CONSCIENCE' SAKE

Romans 13:5−8

Therefore you must be subject, not only because of wrath but also for conscience' sake. For because of this you also pay taxes, for they are God's
ministers attending continually to this very thing. Render therefore to all
their due: taxes to whom taxes are due, customs to whom customs, fear to
whom fear, honor to whom honor. Owe no one anything except to love one
another, for he who loves another has fulfilled the law.

A
t the beginning of Romans 13 Paul set forth the role of civil government. He showed that the secular rulers of the world are God's
ministers. In our last study I tried to draw applications of that text to
issues of civil obedience, capital punishment, and theories of just warfare.

The apostle forges ahead: **Therefore you must be subject, not only
because of wrath but also for conscience' sake** (v. 5). We are not
to submit simply because we are afraid of the law enforcement agencies
of our nation. Rather, we have a responsibility to be submissive to the civil
magistrates as a matter of conscience. If magistrates are oppressive, if we
disagree radically with them, we are still to render obedience because our
consciences are held captive by the Word of God. Since God authorizes our
rulers and places them over us, we are to render obedience as a matter of
principle unless they require us to do something God forbids or forbid us

from doing something God commands. Living by principle lies at the heart of Christian ethics and the Christian life. We are not to live doing whatever our hearts desire; we are to be, in the main, submissive people—submissive ultimately to the law of God and to every other authority that God places over us.

Taxes

Paul turns his attention to the payment of taxes: **For because of this you also pay taxes, for they are God's ministers attending continually to this very thing. Render therefore to all their due: taxes to whom taxes are due, customs to whom customs, fear to whom fear, honor to whom honor** (vv. 6–7). I really admire the apostle Paul for his faithfulness to Christ and his courage in telling people of God to do their duty, even when that duty was something they despised.

The Roman government was, in terms of taxation and tribute policies, an oppressive government. The people who received Paul's admonition had been crushed by the burden of Roman taxation. Nevertheless, Paul said, they were to pay their taxes. Taxes might be unfair and oppressive, but God has given to the civil magistrate the right to levy taxes. The civil magistrate has to have his reign and rule financed. Since governments usually do not produce anything, most of their revenue, if not all, is dependent on the imposition of taxes rather than on voluntary contributions, and the government is allowed by God's decree to collect such taxes by the sword if necessary.

If we in the United States refuse to pay our taxes, we do not have to worry about the government coming after us with a sword. Our government's weapons are a bit more advanced. In any case, every government in every society throughout history has been involved in some form of levying taxes. It is the government's right to levy taxes, and it is our responsibility to pay them. There is a caveat, however. The government, to which God gives the right to levy taxes, has also received from God the responsibility to levy just and righteous taxes. I do not know if any civil government in the history of the world has maintained a righteous system of taxation for any period of time. In the Old Testament, God speaks passionately through the prophets against oppression brought upon the poor by the rich. The rich that God spoke to through the prophets were not the merchants of Israel but the rulers of the nation. Kings and princes used their power to extort burdensome payments from the poor.

King Ahab exercised eminent domain when he confiscated Naboth's vineyard. Naboth had labored strenuously to cultivate his vineyard, and when the king saw that it was a productive operation, he took it as his own possession. God's wrath was poured out against Ahab (1 Kings 21:1–19). Throughout the pages of the Old Testament, we see unjust, unrighteous, and oppressive burdens of taxation levied on the people. We also see that God hates it, whether it is done by a Jewish king, a Babylonian king, a Roman emperor, or the Congress of the United States of America. Every magistrate is called to levy taxes in a just and righteous manner.

The Tyranny of the Majority

Throughout church history and the history of Western civilization there have been different forms of government. There have been autocratic governments, in which the authority and power is invested in one person—a tyrant or dictator. There have been oligarchies, in which all the power and authority is vested in a few people. There have been monarchies, in which a king or queen has exercised authority over subjects.

Americans do not live under a democracy. The fathers of our nation went to great pains to ensure that the United States government would be a republic, not a democracy. In a democracy rule is vested in the majority. In a republic, ultimate authority rests in law. The purpose of the Bill of Rights is to guard against what Alexis de Tocqueville warned would destroy the American experiment—the tyranny of the majority. If everybody in the country except one agrees to stamp out free speech, the First Amendment should rule over that majority. The private rights of individuals are guaranteed by the Constitution and the Bill of Rights.

The founders of America were farsighted, but, in my opinion, not farsighted enough. They failed to protect the individual's rights against unjust taxation. Unjust taxation occurs through a progressive, unequal tax system. When God placed his tax upon the people of Israel, he imposed a tithe. Not everybody paid the same amount. Rich people paid more than poor people, but everybody paid the same percentage. America has politicized economics; we do not have a flat percentage system. Some are required to pay a higher percentage than others. We call that social justice, but it is, in fact, manifest injustice. It is evil and destructive because it gives people the right to vote for taxes on other people that they are not voting to impose on themselves. It creates a politics of envy in which one group is set against another.

Historically this practice has ended in the destruction of the nation, and it will destroy our nation if we do not do something about it. That being said, when we vote, we must do so according to principle. We ought not to use the power of the ballot to pick others' pockets. We must pay our taxes as a matter of conscience while at the same time being scrupulous in supporting righteousness and justice in whatever system of government we live under.

That Which Is Due

The idea of justice is deeply embedded in Paul's words, "Render, therefore to all their due: taxes to whom taxes are due, customs to whom customs, fear to whom fear, honor to whom honor." Mortimer Adler was an important philosopher in twentieth-century America. He published a book that covered concepts we read about in the newspaper every day and words we use in our normal vocabulary, yet, he said, if put to the test we would be hard pressed to render an adequate definition of those terms.[1]

I saw the truth of that when I taught ethics. I would ask my students to write a succinct, accurate definition of *justice*. Most of the answers I received were based upon the concept of merit, rewarding goodness and punishing wickedness. Many of us conceive of a merit structure as the heart of justice. I would then ask the students to consider a beauty contest in which the contestants are judged chiefly by physical beauty. The judges see that an ugly duckling has entered the context and they vote for her from pity. Is that just? If we use the merit system, the answer is no. The woman is not crowned because she deserves it. Aristotle defined justice as giving people their due. Accordingly, in a beauty contest, the most beautiful contestant is due the prize. Even though there is no merit or virtue in being beautiful, the terms of the contest were defined by an aesthetic criterion, so whoever meets that criterion in its greatest dimension is due the prize. Righteousness and justice have a lot to do with *dueness*.

One of the great ethical debates in Christian ethics pertains to the sanctity of truth. Are we always in every circumstance obligated to give the unvarnished truth? Many Christian ethicists answer that question in the affirmative, saying that righteousness demands truth telling with no exception. The Bible gives us Rahab, however, who lied to protect Joshua and his people, and she made the roll call of the saints for her valorous action. The Bible also shows us the midwives of Egypt who were instructed by Pharaoh to kill every male born to a Hebrew woman. The midwives disobeyed and protected the newborn babies and then lied about it to the authorities. Scripture tells us, "Therefore God dealt well with the midwives" (Ex. 1:20). Because of that, many ethics students believe there is a place for a righteous lie.

I had a landlady in Holland who, during World War II, had hollowed out a place under her livingroom floor to hide her teenaged son and a neighbor boy from the Gestapo. The police would arrive unannounced looking for youngsters to send to the labor camps in Germany. Did my

---

1. Mortimer Adler, *The Great Ideas: A Syntopicon of Great Books of the Western World* (Chicago: Encyclopedia Britannica, 1952).

landlady have a moral obligation to tell the guards about the two young men hidden beneath the floorboards? The principle of giving truth to whom it is due—where righteousness and justice require it—would not only allow that woman to deceive the soldiers but require her to do so. The biblical principle is that we should always tell the truth when righteousness and justice require it, but righteousness and justice do not always require it. The principle that defines justice and righteousness is that which is due, owed, or obligatory.

Paul is telling the Roman Christians that we are obliged to pay our taxes. We must give the state what is due the state. Justice and righteousness require that we submit to taxation. Honor is due the king. Even if the king is not honorable, he is to be honored. It is his due. We are to honor our father and mother even if they do not deserve it, because honor is due our parents. We cannot reduce Christian justice and righteousness to the simple formula of merit and demerit. People might not earn honor, but by God's decree it is their due, and I am to give honor to whom honor is due.

My friend John Guest came to the United States as an aspiring evangelist. He had been here less than two weeks when he told me he was unsure how to communicate the gospel in America. When I asked him why, he told me that he had visited an antique store in a section of Philadelphia and had seen signs hanging on the wall proclaiming, "Don't tread on me," and "No taxation without representation," and "We serve no sovereign here." He asked me, "Is that really the American mentality? If so, how can I preach the gospel to a people who have a built-in antipathy toward sovereignty?" We Americans have not been trained in giving honor and respect to those in authority over us.

When one of my graduate school professors would enter the amphitheater where the students had gathered to hear him and walk up to the podium to face the students, it was a silent signal for every student to stand up. We would stand, and then he would nod and give us the signal to be seated. He would deliver his lecture with no interruption. No student ever raised his hand. After his lecture he would close his book and step off the podium, and everybody would stand up again as he left the room. Likewise, at a church I attended in Holland, the minister would come in from the side, and as soon as he appeared, everybody in the congregation would stand up. He would nod, and everyone would sit back down. After his sermon, everyone stood up again as he left the sanctuary. He did not stay to shake hands with people at the back of the church.

During my studies in Amsterdam, one class was held in a very warm room. The students never went to class without a coat and tie, but one day I took my coat off and put it on the chair next to me. Dr. Berkower stopped in the middle of his lecture, looked at me, and said, "Would the American please put his coat back on." He did not know me, but he knew that the only sort of person that would dare to take off his coat in the middle of the lecture had to be an American. We are a cavalier people. The concept of honor is foreign to our culture, yet the biblical culture of ethics is built on honor. Give honor where honor is due—to your boss, your parents, the civil magistrates, and your pastor.

Debt

Owe no one anything except to love one another, for he who loves another has fulfilled the law (v. 8). Paul continues with an exposition of the way in which love fulfills the law. Many see this verse as a mandate against incurring any debt or borrowing money to build churches or homes or to buy an automobile. If we look at the scope of sacred Scripture, however, we will see that there are vast provisions for taking on debt as well as guidelines to protect people who are in debt.

There are strong biblical prohibitions against oppressive usury. Usury is an exploitatively high interest rate that bleeds people dry. If our culture were held up to the law of Israel, the interest rates routinely charged by credit card companies would clearly be seen as usurious and would come under the judgment of God. They are too high, and they exploit people and their weaknesses. Scripture provides a principle with respect to lending and rates of interest.

Scripture also sets out strong considerations for the poor who had to put up personal property as collateral for their indebtedness. If a person put up his garment, which he needed to keep warm at night, the creditor was allowed to keep that garment during the day but was required by law to give it back to its owner before the coldness of the evening (Deut. 24:12–13). Such scenarios in the Bible are all based upon a culture ordained by God that allowed borrowing and lending so long as the lending and borrowing were not exploitive and oppressive.

Every commentator I have examined on this subject says that Paul is instructing Christians to operate only under one perpetual debt or obligation, and that is to love our brothers. The application from the text concerning borrowing and lending is this: there is no sin in borrowing, but there is sin in borrowing something and not paying it back. We are required to fulfill our obligation. People take advantage of loans and do not fulfill their obligation. It does not just happen at Ligonier; it happens at every ministry and in every department store. When Christians incur debt, they, above all others, must move heaven and earth to honor their obligations as a matter of principle and conscience. If you owe somebody something, pay what you owe. Pay your bills and pay them on time. If you enter into a contract, fulfill the terms of the contract. That is basic integrity.

All of this is wrapped, as we will see, in the overarching principle of love. If we borrow our neighbor's rake and do not return it, we are failing to love our neighbor. All the practical applications of righteousness and justice Paul gives us here are rooted and grounded in that overarching responsibility we have to love our neighbor as ourselves. The things Paul sets forth are nothing more or less than practical applications of the Golden Rule.

53

THE FULFILLMENT OF THE LAW

Romans 13:9–14

For the commandments, "You shall not commit adultery," "You shall not murder," "You shall not steal," "You shall not bear false witness," "You shall not covet," and if there is any other commandment, are all summed up in this saying, namely, "You shall love your neighbor as yourself." Love does no harm to a neighbor; therefore love is the fulfillment of the law. And do this, knowing the time, that now it is high time to awake out of sleep; for now our salvation is nearer than when we first believed. The night is far spent, the day is at hand. Therefore let us cast off the works of darkness, and let us put on the armor of light. Let us walk properly, as in the day, not in revelry and drunkenness, not in lewdness and lust, not in strife and envy. But put on the Lord Jesus Christ, and make no provision for the flesh, to fulfill its lusts.

We can pay our debt to the bank, the store, and the credit card company, but our debt to love our neighbor is never discharged until we cross into heaven. Love is a perpetual obligation, an indebtedness given to us by Jesus: "'You shall love the LORD your God with all your heart, with all your soul, and with all your mind.' This is the first and great commandment. And the second is like it: 'You shall love your neighbor as yourself'" (Matt. 22:37–39).

Love and the Ten Commandments

In Romans 13 the apostle links the obligation of love to some of the Ten Commandments. We are not to owe anyone anything except love: **For the commandments, "You shall not commit adultery," "You shall not murder," "You shall not steal," "You shall not bear false witness," "You shall not covet," and if there is any other commandment, all are summed up in this saying, namely, "You shall love your neighbor as yourself"** (v. 9). Paul mentions the commandments often described, particularly by our Lutheran friends, as coming from the second table of the law. The Scripture refers to the Ten Commandments as being given on two tablets of stone. The first few commandments prescribe our duty and behavior with respect to God. We are to have no other gods before him; we are not to make any graven images of him, thereby keeping ourselves from idolatry; we are to make sure that God's name is not taken in vain; and we are to keep the Sabbath. The remainder of the Ten Commandments focuses on how we are to treat one another with respect to marriage, sanctity of life, possessions, truth telling, and the like. The first tablet of the law pertains to our obligations to God, and the second tablet, or table, pertains to our obligations to people, which is a very popular understanding of why the Ten Commandments were given on two tablets. I do not hold that position.

I think the commandments were given on two tablets due to the context in which they were given—the Mosaic covenant. In antiquity, when formal covenants were entered into, the agreement was made in duplicate. One copy was reserved for the sovereign; the other was given to the vassal. The stipulations of the Mosaic covenant were expressed in terms of the Ten Commandments, and therefore the two tablets might reflect the ancient practice of rendering two copies of the agreement. However, neither I nor my Lutheran friends know for sure why the commandments were given this way. Wherever we come out on that question, the commandments Paul mentions in Romans 13 are those that prescribe behavior on the horizontal plain—our behavior toward each other. Whoever loves another has fulfilled the law.

Love and Ethics

The brief passage here in Romans 13 has created lots of consternation, particularly in the second half of the twentieth century in American liberal Christianity. Joseph Fletcher wrote a book called *Situation Ethics*.[1] The basic

---

1. Joseph Fletcher, *Situation Ethics: The New Morality* (Philadelphia: Westminster Press, 1964).

thesis of his book was borrowed from a more sophisticated treatment of ethics, *Ethics in a Christian Context*, by the Princeton scholar Paul Lehmann.[2] In his book Fletcher developed what has become a famous concept of situation ethics: he reduced the entire law of God to one essential precept—the law of love. He wrote that we must always do what love requires in a given situation; hence the title *Situation Ethics*.

Ethical principles and divine precepts are given to us to be obeyed, but doing so requires a context in which to obey them. God's law is given to us for real-life situations. In that sense, all ethics are situational, but that is not Fletcher's point. He went beyond that, saying that God's requirements are determined by the situation. Fletcher drew from Augustine, who said, "Love God and do what you want." There is an even worse application that comes from the lips of Martin Luther. He declared to his friend Philip Melanchthon, "Sin boldly." Luther was not really enticing people to sin but pointing out that they have a Savior who has paid for their sins. We do not have to spend the rest of our lives in total misery as a result of our sin; we have a Savior who has delivered us from the consequences.

According to Fletcher, if we look at concrete life situations in light of the laws written in the Bible, we can envision ethical cases in which it is acceptable to break some of the commandments. One of Fletcher's most famous illustrations is the case of a husband and wife interred in a concentration camp during World War II. The guards wanted to have a sexual relationship with the woman, who was isolated from her husband. The guards told her that if she refused to submit to their advances, they would kill her husband. Knowing her husband's life was at stake, she acquiesced to the desires of the guard. When the camp was liberated, she told her husband what she had done, and he was so horrified that his wife had committed adultery that he sued her for divorce.

When I shared Fletcher's illustration with my students, they all agreed at first that the woman had, in fact, committed adultery. I asked them to consider if they would think similarly if the woman had been attacked by the guards. If she had been wrestled to the ground and raped, would the husband then have the right to divorce on grounds of adultery? Every student said no, because rape victims cannot be accused of adultery. Rape is sex by force, and what greater force could be exhibited against a woman of virtue than to require that she either submit or have her husband killed? That is a worse form of coercion than pointing a gun at her head. When the students considered it from that perspective, they changed their minds about

2. Paul Lehmann, *Ethics in a Christian Context* (New York: Harper and Row, 1963).

the husband's right to divorce her. Fletcher would say that in this situation love not only permitted the adultery but required it. He was wrong about that. Love never requires adultery. However, this situation was not adultery; it was rape, and there is a huge difference ethically.

If our decisions about how to treat others are always motivated by love for God, a singular love for God, we really do not have to worry about the law, because the law reflects what is pleasing to God. That is why Augustine said, "Love God and do what you want." If you love God, you can do as you please, because you will be doing what pleases God. It is that simple. If you really love him, you will be pleased by what pleases him, and what pleases him is revealed to us in his law.

The Rule of Love

The rule of love is this: love God and do what the love of God requires in every human situation. Concerning the love of God, Paul wrote, "Fornication and all uncleanness or covetousness, let it not even be named among you, as is fitting for saints" (Eph. 5:3). Paul could not envision any situation that would justify disobedience to God's law of purity. When Paul writes about love in Romans 13, he is writing about the purpose and goal of the law—the love of neighbor.

Some take the second part of the Great Commandment, "love your neighbor as yourself," as proof that self-love is something to be pursued. Others take it as proof that self-love is inherent. In either case, we are to love our neighbor as much as we love ourselves.

Neighbor Love

Brotherhood is something special in Scripture. It is enjoyed by all who share the same elder brother, Jesus Christ, the only begotten of the Father. The idea that all mankind is a brotherhood and God is the Father of all dilutes the special character of redemption. By nature, Jesus told us, we are children of Satan, and therefore unbelievers are not our brothers. They are, however, our neighbors. The Bible does teach the universal neighborhood of man. The law of the neighborhood, in which God is the supreme mayor, is the law of love, which is to be given to everybody. When Jesus was asked about the greatest commandment, he included in his answer the Old Testament law about love for neighbor. Our question then becomes who is our neighbor. Jesus answered that question this way:

> A certain man went down from Jerusalem to Jericho, and fell among thieves, who stripped him of his clothing, wounded him, and departed, leaving him

half dead. Now by chance a certain priest came down that road. And when he saw him, he passed by on the other side. Likewise a Levite, when he arrived at the place, came and looked, and passed by on the other side. But a certain Samaritan, as he journeyed, came where he was. And when he saw him, he had compassion. So he went to him and bandaged his wounds, pouring on oil and wine; and he set him on his own animal, brought him to an inn, and took care of him. On the next day, when he departed, he took out two denarii, gave them to the innkeeper, and said to him, "Take care of him; and whatever more you spend, when I come again, I will repay you." So which of these three do you think was neighbor to him who fell among the thieves?" And he said, "He who showed mercy on him." Then Jesus said to him, "Go and do likewise." (Luke 10:30–37)

"Neighbor" includes all people. Therefore, "You shall not commit adultery." If we love our neighbor, we will not commit adultery, because adultery is hatred of our neighbor. It is the destruction of our friends and family. Several years ago I counseled a woman who had entered into an ungodly relationship with someone else's husband. When I confronted the woman and her lover, she pushed me away, telling me to mind my own business. I counseled several people because of the trauma brought about by that adulterous relationship. Mothers and fathers, children, and best friends—adultery does not express love to one's neighbor.

"You shall not murder," "You shall not steal," "You shall not bear false witness." We do not love our neighbor by helping ourselves to his possessions, nor do we slander people we love or poison others again them. That kind of behavior violates a specific law of God, and most of all it violates the law of love. I once read an apt illustration pertaining to slander. Think about walking along the streets of New York on a dark night and deciding to take a shortcut. You enter into an alley, and all of a sudden you see somebody come out of the shadows with a knife raised. What do you do? If you have any sense, you run out of the alley and back to the light. The illustration was used to set the stage for warning against those who approach us and say, "Let me tell you something in love." Often that is just a license for a vicious personal attack.

"You shall not covet." If we were given the responsibility of establishing a new nation and were allowed only ten basic laws in which to frame the charter, what laws would we include? Would we think to include a law against covetousness? God did, because God knows what happens when someone is jealous of another, and he knows how destructive envy can be. We can understand an impulse to steal that is fueled by an overwhelming desire to possess the stolen item, but it is something else to say, "If I cannot have it, you cannot either." Vandalism is the worst form of envy and covetousness. God understands what destroys human relationships and fractures love.

Paul sums up: **Love does no harm to a neighbor** (v. 10a). If we love our neighbor, we do not steal from him or slander him, nor do we allow ourselves to be jealous or envious or to bear false witness against him. If we love somebody, we do not want to harm him. That is the way we are to live as Christians; we are to be known by the love that we have for one another.

Therefore, Paul concludes, **love is the fulfillment of the law** (v. 10b). Here Paul provides a terse treatment of the theme. In another epistle he writes an entire chapter about love, 1 Corinthians 13, which was not written as a treatise on romance but on neighbor love.

Time to Wake Up

And do this, knowing the time, that now it is high time to awake out of sleep; for now our salvation is nearer than when we first believed. The night is far spent, the day is at hand. Therefore let us cast off the works of darkness, and let us put on the armor of light (vv. 11–12). In this section Paul enjoins a certain kind of behavior and prohibits another. He prefaces it by reminding the people of the time. The time requires vigilance, alertness, and diligence. Some say that Paul might have been referencing the destruction of Jerusalem. He might have been, but most commentators—rightly so, I think—say that Paul is talking about the consummation of our salvation when we pass into glory.

Do you ever wonder how long you are going to live? I do that more now than when I was younger. Twenty years from now I might still be standing in a pulpit, but there is no doubt about the fact that I am not going to be in the pulpit fifty years from now. Whatever our age, it is time to wake up because the day is approaching, and therefore our salvation is nearer than when we first believed. The verb Paul uses here means "to save." The Greek word appears in the biblical text in every possible tense indicating a sense in which we were being saved and a sense in which we have been saved. The simple aorist tense is rendered "you are saved." The present tense is rendered "you are being saved," and the future tense reads "you shall be saved." The future perfect is rendered "you shall have been saved." Salvation is unfolded biblically in all those increments. Therefore, in the ultimate sense, we do not experience salvation the moment we were born again; that is just one aspect of salvation. The fullness of our salvation will not take place until our glorification when we enter into heaven.

Night and Day

Paul is addressing believers when he writes, "Our salvation is nearer than when we first believed." That is not bad news. It is good news because it means the fullness of our salvation comes closer to us with every passing hour. Paul uses a figure from the normal daily movement of the sun—the difference between night and day. The time already passed is the nighttime. We are now in the last watch of the night, and the dawn of the fullness of our salvation is about to break. This metaphor is used repeatedly in the Scriptures. By nature we are children of darkness. The metaphor is used to describe sin: "The light has come into the world, and men loved darkness rather than light, because their deeds were evil" (John 3:19).

Orlando is a beautiful city until the lights go out. Downtown Orlando in the wee hours of the night has been a bad crime center. Things happen in the darkness that do not happen in the light. People love darkness because it conceals them from exposure. When we are brought into the fullness of day, we are known for what we are.

Let us walk properly, as in the day, **not in revelry and drunkenness, not in lewdness and lust, not in strife and envy. But put on the Lord Jesus Christ, and make no provision for the flesh, to fulfill its lusts** (vv. 13–14). Paul's reference to rioting and drunkenness pertains to the pagan religious worship of the god Bacchus, the god of the grape and the vine. Bacchus was the sponsor of the ancient Bacchanalia, an orgiastic feast involving gluttony and unbridled sexual behavior. Participants set out to get drunk to silence pangs of conscience so they could engage in unbridled sin. In contrast to that, we are to put on the Lord Jesus Christ and make no provision for our flesh. Paul means that we are not to make or provide opportunities for sin.

An old country preacher said that if we desire to overcome drunkenness, we best not tie our horse to the post in front of the saloon. We are not to make provisions. If we struggle with sexual temptation, we ought not to subscribe to *Playboy*. We are not to make provisions for human sin and weakness. Luther put it this way: "I cannot keep sparrows from flying about my head, but I can keep them from making a nest in my hair." We are not to make provision to accommodate our base desires. Instead, we are to provide for our soul by putting on Christ and walking in daylight.

54

THE WEAKER BROTHER

Romans 14:1–13

Receive one who is weak in the faith, but not to disputes over doubtful things. For one believes he may eat all things, but he who is weak eats only vegetables. Let not him who eats despise him who does not eat, and let not him who does not eat judge him who eats; for God has received him. Who are you to judge another's servant? To his own master he stands or falls. Indeed, he will be made to stand, for God is able to make him stand. One person esteems one day above another; another esteems every day alike. Let each be fully convinced in his own mind. He who observes the day, observes it to the Lord; and he who does not observe the day, to the Lord he does not observe it. He who eats, eats to the Lord, for he gives God thanks; and he who does not eat, to the Lord he does not eat, and gives God thanks. For none of us lives to himself, and no one dies to himself. For if we live, we live to the Lord; and if we die, we die to the Lord. Therefore, whether we live or die, we are the Lord's. For to this end Christ died and rose and lived again, that He might be Lord of both the dead and the living. But why do you judge your brother? Or why do you show contempt for your brother? For we shall all stand before the judgment seat of Christ. For it is written:

"As I live, says the LORD,
Every knee shall bow to Me,
And every tongue shall confess to God."

So then each of us shall give account of himself to God. Therefore let us not judge one another anymore, but rather resolve this, not to put a stumbling block or a cause to fall in our brother's way.

A number of years ago I went for dinner to the home of Old Testament scholar Meredith Kline, north of Boston, Massachusetts. At the end of the visit, Dr. Kline prepared to drive me to my home, which was less than a mile away. As we left his house a torrential downpour began. Neither of us had an umbrella, so we dashed the one hundred yards through the rain to the car and got drenched in the process. No sooner had we entered the car than Dr. Kline dashed back out into the rain. He had forgotten something. When he returned to the car, he explained. "I forgot my driver's license."

I was incredulous. "You ran through that rain just to get your driver's license? We are only going down the street!"

He replied, "It is a small thing, but the Lord said if we cannot be faithful in little things, how will he trust us with the big things?"

As a matter of conscience and to submit himself to the civil magistrates, he made sure to have his license with him, as the law required. Without any great fanfare or demonstration of piety he ran back to the house without revealing to me the reason until I interrogated him. Some might say he was a man caught in the bonds of legalism, but I do not think that was the case. Obedience to God in small matters is never a matter of legalism.

Legalism

Legalism is a most destructive distortion of Christianity. There are two major distortions that block our sanctification, flipsides of the same coin. One is the spirit of antinomianism, which abuses Christian freedom by willfully sinning in light of grace. The other is legalism, which binds the freedom grace gives. Legalism makes minor matters the test of true spirituality. We have all encountered Christians who say the essence of spirituality is to refrain from dancing and lipstick and going to movies. The creed becomes "touch not, taste not, handle not." People substitute minor matters for the fruit of the Spirit and use adherence to those minor matters as the test of righteousness. Either distortion can be very destructive to the Christian life.

When Christ set his people free from the curse of the law, he gave them royal liberty, as there was in the garden of Eden, to eat freely from all the trees except those which God has clearly stated we ought not to touch. However, we do not all have the same scruples. Some believe that dancing is a sin; others do not. I knew someone who became convinced that playing ping-pong was a sin because he had gotten so caught up in it. He was addicted to ping-pong, and his work and family began to suffer as a result. For him, ping-pong did become a sin, but that does not mean everyone around him was called to set a prohibition against playing ping-pong. Ping-pong is not inherently evil.

We find in Scripture things about which God has said yes or no, but in between those matters of law there is a host of things that the New Testament describes as *adiaphorous*, morally neutral. In the early Christian church some developed scruples about eating meat, which is adiaphorous.

We read in Paul's letter to the Corinthians about a scandal that emerged among the Christians there that concerned the issue of eating meat that had been used in pagan idol worship. Some of the Corinthian Christians wanted to distance themselves in every conceivable way from every act of idolatry. As a matter of conscience they determined they would never purchase such meat, and they began to look down on their brothers who did purchase it and consume it freely. Those who ate it believed that nothing was inherently wrong with consuming the meat. They ate it without any pangs of conscience. A rift developed in the church between the divided parties, and Paul had to mediate the dispute. Something similar was going on in the Roman community, so in this epistle Paul wants to teach the people a lesson about how to use their Christian liberty. Although Paul taught it to both the Romans and the Corinthians, the lesson must be taught afresh to each generation.

The Weaker Brother

Romans 14 addresses the issue of Christian liberty with respect to the weaker brother. The chapter cannot be considered in isolation from what went before it; this is a continuation of Paul's exposition of love of neighbor, what it means to have fellowship marked by *agape*, spiritual love. Building on that theme Paul writes: **Receive one who is weak in the faith, but not to disputes over doubtful things. For one believes he may eat all things, but he who is weak eats only vegetables** (vv. 1–2).

Some in the early church were convinced that vegetarianism was the right road to follow. They believed that the spiritual measure was not only whether someone refrained from eating meat offered to idols but refrained from meat altogether. The vegetarians thought that exercising such restraint moved them to a higher level of spirituality. Those vegetarians were the ones Paul describes as weaker brothers. They did not understand the fullness of the biblical concept of Christian liberty. They were held captive to elemental principles of "taste not, touch not, handle not." They thought they were being devout when, in fact, they were being infantile and immature in their reasoning.

Some say we should ridicule those who are weaker or have nothing to do with them, but Paul is emphatic that such an approach is wrong: **Let not him who eats despise him who does not eat, and let not him who does not eat judge him who eats; for God has received him** (v. 3). According to Paul, we are not to avoid one another when we differ on matters of *adiaphora*. Paul is not saying that we should be cavalier about heinous sin; he is referring to issues of indifference. The weaker brother has a misinformed understanding of what God allows or forbids, but the weaker one is still our brother and has been received by God. Since he has been welcomed into the family of God, the dispute is a family matter.

As God receives us by grace, we must receive one another by grace. Love covers a multitude of sins as well as a multitude of misunderstandings and weak theology. One who is weak ought not to despise one who manifests liberty, and one who manifests liberty ought not to despise one with a scrupulous conscience.

Paul asks a rhetorical question: **Who are you to judge another's servant?** (v. 4a). Paul is using a marketplace analogy, but the point is that we are all servants of Christ, so who are we to despise another of Christ's servants? If a servant is acceptable to Jesus, how can he not be acceptable to us? The analogy is simple. The weak brother has his scruple unto the Lord; the strong brother has his freedom unto the Lord.

One person esteems one day above another (v. 5a). Paul is not writing about the Sabbath but about certain holy days that Jews observed. Some of the converted Jews had clung to their Jewish traditions and observations. Even though those traditions were no longer enjoined upon the Christian community, some of them, as a matter of conscience, continued those practices. Here Paul gives them freedom to do so.

There are other applications of Christian freedom. Someone I know sits on the board of trustees of a Christian institution, and as a member of that board, he is not allowed to drink wine. The organization has elevated a preference into a rule. They have legislated where God has given freedom. He explained to me that the board was concerned that its members stand out from the culture at large, and I replied, "Do you realize that Jesus and the apostles could not serve on the board of your organization?" We can appreciate their concern to keep the institution unspotted from the world, but their position is one of weakness.

Understanding Christian Liberty

The classical understanding of Christian liberty is this: we are not to try to force somebody with a scruple against something, as uninformed as that scruple may be, to violate his conscience. The basic principle that unfolds here is one of loving sensitivity. If my brother believes that drinking a glass of wine is sin, I ought not to try to coax him into drinking a glass of wine. That would be an attempt to entice him to violate his conscience. The violation of one's conscience, even if it is a misinformed conscience, is a serious matter. That does not mean we should stand back and allow our weaker brother to make his scruple the law of the church. Paul makes clear in his teaching that though we are to be sensitive, loving, and kind to the weaker brother, we ought never to allow him to exercise tyranny over the church.

Paul was constantly confronted with this issue in dealing with the Judaizing conflict. Paul had Timothy circumcised as a matter of indifference, but then the Judaizers came and said that circumcision was necessary for Christians and therefore every Christian must undergo the rite. Paul resisted them with the full force of his apostleship and refused to circumcise those who demanded it. Circumcision was a matter of indifference, but when the weaker brother, the Judaizers, tried to make their weakness the law of the church, Paul put an end to Christian tolerance.

We walk a very thin line. The weaker brother is not to destroy the freedom of all in the church. At the same time, we can forego our freedom for a time out of consideration for our weaker brother. Paul is opposing a spirit of arrogance that leads us to insist on our rights to do whatever we please no matter what. That is the wrong approach. The stronger brother has to be willing to forego his strength for the sake of the weaker brother, yet the church must never allow the weaker one to establish his weakness as law for the Christian community.

That is the essence of what the apostle is setting forth here in Romans 14 and also in 1 Corinthians 8. We are to do what we do to the Lord. **For none of us lives to himself, and no one dies to himself. For if we live, we live to the Lord; and if we die, we die to the Lord. Therefore, whether we live or die, we are the Lord's. For to this end Christ died and rose and lived again, that He might be Lord of both the dead and the living. But why do you judge your brother? Or why do you show contempt for your brother? For we shall all stand before the judgment seat of Christ. For it is written: "As I live, says the LORD, every knee shall bow to Me, and every tongue shall confess to God." So then each of us shall give account of himself to**

God. Therefore let us not judge one another anymore, but rather resolve this, not to put a stumbling block or a cause to fall in our brother's way (vv. 7–13). Simple human kindness and consideration have to go both ways. Again, the application is to things that have no inherent goodness or evil. No one can use this principle to participate in adultery or other sins. These precepts have to do with eating meat, drinking wine, observing certain days that have no direct bearing on the kingdom of God. The great danger is to allow these *adiaphorous* matters to become requirements for Christian spirituality and, even worse, the test for what is spiritual and righteous. Unfortunately, that is what happens again and again.

Christians and Alcohol

I recall a certain dinner I ate with a group at a restaurant. The waitress came to serve us and asked, "May I take your drink orders? Would anybody like a cocktail?" Our hostess cut her off, saying, "No, we are Christians." The smug self-righteousness of our hostess not only embarrassed the waitress, who was simply doing her job, but she gave a wrong message about Christianity. Christianity is not about eating and drinking.

Drinking alcohol is a controversial topic in the Christian community. Many argue that Jesus never drank wine and that when the Pharisees called Jesus a winebibber, they were distorting the truth. They also argue that the wine Jesus made for the wedding in Cana was unfermented. Arguing that way, however, is a hopeless, tortuous treatment of the biblical text, but it happens when people come to the text with a cultural bias. Many are convinced that total abstinence is the only spiritual way, but we learn no such thing from the Scriptures—not from the Old Testament or from the celebration of the Passover. If we were to do a word study of the word *wine* in the Bible, we would see that it was the real thing. God sanctified it and warned against drinking too much of it, because getting drunk is a sin. God did not give that warning against drunkenness to people drinking grape juice.

This view is offensive to many people. To all such who are convinced that they cannot drink wine, then they must never let wine touch their lips, because for them it is a sin. For others it is not. Our brother ought not to judge us, and we ought not to judge our brother.

55

KINGDOM LIFE

Romans 14:14–23

I know and am convinced by the Lord Jesus that there is nothing unclean of itself; but to him who considers anything to be unclean, to him it is unclean. Yet if your brother is grieved because of your food, you are no longer walking in love. Do not destroy with your food the one for whom Christ died. Therefore do not let your good be spoken of as evil; for the kingdom of God is not eating and drinking, but righteousness and peace and joy in the Holy Spirit. For he who serves Christ in these things is acceptable to God and approved by men. Therefore let us pursue the things which make for peace and the things by which one may edify another. Do not destroy the work of God for the sake of food. All things indeed are pure, but it is evil for the man who eats with offense. It is good neither to eat meat nor drink wine nor do anything by which your brother stumbles or is offended or is made weak. Do you have faith? Have it to yourself before God. Happy is he who does not condemn himself in what he approves. But he who doubts is condemned if he eats, because he does not eat from faith; for whatever is not from faith is sin.

Paul continues with the instruction that we began to examine in our last study. We saw that in *adiaphorous* matters, that is, in matters of indifference, the stronger brother is to respond to the weaker brother with patience. Certainly we are not to tolerate gross and heinous evil or disobedience to God's laws, but we are to respect people's differing views in areas where God has left us free.

Nothing Unclean

I know and am convinced by the Lord Jesus that there is nothing unclean of itself (v. 14a). Paul is not giving an educated guess about what is clean or unclean. He writes from apostolic conviction, a basis of certainty, which he grounds not in his own research but on what he received directly from Christ. Paul is passing on to the church what his Lord and Savior has revealed to him. Paul does not mean that there is no inherent evil in the world. Adultery and murder are inherently evil. Paul is still addressing the question about eating and drinking and the disputes that arose about them.

In the Old Testament God called Israel from among the nations to be his chosen people so that they might be a light to the rest of the world. They were called to be different in many respects from the pagan world from which they had come. God had a unique relationship with the people of Israel, and he bound them to himself at Mount Sinai by the giving of the law, the Ten Commandments. The commandments were the provisions of the covenant. To the laws governing his holy nation, God added ceremonial rites and responsibilities. There were great feasts to be celebrated, such as the Passover. He also gave to the children of Israel a list of dietary regulations that they were obliged to keep at all times, and the Israelites were scrupulous about trying to keep those dietary laws.

When Israel was taken away captive to Babylon, the Babylonians did not take every Jew. They selected the crème de la crème of the Jewish people—the most educated, gifted, artistic, and eloquent. The Babylonian monarchy set out to deconstruct these captive Jews by assimilating them into the Babylonian culture. Daniel ended up in the lion's den, and Shadrach, Meshach, and Abednego wound up in the fiery furnace, not just because they refused to bow down to the image of the king but because they refused to break God's dietary laws. During the exile in Babylon, the Jews were ready to pay with their lives if necessary to keep from eating foods that God had declared unclean. Century after century in every Jewish household children were trained about permissible and forbidden foods. The tradition continues to this day among orthodox Jews.

When the New Testament economy appeared, what had been considered unclean was declared clean. In the book of Acts we read that Peter had a vision in which it was revealed to him that things previously deemed unclean were now clean (10:9–16). The whole issue provoked so much debate among the first generation of Jewish Christians that it was necessary to call the first great council of the church. This council, the Council of Jerusalem, addressed whether dietary laws should be imposed upon the Gentile community. After centuries of abstaining from certain foods, God suddenly annulled those laws. Nothing less than a specific revelation, such as Jesus gave to Peter, would have been sufficient to give them liberty of conscience to depart from that ancient tradition. Even after being given his vision, Peter stumbled over it. Later on, under the influence and pressure of the so-called Judaizers, who wanted to continue to enforce the former dietary restrictions, Peter caved in until the apostle Paul rebuked him publicly. After that, Peter regained his courage and agreed to what had been revealed to him in his vision.

Christian Practice and God's Law

To what extent does the Old Testament law have any bearing upon our lives? Has the new covenant, with its accent on grace, completely freed us from obeying the Old Testament law? Many in the church today practice antinomianism, claiming that the Old Testament law has no claim whatsoever upon the New Testament Christian. Are we still to have our consciences influenced by the law of the Old Testament?

Reformed theology has historically divided Old Testament law into three parts: the moral law, the ceremonial law, and dietary law. The church says that certain laws in the Old Testament are no longer applicable in the new covenant, including the dietary laws and the ceremonial laws. We do not slaughter animals and offer sacrifices. In fact, if we were to do that, we would be denying the perfect finished work of Jesus. The ceremonies of the Old Testament have been abrogated. They were fulfilled in Christ and, therefore, set aside. Likewise, the dietary laws are no longer binding on the New Testament Christian. However, it is argued, the third element, the moral law, remains intact; we are still bound by the moral law of God. I have a quibble with that, because obeying those ceremonial and dietary laws was a moral issue of the highest magnitude for Shadrach, Meshach, Abednego, and Daniel. For the Old Testament Jew, keeping every aspect of the law was a great ethical and moral concern. For that reason, we have to be careful when we categorize Old Testament laws.

The law of God reflects his holy character. The historical context in which he gave all his laws was this: "You shall therefore be holy, for I am holy" (Lev. 11:45; 19:2; 20:26; 21:8). Therefore, we are given to understand that God's laws are not arbitrary. He has a holy and sacred purpose for every law he legislates. The law comes from his character.

The nature of God and his character are immutable. Those divine attributes can never be negotiated. He does not change. So then, since the law reflects God's character and his character never changes, how is it possible that any of the Old Testament laws could ever be abrogated? We see that the New Testament does in fact abrogate certain laws of the Old Testament and that it is God himself who abrogates them. If God abrogates a law, it is abrogated. That leaves us asking a question about God's immutable character—does the abrogation of laws contradict God's immutability?

Natural Law and Purposive Law

With respect to the moral law of God, we make a distinction between two kinds of law: God's natural law and God's purposive law. God's law is *purposive* in that God has a sacred and holy purpose for every law he legislates. I use the term *natural law* in a different way from how it has been used historically in philosophy and jurisprudence. When Clarence Thomas went before the Senate Judiciary Committee to be examined for confirmation as a Supreme Court justice, Senator Joseph Biden asked him a provocative question: "Do you believe in natural law?" Clarence Thomas said yes. He affirmed his commitment to natural-law theory, which provoked a hostile response, not only from Senator Biden but from other members of the committee.

The customary meaning of the term *natural law*, the *lex naturalis*, goes back to ancient Rome and even before that to Greece. It means that there are principles of conduct—moral principles and ethics—built into the nature of things that are found in the law of nations. If you look at the civilized nations of the world, all have some law against murder in the first degree and theft, reflecting a common understanding of conscience. That is called *natural law*. Natural law has been thought by philosophers, not just those who are Christian, to be a manifestation of the eternal law of God, the *lex aeterna totus*. God eternally is a God of law. His law is revealed to us not only in the Ten Commandments but in our consciences (Rom. 2:15). Therefore, God's law comes not only from the Bible but from nature itself. That is what is normally meant by the term *natural law*, but it is not what I am referring to here.

When theologians make a distinction between the natural law of God and the purposive law of God, they are not really addressing some transcendent framework for laws enacted in various nations. Rather, God's natural laws are those God gives based on his holy nature, and because they are based on his holy nature, those laws are immutable. For God to abrogate a law that comes from his nature, such as the law against idolatry, he would be compromising his character. God has given other laws for a particular redemptive purpose, which is not necessarily rooted in his eternal immutable being. For example, the dietary laws he gave to Israel were given for a particular reason for a particular time. When that time was fulfilled, God annulled those laws without doing any damage to his character.

God's character was in no way compromised when he put an end to the offering of bulls and goats in the ceremonial rites of the Old Testament. I hope we understand that distinction, because many people in the first century did not understand it. They struggled because they had spent their entire lives being careful not to eat certain foods or drink certain beverages.

As we saw in our last study, pagan religions used both wine and meat in their sacrifices. Wine was used as an oblation and meat was offered on the altars of various deities. Once those religious observances had been completed, the sacrificed wine and meat were taken to the marketplace and sold. Some Christians purchased the food and wine. Others objected to such purchases because the food had been used in pagan rites. It is important to note that the wine itself was not at issue—it was the source of the wine.

That brings us to the question of primary and secondary separation, in which the question of drinking wine applies. We might also consider the use of our tax dollars. Should we pay our taxes if the government uses them to support abortion on demand? Yes, we should. If I separate myself and my family from abortion, it is a primary separation, but if I separate myself from anybody that has something to do with abortion, that is a secondary separation. If we were consistent in secondary separation from evil, we would have to leave the planet, because there is no way to keep ourselves unscathed from what the rest of the world does. If I pay a merchant for his cloth and then he takes my money and uses it in some ungodly way, I am not responsible for what he does with the money after I give it to him, just as I am not responsible for what a corrupt government may do with my taxes after I pay them. That is the difference between primary and secondary separation.

Paul says that there is nothing unclean with respect to food and drink. Food that had once been declared unclean by God did not make that food intrinsically dirty; what made it dirty was God's prohibition, which he had established to show the watching world that his people were different, both internally and externally.

The Rule of Conscience

But to him who considers anything to be unclean, to him it is unclean (v. 14b). I mentioned before the illustration of ping-pong. My former colleague began to believe that he was sinfully addicted to ping-pong, but he did not say that ping-pong is inherently evil so that no one ought to engage in the sport. The principle is that no one should be so engaged in ping-pong that they neglect their family or work. The principle here is clear: if we believe that something is a sin, even if it is not, yet we participate in it, then we have committed a sin because we have done something we believe to be wrong, whether or not it actually is wrong. The sin is not eating the food or wearing the lipstick or playing ping-pong; the sin is doing something that we think is evil. In a word, we act against our conscience.

At the Diet of Worms, Luther was called upon to recant his convictions, but he said, "My conscience is held captive to the Word of God . . . to go against conscience is neither right nor safe." Luther understood the principles that Paul expounds in Romans 14. To act against conscience is neither right nor safe. Neither Paul nor Luther was espousing what I call Jiminy Cricket theology. Jiminy Cricket said, "Always let your conscience be your guide," but unless your conscience is shaped and ruled by the Word of God, we dare not let it be our guide. There are psychopathic murderers and others who commit the most vicious of dastardly deeds who feel no remorse for their actions. If they were to plead "not guilty" in court because they do not feel guilty, they would not be mounting a very strong defense.

Our consciences, the Bible tells us, can be seared and distorted. Jeremiah rebuked the children of Israel for their repeated sins and said, "You have had a harlot's forehead" (Jer. 3:3). They had lost the capacity to blush. They had sinned so often that they no longer felt any pangs of guilt, but that did not excuse them. The fact that their consciences said it was okay did not mean it was okay. If our conscience is informed by Hollywood or popular music—which tells us if it feels good, it is good—we will be without excuse on the day of judgment. The flipside of that is Paul's concern here. If my conscience tells me that something is evil, I may not act against it even if my conscience has not been properly informed. It is not right to do something we believe to be sin.

Yet if your brother is grieved because of your food, you are no longer walking in love. Do not destroy with your food the one for whom Christ died (v. 15). If we are the stronger brother, we are not to parade our freedom in the face of our weaker brother who is convinced otherwise. We are to be sensitive. The one with a misinformed conscience is our brother or sister in faith.

Therefore do not let your good be spoken of as evil (v. 16). We find here another important ethical principle. We have to bend over backwards not to give the appearance of evil. We cannot do that perfectly, and there are some who are going to think we are doing evil no matter how careful we are in our behavior. However, as much as we can, we need to be careful that our good not be spoken of in evil terms. If we were to take that to an extreme, we would have to stop preaching the gospel altogether because some who are hostile to the gospel will consider the preaching of it as evil, just as they did when Jesus and the apostles preached it. We cannot control that, in the final analysis, but we do not have to throw gasoline on the fire by going out of our way to cause offense to those who are watching us.

Kingdom Living

For the kingdom of God is not eating and drinking (v. 17a). The disputes concerning trivial matters that tear churches apart would not happen if we would just grasp the principle that the kingdom of God is not about eating, drinking, lipstick, or any external thing. It is about **righteousness and peace and joy in the Holy Spirit** (v. 17b). We have here a triad of virtues that describes what the kingdom of God is about.

First, the kingdom is about righteousness. Righteousness is misunderstood in the church today, where the goal of so many is to be pious or spiritual. The goal of the kingdom is not spirituality. The goal of our Christian life is not spirituality. Spirituality is a good thing, but it is not the goal; it is a means to the goal. The goal of the Christian life is righteousness, and we are to seek it. We are to strive to be righteous people.

The Pharisees majored in the pursuit of righteousness, but true righteousness is not a pharisaical parading of a holier-than-thou attitude. Jesus said, "Seek first the kingdom of God and His righteousness, and all these things shall be added to you" (Matt. 6:33). Our first priority is to pursue God's kingdom and his righteousness. Jesus also said, "Unless your righteousness exceeds the righteousness of the scribes and Pharisees, you will by no means enter the kingdom of heaven" (Matt. 5:20). We know, however, that all our righteousness is as filthy rags. The epistle of Romans was written to show that the only way we can stand before God is if we are clothed not in our own righteousness but in the righteousness of Christ.

Since by faith we have his righteousness, why would we bother seeking our own? Justification is not the end of the Christian life; it is the beginning, and it is to be followed by a rigorous pursuit of holiness. That is what righteousness is. To be a mature Christian is to live according to the principles of God. Righteousness is not defined in categories of eating and drinking. Churches that elevate trivial matters as the true test of Christian living are destructive. To say people are Christian only if they do not go to movies or dances is nonsense. Anybody can refrain from those things. It is the fruit of the Spirit that Christ wants for us—love, patience, longsuffering, meekness, humility. Paul is basically telling the church at Rome to grow up.

Second, the kingdom of God is about peace. Jeremiah decried those who proclaimed, "Peace, peace!" when there was no peace (Jer. 6:14; 8:11). There are so-called peacemakers in the church who say that since doctrine divides, we must not enter into debates about theological matters. Luther called that *carnal* peace, because it is born of the flesh and comes from fear of conflict or cowardice. Of course, we are not to be bellicose people, looking for a fight and being contentious over every minor point, which happens when immature people major in minors.

Third, the kingdom of God is about joy. It does not consist of a company of sourpusses. We should be happy people. The kingdom of God is about the joy that has been shed abroad in our hearts because we have been redeemed by the Lord our God. Why should we be glum and fuss over who eats meat and drinks wine? Such things are not what the kingdom of God is about, according to Paul. Life in the kingdom is about loving the things of God and loving those for whom Christ died. That is the recipe for mature Christian unity.

56

THE PURSUIT OF PEACE

Romans 14:19–15:13

Therefore let us pursue the things which make for peace and the things by which one may edify another. Do not destroy the work of God for the sake of food. All things indeed are pure, but it is evil for the man who eats with offense. It is good neither to eat meat nor drink wine nor do anything by which your brother stumbles or is offended or is made weak. Do you have faith? Have it to yourself before God. Happy is he who does not condemn himself in what he approves. But he who doubts is condemned if he eats, because he does not eat from faith; for whatever is not from faith is sin. We then who are strong ought to bear with the scruples of the weak, and not to please ourselves. Let each of us please his neighbor for his good, leading to edification. For even Christ did not please Himself; but as it is written, "The reproaches of those who reproached You fell on Me." For whatever things were written before were written for our learning, that we through the patience and comfort of the Scriptures might have hope. Now may the God of patience and comfort grant you to be like-minded toward one another, according to Christ Jesus, that you may with one mind and one mouth glorify the God and Father of our Lord Jesus Christ. Therefore receive one another, just as Christ also received us, to the glory of God. Now I say that Jesus Christ has become a servant to the circumcision for the truth of God, to confirm the promises made to the fathers, and that the Gentiles might glorify God for His mercy, as it is written:

> "For this reason I will confess to You among the Gentiles,
> And sing to Your name."

And again he says:

> "Rejoice, O Gentiles, with His people!"

And again:

> "Praise the LORD, all you Gentiles!
> Laud Him, all you peoples!"

And again, Isaiah says:

> "There shall be a root of Jesse;
> And He who shall rise to reign over the Gentiles,
> In Him the Gentiles shall hope."

Now may the God of hope fill you with all joy and peace in believing, that you may abound in hope by the power of the Holy Spirit.

How are we to treat weaker brothers in terms of *adiaphorous* matters, that is, in things that are not inherently wrong but nevertheless bother the consciences of some? This is such a serious matter that Paul deals with it not only here in Romans but also in his correspondence to the Corinthian church and in his writing to the Galatians. The issue was also at the center of debate in the first-century church. The concern there was how the Jewish converts were to receive and deal with the Gentiles coming into the covenant community. It was a matter of great urgency to the apostle.

A Call to Action

Therefore let us pursue the things which make for peace and the things by which one may edify another. Do not destroy the work of God for the sake of food (vv. 19–20a). Here we find a conclusion that comes from Paul's previous reasoning. It is a call to action. When we pursue something, we chase after it not casually but with a degree of earnestness.

When I was three years old, the most exciting toy I received for Christmas was a metal plane in which I could sit and peddle around the streets. It was called a pursuit plane. That was the first time I heard the word *pursuit*. Not until much later did I understand that pursuit planes were designed to search out and destroy the enemy. That is the action to which Paul is calling us. We are to chase after and seek diligently the things that make for peace.

The opposite of peace is war; it is conflict. God's people are not to chase after fights and look for conflict. We are to search for things that make for peace, and the sort of peace we are to chase is peace that passes understanding. It is the peace that Jesus left as his legacy: "Peace I leave with you, My peace I give to you; not as the world gives do I give to you" (John 14:27). There is a reason why our Lord is called the Prince of Peace. In fact, his ultimate mission was to bring us peace with God, to reconcile us to him.

There is a sharp contrast between two words in verse 19—*edify* and *destroy*. Most of us have a vivid mental picture of what happened in New York City on 9/11. We saw video of the planes crashing into the World Trade Center towers and we witnessed the implosion of those magnificent buildings. One thing we will never forget about the Twin Towers is how quickly they fell to the ground. Ever since, there have been plans for rebuilding the towers, but it takes much longer to build a building than to destroy one. To edify, to produce an edifice, involves building, which is the stark opposite of destroying.

Paul is concerned about that when it comes to manifesting love in the body of Christ. He wants his readers to recognize that it is much easier to destroy our brother than to edify him. Christ came not to destroy us but to destroy the works of the Devil. He came to build for himself a people that will manifest his image. That is what we are to pursue in the church. We are not to be known for being critical, for attacking each other and gossiping. Slander is the principle work of Satan, which is why his title is Slanderer. He is the destructive one who brings false claims to tear people apart. We are called in the name of Jesus to build up, not tear apart.

Man Pleasers

All things indeed are pure, but it is evil for the man who eats with offense. It is good neither to eat meat nor drink wine nor do anything by which your brother stumbles or is offended or is made weak (vv. 20b–21). Paul is repeating the principle of considering our weaker brothers and sisters. If we understand the freedom we have in Christ, we are not to flaunt our liberty before our weaker brothers who may not understand their freedom. We can eat our meat in private, before the Lord, who sees all things: **Have it to yourself before God. Happy is he who does not condemn himself in what he approves. But he who doubts is condemned if he eats, because he does not eat from faith; for**

whatever is not from faith is sin (vv. 22b–23). It bears repeating that there is danger and impropriety in acting against conscience.

Paul continues that line of thought into chapter 15 with this admonition: **We then who are strong ought to bear with the scruples of the weak, and not to please ourselves. Let each of us please his neighbor for his good, leading to edification** (15:1–2). When the Galatians compromised the gospel, Paul wrote some of the strongest language we find anywhere in his epistles:

> I marvel that you are turning away so soon from Him who called you in the grace of Christ, to a different gospel, which is not another, but there are some who trouble you and want to pervert the gospel of Christ. But even if we, or an angel from heaven, preach any other gospel to you than what we have preached to you, let him be accursed. (Gal. 1:6–9)

Let him be *anathema*, let him be damned. Paul follows up those strong words with a sharp warning: "Do I now persuade men, or God? Or do I seek to please men? For if I still pleased men, I would not be a bondservant of Christ" (v. 10).

Paul's words to the Galatians seem to be a direct contradiction to what we just read from Romans, where he writes that we are not to please ourselves but to please our brother. To the Galatians he says that if he is pleasing man, he cannot be a disciple of God. He is talking about two different types of pleasing. In Galatians he is talking about a sin: compromising or distorting the gospel for the sake of man-pleasing, which has occurred repeatedly down through church history. The gospel is foolishness to those who are perishing. Human beings have a built-in hostility against the truth of God. If we seek the sort of carnal peace that attempts to avoid conflict at any cost, and if we seek to please men rather than God, we are enemies of the gospel.

In the context of the Galatians' struggle, Paul referred to man-pleasing as a dreadful vice, not a virtue. To the Ephesians he wrote against offering mere sight service: "Bondservants, be obedient to those who are your masters according to the flesh, with fear and trembling, in sincerity of heart, as to Christ; not with eyeservice, as men-pleasers, but as bondservants of Christ, doing the will of God from the heart" (Eph. 6:5–6). We talk about giving "lip service," which means that we say one thing while really thinking another. Those who give sight service work diligently when the eye of the supervisor is directed toward them, but as soon as the boss leaves the worker takes his ease and gives little effort to do what is right. That is man-pleasing of the worst sort, but it is not what Paul is talking about here in Romans. Here

Paul is saying that we ought to bear with the scruples of the weak rather than please ourselves.

The Zeal of Christ

We do not try to please people for the sake of personal gain. That is the principle underlying this discussion about being patient with one another. Paul gives the supreme model for doing so, quoting from Psalm 69: **For even Christ did not please Himself; but as it is written, "The reproaches of those who reproached You fell on Me"** (v. 3). Jesus did not find his pleasure in doing what he wanted to do. Later in that psalm we read:

> You know my reproach, my shame, and my dishonor;
>> My adversaries are all before You.
> Reproach has broken my heart,
>> And I am full of heaviness;
>> I looked for someone to take pity, but there was none;
>> And for comforters, but I found none
> They also gave me gall for my food,
>> And for my thirst they gave me vinegar to drink. (vv. 19–21)

Psalm 69 is a psalm of messianic expectancy:

> Because for Your sake I have borne reproach;
>> Shame has covered my face.
> I have become a stranger to my brothers,
>> And an alien to my mother's children;
> Because zeal for Your house has eaten me up,
>> And the reproaches of those who reproach You have fallen on me.
> (vv. 7–9)

The Messiah was known for his singular zeal for his Father's house. Zeal for his Father's house consumed him; it ate him alive. Jesus is described that way in the Scriptures. He was so passionately committed to doing the will of the Father that he was consumed by it. His meat and drink was to please the Father, and as a result, the reproaches that were directed against God came upon him. Paul directs the Romans to the supreme example of Jesus. He was willing to suffer the reproach of the world and not please himself so that his people would be redeemed and edified, which is so unlike our natural selfishness. We want to please ourselves rather than others. Who among us has grace so sown in our soul that we are consumed by a passion to put others before ourselves?

Formula for Joy

As a board member of Prison Fellowship, some years ago I visited a maximum-security prison in Minneapolis, Stillwater State Prison, which was the most ungodly place I have ever been. Human beings behaved like animals; it was beastly to behold. A fellow board member visiting the prison with me was Lem Barney, all-pro defensive back for the Detroit Lions. This veteran of the wars of the National Football League came to an audience that overall was profoundly hostile. Barney stood up before the prisoners and began to sing:

> Lord, help me to live from day to day
> In such a self-forgetful way,
> That even when I kneel to pray
> My prayer shall be for others.
>
> Others, Lord, yes others,
> Let this my motto be,
> Help me to live for others,
> That I may live like Thee.

You could have heard a pin drop. Barney sang a children's song that captured the essence of Christian love. We are called to live for others.

JOY is a well-used acrostic: *J*esus first, *O*thers second, *Y*ourself last. We do not need a PhD in theology to get that message. That is the formula for joy. When we do what the apostle enjoins here, seeking to please others for their edification, the by-product for us is not loss but gain. We ourselves are edified in the process.

For whatever things were written before were written for our learning, that we through the patience and comfort of the Scriptures might have hope (v. 4). I know of nothing more comforting to the soul than the Word of God. When my soul is cast down (and it is cast down from time to time, as everyone's is), there is no greater panacea than to immerse myself in the Word of God.

When Simeon saw Jesus in the arms of his mother, he sang the Nunc Dimittis:

> Lord, now You are letting Your servant depart in peace,
> According to Your word;
>> For my eyes have seen Your salvation
>> Which You have prepared before the face of all peoples,
>> A light to bring revelation to the Gentiles,
> And the glory of Your people Israel. (Luke 2:29–32)

Most think the Paraclete, the Comforter, the Helper is the third person of the Trinity, the Holy Spirit, but he is the other Paraclete, "another Helper" (John 14:16). The primary Paraclete is Jesus, and he bestows his comfort to his people through his Word. People have asked me why I fight tenaciously to maintain the integrity of Holy Scripture in an age of skeptical cynicism, and I ask in response, "Do you want to take away my comfort, which is here in the inspired Word of God?" When God speaks, even in judgment, there is comfort.

There is a difference between the accusations of Satan, when he calls attention to our sin, and the conviction of the Holy Spirit. When Satan comes to accuse us, he comes to destroy. There is no comfort in it. When the Spirit convicts us of sin, as painful as it may be, he never leaves us destroyed. Even in his conviction, he brings comfort and consolation, never leaving us without hope. Along with the conviction he brings certainty of the forgiveness available to us.

Here Paul speaks of the comfort of the Scriptures in order that we might have hope. Without the patience and comfort that is delivered to our hearts by the Word of God, we would be like the rest of the world—without hope. The world is perishing before our very eyes. People parade in eloquent pride presenting thin disguises of their sad hopelessness. Those without Christ are without hope; those in Christ are never without hope.

Like-minded in Hope

Paul continues in the terms of a benediction: **Now may the God of patience and comfort grant you to be like-minded toward one another, according to Christ Jesus, that you may with one mind and one mouth glorify the God and Father of our Lord Jesus Christ** (vv. 5–6). This is what heaven will be like. When we get to heaven, the saints will be of one mind and voice, singing together to the honor and glory of God, but that is also what the church in this world is supposed to look like.

We come to another conclusion: **Therefore receive one another, just as Christ also received us, to the glory of God** (v. 7). When we receive one another in our various weaknesses and strengths, we do it to the glory of God. It is not simply a matter of showing kindness; it is about glorifying Jesus.

Now I say that Jesus Christ has become a servant to the circumcision for the truth of God, to confirm the promises made to the fathers, and that the Gentiles might glorify God for His mercy (vv. 8–9a). Paul comes back to the place and function of the Gentiles in the kingdom of God in the new covenant. He then cites several passages from the Old Testament.

> **For this reason I will confess to You among the Gentiles,**
> **And sing to Your name . . .**
>
> **Rejoice, O Gentiles, with His people!** (vv. 9b–10)

Jew and Gentile come together with one voice, one mind, one Lord, one faith, and one baptism. Then:

> **Praise the LORD, all you Gentiles!**
> **Laud Him, all you peoples! . . .**
>
> **There shall be a root of Jesse;**
> **And He who shall rise to reign over the Gentiles,**
> **In Him the Gentiles shall hope.** (vv. 11–12)

Someone from the family of Jesse, from the seed of David, would come centuries later and rise to reign over the Gentiles. That one was Christ, and in him the Gentiles found hope. **Now may the God of hope fill you with all joy and peace in believing, that you may abound in hope by the power of the Holy Spirit** (v. 13). We are given the slightest hint here of what Paul will cover in great detail when he writes to the Corinthians and to the Galatians—the fruit of the Spirit. The Holy Spirit works in our hearts to shed love abroad and to produce the fruit of joy, peace, hope, forbearance, patience, kindness, goodness, and humility. That is what the God of all hope does when he fills us with his love in the power of the Holy Spirit.

57

A MINISTER OF GOD

Romans 15:14–33

Now I myself am confident concerning you, my brethren, that you also are full of goodness, filled with all knowledge, able also to admonish one another. Nevertheless, brethren, I have written more boldly to you on some points, as reminding you, because of the grace given to me by God, that I might be a minister of Jesus Christ to the Gentiles, ministering the gospel of God, that the offering of the Gentiles might be acceptable, sanctified by the Holy Spirit. Therefore I have reason to glory in Christ Jesus in the things which pertain to God. For I will not dare to speak of any of those things which Christ has not accomplished through me, in word and deed, to make the Gentiles obedient—in mighty signs and wonders, by the power of the Spirit of God, so that from Jerusalem and round about to Illyricum I have fully preached the gospel of Christ. And so I have made it my aim to preach the gospel, not where Christ was named, lest I should build on another man's foundation, but as it is written:

> "To whom He was not announced, they shall see;
> And those who have not heard shall understand."

For this reason I also have been much hindered from coming to you. But now no longer having a place in these parts, and having a great desire these many years to come to you, whenever I journey to Spain, I shall come to you. For I hope to see you on my journey, and to be helped on my way there by you, if first I may enjoy your company for a while. But now I am going to Jerusalem to minister to the saints. For it pleased those from Macedonia and Achaia to make a certain contribution for the poor among the saints who are in Jerusalem. It pleased them indeed, and they are their debtors. For if the Gentiles have been partakers of their spiritual things, their duty is also to minister to them in material things. Therefore, when I have performed this and have sealed to them this fruit, I shall go by way of you to Spain. But I know that when I come to you, I shall come in the fullness of the blessing of the gospel of Christ. Now I beg you, brethren, through the Lord Jesus Christ, and through the love of the Spirit, that you strive together with me in prayers to God for me, that I may be delivered from those in Judea who do not believe, and that my service for Jerusalem may be acceptable to the saints, that I may come to you with joy by the will of God, and may be refreshed together with you. Now the God of peace be with you all. Amen.

We can tell from Paul's tone that he is gradually drawing the letter to a close. He expounded weighty theological matters in the first eleven chapters, and then he transitioned to practical application. Now Paul begins to speak of his personal relationships with those who will receive the epistle. We tend to skip over the personal parts of the epistles, as if they contain no great weight of divine revelation. I was once heard a taped sermon, now a classic, by the late Clarence McCartney. That magnificent sermon, entitled "Come before Winter," was preached from a simple phrase Paul used in his final requests to Timothy in the second and last epistle he wrote to his beloved disciple. The treasures found by McCartney in those seemingly desultory remarks are a good reminder not to take lightly anything that Paul mentions in passing.

Paul has just finished writing that the Christian life is to be characterized by a fullness of joy, a completeness of peace, and a dimension of hope worked in our soul by the power of the Holy Spirit. He continues: **Now I myself am confident concerning you, my brethren, that you also are full of goodness, filled with all knowledge, able also to admonish one another** (v. 14). This might well be viewed as a thinly veiled apology. Paul is aware that those who will receive this theological treatise—the weightiest epistle to come from the pen of the apostle— already know all he is writing to them about. **Nevertheless, brethren, I have written more boldly to you on some points, as reminding you** (v. 15a).

The Minister's Burden

From the beginning of his ministry to the very end Paul was acutely conscious of the burden that Christ had put upon him as an apostle of God's gospel. He knew that his duty was to communicate the full counsel of God. That burden has been shared by every earnest minister of the gospel ever since. The pulpit is not a place for the minister to orate or opine on his personal preferences or insights. The pulpit is where the Word of God is to be proclaimed, and the burden of everyone who stands in it is to make sure that the whole counsel of God is to be given to the people of God.

Paul understood that his very engagement in ministry was a matter of grace: **because of the grace given to me by God, that I might be a minister of Jesus Christ to the Gentiles, ministering the gospel of God** (vv. 15b–16a). He had not earned his role as the apostle to the Gentiles. Christ called him on the road to Damascus in the midst of the hatred and venom he was spewing out against the church of Jesus Christ. The only thing Paul had earned was the title he gave himself later—the chief of sinners (1 Tim. 1:15). He became an apostle and spokesperson for Christ by grace, not merit. The same is true for all who dare to open the Bible and presume to preach or teach from it. Paul comes full circle from Romans 1 where he introduced himself as "Paul, a bondservant of Jesus Christ, called to be an apostle, separated to the gospel of God" (v. 1). Paul is an apostle called to proclaim not his own message but the message that belongs to God and comes from God. Now he uses that very same language here toward the close of the epistle.

In the New Testament those appointed to preach and teach are usually called elders or servants or pastors or shepherds; on rare occasions they are called ministers. *Minister* is the common term we use today, but it was not used frequently to describe the role of pastor in the early Christian community. Strikingly absent here is another word often used to describe those who minister to the people of God—*priest*. That word is almost completely absent from the New Testament, and yet it was regularly applied to those who stood between the people and God as intercessors to offer the sacrifice of worship in the Old Testament. The only reference to priesthood in the New Testament is Peter's mention of the royal priesthood to which Israel was called (1 Pet. 2:9). The office of *pastor* is not called the office of *priest*, because the function of the priest in the Old Testament had reached its fulfillment in the offering of the perfect sacrifice of Jesus on the cross. The entire sacrificial, or sacerdotal, system of the Old Testament was done away with once for all in Christ.

The Minister's Offering

Some churches today still practice sacerdotalism. Salvation is mediated through the sacraments and, therefore, through the priesthood. In such cases, the church is seen as the instrument that brings people to salvation. This was a central issue in the sixteenth-century Reformation. The priesthood of Christ was fulfilled on the cross, so we are not priests. Paul does not consider himself a priest; he calls himself "a minister of Jesus Christ to the Gentiles, ministering the gospel of God."

Although Paul does not call himself a priest, he borrows the language of the priesthood and uses it in a metaphorical way. Earlier in the letter Paul had written, "I beseech you therefore, brethren, by the mercies of God, that you present your bodies a living sacrifice, holy, acceptable to God, which is your reasonable service" (12:1). We do not offer bulls and goats anymore, but we are called to make a sacrifice to Christ, an offering of our very lives, as our response to the gospel. In that sense, every Christian is a priest, but the offering is a sacrifice of praise, not of atonement. It is a sacrifice of worship, which is what we are called to do when we gather together as the Lord's people.

Here Paul uses the concept of the offering in a somewhat unusual way. He is ministering Jesus Christ to the Gentiles for this purpose: **that the offering of the Gentiles might be acceptable, sanctified by the Holy Spirit** (v. 16b). We can understand that sentence in two possible ways, but only one can be right. Some say that Paul is asking that the Gentiles' sacrifices of praise and worship would be acceptable to God as they are consecrated by the work of the Holy Spirit. I do not think the text should be interpreted that way. Paul is talking about his offering of the Gentiles to Christ.

Paul had been set apart to go to the Gentiles, and he had done that. As Paul had proclaimed the gospel of God to the Gentiles, the Holy Spirit had attached himself to the proclamation of that word and worked to bring those Gentiles to conversion. That, Paul is saying, is his sacrifice, the fruit of his ministry. His sacrifice is the Gentile converts. Not for a minute was he claiming that he had the power to convert them. Paul knew that such power comes only through the Holy Spirit. Nevertheless, as a minister, he offers the fruit of his ministry to the Lord. In that sense Paul exercises the office of priest.

The Minister's Glory

Therefore I have reason to glory in Christ Jesus in the things which pertain to God (v. 17). Paul wrote to the Corinthians, quoting Jeremiah,

"He who glories, let him glory in the LORD" (1 Cor. 1:31). Paul has reason to glory because all glory he has experienced is rooted and grounded in Christ Jesus. He understands it is not of himself.

> I, brethren, when I came to you, did not come with excellence of speech or of wisdom declaring to you the testimony of God. For I determined not to know anything among you except Jesus Christ and Him crucified. I was with you in weakness, in fear, and in much trembling. And my speech and my preaching were not with persuasive words of human wisdom, but in demonstration of the Spirit and of power, that your faith should not be in the wisdom of men but in the power of God. (1 Cor. 2:1–5)

For I will not dare to speak of any of those things which Christ has not accomplished through me, in word and deed, to make the Gentiles obedient (v. 18). The only thing Paul has to talk about is what Christ has done. Paul is not just being humble; he is being truthful, accurate, and theologically sound.

Good preachers work hard with the text. They want to make the sermon as accurate as possible. They also want to make it as interesting as possible. They want to persuade, admonish, and exhort, yet nothing happens as a result of their skill. Nothing can happen—at least, nothing good. The Holy Spirit, who attends the preached Word, is the only one who moves people to changed lives and growth. The Word is where the power is. It is not in programs or human skills. We can preach this Word till we are blue in the face, but if the Holy Spirit does not work through the Word preached, nothing happens.

Paul is looking at the results of his ministry, and he understands that those results have been wrought by God. Paul offers to God a return of the gifts that God himself has given. That is all we can ever do. What can we give to God that we have not first received from his hand? We do not give God our money so that he will make us rich, give us something we want, or forgive us our sins. We acknowledge that God owns it all. Everything we possess belongs to him, and he asks for just a small portion, a tenth. We all must be ready to give and be given at a moment's notice as an offering of praise to the Lord God.

Miracles

Paul calls attention to his missionary outreach, which has been carried out **in mighty signs and wonders, by the power of the Spirit of God** (v. 19a). There is no word for *miracle* in the New Testament, but we find the words *signs*, *wonders*, and *powers*. We extrapolate from those words a concept that we call *miracle*. We use the word *miracle* in a generic sense, but there is a narrow, technical, theological definition of the word. In terms of general miracles, I believe that they do occur—all the time—but such "miracles" are not technically miracles. A miracle is a sign or power that signifies something. Such signs, or miracles, in the apostolic age were meant to signify the breakthrough of God's kingdom and, most importantly, to signify the agents of that breakthrough. Moses, for example, was given power to perform miracles so that his credentials would authenticate his role as God's ambassador.

Nicodemus came to Jesus at night and said, "Rabbi, we know that You are a teacher come from God; for no one can do these signs that You do unless God is with him" (John 3:2). Nicodemus understood that the Devil is a liar and that he can perform counterfeit signs such as those of the magicians of Egypt. Although Satan has more power than we do, he does not have the power of God. Satan cannot bring something out of nothing. Satan cannot bring life out of death. Only God can do that and those whom he empowers to do it, and he empowers them to authenticate them as agents of revelation.

Therefore, how can those who perform miracles be authenticated as God's agents if others, including Satan, can do the same things? God answers prayers and heals the sick today, but I do not expect that someone today can go to the house of Lazarus and raise him from the dead. I do not expect to see anybody today bringing something out of nothing—not until the Lord comes back. There was a purpose and set time in redemptive history for that special, tight category of miracles.

Paul gives his reason for mentioning the signs and wonders the Holy Spirit has done through him: **so that from Jerusalem and round about to Illyricum I have fully preached the gospel of Christ** (v. 19b). Illyricum was in Asia Minor, far north of Jerusalem. Paul's ministry has extended far and wide. In every place he has traveled the power of the Holy Spirit has been there to authenticate his ministry with signs and powers and wonders.

Paul's Travels

And so I have made it my aim to preach the gospel, not where Christ was named, lest I should build on another man's foundation, but as it is written: "To whom He was not announced, they shall see; and those who have not heard shall understand" (vv. 20–21). There is nothing wrong with preaching on somebody else's foundation. Ministers build on the ministry of those who have gone before. Very rarely does a church begin and end with a single pastor, and it is customary in the ministry to build on another's foundation. Paul, however, was not a pastor; he was an apostle and a missionary, and he was sent to places where the gospel had not been preached and where no one else had laid a foundation. That was his aim—to preach the gospel not where Christ was already named, lest he should build on another man's foundation.

Paul's travels have impacted his relationship with the Christians at Rome: **For this reason I also have been much hindered from coming to you. But now no longer having a place in these parts, and having a great desire these many years to come to you** (vv. 22–23). Whether Paul ever got to Spain we do not know. Scholars are divided on that point, but we have no certain evidence that his desire to get to Spain was fulfilled. He got to Rome, but he did not get there while traveling to Spain. He went to Rome in chains after getting in trouble with the Jews and then with the Romans, as we discover in the book of Acts.

Whenever I journey to Spain, I shall come to you. For I hope to see you on my journey, and to be helped on my way there by you, if first I may enjoy your company for a while (v. 24). The fame of the church in Rome had gone into the whole world (1:8). Paul counts the Christians at Rome as his brothers and sisters in the Lord, and he longs to see them in person. He is optimistic about being able to do so in the near future.

First, however, he plans to go to Jerusalem to minister to the saints. **For it pleased those from Macedonia and Achaia to make a certain contribution for the poor among the saints who are in Jerusalem** (v. 26). Paul has collected an offering from Gentile converts and plans to take it to Jerusalem and distribute it to the Jewish believers living in the midst of hostility and poverty.

It pleased them indeed, and they are their debtors. For if the Gentiles have been partakers of their spiritual things, their duty is also to minister to them in material things (v. 27). The Gentile converts have been supremely blessed to receive what they had received from Israel. They understood that they were the wild olive branch that had been grafted into the root of Israel. The Gentiles were the heirs of the spiritual promises brought to them by the apostle Paul, and they see themselves as debtors to their Jewish brothers and sisters suffering in Jerusalem. The Gentiles were pleased to give a contribution for those saints. Since the Gentiles had been partakers of Israel's spiritual things, they saw it as a matter of duty to minister to the Jews in material things.

Therefore, when I have performed this and have sealed to them this fruit, I shall go by way of you to Spain (v. 28). After Paul goes to Jerusalem, he wants to visit Rome on his way to Spain. **But I know that when I come to you, I shall come in the fullness of the blessing of the gospel of Christ** (v. 29). Paul would arrive at Rome in chains and still rejoice that he was there because of the privilege of being a minister of the gospel.

Now I beg you, brethren, through the Lord Jesus Christ, and through the love of the Spirit, that you strive together with me in prayers to God for me, that I may be delivered from those in Judea who do not believe (vv. 30–31a). Paul begs the Roman Christians to pray for him as he undertakes his journey to Jerusalem. He knows there is a price on his head and a bull's-eye on his back. He knows there are multitudes of unbelieving Jews eager to get their hands on him and, if possible, stone him to death. So he asks the saints in Rome to pray for him, **that my service for Jerusalem may be acceptable to the saints, that I may come to you with joy by the will of God, and may be refreshed together with you** (vv. 31b–32). He is going to Jerusalem to deliver the offering designed to bring relief to the saints there, but he is going to need safe conduct to get in and out of that city.

The God of Peace

Paul closes this section with a brief benediction. It is not the ultimate benediction but the penultimate one: **Now the God of peace be with you all. Amen** (v. 33). The primary concern of the apostle—and of every Jew—was the experience of the peace of God. Jews greet another with *Shalom alachem, alachem shalom*, "Peace be unto you and unto you be peace."

> The LORD bless you and keep you;
> The LORD make His face shine upon you,
>   And be gracious to you;
> The LORD lift up His countenance upon you,
>   And give you peace."' (Num. 6:24–26)

At the heart of virtually every Jewish benediction was the constant plea that God would give peace to his people.

58

FINAL GREETINGS

Romans 16

I commend to you our sister Phoebe, a servant of the church at Cenchreae, that you may receive her in the Lord in a manner worthy of the saints, and assist her in whatever business she has need of you; for indeed she has been a helper of many and of myself also.

Greet Priscilla and Aquila, my fellow workers in Christ Jesus, who risked their own necks for my life, to whom not only I give thanks, but also all the churches of the Gentiles. Likewise greet the church that is in their house. Greet my beloved Epaenetus, who is the firstfruits of Achaia to Christ. Greet Mary, who labored much for us. Greet Andronicus and Junia, my countrymen and my fellow prisoners, who are of note among the apostles, who also were in Christ before me.

Greet Amplias, my beloved in the Lord. Greet Urbanus, our fellow worker in Christ, and Stachys, my beloved. Greet Apelles, approved in Christ. Greet those who are of the household of Aristobulus. Greet Herodion, my countryman. Greet those who are of the household of Narcissus who are in the Lord.

Greet Tryphena and Tryphosa, who hyave labored in the Lord. Greet the beloved Persia, who labored much in the Lord. Greet Rufus, chosen in the Lord, and his mother and mine. Greet Asyncritus, Phlegon, Hermas, Patrobas,

Hermes, and the brethren who are with them. Greet Philologus and Julia, Nereus and his sister, and Olympas, and all the saints who are with them.

Greet one another with a holy kiss. The churches of Christ greet you.

Now I urge you brethren, note those who cause divisions and offenses, contrary to the doctrine which you learned, and avoid them. For those who are such do not serve our Lord Jesus Christ, but their own belly, and by smooth words and flattering speech deceive the hearts of the simple. For your obedience has become known to all. Therefore I am glad on your behalf; but I want you to be wise in what is good, and simple concerning evil. And the God of peace will crush Satan under your feet shortly.
    The grace of our Lord Jesus Christ be with you. Amen.

Timothy, my fellow worker, and Lucius, Jason, and Sosipater, my countrymen, greet you. I, Tertius, who wrote this epistle, greet you in the Lord. Gaius, my host and the host of the whole church, greets you. Erastus, the treasurer of the city, greets you, and Quartus, a brother. The grace of our Lord Jesus Christ be with you all. Amen.

Now to Him who is able to establish you according to my gospel and the preaching of Jesus Christ, according to the revelation of the mystery kept secret since the word began but now made manifest, and by the prophetic Scriptures made known to all nations, according to the commandment of the everlasting God, for odedience to the faith—to God, alone wise, be glory through Jesus Christ forever. Amen.

As Paul concludes the epistle, he sends greetings to friends in the church at Rome. The apostle has finished the instructional content of the epistle, and he is winding down now in his customary manner. Even in these greetings we can learn something of value for our souls. We know the promise of God: "All Scripture is given by inspiration of God, and is profitable for doctrine, for reproof, for correction, for instruction in righteousness, that the man of God may be complete, thoroughly equipped for every good work" (2 Tim. 3:16–17).

Phoebe

This lengthy list of greetings and mentions of various people begins with a special commendation of a woman named Phoebe. She is described as a servant of the church in Cenchrea, which is on one of the coasts of Corinth. **I commend to you Phoebe our sister, who is a servant of the church**

in Cenchrea, that you may receive her in the Lord in a manner worthy of the saints, and assist her in whatever business she has need of you; for indeed she has been a helper of many and of myself also (vv. 1–2). Paul's brief commendation has received no small amount of attention by those trying to glean from the New Testament an understanding of the role of women in the life of the church.

Phoebe's name is taken from a pagan goddess. In the early church, Christians who had been named for pagan deities retained those names after conversion because the names' origins no longer had any religious or theological significance. We need to bear that in mind, because disputes over any sort of Christian link to anything with pagan roots occasionally arise in the church today. *Easter* sounds close to the pagan deity Ishtar, and the celebration of Christmas on December 25 corresponds to the time in ancient Rome when celebration was held for the pagan god Mithras. Christians decided at one point to use the occasion to celebrate the birth of Christ. That was a noble endeavor, but some still are scandalized by the historic relationship to the Mithras cult.

It is understandable that many things in our culture have roots in paganism, yet those roots have long since been overlooked, and we do not need to have scruples about them. The days of the week were named for pagan gods. Monday was named for the moon. Wednesday came about in honor of the Scandinavian Norse god Woden. Thursday comes from the celebration of the pagan deity Thor. Saturday goes back to the celebration of the Roman god Saturn. We use those designations, but we do not attribute to the names of the days of the week any particular religious homage.

Phoebe is identified as our sister in the faith and a servant of the church in Corinth. This descriptive term "servant of the church" comes from the Greek work *diakonia* and is rendered in some translations as "deaconess." Many churches in our day are organized by elders, ministers, deacons, and deaconesses, who are female deacons. Over the years there have been disputes, even within Reformed communities, about whether the office of deaconess should be an ordained office.

Years ago I was asked to write a theological position paper with respect to the role of women in the church and with specific reference to the meaning of a church office. In that paper I pointed out that there is no connotative description of the term *church office* to be found anywhere in the New Testament. The concept of *church office* is something we extrapolate from the examples given to us biblically. The most generic term for a church worker in the New Testament is *diakonia*, which describes a position of service to which all of us in ministry are called. In my paper I wrote that the New Testament is replete with examples of women being deeply involved in the life of the church as well as in the ministry of the apostolic expansion of the church, though no woman was selected to the office of apostle, and restrictions were placed on women in Paul's letters to Timothy and Titus. Nevertheless, we see that women were profoundly involved in the life of the church. Women were the last to remain at the cross and the first to greet the risen Savior in the garden at the tomb.

We see throughout Paul's greetings his profound appreciation for the assistance he received from women who were serving the cause of Christ and the church in very significant ways. What the church does today in terms of ordination is a different matter, which I will not address here. The point is that we must not underestimate the very important role that women have in the life of the church of Christ.

Paul directs the Christians in Rome to receive Phoebe in the Lord in a manner worthy of the saints. She is to be assisted in whatever she needs because of the high honor bestowed on her as a helper of many. The term "helper" is a very weak translation of the Greek, which indicates someone with a specific office, one of important assistance to the apostolic ministry. Phoebe is an assistant to Paul and part of his apostolic ministry, so he directs the people in Rome to receive her with all honor and assistance.

Priscilla and Aquila

Paul sends more greetings: **Greet Priscilla and Aquila, my fellow workers in Christ Jesus, who risked their own necks for my life, to whom not only I give thanks, but also all the churches of the Gentiles. Likewise greet the church that is in their house** (vv. 3–5a). We hear of Priscilla and Aquila in the book of Acts (see Acts 18). They ministered with the apostle in Ephesus. Apparently Priscilla and Aquila had been in Rome and had to flee when Christians were banished by the emperor Claudius. They went from Rome to Ephesus, where they met with the apostle Paul and assisted him in his ministry. We do not have a specific record of the risks they took for the apostle, but from the Acts record of Paul's sojourn in Ephesus we know the time was a tumultuous one and that his life was in danger more than once.

Paul also sends a greeting to the church that was in their house. In the first-century community there were not only the *ekklēsia*, the churches, but *ekklēsioli*, little churches that met in homes. Those were not representative of today's so-called house church. Today's home-church movement generally, though not always, tends toward disenchantment with the organized visible church. There were home churches in the first century because there were no other places to meet. Those with larger homes would open them so people could assemble together for worship and instruction. The family of Priscilla and Aquila did that.

Further Greetings

Greet my beloved Epaenetus, who is the firstfruits of Achaia to Christ (v. 5b). Some controversy surrounds this greeting. Elsewhere Paul writes about Stephanas, whom he also calls the "firstfruits of Achaia" (1 Cor. 16:15). A textual variant could explain the tension. The wording could be taken as referring to the firstfruits of Paul's ministry in Asia rather than in Achaia. Even if it was in Achaia, the firstfruits presumably would include more than one person, perhaps members of his family or a related group.

Greet Mary, who labored much for us. Greet Andronicus and Junia (vv. 6–7a). Junia could be a man or a woman, depending on how the Greek is rendered. Paul also sends greetings to: **my countrymen and my fellow prisoners, who are of note among the apostles, who also were in Christ before me** (v. 7b). Apparently these believers had been part of Paul's entourage and had suffered imprisonment with the apostle. He gives them tribute for their fidelity and also points out that they were Christians before he was; they were older in the Lord.

Greet Amplias, my beloved in the Lord. Greet Urbanus, our fellow worker in Christ, and Stachys, my beloved. Greet Apelles, approved in Christ. Greet those who are of the household of Aristobulus. Greet Herodion, my countryman. Greet those who are of the household of Narcissus who are in the Lord. Greet Tryphena and Tryphosa, who have labored in the Lord. Greet the beloved Persis, who labored much in the Lord (vv. 8–12). Tryphena, Tryphosa, and Persis were women, so again we see Paul's concern to give his apostolic good wishes to women who had labored with him.

Greet Rufus, chosen in the Lord, and his mother and mine (v. 13). Jesus' cross beam was carried by Simon of Cyrene, who is identified as the father of Alexander and Rufus (Mark 15:21). It was unusual for Mark to insert that kind of detail in his narrative, and we have to wonder why he did it. Mark's Gospel was sent to the church at Rome. Mark was likely aware that Rufus and perhaps his brother Alexander were members of the church at Rome when the Gospel was sent there. Mark, under the influence of the Holy Spirit, honored those local church members, the sons of the man who had carried the cross of Jesus. Rufus is described as "chosen in the Lord." In this context it is unlikely that Paul means that Rufus is one of the elect, because all of them were elect. The context indicates that Rufus had a particular role and influence with the apostle and with the apostolic community in Rome.

Paul also sends greetings to Rufus's mother, presumably the wife of Simon of Cyrene, whom Paul calls his own mother. Paul was not speaking literally here; rather, he considered her his mother in the faith.

Greet Asyncritus, Phlegon, Hermas, Patrobas, Hermes, and the brethren who are with them. Greet Philologus and Julia, Nereus and his sister, and Olympas, and all the saints who are with them (vv. 14–15). After acknowledging others numbered among the saints, Paul adds, **Greet one another with a holy kiss. The churches of Christ greet you** (v. 16). That was the custom, particularly at the celebration of the Lord's Supper. Upon completion of the Lord's Supper meal, the people would customarily greet one another with a kiss on the cheek. We still see that form of greeting in the Middle East today. We do not know when or why that custom passed out of practice in the church, but it must be considered as a custom, not a principle.

A Final Warning

Paul turns his attention to a serious apostolic admonition. This is perhaps the last apostolic entreaty we find in the book of Romans. **Now I urge you, brethren, note those who cause divisions and offenses, contrary to the doctrine which you learned, and avoid them** (v. 17). He admonishes the Christians at Rome to notice the troublemakers in the church. They are to watch out for those who sow seeds of dissension, particularly those who disrupt the body of Christ with false doctrine.

In the church today doctrine is decried. Doctrine divides, some say, so we ought not to give much concern to it but focus instead on loving, peaceful relationships. They forget that we do not know what a loving relationship looks like apart from how it is described by the truth of biblical doctrine. Paul does not say to avoid doctrine here; he says to avoid heretics. We are to avoid those who would come into the church teaching false doctrine. **For those who are such do not serve our Lord Jesus Christ, but their own belly** (v. 18a). Such people are not in it for the building of the kingdom of God but for their own gratification, wealth, pleasure, and status in the community.

Paul is quite critical of them, who **by smooth words and flattering speech deceive the hearts of the simple** (v. 18b). James warns that not many should become teachers, for with teaching comes the greatest judgment (James 3:1). When I first started my teaching career, I struggled when students would ask me a particularly difficult theology question. Each time they asked, I had the option of giving them an answer that might satisfy them but be unsound. I knew I could dazzle them and gain their respect and admiration, and sometimes I was tempted to do so. I knew if I caved in to the temptation, I would be positioning myself for judgment at the hands of Christ. I had to examine myself, asking whether my teaching was the unvarnished truth of the Word of God or my favorite hobbyhorse. Every minister of the gospel must face and examine himself continually, lest he be guilty of deceiving the simple.

Most people in the congregation, even if they have PhDs in unrelated fields, are still simple with respect to the things of God. Jesus warned that it would be better to have a millstone tied around one's neck and be thrown into the abyss than to cause one of the sheep to stumble (Matt. 18:6). Watch out, says Paul. **I want you to be wise in what is good, and simple concerning evil** (v. 19c).

There are many Christians who do not want to be engaged in a laborious study of the Word of God. They say that they want to keep their faith simple and childlike, but there is a difference between a childlike faith and a childish faith. We are to be childlike in terms of our acquiescence to the authority of God, but we are to be adults in our understanding. The Christians of the New Testament were rebuked for being satisfied with spiritual infancy, with milk, when they should have been seeking after the deeper things of God, the meat of the Word (1 Cor. 3:2; Heb. 5:12). All we have been examining in Romans is not pabulum. We have been looking at the weightier things of God's Word so that we might not be simple in our understanding.

Final Greetings

And the God of peace will crush Satan under your feet shortly (v. 20a). That prophetic statement may have specific reference to the destruction of Jerusalem, which would take place shortly after this letter was received. When it came, the great threat of the Judaizing heresy was removed from the church, the temple was destroyed, and those persecuting the early church were dispersed among the nations. However, Paul might have been referring to something altogether different. He does not tell us.

Paul gives a preliminary brief benediction: **The grace of our Lord Jesus Christ be with you. Amen** (v. 20b). Paul's greatest hope was that the people would continue to have the grace of God in their presence. He told us earlier that we move from faith to faith, from life to life, from grace to grace. Our Christian pilgrimage begins in grace, is sustained by grace, and is finished by grace.

Timothy, my fellow worker, and Lucius, Jason, and Sosipater, my countrymen, greet you (v. 21). Next we find out who really wrote Romans: **I, Tertius, who wrote this epistle, greet you in the Lord** (v. 22). After all the greetings are communicated to Paul's friends in Rome and from his coworkers in Corinth, Tertius adds his personal greetings, identifying himself as the one who wrote the epistle. In the vast majority of cases, Paul did not write with his own hand. He had significant problems with his vision. On one occasion he did write his letter: "See with what large letters I have written to you with my own hand!" (Gal. 6:11), but typically he, as well as many others, used a personal secretary called an amanuensis. The practice dates back to the Old Testament prophets. Jeremiah had an amanuensis who took down his words. Here Paul has been dictating the letter to the church at Rome, and Tertius, which means "the third," has been recording this magnificent epistle dutifully and carefully under the inspiration of the Holy Spirit.

Gaius, my host and the host of the whole church, greets you. Erastus, the treasurer of the city, greets you, and Quartus, a brother (v. 23). Not many in the early Christian community were in societal positions of honor or authority, but there were some, and here we learn of one such, the treasurer of the city. He sent his greetings, along with Quartus, a brother. Then: **The grace of our Lord Jesus Christ be with you all. Amen** (v. 24).

Benediction

Paul gives the final benediction: **Now to Him who is able to establish you according to my gospel** (v. 25a). He frequently uses the term *edification*. It is a term borrowed from the building industry. The teaching of our Lord at the end of the Sermon on the Mount warns against building a house upon the sand. Those who do so will find that when the floods come the house will be swept away because its edifice had not been established. By the same token, Jesus said, the wise man is one who builds his house upon a rock so that when the storms come and beat against it, the house stands (Matt. 7:24–27). We are warned not to be tossed to and fro by every wind of doctrine. As we grow in grace, as our sanctification proceeds, we are to be edified and built up to the point at which our faith, our character, and our devotion are established (Eph. 4:11–13).

In this benediction, the apostle reminds the people at Rome about who is able to make that happen: **the preaching of Jesus Christ** (v. 25b). We are to be established according to Paul's gospel. Countless essays, articles, and books have been written in the last ten years about the gospel. The biblical gospel is under attack today. The doctrine of justification by faith alone, which we have examined in much detail in Paul's letter, has been and continues to be attacked in the church today—not just from the so-called liberal wing of the church but from the evangelical and even the Reformed wings. At the heart of the dispute is whether our salvation rests upon the imputation of the righteousness of Jesus.

Without the righteousness of Christ, you and I are finished. Without imputation there is no justification, and without justification by faith alone, there is no gospel. The only gospel is Paul's gospel, the one he was authorized and set apart to proclaim. Being established in the Christian life is to be established according to that gospel. The doctrine of justification by faith alone is easy to get from an intellectual standpoint, but to get it in the bloodstream takes a lifetime.

This is Paul's final benediction, that God is able to establish them in the gospel and in the preaching of Jesus Christ, **according to the revelation of the mystery kept secret since the world began but now made manifest, and by the prophetic Scriptures made known to all nations, according to the commandment of the everlasting God, for obedience to the faith** (vv. 25c–26). The final benediction of the final line of Paul's epistle repeats in succinct terms the quintessence of the message that he has labored to communicate throughout the epistle, the principle of soli Deo Gloria: **to God, alone wise, be glory through Jesus Christ forever** (v. 27a).

In every generation all over the world, the gospel that Paul lovingly, jealously, passionately sets forth here in his magnum opus is obscured, attacked, and brought almost to ruin, but Paul's prayer—that people would be established in that gospel forever—has borne witness by the history of the church. Despite all heresies, persecutions, and distortions, the gospel that was revealed here continues to be manifested by the wisdom, power, and establishment of God, who alone receives the glory.

The final word of the apostle's letter comes from the Hebrew *aman*, which is translated "truth." That word is **Amen** (v. 27b). So all God's people say, "Amen."

FOR FURTHER STUDY

Cranfield, C. E. B. *Romans 1–8*. International Critical Commentary. London: T. & T. Clark, 2004.

_____. *Romans 9–16*. International Critical Commentary. London: T. & T. Clark, 2004.

Hodge, Charles. *Commentary on the Epistle to the Romans*. Grand Rapids, MI: Eerdmans, 1950.

Moo, Douglas. *The Epistle to the Romans*. New International Commentary on the New Testament. Grand Rapids, MI: Eerdmans, 1996.

Morris, Leon. *The Epistle to the Romans*. Pillar New Testament Commentary. Grand Rapids, MI: Eerdmans, 1988.

Murray, John. *The Epistle to the Romans*. Grand Rapids, MI: Eerdmans, 1997.

INDEX OF NAMES

Aaron, 144, 167

Abraham, 75, 108, 336, 350, 367, 376; call of, 72, 177, 324; covenant with, 72–73, 123, 177, 179, 308, 375, 449; excluded from boasting, 106; faith of, 106–7, 122, 130–32; justification of, 106, 111, 122; and Melchizedek, 167–68; offering of Isaac, 296; Paul's appeal to, 103–13, 116, 121–22, 126; promise to, 72–73, 107, 130, 178, 342, 391–92; seed of, 126, 129, 168, 262, 313, 367–68, 391

Adam, 251; abilities of, 175; covenant with, 308; death through, 166–67, 172–73, 175, 179–80, 206; fall of, 172; as federal head, 168–70; nature of, 259; sin of, 174–76

Adam and Eve, 117; abilities of, 176; access to God, 143; covenant with, 177–78, 207; curse of, 18, 268; death through, 206; fall of, 154, 172, 175, 207, 219, 279, 448; sin of, 120–21, 334, 448; uncovered, 64; and worship, 406

Adler, Mortimer, 458

Agricola, Ganeus, 129

Ahab (king), 368–69, 345–57

Alexander, 505

Ambrose, 13

Aquila, 504–5

Aquinas, Thomas, 43, 89, 433, 451

Aristotle, 51, 101, 395, 458

Arminius, 286

Athanasius, 136, 298

Augustine, Aurelius, 13–14, 33, 43, 54, 62, 148, 189, 192, 229, 240, 276, 286, 287, 312, 235, 342, 343, 344, 433, 451, 465, 466; debate with Pelagius, 154, 175–76, 196

Baal, 368

Bacchus, 469

Barney, Lem, 490

Barth, Karl, 279, 293

Bathsheba, 81

Benjamin, 367

Berkouwer, G. C., 203

Biden, Joseph, 480

Boice, James, 306, 336

Bundy, Ted, 330

Bunyan, John, 136

Burns, Robert, 281

Caiaphas, 155, 324

Calvin, John, 14, 42, 53, 91, 98, 158, 172, 212, 240, 277, 286, 287; and baptism, 185; disagreement with Luther, 208–11; dispute with Pelagius, 236; doctrine of election, 327; teaching of, 393

Camus, Albert, 43

Chamberlain, Neville, 140, 434

Charles II (king), 136

Claudius (emperor), 30, 504

Cleopatra, 93

Cranfield, C. E. B., 511

Cromwell, Oliver, 136

Daniel, 478–79

David (king), 112, 113, 117, 120; covenant with, 177, 308; lineage of, 20; and Mephibosheth, 391; Paul's example of, 116, 118–19, 121, 371; promises to, 178; psalm of, 81; repentance of, 81–82; seed of, 21, 309, 492; sin of, 81

Descartes, René, 109, 319

Devil. See Satan

Dostoyevsky, Fyodor, 127

Edwards, Jonathan, 14, 58, 196, 234, 304, 423; and doctrine of seeking, 80; and the Great Awakening, 79; exile of, 435–36; identity theory of 169–70, and the will, 236, 240

Eli, 82

Elijah, 368–69

Eliezer, 130
Erasmus, Desiderius, 129, 190, 196, 236, 286,
    401
Erikson, Erik H., 208, 209
Esau. *See under* Jacob
Ezekiel, 308, 377
Ferguson, Sinclair, 164
Fields, W. C., 60
Fletcher, Joseph, 464–65
Freud, Sigmund, 45
Gabriel (angel), 131
Gaius, 508
George (king), 169
Gerstner, John, 304
Graham, Billy, 19, 71, 190
Green, Nick, 54
Guest, John, 459
Habakkuk, 34, 121
Hammurabi, 308, 324
Herod, 155, 307
Hitler, Adolf, 140, 300, 309, 330, 451
Hodge, Charles, 150, 362, 511
Hodges, Zane, 183
Hoffman, Dustin, 257
Horton, Michael, 112
Hosea, 338, 341
Hughes, Howard, 220–21
Hume, David, 319
Isaac, 111, 126, 129, 168, 177–78, 179, 296, 313;
    covenant with, 308; faith of, 122; Jews
    descended from, 314
Isaiah, 19, 22, 28, 88, 345, 354, 355, 358, 361,
    395, 433
Ishmael, 313, 368; Arabs descended from, 314
Jacob, 168, 177, 178, 179, 278, 308, 390, 392,
    449; and Esau, 291, 311–17, 323–24,
    340
James (apostle), 26, 352, 396; vs. Paul, 107–11,
    122
Jenkins, Jerry B., 366
Jeremias, Joachim, 263
Jeremiah, 64, 354, 395, 434, 482, 484, 496, 508
Jesus, active obedience of, 135–37; and
    adulterous woman, 247–48; and
    alcohol, 476; anger of, 336; birth of,
    307–8, 430, 441; enemies of, 324; and
    Lazarus, 292, 496; name of, 16; and
    Nicodemus, 190, 196, 255, 498; and
    Olivet Discourse, 383–86; parables
    of, 68–69, 435; and Peter, 362, 479;
    priesthood of, 167; resurrection of, 19,
    21, 135; return of, 381–82; on Sea of
    Galilee, 45; and Sermon on the Mount,
    92, 117–19, 258, 421, 426, 450, 508;
    warnings of, 31, 64, 78, 342–43, 347,
    507; in the wilderness, 35, 49, 207
Jezebel, 368–69
Job, 49, 166, 278, 331, 425, 436
John (apostle), 17, 244, 309, 398, 417
John the Baptist, 28, 32
Jonah, 375
Jonathan (son of Saul), 391
Joseph (adoptive father of Jesus), 21, 307, 441
Joseph (patriarch), 278, 282, 301
Josephus, 386
Joshua, 458
Judah, tribe of, 167
Judas Iscariot, 84, 155, 360, 370
Junia, 505
Kant, Immanuel, 41, 54, 59, 60, 319, 395
Kennedy, James D., 109–10
Kierkegaard, Søren, 399
King, Larry, 450
Kline, Meredith, 472
LaHaye, Tim, 366
Lazarus, 292, 426, 498; tomb of, 131
Leah, 317
Lehmann, Paul, 465
Levi, 168; tribe of, 167
Lindsey, Hal, 366
Locke, John, 400
Luke, 20, 383, 384
Luther, Martin, 31–32, 108, 128, 158, 172, 182,
    189, 240, 287, 309, 329, 371, 434, 469,
    484; and baptism, 185; conversion of,
    14, 33, 68, 100; at Diet of Worms, 482;
    and Erasmus, 128, 190, 236, 286, 401;
    and faith, 110, 352; on justification, 98,
    100, 109–10, 113, 184; and the law,
    208–12; and sin, 465
MacArthur, John, 184
Machen, J. Gresham, 136–37
Maltz, Maxwell, 238
Manson, Charles, 330
Mark, 505
Martha, 426
Martyr, Justin, 441
Marx, Karl, 269–70
Mary (Paul's co-laborer), 505
Mary (mother of Jesus), 21, 32, 131, 307, 430,
    441
Mary (sister of Lazarus), 426
McCartney, Clarence, 494
McGee, J. Vernon, 308
Melancthon, Philip, 287
Melchizedek, 167–68
Mephibosheth, 391
Micah, 441
Michelangelo, 101
Mill, John Stuart, 43, 268, 395
Mithras, 503
Moo, Douglas, 511
Morris, Desmond, 120
Morris, Leon, 511
Moses, 63, 143, 167, 175, 178, 179, 199, 206,
    287, 308, 330, 350, 449, 498; law given
    through, 166
Murray, John, 137, 511
Naboth, 456
Nebuchadnezzar, 324
Nero, 273, 443
Nicklaus, Jack, 71

Nicodemus, 190, 196, 244, 255, 314, 498
Nicole, Roger, 303
Nietzsche, Friedrich, 43, 299–300
Noah, 122, 450; covenant with, 177, 179, 308
Owen, John, 136
Packer, J. I., 98
Paul, attacks on, 426; call of, 292, 495;
    conversion of, 18, 20, 90, 324, 361;
    grief of, 305–6; identity of, 16–18, 27,
    496; longing of, 29–31; perplexity of,
    personal relationships of, 494, 502–8;
    228; struggle with sin, 220, 224–26,
    242–43; trials of, 498–500; vow of,
    26–27
Pelagius, 154, 172, 175, 196, 236
Persis, 505
Peter, 309, 362, 417, 441, 442, 495; vision of,
    478–79
Pharaoh, 278, 281–82, 307, 325, 342, 458; and
    God, 329–30; hardening of, 330–31
Pheidippides, 355
Phoebe, 502–4
Pilate, Pontius, 155, 299, 324, 400
Piper, John, 136
Pius, Antoninus, 441
Plato, 192, 245, 395, 432
Priscilla, 504–5
Quartus, 508
Rachel, 317
Rahab, 458
Rembrandt, 102
Rosen, Moshe, 376
Rosewell, Rosie, 238
Rousseau, Jean-Jacques, 170
Rufus, 505–6
Russell, Bertrand, 385
Ryrie, Charles, 183
Samuel, 82
Sarah, 130
Sartre, Jean-Paul, 43
Satan [Devil], 18, 109, 130, 131, 189, 198, 199,
    211, 218, 219, 237, 238, 277, 299, 301,
    352, 498; as accuser, 210, 227, 297,
    491; children of, 262, 466; delivered to,
    50, 379; and Jesus, 35, 207, 487; and
    Job, 49, 278, 331; and Martin Luther,
    32, 185, 401; lie of, 276; obedience to,
    262; servants of, 198; as slanderer, 218,
    297–98, 487; temptations of, 229
Saturn, 503
Saul (king), 391
Schaeffer, Francis, 399

Serling, Rod, 53–54
Shadrach, Meshach, and Abednego, 478–79
Shaw, George Bernard, 366–67
Simeon, 490
Simon of Cyrene, 505–6
Socrates, 432
Sproul, R. C., and alcohol, 476; at atheists'
    club, 40; and baptism, 185; and battle
    against sin, 260; and birth of son, 180;
    at booksellers' convention, 160–61;
    childhood of, 75, 79, 140, 367, 369,
    413–14; confronting sin, 50, 219, 467;
    conversion of, 90, 120, 226; and ECT,
    112, 173–74; disappointment of, 151;
    and election, 304, 321, 337; end times
    view of, 386–87; father of, 407, 426;
    and fear of God, 336–37; and friend
    in Boston, 131–32; grief of, 306; life
    verse of, 73, 424; at moment of self-
    awareness, 199–200; and mother's
    death, 180–81; at Nick Green's orchard,
    54; playing golf, 71; as preacher, 11–12,
    352, 361, 416, 435; quoted in movie,
    217; on radio, 327, 409; as seminary
    student, 129, 304, 354, 385, 425, 437,
    459–60; and Sherrie Sproul, 119–20,
    155, 181; as smoker, 226–27; as teacher,
    11, 171–72, 319–20, 351, 407, 458, 507;
    and thirst for Scripture, 230; and Weight
    Watchers, 211–12, 239; on women in
    the church, 503–4
Sproul, R. C., Jr., 407
Sproul, Sherrie, 119, 155, 181
Sproul, Vesta, 131, 155
Spurgeon, Charles, 240, 393
Stendhal, Krister, 208
Stephanas, 505
Stephen, 298
Tertius, 508
Thielicke, Helmut, 422
Thomas, Clarence, 480
Timothy, 361, 418, 475, 494, 504
de Tocqueville, Alexis, 457
Toplady, Augustus, 210
Tryphena, 505
Tryphosa, 505
Uzziah (king), 418
Warfield, Benjamin Breckinridge, 228–29
Washington, George, 109
Wesley, John, 14, 224, 227
Woden, 503

About Ligonier Ministries

Ligonier Ministries, founded in 1971 by Dr. R. C. Sproul, is an international teaching ministry that strives to help people grow in their knowledge of God and His holiness.

"We believe that when the Bible is taught clearly, God is seen in all of His majesty and holiness—hearts are conquered, minds are renewed, and communities are transformed," Dr. Sproul says.

From its base in Lake Mary, Florida, Ligonier carries out its mission in various ways:

- By producing and broadcasting solid, in-depth teaching resources.
- By publishing and promoting books true to the historic Christian faith.
- By publishing *Tabletalk*, a monthly theological/devotional magazine.
- By publishing *The Reformation Study Bible*.
- By training and equipping young adults, laypeople, and pastors through the Ligonier Academy of Biblical and Theological Studies.
- By creating and releasing recordings of beautiful music.
- By producing and promoting conferences.

For more information, please visit www.ligonier.org.